THE HISTORY of an ENGLISH BOROUGH

Publications of
The Shakespeare Birthplace Trust
in association with
Sutton Publishing Limited

Robert Bearman
Shakespeare in the Stratford Records
1994

Joan Lane
John Hall and his Patients:
The Medical Practice of Shakespeare's Son-in-Law
1996

Philip Tennant
The Civil War in Stratford-upon-Avon:
Conflict and Community in South Warwickshire 1642–1646
1996

Jeanne Jones
Family Life in Shakespeare's England:
Stratford-upon-Avon 1570–1630
1996

Robert Bearman, ed.
The History of an English Borough:
Stratford-upon-Avon 1196–1996
1997

THE HISTORY of an ENGLISH BOROUGH

STRATFORD-UPON-AVON 1196–1996

EDITED BY ROBERT BEARMAN

SUTTON PUBLISHING
THE SHAKESPEARE BIRTHPLACE TRUST

with the support of
THE STRATFORD-UPON-AVON TOWN COUNCIL

First published in the United Kingdom in 1997 by
Sutton Publishing Limited · Phoenix Mill
Thrupp · Stroud · Gloucestershire · GL5 2BU
in association with
The Shakespeare Birthplace Trust
The Shakespeare Centre · Henley Street · Stratford-upon-Avon · CV37 6QW

British Library Cataloguing in Publication Data
A catalogue record for this book is available from the British Library

ISBN 0 7509 1535 8

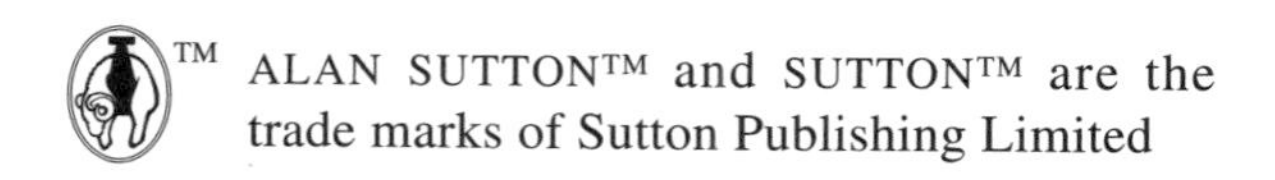

Typeset in 10/12pt Times.
Typesetting and origination by
Sutton Publishing Limited.
Printed and bound in Great Britain by
MPG Books Ltd, Bodmin, Cornwall

Contents

General Editors' Preface

The objects of the Shakespeare Birthplace Trust, as defined by the Act of Parliament under which it operates, are:

a) to promote in every part of the world the appreciation and study of the plays and other works of William Shakespeare and the general advancement of Shakespearian knowledge;

b) to maintain and preserve the Shakespeare birthplace properties for the benefit of the nation;

c) to provide and maintain for the benefit of the nation a museum and a library of books, manuscripts, records of historic interest, pictures, photographs and objects of antiquity with particular but not exclusive reference to William Shakespeare, his life, works and times.

It is from these objectives that the series of publications, of which this volume is part, derives. The central focus of the series is Shakespeare: his plays and their performance, his life and the environment, historical, topographical, and domestic, in which he lived; and the raw material for volumes in the series is derived largely from the rich Shakespearian holdings of the Trust's Library and Records Office, in the form of printed books and archival and pictorial material relating to Shakespeare's life in Stratford, to the history of the town, to scholarship and criticism on his writings, and to the performance history of his plays. Such a collection of volumes, covering a wide range of topics – theatrical, literary and historical – cannot, of course, observe rigid editorial uniformity. To a considerable extent, therefore, treatment and approach from volume to volume are determined by the aims and needs of individual authors and editors. Within this rather broad scope, however, we seek to produce a series of volumes that will be of interest to the general reader while maintaining a high standard of scholarship in the furtherance of that basic objective of the Shakespeare Birthplace Trust, the general advancement of Shakespearian knowledge.

The present volume might at first be thought to fall outside this broad definition; but the Trust, not least because its Records Office houses much of the source material for the history of Shakespeare's town, had long wished to commemorate in some way the 800th anniversary of the grant of Stratford's first charter of 1196. In October 1996, it therefore organized a three-day conference at which twelve papers were given on various aspects of the town's history. It is these, many of which draw extensively on the Trust's archive collections, which form the basis of the present volume.

Robert Bearman
Robert Smallwood

Foreword by the Mayor of Stratford-upon-Avon

Scholars may dispute exactly when the charter granted by John of Coutances, Bishop of Worcester, founding the borough of Stratford-upon-Avon, was executed. There is, however, no doubt that a market charter was granted by King Richard I on 25 June 1196, and Bishop John's grant was almost certainly made shortly afterwards. In all events, the citizens of Stratford-upon-Avon had no doubt that the year of Our Lord one thousand one hundred and ninety-six marked the 800th Anniversary of the town's beginnings. Throughout this momentous year the Town Council, in conjunction with organizations, societies, groups and individuals representing all aspects of the town's life, engaged in a year-long celebration.

The celebrations included:

January: televised launch.
February: historic council meeting at Big School, King Edward VI Grammar School (where the Town Council used to meet until gas lighting was installed at the Town Hall in 1843).
March: civic service led by the Bishop of Coventry at Holy Trinity Church involving local residents in music, drama, readings, morris dancing and vintage cars.
April: Shakespeare's Birthday Weekend with special reference to the 800th Anniversary.
May: revival of Swan-Upping Ceremony 'to count the swans on the River Avon'.
July: celebratory street market in original location in Bridge Street with medieval dress, steam fair and street party rounded off with fireworks.
September: carnival and pageant.
October: 800th Anniversary Mop and Runaway Mop, and Beating the Bounds.
November: visit of Her Majesty the Queen and His Royal Highness the Duke of Edinburgh to unveil the 800th Anniversary Celebratory Fountain, visit Big School and the Guild Chapel, attend the special council meeting at the Town Hall, followed by balcony appearance and cutting of the 800th Anniversary cake with the sixteenth-century broadsword from the town collection.
December: The Mayor's New Year's Eve Charity Ball to complete the Octocentenary.

In addition, 1996 marked the 500th anniversary of the death of Hugh Clopton. His fine monument is in the Guild Chapel and his benefactions all around us, notably the Clopton Bridge which to this day remains the town's main river crossing. The Quincentenary was marked by a civic service at the Guild Chapel led by the Bishop of Worcester at which new church furnishings were dedicated as a permanent commemoration.

This list of activities, however, is only a fraction of the total celebrations organized by townspeople, not least by our good friends at the Shakespeare Birthplace Trust.

It is thanks to the Trust that we enjoyed the splendid weekend symposium in October 1996, during which eminent academics opened up the riches of Stratford's fascinating history. It is good to know that the research has been preserved and made available to an even wider audience by the publication of this volume.

As Mayor of Stratford-upon-Avon it gives me great pleasure to commend this book to residents of the town and our many visitors from across the world.

Charles H Bates

The Worshipful the Mayor of Stratford-upon-Avon, May 1996–May 1997
Councillor Charles H. Bates

List of Illustrations

List of Figures and Tables

Figures

Tables

List of Contributors

Robert Bearman is Senior Archivist at the Shakespeare Birthplace Trust and, in addition to books and articles on local history topics, is the author of *Shakespeare in the Stratford Records* (1994) and editor of *Charters of the Redvers Family and the Earldom of Devon, 1090–1217* (1994).

Christine Carpenter is Reader in History at the University of Cambridge and a Fellow of New Hall. She has worked extensively on fifteenth-centry gentry families in the Midlands and among her publications is *Locality and Polity: A Study of Warwickshire Landed Society, 1401–1499*, winner of the Whitbread Prize for 1992.

Alan Dyer is Senior Lecturer in History at the University of Wales, Bangor, and is well-known for his work on sixteenth- and seventeenth-century urban society, with particular reference to disease and demography. His publications include *The City of Worcester in the Sixteenth Century* (1974).

Christopher Dyer is Professor of Medieval Social History at the University of Birmingham. His most important articles, many with a Midlands bias, have recently been re-published under the title *Everyday Life in Medieval England* and among his other works is *Lords and Peasants in a Changing Society: The Estates of the Bishopric of Worcester, 680–1540* (1980).

Nicholas Fogg, author of *Stratford-upon-Avon: Portrait of a Town* (1986), has written several other books and articles on Stratford-upon-Avon. Formerly a teacher at Marlborough College, he is now a freelance writer and is currently working on a history of SS *Great Britain*.

Ann Hughes is Professor of Early Modern History at the University of Keele. She has written extensively on seventeenth-century social and religious conflict in the Midlands including *Politics, Society and Civil War in Warwickshire, 1620–1660* (1987), and is also author of *The Causes of the English Civil War* (1991).

Joan Lane, Senior Teaching Fellow in the Centre for Social History at the University of Warwick, is the author of many articles and monographs on eighteenth-century medical and social history. Among her other published works are *John Hall and his Patients: The Medical Practice of Shakespeare's Son-in-law* (1996) and *Apprenticeship in England 1600–1914* (1996).

Nicholas Palmer is Senior Field Archaeologist at Warwickshire Museum and has conducted many excavations throughout the county. These have included several in Stratford-upon-Avon, with particular reference to the Romano-British settlement at Tiddington.

Roger Pringle, whose published works include an edited anthology, *Poems for Warwickshire, A Portrait of Queen Elizabeth I* and *Portrait of a Stratford Year*, has been Director of the Shakespeare Birthplace Trust since 1989. He is currently editing an anthology of literary visitors' impressions of Stratford for publication.

T.R. Slater is Reader in Historical Geography at the University of Birmingham. He has published extensively on landscape history and medieval town-planning, and is also the author of *A History of Warwickshire* (1981), shortly to be re-published.

Philip Tennant, until retirement a lecturer in nineteenth-century French literature and painting at the University of London, has since studied in detail the effects of the Civil War in the Midlands. His published works include *Edgehill and Beyond: The People's War in the South Midlands 1642–1645* (1992) and *The Civil War in Stratford-upon-Avon: Conflict and Community in South Warwickshire, 1642–1646* (1996).

Introduction

ROBERT BEARMAN

There can be few towns of Stratford-upon-Avon's modest size which are so well known, not only in this country but throughout the world. This is to be attributed, of course, to the fact that England's national poet and playwright was born, brought up and buried here, and the town today both enjoys the benefits and suffers the consequences of this famous association. Yet this alone does not make Stratford an historic town, if by such a term we mean a town which reveals to us various episodes of its past through visible features in its existing urban fabric. Moreover, the town's Shakespearian associations, although appreciated by increasing numbers of people from the early eighteenth century onwards, had little significant effect on the town's economy until early this century; indeed, some would argue that visitor patronage has only had a major impact in this respect since the Second World War. Be that as it may, it is clear that for at least the first 700 years of its existence – that is, from the grant of borough status in 1196 – Stratford's history is that of a Midlands market town, its fortunes fluctuating in response to influences largely outside its control, but never succumbing to those forces which set other urban settlements on the path of irreversible decline. And this history is still reflected in many of the town's surviving features; its physical relationship with its rural hinterland, its medieval street pattern, the fine range of buildings associated with its medieval Guild of the Holy Cross, its parish church rebuilt and extended in response to changing needs, its timber-framed buildings, many dating from after the fires of the late sixteenth and early seventeenth centuries, and its public buildings of eighteenth- and nineteenth-century date, reflecting the developing responsibilities of local government and the townspeople's more complex spiritual and recreational needs.

A by-product of Stratford's fame as a place of literary pilgrimage has been the preservation of its records. From the second half of the eighteenth century, antiquarians were burrowing into what had survived in the hope of unearthing new material relating to Shakespeare and his family. By a process of association, any material relating to Stratford acquired a status that it might otherwise not have achieved. Private collections were formed and public ones zealously preserved and catalogued. The purchase of Shakespeare's Birthplace in 1847, with the intention not only of preserving the house as a national memorial but also of assembling within it a collection of books, documents and artefacts relating to Shakespeare, provided a focal point for the collection of the town's archives at a time when local record-keeping was otherwise virtually non-existent.[1] As a result there is still preserved in the town a fine body of material relating to its history which might otherwise have been destroyed. There are, of course, archival collections elsewhere which contain material essential for the study of the town's past, but it remains the case that, just as Stratford's fame is disproportionate to its size, so is the survival rate of its archives the envy of larger towns. It is the purpose of this volume to bring together a collection of essays which draw on these rich resources. Taken together they provide us with a new history of the town but individually they also set Stratford in a broader context at various crucial periods in its history.

Charters of incorporation, conferring a measure of self-government on a town's inhabitants, are justly commemorated as milestones in any borough's development. Stratford received such a charter in 1553. Yet, if we wish to account for the existence of a town in the first place, it is almost invariably necessary to begin our study several centuries earlier. As a generalization, it can be said that most sixteenth-century towns owed their origin to a grant of borough status at some point in their medieval past. Such a grant conferred on the people who lived there (the burgesses) certain rights and privileges which encouraged them to manufacture and trade. One such privilege was that the burgesses became free, in contrast to those – the vast majority – who lived and worked on the land, and whose lives were controlled at every turn by the lord of the manor on which they resided. A grant of borough status was therefore fundamental to the evolution of a market town. Before such a grant, local inhabitants would be almost exclusively engaged in agriculture: afterwards, a community would evolve made up predominantly of those engaged in urban trades and activities.

The first essay which follows is therefore a detailed study of the charter by which, in 1196, John of Coutances, the Bishop of Worcester, established a borough on his manor of Stratford, touching on the political circumstances surrounding the grant, explaining how it fits into the general pattern of borough plantation during this period and why such grants were made, and analysing exactly what privileges the charter conferred. To this is linked a study of an almost contemporary charter by which the king, Richard I, granted to the bishop the right to hold a market at Stratford; for to a great extent the new town would depend for its success on the amount of trade it could attract.

In the wake of this grant of borough status, a town rapidly grew up where no town had existed before and, if we are concerned here only with the study of the fortunes of an urban community, its history cannot therefore really be pushed back beyond this point. But the pre-urban period cannot be ignored entirely, for there were certain influences at work which explain why the town of Stratford was established where it was. In the next essay, Nicholas Palmer therefore reviews the evidence for the earlier settlement of the area, beginning with a nucleated Romano-British village to the south-east of the River Avon. This eventually covered some twenty-two hectares, its site today bisected by Tiddington Road. It is first in evidence in the first century AD and may, although the evidence is inconclusive, have evolved out of a Late Iron Age settlement, thus predating the Roman Conquest. Its position seems to have been determined by the intersection of a road on the line of the present Tiddington Road with another crossing the Avon by a ford. It flourished into the fourth century but by the fifth was in decline and, indeed, may have been all but abandoned. However, a place of local importance grew up nearby, at Bridgetown, where a Roman road from Alcester to the Fosse crossed the Avon on the site of the present Clopton Bridge, indicated by an extensive Anglo-Saxon pagan cemetery of late fifth- to seventh-century date on land to the east of the present Alveston Manor Hotel. A settlement may have existed nearby but, if it did, it was in turn abandoned, to be replaced eventually by one around the present parish church, the presumed site of an Anglo-Saxon minster established by the end of the eighth century, close to two further fords. This shift could be explained on ideological grounds, a desire by the new Christian community to distance itself from the pagan cemetery at Bridgetown. However, we cannot assume that a nucleated settlement existed here, or indeed at Bridgetown, during this early period: a far more common pattern would be for the local population to have lived in scattered farms and hamlets. It is certainly the case that the church had become the focal point of such a village by the twelfth century, but Nicholas Palmer's review of the archaeological evidence from this area makes it clear that a case for a large village here earlier than around 1100 cannot yet be substantiated.

In 1086, when Domesday Book was compiled, there were only twenty-nine householders recorded on the Bishop of Worcester's manor of Stratford – rising to some fifty-five by the time of a mid-1160s survey – spread throughout a very large parish, but with concentrations in Shottery, Welcombe and Stratford itself. But in 1196, the then Bishop of Worcester, John of Coutances, decided to establish a town on the manor. This did not displace the purely rural community, living by now in a cluster of dwellings around the church, but was laid out alongside it on what had hitherto been agricultural land. Dr T.R. Slater's contribution to this volume explores the reasons behind the bishop's choice of this particular site for his 'new town' development, and also outlines the problems these early town-planners faced. These included the geology of the area, the flood plain, the existing road network and the location of the village. Nevertheless, a regular, though not a right-angled, grid-pattern was achieved, lined with burgage plots of a uniform size defined in the borough charter. Dr Slater then looks more closely at this pattern to determine the original orientation of the burgage plots and to show in particular how those on prime corner sites became broken down into profitable subdivisions. He also describes the type of houses which would first have been built upon them. This study is also important in demonstrating how Stratford's present town plan is still essentially that laid down 800 years ago, even though developments over the last hundred years have in many cases obliterated the boundaries of the medieval burgages behind the street frontages.

The bishop's venture was a great success. From a survey of 1251/2, we know that some 230 householders had by then been attracted into this new town. Their names give us clues to their places of origin – mostly within sixteen miles of Stratford – and the wide variety of urban trades and activities in which they were engaged. Yet even in the 1220s, there is evidence of a vigorous, if rather disorderly, community and as early as 1214, the Bishop of Worcester had applied to the king for a licence to hold a three-day fair, a sure indication that the town was developing as an important place of exchange. We can only conclude, therefore, that the laying out of a new town in, or very soon after 1196, and the grant of the rights of free burgesses to those who came to live there, had proved an irresistible attraction. In the next essay, Christopher Dyer gives further evidence of the remarkable success achieved by this new town, with a population of between 1,000 and 2,000, at least until the Black Death in the middle of the fourteenth century, and a pre-eminence in the local area over all but the ancient boroughs of Coventry, Warwick and Worcester. This, of course, was almost entirely due to its success as a trading centre, of which the grants of charters for the holding of three additional fairs, in 1239, 1269 and 1309, are an obvious manifestation. This success can be attributed partly to the town's strategic siting at a river crossing, where several important routes converged, and the construction of a bridge over the old ford, certainly by 1235 and perhaps nearer to the time of the founding of the borough, is an indication of the importance of good communications for a flourishing town. But Stratford also stood on the boundary between two distinct regions, the Arden and the Feldon, providing a place of exchange for goods from the more wooded Arden to the north-west with those from the arable landscapes of the Feldon to the south-east, and this was also undoubtedly a factor in its success. Civic institutions within the town were also soon in evidence. The Guild of the Holy Cross, for example, was licensed to found a hospital in 1270, but there were also two other guilds in existence by this time. Their original function was to generate income to employ priests to say masses for the safety of the members' souls, but they also developed a social role and later played a part in the governance of the town. In the early fourteenth century the parish church was largely rebuilt and became collegiate, thanks to the patronage of three members of a very influential local family, John, Robert and Ralph Stratford, who between them held the highest offices in church and state.

Following the Black Death there are signs of economic difficulties, and these are also analysed in Christopher Dyer's essay. However, though it is clear that the population declined and that some properties fell into disrepair, it would also seem that, at the very least, the town's earlier success had placed it in a strong enough position to weather the storm. There is also reason to believe that some of this 'decay' could have been linked to inefficiency on the part of the bishops' officers whose influence declined as that of the Guild of the Holy Cross increased. In 1403 the Guild had amalgamated with other similar institutions in the town, and soon after built for itself a new Guild Hall and a row of almshouses, all of which survive today. Thereafter, there are indications of its increasing authority and influence within the town and before the end of the century, building work not only in connection with the Guild Chapel but also the parish church, Clopton Bridge and some of the town's residential properties, all contributes to the impression of a town which, though experiencing some short-term difficulties, was more than holding its own in the local hierarchy.

The importance of the Guild in medieval Stratford can hardly be exaggerated and it is fortunate indeed that the survival of its register of members, an impressive series of rentals and accounts, and many of its deeds and leases allow us to examine its activities in detail. Christopher Dyer describes some of these, emphasizing in particular the beneficial 'bonding' effects of such occasions as the annual feasts, and the social benefits conferred by the school and almshouses which the Guild administered. In her contribution, Christine Carpenter develops these points in relation to the membership of the Guild and, in particular, gentry membership. It is clear from even a cursory study of the records that membership, far from being confined to the town's élite, was frequently sought by local gentry families and on occasion bestowed on some of the greatest figures in the Midlands, George, Duke of Clarence, for example, in 1477/8 and Edward, Prince of Wales in 1478/9. Two questions arise: what benefits did the Guild hope to derive from such recruitment and, the other side of the coin, what advantages were there in it for the gentry? In terms of direct involvement, these gentry members, with one or two notable exceptions, played little part in the Guild's affairs, nor, in fact, did they show the Guild any great favours by way of gifts or bequests. Nevertheless, these local gentry, though by no means from the upper echelons of landed society, gave the Guild (and through it the town) a point of contact with the country's ruling class, and thus a path to favour and protection. The benefits to the gentry of Guild membership are less easy to discern but Christine Carpenter points out the commercial advantages of their establishing links with the principal traders in the area. She also emphasizes the role of the Guild as a means whereby gentry members could maintain or develop contacts with their own social equals, drawing attention at the same time to a political affinity they shared with the most potent landowning family in the vicinity, the Earls of Warwick. In this sense, the Guild served almost the purpose of a club where local gentry could expect deferential treatment when visiting town to discuss matters of business with fellow members of the local landowning élite. In any event, we are left in no doubt as to the importance and influence of the Guild on the life of the town.

This state of affairs came to a sudden end in 1547. In that year, the Guild of the Holy Cross, as a religious foundation, was suppressed as part of the English Reformation and its property confiscated by the Crown. This caused problems for the town, not only because the Guild, through its school and almshouses, had provided some social services, but also because its officers had, in effect, become the town's unofficial governing body. The bishop, of course, had remained the lord of the borough throughout the medieval period; the day-to-day running of the town was in the hands of his bailiff, and his court, under his steward, had continued to meet. But the court's personnel came to be drawn almost exclusively from the Guild's own masters and aldermen, evolving into an oligarchy of the town's élite who managed the town's affairs to suit its own, rather than the bishop's, agenda. The suppression of the Guild in 1547 must therefore have been a matter of some concern, and the surrender of the lordship of the manor, two years later, by the Bishop of Worcester, a cause of further uncertainty. This is the starting point for Alan Dyer's essay on the challenges which faced the town and the way in which they were met and largely overcome over the following hundred years. The particular problem of town government was partially solved in 1553, when Stratford received from the king, Edward VI, a charter of incorporation. Under this, a high bailiff and fourteen aldermen, endowed with the confiscated property of the Guild, took over the running of the school and almshouses, and were also made responsible for the maintenance of the bridge and for paying the vicar. This left unresolved the problem of the relationship between this new Corporation and successive lords of the manor, and it was not until the grant of a second charter of 1610 that this was sorted out. In the meantime, however, the town had other worries on its mind, the result of nationwide economic and social change. There were also catastrophic outbreaks of disease, particularly in 1564 and 1597, the first bubonic plague and the second the result of malnutrition in the wake of four disastrous harvests. There were also four very damaging town fires, in 1594, 1595, 1614 and 1641. Petitions to the government for tax exemptions and other concessions paint a particularly bleak picture of a town overrun with poor people. No doubt there was an element of special pleading here, but other sources reveal that when food was scarce or the town's commons threatened with enclosure, the more desperate of the townsfolk came close to rebellion.[2] Yet, just as Stratford survived the upheavals in the wake of the Black Death, so did it once more overcome these new difficulties and again this is attributed to its role as one of the main market towns in the region. Although the road network may in some respects have been deficient (the town, for instance, was not linked by a major route to the capital), its key position on the dividing line between the Arden and Feldon, with their different agricultural economies, is again seen as crucial in enabling the town to survive this difficult period. One indication of this is the increase in the number of fairs authorized under the 1610 charter, from two to five.

This was, however, also a period of great cultural and spiritual change. The Reformation had brought in its wake not only a crisis in local government and a turbulent land market, but also a fundamental change in the country's religious outlook. The intention of the early Protestant reformers, it seems, was merely to secure independence from Rome. But such tampering with orthodoxy opened the floodgates for new ideas and by the early seventeenth century, the main threat to the new Protestant church came not from families who had refused to abandon their Catholic faith but from zealous Puritans who wished to carry the Reformation into every corner of people's lives, with particular emphasis on their moral and social behaviour. This is the theme of Ann Hughes's essay, 'Building a Godly Town', where the point is made that, although Catholic recusants (including in all likelihood Shakespeare's father, John) were a source of some anxiety, it was the manifestations of extreme Protestantism, or Puritanism as it became known, which eventually brought about real division in the town. As far as the Corporation was concerned, an early expression of sound Protestant thinking is found in such acts as the defacing of the images in the Guild Chapel in 1564. Later, in 1602 and 1612, by-laws were promulgated which attempted to exclude companies of travelling players from the town. The complementary workings of the vicar's ecclesiastical court, with its jurisdiction over sexual as well as religious matters, also reveal a general enthusiasm for the punishment of moral backsliders. Thus far, the church and Corporation might be seen to be working together, even though personal quarrels between townsmen with differing religious views might surface from time to time. But the Corporation's appointment as vicar, in 1619, of the radical Thomas Wilson led to more open conflict, characterized by rioting and accusations of libel and defamation. Even so, Wilson seems to have retained the confidence of the majority of the Corporation for nearly a decade. In the end, however, his reforming zeal, aggravated, we may suspect, by a conflict of personalities, led to his increasing isolation and, in the final analysis, failure to 'reform' the town in the manner he had intended. The townspeople may have been willing to acquiesce in, and even support, the establishment of moderate Protestantism in Stratford but eventually drew the line at the sort of extremism which Wilson represented.

Serious as these economic difficulties and cultural conflicts were, there was, of course, worse to come; Stratford, like most other communities throughout the land, had yet to experience the effects of the Civil War. The town had the good fortune not to be defensible and so escaped the widespread damage which crippled towns like Banbury. But, as Philip Tennant shows in his essay 'Stratford-upon-Avon in the Civil War', it was not without its moments of crisis and, more importantly, it could not escape the less dramatic but all-pervading misfortunes of heavy taxation and the requirement to billet soldiers and otherwise provide for the military (of both sides) on a more or less permanent basis. In the latter respect, the town seems to have been particularly unfortunate. Between 1642 and 1646 the Midlands, and especially Warwickshire, was the scene of major troop movements on both sides, with armies crossing the county, on average, some four or five times a year. After the war was over, those who had suffered losses at the hands of the Parliamentarian armies were able to claim compensation and these claims bear witness to the constant drain on the town's resources caused by billetting and requisitioning. The town was not without experiences of a less negative kind: Queen Henrietta's three-day visit, for instance, in 1642, when she was met by Prince Rupert on her way to join her husband, Charles I.[3] But the picture which emerges is one of persistent harassment and oppressive taxation.

Nevertheless, it seems that Stratford's commercial base was once again strong enough to carry the town forward to more prosperous times. Despite a serious fire in 1641 and an outbreak of plague in 1646, and even though Clopton Bridge had been breached in 1645 during the closing stages of the war, the town's markets continued to function effectively; indeed the buying and selling of horses at four fairs in 1646 stood at record levels.[4] When

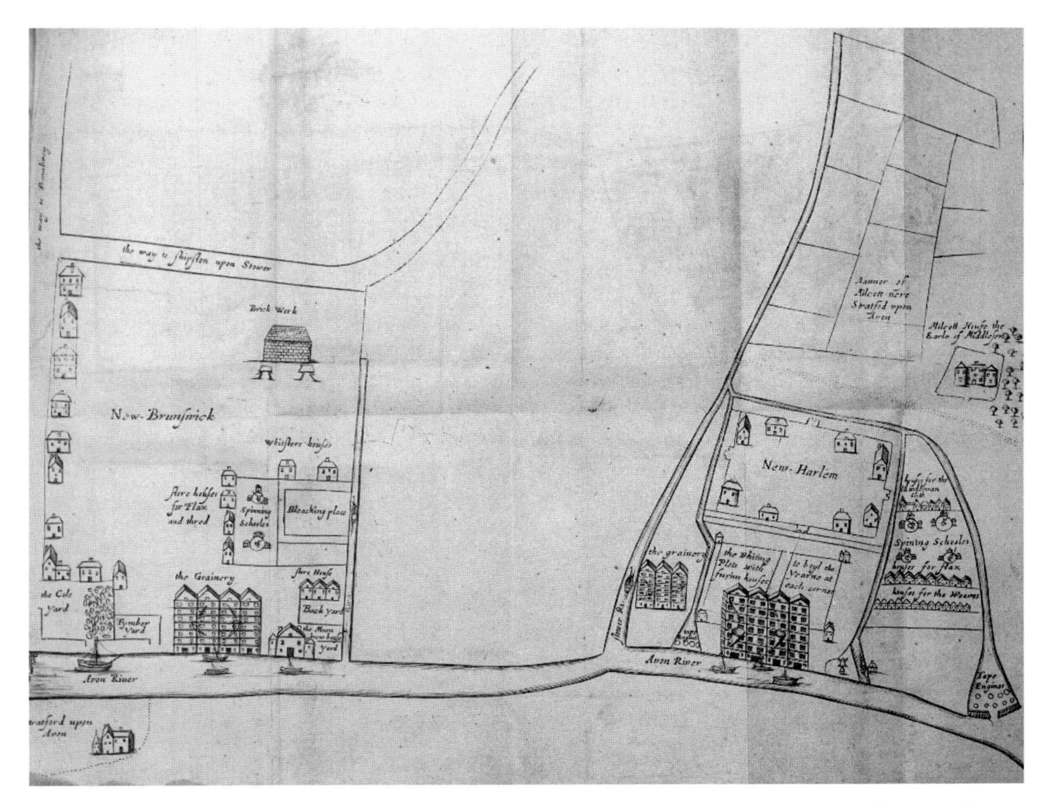

Plate 1. Plan of the proposed 'New Brunswick' at Bridgetown, Stratford-upon-Avon, from Andrew Yarranton's *England's Improvement by Sea and Land*, 1677.

peace was finally restored, the town resumed its traditional trading role and, after the Restoration in 1660, its trade was given a further boost as a result of the permanent opening up of the River Avon to navigation. An earlier scheme, barely complete by the time the Civil War had broken out, had fallen into disuse, but entrepreneurs, sensing the potential of Stratford's trading position, embarked on a more ambitious scheme in the 1670s, to be linked, it was hoped, to the building of two new towns, one at Milcote (a mile or two downstream from Stratford) to be called New Haarlem and one at Bridgetown, to be called New Brunswick.[5] The scheme proved far too ambitious but there was some building at Bridgetown (of which the present Forte Posthouse Hotel is a surviving example) and the added prosperity which the navigation brought to the town is also reflected in a mini-building boom of late seventeenth- and early eighteenth-century date. The lead was taken by the local squires, the Cloptons, who rebuilt their family home, Clopton House, just outside the town in the 1660s, and their town house, New Place, around 1700. Of the others, built mostly by lawyers pre-eminent in the ranks of a rising class of town gentry, many still survive in Old Town and Church Street.[6] But this was short-lived, and by the middle of the eighteenth century it is clear that the borough, in common with many other towns, was in decline. There was a reduction in the number of fairs (to three) and in the amount of business transacted in those that remained, and a decrease in the volume of traffic on the Avon to a point where it was feared it may 'in a short time utterly cease'.[7] In 1781 one in ten houses stood empty. At the same time, the corporate body governing the town was clearly in difficulties. From 1731, there were vacancies in the ranks of both aldermen and chief burgesses, with only two of the latter being persuaded to serve in 1789. As a result, it was often difficult to muster sufficient members for the conduct of business; after 1783, nearly a third of council meetings were abandoned for want of a quorum. The Corporation became increasingly burdened with debt, and several of its members also ended up personally bankrupt.[8]

The general impression of eighteenth-century Stratford is one of stagnation, if not decline, from which the town was only rescued, towards the end of the century, by improved communications and the knock-on effects of the country's increasing industrialization. This provides the background for Joan Lane's essay on poverty and disease in the town during this period. The sources for this aspect of town life are less plentiful and require careful interpretation, but she is able to point up periods of crisis associated with particular outbreaks of disease and to outline what services and treatments (including inoculation) were available to the townspeople, especially the disadvantaged among them who needed to ask assistance from the Poor Law overseers. Central to her study is a unique census of the town taken by order of the overseers in 1765, ostensibly to discover how many of the population had had smallpox and where the townsfolk were legally settled, but yielding at the same time other important demographic information.

Plate 2. Early eighteenth-century houses in the Old Town area. (Photo: Malcolm Davies)

Municipal government was reformed in 1835. Until that time most of the old corporations, Stratford among them, had been governed by bodies of men who chose 'suitable' colleagues from the ranks of the townsmen to fill any vacancies which might occur. Under the Municipal Corporations Act of 1835, these self-perpetuating oligarchies were swept away to be replaced by elected councils chosen by the ratepayers. It would be easy to attribute Stratford's revival to this measure, but in fact recovery was already under way. The turnpiking of the major roads into the town was completed by 1773 and in 1816 a canal eventually reached the town, though only after much difficulty. This led to a revival of the Avon Navigation and the building of the horse-drawn tramway to Moreton in Marsh, opened in 1826.[9] But rising prosperity also brought its problems for, like all successful urban settlements, Stratford was on the brink of massive change. In a hundred years, between 1801 and 1901, its population was to treble, from some 3,000 people to nearly 9,000. Existing mechanisms for caring for the sick and the poor were unable to cope with these new demands, and a housing crisis led to overcrowding and insanitary slums. This aroused in some a sympathy for the plight of the urban poor and in others a fear of social disorder. It also sparked off a debate within the church between those whose convictions led them into the field of social reform and those who saw the defence of the Church of England's privileged ascendancy as essential in the fight against social disintegration. This is the starting point for Nicholas Fogg's essay on religion and politics in nineteenth-century Stratford. He points out that the early reformers, devout churchmen, at first worked within a charitable or voluntary framework. A free dispensary for the poor was established in 1823, funded by donations from the more well-to-do. This was the brainchild of a young doctor, John Conolly, who was later to win national recognition for his pioneer work in the humane treatment of the insane. Day schools were also set up in the 1820s, again relying on voluntary subscriptions.[10]

Gradually, however, government, both central and local, was obliged to intervene as problems multiplied and, as Nicholas Fogg goes on to show, social reform became a political issue. In 1834 the old parish system of poor relief was scrapped and replaced by one overseen by centrally-appointed Commissioners. Parishes were grouped into unions served by one workhouse. Stratford became the centre of one such union, with its new workhouse in Arden Street built in 1836. To reduce costs, conditions within were made deliberately harsh in an effort to deter all but the most destitute from seeking assistance. Public health was the next major public issue to interest central government, largely in response to the then serious threat of cholera. Under an Act of 1848 a General Board of Health was established to which local boards were answerable. These local boards, usually associated with towns, could be established in a number of ways. One method was for a tenth of the rate-payers to petition for a visit by a government inspector, on whose recommendation, if he thought the situation warranted it, the appointment of a local Board would be authorized. This was what happened in Stratford, not, however, without controversy; for by the time the inspector's report had been received and the local Board authorized, the cholera scare had come and gone.[11] There had been no deaths in Stratford, but at the same time it had dawned on local people how much it would cost to construct the drainage and water system recommended in the inspector's report. Attempts were therefore made to disband the local board even before it met and, although this failed on legal grounds, the improvements to the town's infrastructure were fought all the way by the 'economists' and not completed until 1884.

A similar situation arose with regard to education. An Act of 1870 required local communities to provide sufficient places for all school-age children: if they could not do this, a local School Board would have to be set up with powers to raise a rate to pay for the necessary additional provision. However, until attendance was made compulsory (in 1880), existing voluntary schools could make out a case that no such provision was needed. After 1880 this was more difficult, especially when the government refused to 'count' certain voluntary school places on the grounds that they were 'inadequate'. By such means, they were able to force School Boards onto reluctant ratepayers, despite stout resistance. The battle in Stratford was particularly lively: at stake was not only the cost to the ratepayers of providing new facilities but the threat to the ascendancy of the Church of England over education.

The Victorians are often praised for the manner in which they succeeded in paving, draining and lighting their towns, but this rather overlooks the fact that at local level at least such improvements were often resisted by many ratepayers. Nicholas Fogg's essay reveals how in Stratford this resistance influenced local elections, at both municipal and parliamentary level, but bearing in mind, of course, that for much of this period the electorate was only a fraction of the total population. He also shows how the link between religion and politics extended into controversies unconnected with social reform; the issue of church rates in the 1830s and 40s, for example, and the influence of Methodism on Joseph Arch and his fellow co-founders of the Warwickshire Agricultural Labourers' Union in the 1870s.

The history of nineteenth-century Stratford, however, has another aspect, its growing reputation as a literary shrine. This had its origins in occasional recorded visits in the seventeenth and early eighteenth centuries, and was given a great boost by the three-day Jubilee in honour of Shakespeare which the leading actor of the day, David Garrick, organized in the town in 1769. Even so, at the end of the nineteenth century, the number of visitors to Shakespeare's Birthplace still totalled only 28,000 a year, modest when compared with current figures of around half a million. It was thus still the case that, in terms of the town's economy, visitor patronage was not a dominant factor. At the same time, however, it was during the nineteenth century that Stratford's name became inextricably linked with Shakespeare. The purchase of Shakespeare's Birthplace in 1847, the elaborate celebrations held in the town in 1864 to commemorate the 300th anniversary of his birth, and the opening of the Shakespeare Memorial Theatre in 1879, though owing much, if not all, to the enthusiasm and dedication of local people, brought Stratford to the attention of not only the nation but the world. In the final essay, Roger Pringle plots the course of this remarkable story into the early years of this century, drawing attention in particular to the manner in which it reflects more general trends; a growing interest in matters antiquarian in the eighteenth century, a need to celebrate cultural heroes in the fervently patriotic atmosphere of the mid-nineteenth century, and the growing concern as the century closed to protect the nation's heritage. Developments in the transport system are also seen as of major importance.

Since 1900 Stratford's growing popularity as an inland resort has probably been the most significant factor in its development. This is not to say that Stratford does not have a thriving commercial and business life unrelated, at least on the face of it, to visitor patronage. But it is an undoubted fact that tourism is now one of the country's most important industries and Stratford's success can be attributed now, as it can in the past, to its good fortune in possessing the right attributes at the right time. For a town to thrive, it needs to trade in what people wish to buy and this, it would appear, has always been Stratford's good fortune.[12]

CHAPTER 1

The Charter of 1196

ROBERT BEARMAN

In 1086, when Domesday Book was compiled, the number of householders within the manor of Stratford, at that time forming part of the Bishop of Worcester's estates, was given as twenty-nine.[1] A more detailed survey of the late 1160s lists some fifty to fifty-five households and also reveals three main centres of local population within the manor; around thirty in Shottery, ten at Welcombe and twenty in Stratford itself.[2] If these figures can be taken at or near their face value, there had, then, been some growth during this period. But by 1251/2, from the evidence of a survey of that date, something far more dramatic had taken place. This survey is in two parts: first, the rural manor, including, as before, tenants living not just in Stratford itself but at Shottery and Welcombe too. Again, there had been a significant increase, from around fifty households to some seventy. But alongside this is a survey of what is called the 'borough' of Stratford, with over 230 householders listed.[3] Together, these figures represent about a six-fold increase in the number of households within the space of a hundred years. Such an increase cannot, of course, be accounted for by natural growth: it was instead almost entirely due to this novel component of a borough within the Stratford estate. The establishment of this borough can be dated fairly precisely: as we shall see, it was not there in June 1196 but it was by September 1198. Between these two dates the lord of the manor, John of Coutances, the Bishop of Worcester, issued a charter defining the legal basis on which this borough had been established. There are very good reasons for believing this decision was taken at the beginning of this period rather than the end, hence the traditional dating of it to 1196.

The development of this new borough began fairly quickly and along highly organized lines, and this will be fully discussed later.[4] But we need to explore first what was special about a borough and why it required a charter to become established. The answer to this concerns the terms on which the inhabitants of such boroughs (the burgesses) held their land (the burgages) within them. This varied from borough to borough but, as a generalization, burgesses can be said to have held their land more freely than those who lived and worked in purely rural settlements. This can be simply illustrated by looking again at the 1251/2 survey. Here the burgesses of Stratford are listed as holding their burgages (or subdivisions of them) at an annual rent of twelve pence, and with an obligation to attend the borough court three times a year. In contrast, the customary tenants on the rural estate were burdened with a whole range of irksome duties and payments to the lord of the manor. They paid a toll, for instance, on every native-born horse or ox born or sold within the manor, and on any ale similarly sold. They could not sell pigs between August and November. On their death, the best animal had to be handed over to the lord if the family were to keep the land. Their daughters could not be married without their lord's consent. If they were not paying the full rent of 8*s* a virgate for their lands, then they were also liable to a whole string of onerous labour services: from September to June, for instance, they had to work on the lord's lands for one day a week and from June to September for four days a week, providing at the same time a man to assist. But we must be careful not to paint too bleak a picture. By 1251/2, most of the Stratford tenants paid only money rents and were thus free of these labour services. The actual enforcement of the other dues and customs must also have been very difficult. Moreover, nearly two thirds of these tenants held at least half a virgate of land, and a third of them a virgate or more. With a virgate sometimes taken to represent as much as thirty acres, these were substantial holdings, sufficient to maintain a family in reasonable style provided crop yields were good. Nevertheless, their tenure depended almost entirely on their lord's goodwill and, above all, they were not free, the most obvious manifestation of this being that they and their chattels could still be sold by one lord to another. In contrast, the burgess held freely; that is, his burgage would be automatically inherited by his heir or he could sell it, sublet it, subdivide it, or develop it as he pleased. As long as he paid his rent and appeared at the borough court three times a year, he and his family could count on being more or less left in peace. Stratford's borough charter of 1196 is therefore of great significance; it gave to the people who came to live in the new town a legal status which they would be very unlikely to have achieved as rural tenants. Villeins (as the unfree tenants in rural settlements were called) were very occasionally granted their freedom by a lord (by a process known as manumission) but this was always an unlikely route to the improvement of one's status. Burgage tenure was a far more attractive proposition.

Our knowledge of the text of Stratford's borough charter depends on a transcript of it copied into one of the Bishop of Worcester's cartularies.[5] The title page of this volume is dated the ninth year of the reign of Henry IV (1407/8) and the hand of the scribe is consistent with an early fifteenth-century date. We are not, then, dealing with an original charter, but a copy made some 200 years later. This copy must have been made from an earlier version, but of this no trace now survives. It could perhaps have been the original, the copy which the beneficiaries of the grant, the burgesses of Stratford, should have received, written out on a piece of parchment and authenticated by the Bishop of Worcester's seal. Such an item, however, one would not have expected to have remained in the bishop's archives for it to have been conveniently copied some 200 years later. Surely, this would have been given to the burgesses and (as there is no trace of it today) subsequently lost by them. We are therefore on fairly safe ground in assuming that the text in the register was taken from an earlier administrative copy which the bishops had retained in their archives for reference purposes. The original – the burgesses' copy – was said to have been shown to Bishop Mauger, John's successor, who at some point between 1200 and 1210, issued his own charter confirming it.[6] Be that as it may, it is not heard of again. It must also be borne in mind that, in the uncertain situation of 1196, when no one knew whether or not the new borough would succeed or even get off the ground, the drawing up of a solemnly sealed original might well have been thought an extravagance, or even tempting fate. It is therefore much more likely that the bishop's charter records a setting down in writing some time after the event, as was common with most other written records of the time, the conditions on which his new borough had been established, attested by those of the bishop's officials who had been present when he announced his intention. This would have become necessary when it was clear that the bishop's new venture was going to be a success or, at least, that it was not going to fail. Seen in this

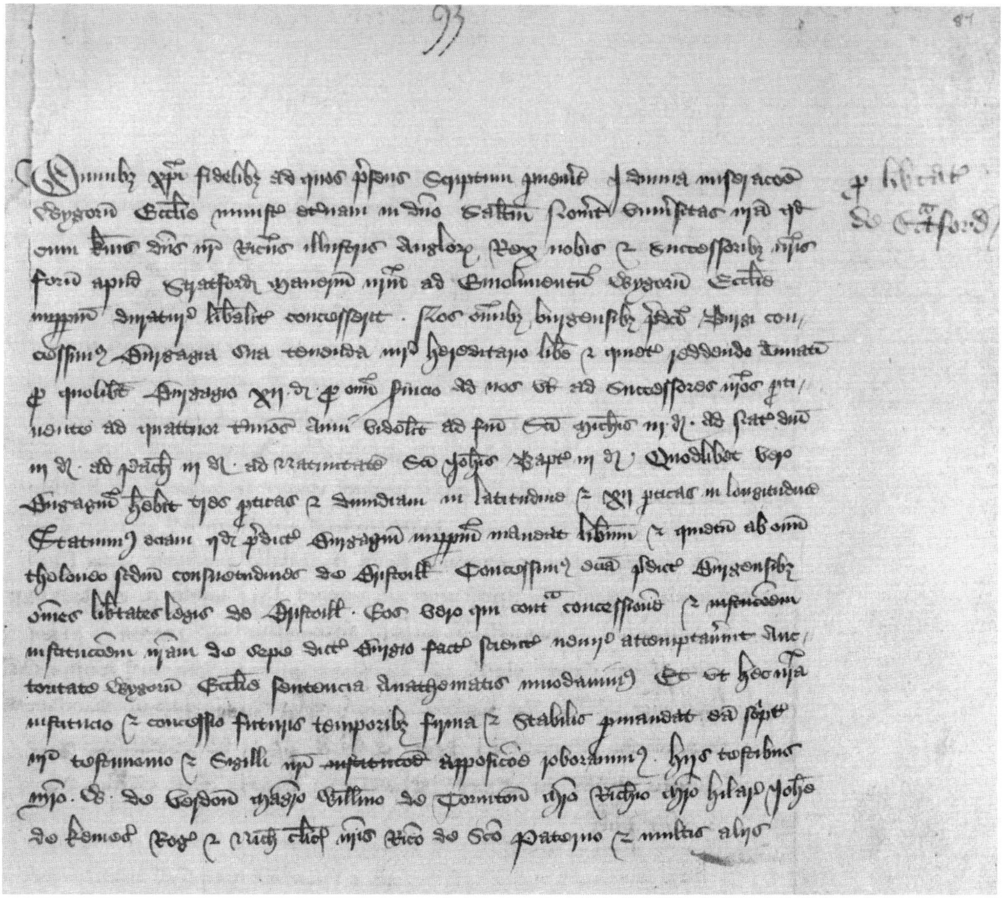

Plate 3. The charter of John of Coutances, Bishop of Worcester (as copied into an early fifteenth-century cartulary) establishing a borough on his manor of Stratford. (HWCRO, BA 2636/9 iv ref. 009.1, fol. 93)

light, the charter takes on the nature of an administrative convenience for the bishops and their officers who saw the advantage in a written record of the terms on which the new burgesses held their lands, rather than that of a solemn grant of privileges conferred upon them. It should therefore come as no surprise to find that the burgesses' rights, as we shall see, were left rather imprecise while their obligations to the bishop were much more clearly specified.

The first historian to draw attention to Stratford's charter was William Dugdale who, in his *Antiquities of Warwickshire*, published in 1656, gave a summary in English of its contents.[7] His marginal reference reads 'ex autographo in armario Wigorniensis episcopi' (from an autograph in the Bishop of Worcester's study). This is usually how Dugdale described original charters and has given rise to the assumption that Stratford's original borough charter had, for some reason, survived in the bishop's archives.[8] This, as we have seen, is not what one would have expected and in any case, on this occasion, Dugdale might be misleading us.

It has long been recognized that Dugdale depended on a network of collaborators to compile his *Antiquities*. Probably the most important of these was the Warwickshire antiquary, Sir Simon Archer of Umberslade.[9] Yet Archer himself also relied on help from other quarters, especially when it came to examining material outside the county. The diocesan archives at Worcester were an obvious quarry, as some half of Warwickshire lay within the bishopric. The man who apparently combed these on Archer's and Dugdale's behalf was an antiquary by the name of Thomas Habington. On 16 September 1636 Habington wrote to Archer: 'My Lord Bishop grauntethe mee the perusall of hys Leger bookes wheare I find some lytell of Warwyckshyre: when I have reade them (for I am yet in the fyrst) I wyll present to you what I fynd of yor county.'[10] On another occasion, he wrote: 'I could neaver see any legers in our shyre but onely of the Bishopricke & Priory of Worcester, wheareuppon I dyd wryte a short treatise of the Churche & a tedyous discourse of theyre manors, of Stratford uppon Avon being one, & of thease I have enoughe yf not to muche.'[11] This 'tedyous discourse' still survives in Habington's papers and includes a detailed abstract in English of the town's borough charter.[12] He must have sent Archer a copy of not just this but the whole of his Stratford account, for the latter copied it, almost word for word, into his manuscript history of Warwickshire.[13] Archer must then have passed the information to Dugdale for, on a page of one of Dugdale's notebooks, headed 'Perticulers concerninge Stratford super Avon observed by Mr Abington . . . out of ye old registers in ye B:^pp of Worcester's custodye' we find another, though slightly less complete, copy of Habington's abstract of the borough charter.[14] This, in turn, and further shortened, is what eventually appeared in the *Antiquities*. So, far from Dugdale discovering the text of the charter himself, and from the original, as his marginal note implies, it seems that his account of it was a third-hand version of an abstract from the cartulary.

There is a tailpiece to this complicated story. Nowhere in Habington's, Archer's or Dugdale's surviving papers is there a copy of the actual Latin text. From Dugdale's time until the rediscovery of the cartulary entry in the 1970s, historians relied solely on the abstract published by Dugdale on which to base their statements about the charter's contents. But among the papers of an early nineteenth-century antiquary, Captain James Saunders of Stratford-upon-Avon, there is a full Latin copy.[15] This is in Saunders's hand and he does not name his source. However, there is very little evidence that Saunders ever

Plate 4. Thomas Habington as a young man. Suspected in 1605 of involvement in the Gunpowder Plot, Habington was confined for the rest of his life to his native county of Worcestershire. Dedicating himself thereafter to antiquarian research, it was he who discovered the text of Stratford's first charter.

went any distance to search out material. The bulk of his copying was from documents in the town and for a few years, from 1812 to 1815, these included the papers of Simon Archer.[16] It would therefore not be unreasonable to assume that Habington did indeed send a copy of the charter, as well as an abstract, to Archer and that, although now lost, this copy was still among his papers when examined by Saunders.

Towards the end of the nineteenth century, the cartulary from which Habington had worked passed into the hands of the Ecclesiastical Commissioners, becoming in effect inaccessible to researchers. It was not deposited at the Worcester (now Hereford and Worcester) County Record Office until 1959, and it was another ten years or so before the fact that it contained the text of the Stratford charter was recognized.[17]

The charter, issued in the name of Bishop John, must obviously date from before his death in office on 24 September 1198. The earliest date possible is 25 June 1196; it was on this day that King Richard, by a dated charter, granted to the bishop his right to hold a weekly market in his manor of Stratford;[18] and, as this grant is mentioned in the preamble of the bishop's charter to his new borough, then the latter must be later. In fact in June, John of Coutances was only bishop-elect; he had been chosen for the office but not yet consecrated. Convention demands that any charter issued by him as bishop (as in this case) rather than bishop-elect, should be dated after his consecration. In John's case this would be after 20 October of the same year.[19] However, if, as already suggested, John's act of setting up his borough was not actually committed to writing until some time after the event, the niceties of whether he was bishop or just bishop-elect at the time might have seemed an irrelevance to the clerks who drafted it. The chances are that, if, in June, John had gone to the trouble of establishing his right to hold a weekly market, then his decision to establish a borough had probably already been taken. It might seem odd that John, within months of his election, had formulated such a policy, and it could even be suggested that he was merely carrying into effect something his predecessor had initiated.[20] In all events, the act which his charter records can with some confidence be dated to the summer of 1196, even though it may not have been committed to writing until later; after his consecration as bishop on 20 October and before his death in September 1198.

The political background to the granting of this charter is worth examining for it has a bearing, if not on John's establishment of his new borough, then at least on his election as bishop and the king's confirmation to him of his market rights in June 1196. John's uncle was Walter of Coutances, Archbishop of Rouen.[21] Until early 1196, Walter had been high in the king's favour, having for many years served both him and his father Henry II as a leading administrator: indeed, he had been regent during Richard's absence on Crusade and subsequent captivity.[22] But in January the king and archbishop fell out. Since his release, Richard had been periodically at war with Philip, King of France, struggling to recover lands in Normandy which Philip, in Richard's enforced absence, had overrun. In January the two kings negotiated a peace treaty at Louvieres which attempted to fix a new boundary between them. On the proposed new frontier lay the archbishop's most valuable estate, L'Ile d'Andeley, on the River Seine, dominated by a huge rock outcrop which both kings dearly wished to fortify. A complicated clause in the treaty allowed either king to seize this property if the archbishop should place an interdict on their lands.[23] This was more than likely. Philip's lands within the archdiocese were already under an interdict as a punishment for the damage he had inflicted on church property during the recent war. Walter was determined not to submit to such an arrangement and left Richard's court, going first to

Rouen and then taking refuge at the abbey of Cambrai. Various diplomatic manoeuvres ensued, including a visit in April by the archbishop to Paris to flirt with the king of France. King Richard was therefore forced to accept that he must come to terms with the archbishop. This he had done by 7 July, on which date, as the archbishop wrote to the English churchman, Ralph of Diceto, he re-entered his church at Rouen, after receiving reparations from both kings and where he was greeted by the Bishops of Lincoln, Salisbury and Exeter.[24]

These events were exactly contemporary with the marks of royal favour shown to Walter's nephew, John of Coutances, namely his appointment as bishop and the king's grant to him of his Stratford market. John had already benefited considerably from his uncle's patronage: it was Walter who, apparently, when Bishop of Lincoln in 1183–4, had appointed John as his archdeacon of Oxford.[25] Later, as Archbishop of Rouen, he had given John the office of dean there. From the witness lists to Henry II's charters, it is also clear that, like his uncle, John was a valued royal administrator and promotion to a bishopric was frequently the reward for service of this kind. The bishopric of Worcester had fallen vacant on the death of Bishop Henry de Soilli in October 1195. In theory, the monks of Worcester would have been free to elect their new bishop but, as the king could block any appointment of which he did not approve, a royal nominee was, to say the least, in a very strong position. The king's choice on this occasion was clearly John of Coutances and the prior and convent, at a cost of twenty marks, had to travel to Normandy to 'elect' him.[26] Richard I then wrote to the Archbishop of Canterbury, informing him of this. His letter is found among a number of other documents concerning the dispute between the king and archbishop, collected together in a chronicle of the time by Ralph of Diceto, the Dean of St Pauls, with whom Archbishop Walter had corresponded throughout this difficult period.[27] There is surely enough circumstantial evidence here to warrant the assumption that John's election, some time in the first half of 1196, and the grant to him of a market in Stratford on 25 June, was part and parcel of the settlement between the king and archbishop, known to have been negotiated before 7 July.

The terms on which the bishop established his borough at Stratford are laid down in his charter, which may be translated as follows:

> To all the faithful in Christ, to whom this present writing shall come, John by divine mercy minister of the church of Worcester eternal greetings in the Lord. Be it known to all that, whereas our dear lord Richard, the illustrious king of the English, has granted to us and our successors, freely and forever, a market at our manor of Stratford for the benefit of the church of Worcester, we have granted to all our burgesses of the said borough their burgages, to hold by hereditary right freely and quietly, rendering annually for each burgage twelve pence for all services pertaining to us or our successors, at four terms of the year; namely, at the feast of St Michael, three pence, at the feast of the Nativity of Our Lord three pence, at Easter three pence, and at the Nativity of St John the Baptist three pence. Each burgage shall have three and a half perches in width and twelve perches in length. We have declared also that the said burgage shall remain forever free and quit from all toll according to the customs of Bristol. We have conceded also to the said burgesses all the free laws of Bristol. Those who should attempt knowingly to contravene our grant and foundation made of the said borough, we shall condemn by the authority of the church of Worcester by the sentence of anathema. And so that, in future times,

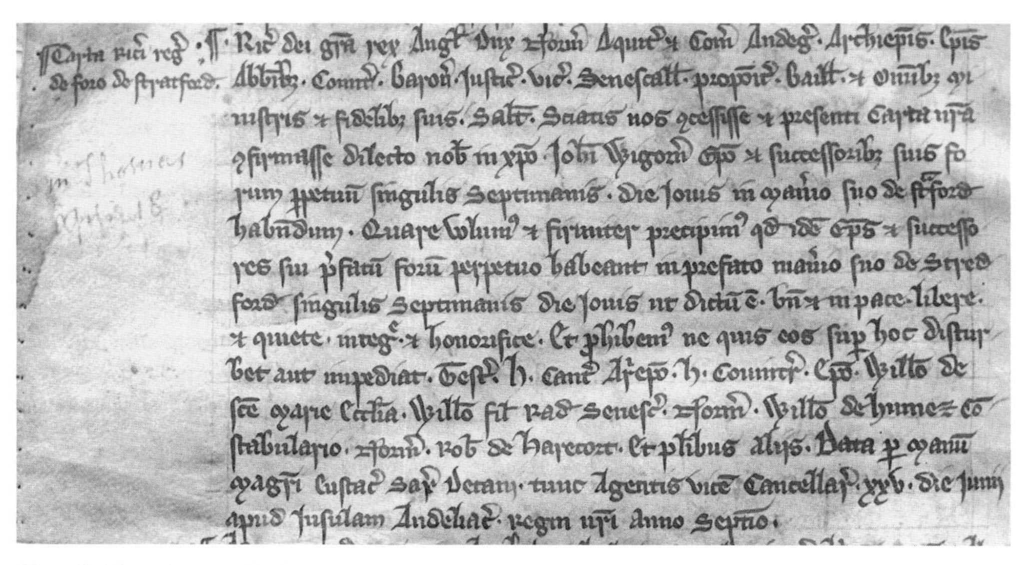

Plate 5. The charter of King Richard (as copied into the 'White Book') granting the Bishop of Worcester the right to a weekly market on his manor of Stratford, 25 June 1196. (HWCRO, ref. 821 BA 3814, fol. 42)

> this our ordinance and grant shall remain firm and stable, we have strengthened it with the testimony of our writing and our seal. With these witnesses: Master William of Verdon, Master William of Torinton, Master Richer, Master Hilary, John of Kempsey, Roger and Nicholas our clerks, Richard of St Paterno and many others.[28]

The first item requiring discussion is the mention of the grant of a market. This had been recorded in a royal charter dated 25 June 1196. Its text adds the further detail that this market was to be held weekly on a Thursday.[29] It would be natural to assume that this charter signified the market's inauguration. This, however, may be an oversimplification. By the late twelfth century, it was accepted that the holding of formal markets was a royal prerogative and consequently that consent from the crown was required if new markets were to be established.[30] This prerogative appears to have developed out of the circumstances in which markets originated at a period before the Norman Conquest. The primary administrative division of the country by then to have evolved was the shire, but within this there were further subdivisions, the hundreds. Each hundred had a main manor, the hundredal manor, usually belonging to the king, where the hundred court was held. Markets, it seems, were also conducted there, with the tolls on sales passing into the king's hands and it was this which gave rise to the notion that markets were a royal prerogative. However, the king could grant away these hundredal manors and the jurisdiction and market rights which went with them. Could this, or something like it, have happened in Stratford, thereby making the king's grant of 1196 more of a ratification of what was already going on?

Stratford lay in the hundred of Pathlow. When Domesday Book was compiled this comprised ten manors of which the Bishop of Worcester held Hampton Lucy, Stratford, Alveston and Loxley. Of the others, Clopton, Luddington, Milcote and Ruin Clifford had also once been, or were alleged to have been, part of his estates.[31] These had come to the bishop mainly as the result of royal grants in the late seventh and early eighth centuries.[32] Later, in 1285, the bishops claimed the jurisdiction of the Pathlow hundred court, or the Liberty of Pathlow as it was then known, from time out of mind and there is evidence from the late 1160s to substantiate this.[33] The bishops' right to hold a market within the hundred may therefore have been taken for granted well before Bishop John obtained formal consent in 1196 for its establishment at Stratford. The parallel with other hundreds is not exact as Pathlow itself was not even a manor, let alone the hundredal one. But the bishops may nevertheless have believed their tenure of the hundred gave them market rights within it and where more likely for one to have grown up than the river crossing at Stratford? A place to exchange goods must always have been required by the inhabitants of all but the smallest of settlements. By 1196 activity of this sort, possibly outside the gates of the old minster church at Stratford, though on a modest scale and not necessarily on a regular basis, might have been just what persuaded the Bishop of Worcester, or his staff, that a new town would do well there, rather than, say, at his manor of Hampton Lucy a few miles upstream.[34] In other words, it may be unwise to regard the king's grant of market rights as inaugurating the market itself. It could just as easily have been a retrospective acknowledgement of what was already taking place, albeit informally. But it is equally clear why the bishop made sure of his position by securing this royal confirmation. If a 'new town' venture was indeed in his mind, he needed to make sure that the holding of a market, on which its success would depend, was legally beyond question.

Of the remaining clauses of the charter, the most significant relates to the size of the burgage plots, but this, and its effect on the town's topography, will be discussed in a later chapter.[35] Suffice to say now that if each burgage was indeed to take up plots of land of identical size (i.e. three and a half perches wide and twelve deep, or approximately eighteen by sixty metres), then one would expect the town plan to conform to a neat pattern. As we shall see, it does; it is a grid of streets, the distance between parallels defined by the need to accommodate two of these plots end to end. For the rest, with the exception of the twelve pence rent, matters were left rather vague, although two key principles were established: firstly, that the burgesses should hold freely and by hereditary right (in marked contrast to villein tenure), and secondly, that the burgages would be free from toll. This was more than an emancipation from the irksome and stifling requirement of villein tenure that, out of the profits of the sale of merchandise, a percentage had to go to one's lord. It also exempted the burgesses from the tolls paid by those trading at the town's market. The remaining privileges of burgage tenure are summed up as corresponding to the 'free laws of Bristol'. There is no doubt that this is how the clause now reads, but many years ago Mary Bateson demonstrated beyond reasonable doubt that Bristol, or 'Bristoill' as it appears in the text, was a misreading by the early fifteenth-century copyist of the Latinized form of Breteuil (usually 'Britolium').[36]

Breteuil is now a small town in the department of Eure, some twenty-five miles southwest of Evreux, but its size belies an earlier importance. It was founded by William fitz Osbern in about 1060 and its customs were adopted by at least seventeen and perhaps twenty-five boroughs subsequently established in England. Moreover, the customs of some of these first-generation boroughs were used as models for subsequent foundations, thereby extending the

Breteuil family even more widely. Why this happened, we need not explore in detail here; the earliest references occur in Domesday Book (1086) and relate to boroughs established on the Welsh Marches. Hereford was one of these, granted by the Conqueror to William fitz Osbern, also the Lord of Breteuil.[37] The connection here is therefore obvious, and similar links can be established for some other early foundations. The customs, as originally granted to Breteuil, do not survive, but Mary Bateson reconstructed them by comparing the known customs adopted in the boroughs which acknowledged Breteuil as their parent. They ran to some thirty clauses. However, it would seem doubtful that any of Stratford's burgesses in 1196 would have had much idea of what the Bishop of Worcester was conferring on them when he added this clause to their charter. It would seem more likely that there was by then, some 130 years on, a general acceptance, in the bishop's or his administrators' eyes, that the grant of the laws of Breteuil, because they had been adopted by so many other towns, was just a convenient way of summarizing the privileged status which the new burgesses were to enjoy. What the bishop needed to make clear, he did: the size of the plots and the rent due. What the burgesses needed to know was that they held their burgages freely by inheritance and that they could trade free of toll. These four requirements are clearly spelt out. The rest was probably not of so much concern at the time: suffice to say that the laws of Breteuil generally concerned the burgesses' freedom over the disposal of their property and limited the rights of the lord over them.

What was the immediate effect of the grant of this charter and why had the bishop decided to set up a borough in the first place? The later twelfth century was a time of inflation and the effect of this on the great landholders of the day was considerable. The estates that they did not work were farmed out to others at fixed rents (or assized rents as they were known). As the century progressed and inflation began to bite, their income from this source, though the same in cash terms, began in effect to fall. They therefore began to look round for a means of offsetting these losses. One option was to bring back land under their own management and there is some evidence of this on many estates, including the Bishop of Worcester's.[38] Another was to set up new boroughs, and this is the context in which we must see Stratford's charter of 1196. For a borough not only brought the advantages of greater freedom to those who came to live there, it also benefited the lord of the manor. He was able to concentrate in a small area a group of people paying together much more in rent than he could get for the same land if let to peasants as agricultural holdings. If a borough prospered (and the best way to ensure that it did was to offer the new townsmen attractive rights and privileges) then the lord's income would be further boosted. This was because he had a right to the tolls payable by visitors to the fairs and markets and the income from fines imposed in the borough courts. So the more successful the market, the more money he would get; and the best way to ensure that the market prospered was to remove from the shoulders of the people who lived there the irksome restrictions on their rural counterparts. There was a further advantage, of course, if the lord of the manor also held large rural estates in the vicinity: a thriving town could stimulate demand for food and industrial raw materials, like wool and hides, thereby increasing his income from his other manors. Given this general background, we should not therefore be surprised to find that the establishment of a borough at Stratford was part of a nationwide phenomenon. Over seventy new towns were founded in the period between 1160 and 1230, forty-five of them (over half) after 1190 and thirteen in the 1190s.[39]

Within fifty years or so, as we have already seen, it is clear that the bishop's venture had been an outstanding success. In the late 1160s there were some fifty householders scattered through estates in Stratford, Shottery and Welcombe. By 1251/2, the situation had changed dramatically. The population of the manor of Stratford, now called Old Stratford, had indeed increased to about seventy households but alongside this, and in sharp contrast, was an entirely new element, the borough, with no less than 234 tenants. Here, then, is a textbook example of how the less burdensome demands of burgage tenure had attracted a population of some 1,000 souls within fifty years and which must also have swelled the bishop's coffers considerably: in 1251/2 he was gaining from rents alone £16 0*s* 6*d*, rising to £17 3*s* 6¾*d* by 1268–9.[40] These may sound trifling sums today but before the advent of the new town the agricultural land on which it was laid out would have been worth only a pound or two to the bishop.

The names of these people also give us valuable clues on two other points. Of the 234 tenants in 1251/2, eighty-two have place surnames. Excluding such vague types as 'de Bosco', we are left with fifty-seven (some occurring more than once) of which fifty can be identified with some certainty. Of these, only five are more than sixteen miles distant from Stratford, and thirty-five are less than eight.[41] If this is a representative sample, then the overwhelming majority of these new settlers were from Stratford's medieval catchment area. A further sixty-four surnames are occupational, giving further insights into life in the early town. This is in marked contrast to the names on the old rural manor. Here only seven (if we exclude the rural officials, the reeve, hayward and woodward) had occupational surnames. But within the borough, the difference is striking, with sixty-four names indicating artisans supplying essential goods and services. The clothing trades predominate, with six tanners, two shoemakers, two glovers, two weavers, two fullers, three dyers and three tailors. Metal-workers include three whitesmiths, two blacksmiths, and one locksmith. The woodworking and building trades are represented by a carpenter, three tilers, four coopers and one wheelwright. A butcher, a baker and a cook also occur, and so do a doctor, a clerk, a palmer, a carter and a farrier. These occupational names, of course, represent only a quarter of the households listed and are therefore not an indication of the total numbers engaged in any one trade. But they do reveal the wide range of artisan crafts now being practised in the new community, thus emphasizing its urban, as opposed to rural, nature.

Where did all these people set up house? The old rural settlement, we can safely assume, by then lay clustered around the church. The new town did not displace this community; as we have seen, it was still there in 1251/2 and listed separately. Instead the new town was laid out alongside it, presumably on land previously used for agriculture, within a closely defined boundary.[42] Within this the inhabitants were burgesses with the advantages of burgage tenure. Outside it they were tenants of the rural manor. This new town is represented today by the grid pattern of streets in the town centre linked to the former settlement by a street still known as Old Town, a nice reminder that the burgess proceeding along it to the church was indeed passing out of the new borough into the old settlement, with its different history and traditions.

By 1251/2, then, we know how successful the bishop's venture had been. What we do not know, of course, is how soon after 1196 these settlers arrived and what status they had enjoyed before they had become burgesses. A peasant farming thirty acres, or even twenty, was not likely to have given up his holding before he was fairly sure that life in a town would bring him a better return, even though burgage tenure was theoretically less burdensome. The answer may be that many of these settlers were younger sons from peasant communities with little hope of acquiring any sizeable holding in the country. Even they may have hesitated, but clearly they had a greater incentive to try their luck elsewhere. Nor would the lord of the manor necessarily have wished to prevent this. A custom did exist whereby a villein could gain his freedom by escaping to a town and remaining there undetected for a year and a day, and perhaps there were a few refugees of this sort in early thirteenth-century Stratford. But this was a period not only of inflation but also of population growth. Quantifying this with any accuracy is impossible but it seems that a Domesday population of about two million (1086) had increased some threefold to six million by 1300.[43] It was not necessarily in a lord's interest to see his villagers increasing in number if there was no land available for them to work. So in most cases peasants would have doubtless just been allowed to leave, especially if they were from estates belonging to the bishop whose main interest it was to ensure the new venture flourished. Alternatively, some villagers from the existing settlement at Stratford may have taken a lease of a burgage plot to try their hand at trading before relinquishing their rural holding. It may, therefore, have taken a year or two before colonization really took hold, increasing to a steady stream once it was clear that the borough was going to succeed. Only then would the more cautious have been prepared to give up their life on the land, which, despite its onerous obligations, provided reasonable security, for the greater uncertainties of a freer life in the town. In all events, it is clear that within a decade or so a true town, colonized by people from the neighbouring district and engaged in predominantly urban activities, had begun to overshadow the older community around the church. In 1214 a later bishop, Walter de Gray, made his own approach to the king, this time for permission to hold an annual three-day fair on the eve, feast and morrow of Holy Trinity in June.[44] Fairs were much grander than markets and the need for traders to be accommodated, fed and entertained stimulated the service industries too. The grant of a fair so soon also indicates that Stratford had quickly developed more than a local clientele for the exchange of goods.

The popular concept of dramatic events transforming the lives of communities is not always borne out by a detailed examination of the available evidence; this often reveals instead more gradual processes at work. As far as events in Stratford in 1196 are concerned, it may indeed have been the case that Richard I's grant of a market to the bishop was merely regularizing what was already happening, albeit on a modest scale; and, despite the fact that from 1196, those people settling in Stratford were to enjoy the status of free burgesses, they may not have arrived in any great numbers for a few years. As for the charter itself, this is likely to have been drawn up some time after the event, and only when it was clear that there was going to be a body of burgesses whose relations with the bishop needed to be placed on a legal footing. But this is far from saying that the events of 1196 were of no significance at all. At some point in the year a decision was clearly made that Stratford was to be developed as a borough. To safeguard against any calling into question of the bishop's market rights, a confirmation of them was secured from the king in June. An area of land was then marked out for development, and settlement encouraged on the basis that the new tenants would be free burgesses. This status, of great advantage to those who acquired it, was also crucial to the success of the venture; it was designed to stimulate trade and by doing so brought increased wealth to the borough's founder. In the longer term this also paved the way for the development of Stratford as a thriving market town and there can therefore be no doubt that the charter of 1196, enshrining the decision which the bishop made that year, is indeed of crucial importance in Stratford's history.

CHAPTER 2

Origins: the Romano-British and Anglo-Saxon Settlements

NICHOLAS PALMER

With the knowledge that the name Stratford derives from the Old English word *streat*, a paved road – usually Roman – and ford, and means 'where the Roman road crosses the river', it might be thought that the origins of the settlement are relatively straightforward. In fact, the full story is more complicated and involves at least three successive centres of settlement (not including the borough of 1196), three fords, a number of possible Roman roads and a Roman fort (Fig. 1).

Any account of the early history of Stratford must acknowledge the contribution of earlier researchers such as Robert Wheler and Cuthbert Cove Jones who in the eighteenth and nineteenth centuries collected the Roman coins[1] that gave the first indication of the existence of the Romano-British settlement at Tiddington, east of the river, about 1.5 km east of the modern centre. In particular it was Frederick Wellstood, librarian and secretary to the Shakespeare Birthplace Trust, who laid the foundations of our knowledge of the early settlements, spending apparently all his spare time through the 1920s and 1930s recording the Romano-British and Anglo-Saxon remains revealed by building work and gravel extraction in the vicinity.

In 1923–4, as housing development spread along the Tiddington Road, a Romano-British cemetery containing over 200 graves and some cremations was excavated around the site of no. 77 Tiddington Road (Fig. 2). When the Stratford golf course was laid out in 1925 on the south-east side of the Tiddington Road, the earth-moving along the northern edge produced more Romano-British material. Wellstood was able to record this evidence and then to excavate an area in the north corner of the course revealing dense domestic occupation and a group of twenty more burials.[2] In 1927, with financial backing from W.J. Fieldhouse, Wellstood was joined by Thomas May, a leading Romano-British archaeologist and an expert on pottery, to excavate a further strip along the north-east boundary of the golf course. This revealed a stone building (Plate 6) and features that were interpreted as evidence of iron and lead smelting and tile manufacture. This excavation was published in 1931,[3] following May's death, and Tiddington entered the literature as an 'industrial settlement'. This interpretation was challenged in 1974 by Graham Webster who pointed out that the supposed 'tile kiln' in the stone building was probably a corn-drying oven, the iron working was probably blacksmithing, of a kind to be expected on any settlement, and the evidence for lead smelting was unconvincing.[4]

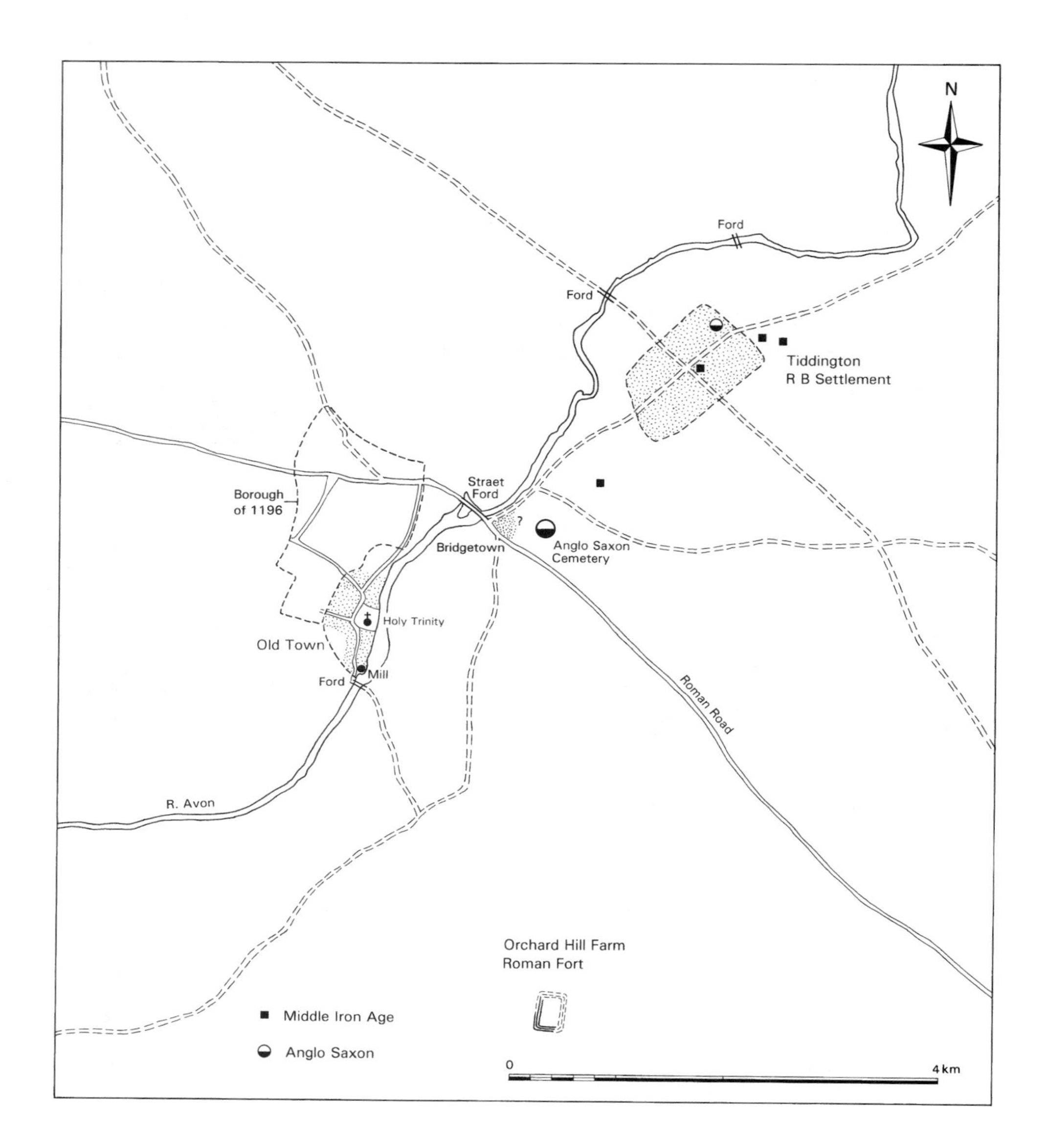

Fig. 1. Early settlements at Stratford-upon-Avon.

Plate 6. Stone building with corn-drier/ 'tile kiln', from 1927 Golf Course excavation. (Photo: Shakespeare Birthplace Trust)

In 1932 Wellstood turned his attention to the Bridgetown area east of Alveston Manor where an Anglo-Saxon cemetery had come to light in a gravel pit. Between 1932 and 1935 he recorded over a hundred inhumation and cremation burials, many with elaborate jewellery and weaponry as grave goods.[5] In 1937–8 he returned to Tiddington, excavating a small area in the field adjacent to the golf course site and then a much larger area on the site of no. 102 Tiddington Road. In 1938 a Roman well was excavated on an uncertain site in the centre of the settlement, followed in 1939 by a small excavation on the site of no. 86 Tiddington Road.[6]

The next phase of archaeological investigation accompanied the development boom of the late 1960s/early 1970s. In 1969 W.J. Ford excavated part of the site of the new vicarage in Old Town, the trenches producing pottery identified as late Saxon.[7] In 1971–2 Ford directed further work at Alveston Manor in advance of proposed hotel extensions. The south-west limit of the Anglo-Saxon cemetery was established and a further nine inhumations and seven cremations were excavated.[8] In 1977 the first detailed survey of the archaeological evidence for the origins of Stratford was published by T. Slater and C. Wilson.[9] In the twenty years since this was produced, knowledge has moved on significantly in some areas, although in others the problems set out there remain unresolved.

The main area where there has been progress is in our understanding of the Romano-British settlement at Tiddington (Fig. 2). In 1980–1 and 1982 two large developments, the new NFU Mutual and Avon Insurance Head Office east of Wellstood's golf course excavations, and the Reading Court Sheltered Housing north of Tiddington Road, were preceded by large-scale archaeological excavations.[10] The opportunity was also taken to re-examine the material from Wellstood's excavations, much of which had never been studied. Further smaller excavations took place in 1983 in Knight's Lane, east of the NFUMAI site, and in 1988 adjacent to the 1982 Reading Court site.[11] For the Anglo-Saxon period the main advances have come from Della Hooke's studies of the landscapes revealed by the charter evidence.[12] In the 1990s there has been more development-related archaeological work at Tiddington, Bridgetown, Old Town and within the medieval borough, but it has all been quite small-scale and consequently has brought only modest advances in knowledge.

The light well-drained soils of the gravel terraces of the Avon Valley have been cultivated since the Neolithic period (*c.* 3,500–2,000 bc) and by the Middle Iron Age (*c.* 300–50 bc) they were relatively densely settled with scattered farmsteads. Evidence for a number of these is known south-east of the river in the vicinity of Stratford (Fig. 1). In the 1920s Wellstood collected pottery of this date from a gravel pit in Loxley Lane (now

Plate 7. Cropmark of probable Roman fort at Orchard Hill Farm, July 1994. (Photo: N. Palmer)

occupied by the rugby ground) and further pottery came from his 1937–8 excavation on the site of no. 102 Tiddington Road. There were also two clusters of pits and ditches on the 1980–1 NFUMAI site to the east of the later settlement.[13] These all seem to have represented separate farmsteads and not a nucleated settlement.

The first proper nucleated settlement in the vicinity of Stratford seems to have developed at Tiddington in the first century AD. It consisted of an irregular spread of timber round houses set in curvilinear enclosures, extending westwards from the north-west corner of the 1980–1 NFUMAI excavation, and covering an area of over eight hectares. It is likely that it developed along a road on the south bank of the Avon following the line of the modern Tiddington Road where it met another running north–west/south–east, crossing the river by a ford at a point where Roman coins and metalwork were dredged up in 1982 (Fig. 2). Because the pottery from the earliest phase can only be dated generally to a period spanning the Roman Conquest (AD 30–70) it is not possible to say with certainty whether the settlement originated in the Late Iron Age before the Conquest or developed after the arrival of the Romans in the area. A total of six Iron Age coins found in the settlement, four of the Dobunni, a tribe centred on Cirencester, and two of the Corieltauvi, a tribe centred on Leicester, would appear to argue for a Late Iron Age origin but these coins circulated into the Roman period and are more commonly found on Roman sites than Iron Age ones.

Most Romano-British nucleated settlements are believed to have developed round forts, their inhabitants subsequently remaining behind when the army moved on. After the invasion in AD 43 the Roman legions overran the south-east part of the country arriving in the Midlands by about AD 47 and establishing a frontier zone in the area just beyond the newly-built Fosse Way road. A series of forts was established across the area supported by other new roads. There was one at Alcester, on the hill south of the river, and probably another at Orchard Hill Farm, south of Stratford (Fig. 1). This site, which was discovered by A. Baker in 1970, regularly shows as a cropmark enclosure defended by three ditches (Plate 7).[14] It has, however, not been excavated and field-walking by Della Hooke in 1976 failed to find any material on its surface.[15] The fort was supported by a new road running from the Fosse Way and then on to Alcester, crossing the Avon at the modern crossing place, the *Streat*-ford. This ford may already have existed, serving an early east-west route. The river appears to have been relatively easy to ford in this area and a number of crossing places are recorded in use at different periods.

At Alcester the early fort is believed to have been replaced with another down on the crossing of the Arrow where the Roman town later grew up. It is possible that the same sequence of events took place at Tiddington although no trace of a fort has been found. However, there is an important difference in the finds assemblage from the earliest phase at Tiddington compared with those from Alcester and other forts in Warwickshire, at The Lunt, Baginton, and Mancetter, in that it lacks the distinctive range of Roman pottery and military metalwork found on these sites. One can also point to the wide extent of the early/mid-first-century occupation and evidence for multiple phases within it, which it would be difficult to compress into a short period after the abandonment of the Orchard Hill Farm fort. Furthermore, had the settlement been a Roman foundation, it would probably have been located where the new military road crossed the river and not at Tiddington. All this suggests therefore that the origins of the Tiddington settlement lay in the Late Iron Age rather than the early Roman period.

Plate 8. Late first-century pottery kiln from 1982 Reading Court excavation. (Photo: N. Palmer)

Whatever its origins, the settlement grew fairly rapidly through the later first and second centuries. The late first century saw the introduction of Romanized pottery such as 'greywares', some of which was manufactured in two kilns excavated on the 1982 Reading Court site, one dating to the late first century (Plate 8), the other to the early second. By the mid-second century Iron Age-type round houses had given way to rectangular buildings. On the 1980–1 NFUMAI site, occupation spread southwards and a road was built out of the settlement to the east with rubbish pits alongside it, both inside the settlement. A hiatus in development appears to have occurred during the early/mid-third century with little new building in this period, and thereafter the fortunes of the two main excavated areas varied markedly. On the 1982 site the properties were abandoned, although their boundaries and the roads alongside them remained in use. Subsequently, probably in the fourth century, a number of small groups of burials were scattered across the site. On the 1980–1 NFUMAI site, in contrast, the occupied area did not contract and new buildings were constructed in the late third/early fourth century.[16]

In the mid-fourth century the settlement, or at least its eastern part, was defended by a large irregular ditch. This was traced across the NFUMAI site; it varied in width from 3–7 m and in depth from 1–2 m and would have been accompanied by an internal bank although little or no trace of this remained. The ditch cut across the line of the former road out of the settlement which fell out of use. The area within the settlement was reorganized with boundaries across the former road line and a series of new buildings was built across it.[17]

The settlement seems to have covered a total area of about twenty-two hectares.[18] Its extent (Fig. 2) can partly be gauged by the spread of excavated occupation deposits and partly by the extent of its cemeteries, which according to Roman law should lie outside the settlement. To the south-west the 1923–4 cemetery gives one limit, although trial trenching in 1996 suggested that occupation may extend further, south of the road.[19] To the north-east, scatters of burials on the 1980–1 site and one seen in 1988 at the Bowling Club give another limit. Occasional burials do occur within the settlement on the golf course and on the 1982 Reading Court site but these appear to be late Roman and in areas where the settlement had contracted. The fourth-century defensive ditch, although a late feature, enclosed the built-up area and gives definite south and east limits. To the north-west occupation did not extend beyond the edge of the gravel terrace as the flood plain would have flooded in winter, then as now.[20] It is noticeable that the distance from the Tiddington Road to the edge of the flood plain is similar to that between the road and the south-east arm of the defensive ditch. This suggests that the road lay down the centre of the settlement. It is also noticeable that the road kinks at the point where the north-east arm of the ditch would intersect with it. A similar kink is evident by the 1923–4 cemetery and, as such kinks are common topographical features at the edges of settlements, it is possible that these mark the entrances to the Romano-British settlement.

Although the settlement covered a large area it was not densely built up; the excavated buildings were widely spaced and appear to have sat within their own plots. A fairly typical arrangement is represented by a later second-century property on the 1982 Reading Court site which sat in a triangular plot, fronting the Tiddington Road, bounded by trackways on the other two sides (Fig. 3). Sitting within the plot there was a timber house with at least two rooms, its walls supported partly on horizontal beams and partly on posts. Behind the house was a timber barn building, fifteen metres by six metres, its walls supported on posts, with a porch on one side, containing a corn-drier at one end and a bread oven at the other (Plate 9). Between the house and the barn there was a well with a timber lining, and a pit lined with clay, possibly for steeping grain preparatory to malting.[21]

Most of the buildings in the settlement were of timber and presumably with thatched roofs. A single stone building was excavated in 1980–1, an aisled building with small rectangular rooms projecting from two of its corners, and not dissimilar to a humble villa (Fig. 4). The stone building with the corn-drier excavated by Wellstood and May (Plate 6) was adjacent to this and may have been associated with it.[22] A handful of fragments of hypocaust tile and architectural details in oolitic limestone attest to buildings of more pretension somewhere in the settlement.

Outside the settlement, the 1980–1 excavations revealed field systems aligned on the road out of the settlement. These contained small paddocks some of which contained wells, presumably for watering stock. About 100 metres east along the road and downwind of the settlement there was a large area of pits, perhaps originally dug as gravel pits to provide material for road and floor surfaces, but then used for the disposal of rubbish.[23]

Although Tiddington was originally published as an industrial settlement, this interpretation owed more to the enthusiasm of the early excavators than to solid evidence. The recent excavations produced none for the claimed iron or lead smelting, glass-making

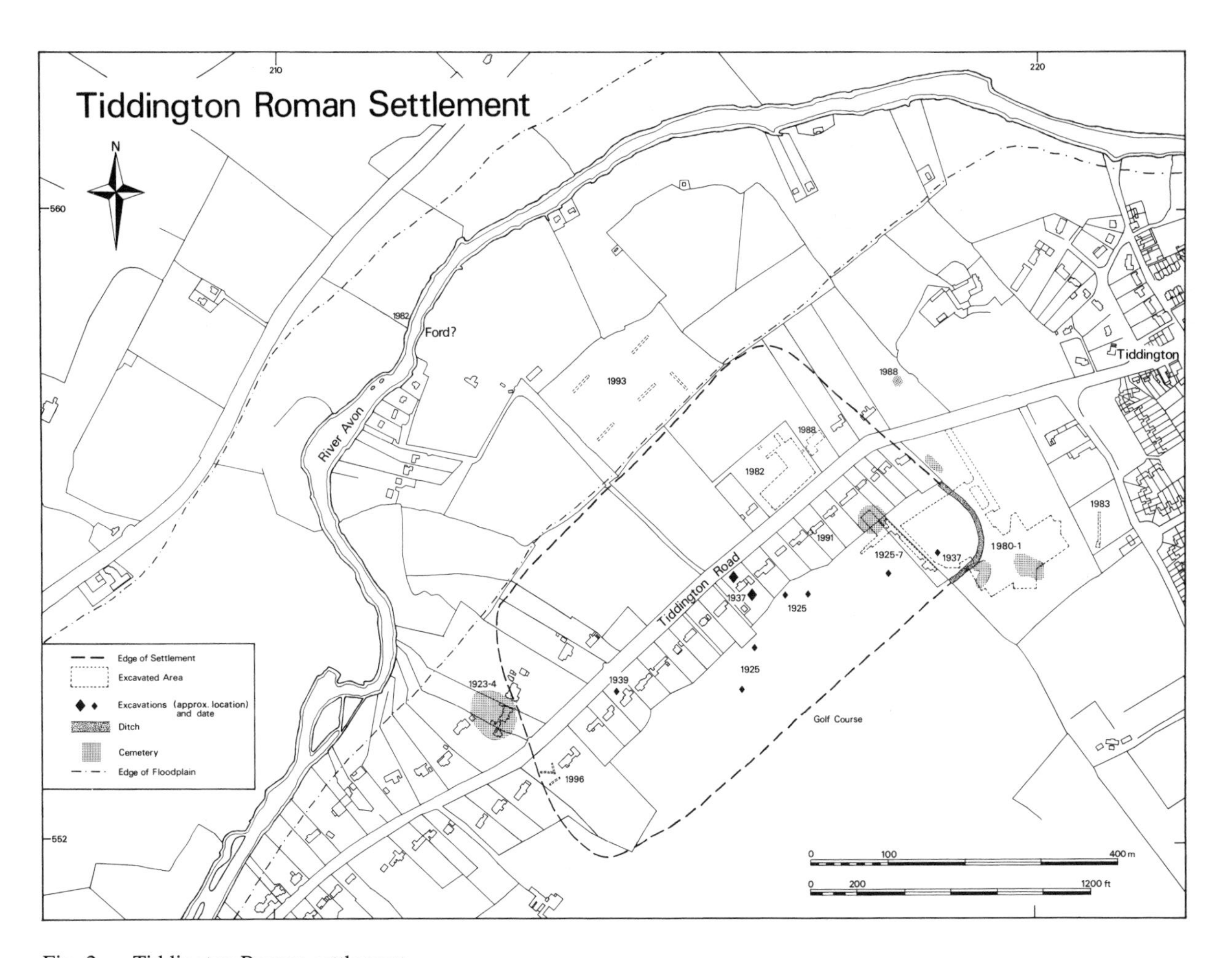

Fig. 2. Tiddington Roman settlement.

Plate 9. Late second-century barn with corn-drier, under excavation, 1982 Reading Court excavation. (Photo: N. Palmer)

or tile manufacture. There is evidence for blacksmithing and a small amount of non-ferrous metalworking, in the form of tools, stock and slag, but the former was only on a scale to be expected on a settlement of this type and the latter was probably no more than waste left by an itinerant smith. Even the fragment of 'Roman' cast iron from the golf course is likely to be recent and to have come from a later furrow cutting into the Roman levels, similar to those excavated on the adjacent site in 1981.[24] The recent excavations also produced relatively small quantities of tile, suggesting that it was not much used on the site, and making the possibility of its manufacture in the vicinity very unlikely.

The economic base of the settlement was mixed agriculture, although it probably also served as a minor market for the settlements of the immediate vicinity. Study of charred plant remains from the settlement suggests the crops grown were wheat (mainly spelt, less emmer and very small quantities of bread wheat), barley, a few peas, and possibly some rye.[25] Six corn-drying ovens have been excavated, some of which may have served also as malting kilns.

The animal bone from recent excavations represents a typical 'producer' group from a rural site where animals were raised. In terms of numbers (calculated as Minimum Number of Individuals) the proportion of sheep remained constant over the Roman period

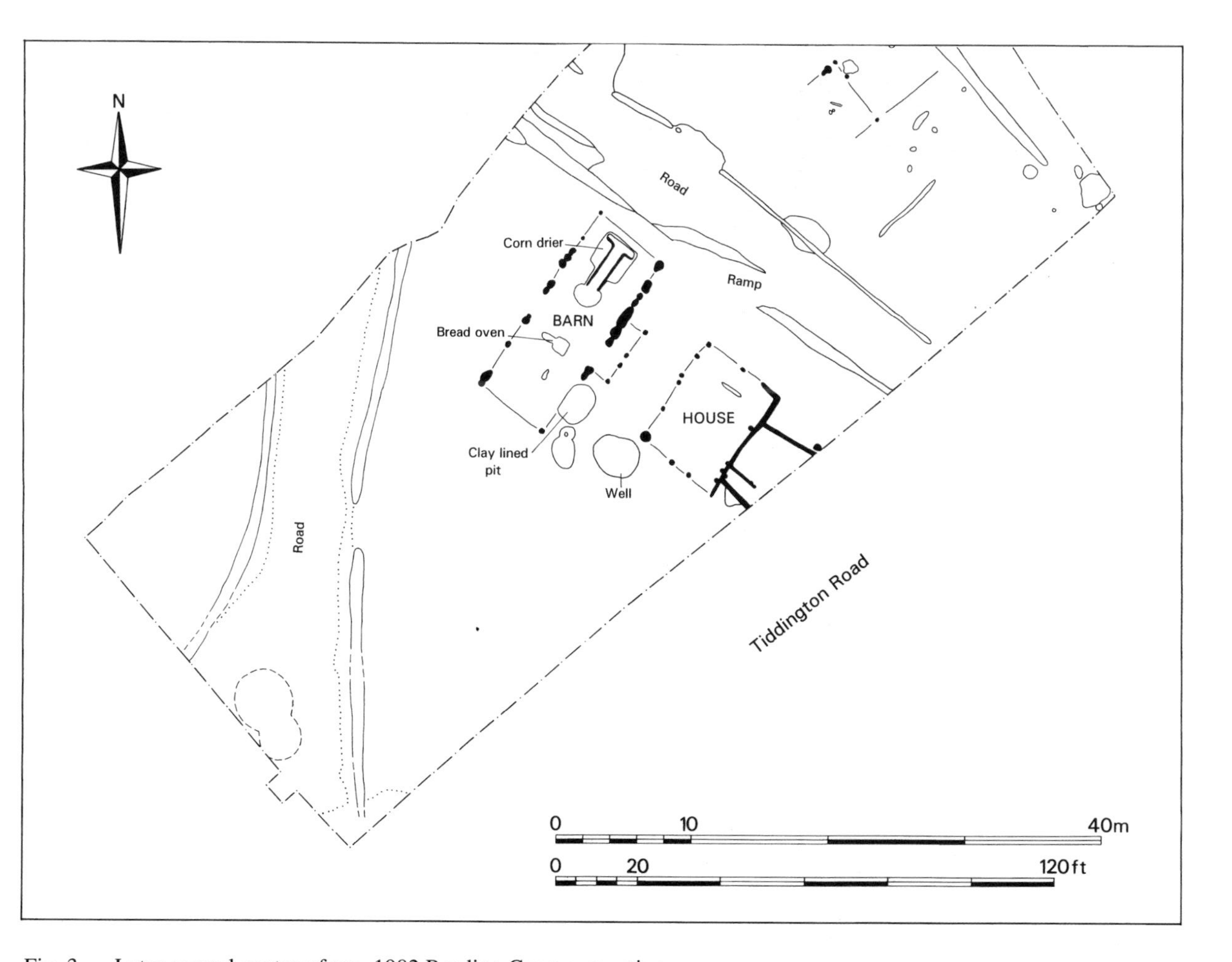

Fig. 3. Later second-century farm, 1982 Reading Court excavation.

at 50 to 53 per cent of the three main species. Pig declined from 22 per cent in the first century to about 10 per cent in the second to fourth centuries, the differences being made up by cattle which increased from 25 to 40 per cent. In terms of meat weight, cattle accounted for about 65 per cent of the assemblage. Most males were killed at two to three years with some older animals retained as bulls to maintain the herd and as castrates to provide traction. Over half the adult cattle were females, vital to maintain the herd. Milk production does not seem to have been a major concern. Although more numerous than cattle, sheep contributed only 20 to 25 per cent of the meat weight. A high kill-off rate in the first two to three years suggests that they were reared mainly for meat, rather than for wool. Pigs were also kept for meat, most being killed in their first year and few surviving their second year. In spite of their considerably lower numbers they represented about 15 per cent of the meat weight.[26]

Agricultural implements such as ox-goads, a ploughshare and a spade iron among the finds complement the environment data for the main economic activity. There was also some evidence on the site for domestic and craft activities such as sewing, spinning, weaving, carpentry and bone working, but these, like the pottery production, were carried out on a relatively small scale.

Some hint of a minor administrative function may be given by the contents of the well excavated in 1938. As well as some fourth-century pottery this contained a complete bronze bowl, fragments of a turned wooden chair or stool, and a group of four styli for writing on wax tablets, almost suggesting the contents of an office. A total of thirty-one styli and fragments are known from the settlement which perhaps indicates a surprisingly high level of literacy. The same well group also contained religious objects in the form of two carved stone heads, one of Jupiter, in a crude classical style, possibly from a 'Jupiter column', the other a much cruder 'Celtic' type. A few other finds give further hints of religious belief, including a brooch in the form of a horse, of a type often linked with the cult of Epona,[27] and a miniature bronze axe, perhaps a votive offering or good luck charm.[28]

Generally the finds from the settlement reflected a middling level of prosperity. There were no outstandingly rich items, but a good collection of copper alloy and bone ornaments and domestic items was found. The pottery from the site was drawn from a relatively wide variety of sources, but it included few real exotica. Apart from the locally produced material, there were Severn Valley wares, black burnished wares from Dorset, pink grogged ware from Milton Keynes, East Midlands shell tempered ware, and Mortaria and white wares from Verulamium, Mancetter-Hartshill, Oxfordshire and the Nene Valley. Foreign imports included samian ware from Gaul, Central Gaulish wares, Rhenish wares, and amphorae from Spain and Southern France. Fine and specialist wares represent about 8 per cent of the total collection. This is markedly less than at small towns such as Alcester, Chesterton and Tripontium where these form between 18 and 24 per cent of the assemblages. On the other hand in rural groups such as those from Wasperton, and Crewe Farm, Kenilworth, these wares form only 3.4 and 4.9 per cent respectively.[29]

The picture of the settlement presented by the evidence is thus of a large village rather than a small town. Its economy was overwhelmingly agricultural and, in spite of its extent, the low density and character of its buildings suggest a non-urban environment. The place may have served as a minor market and had some administrative and/or religious functions but these would have been insufficient to raise it above village status.

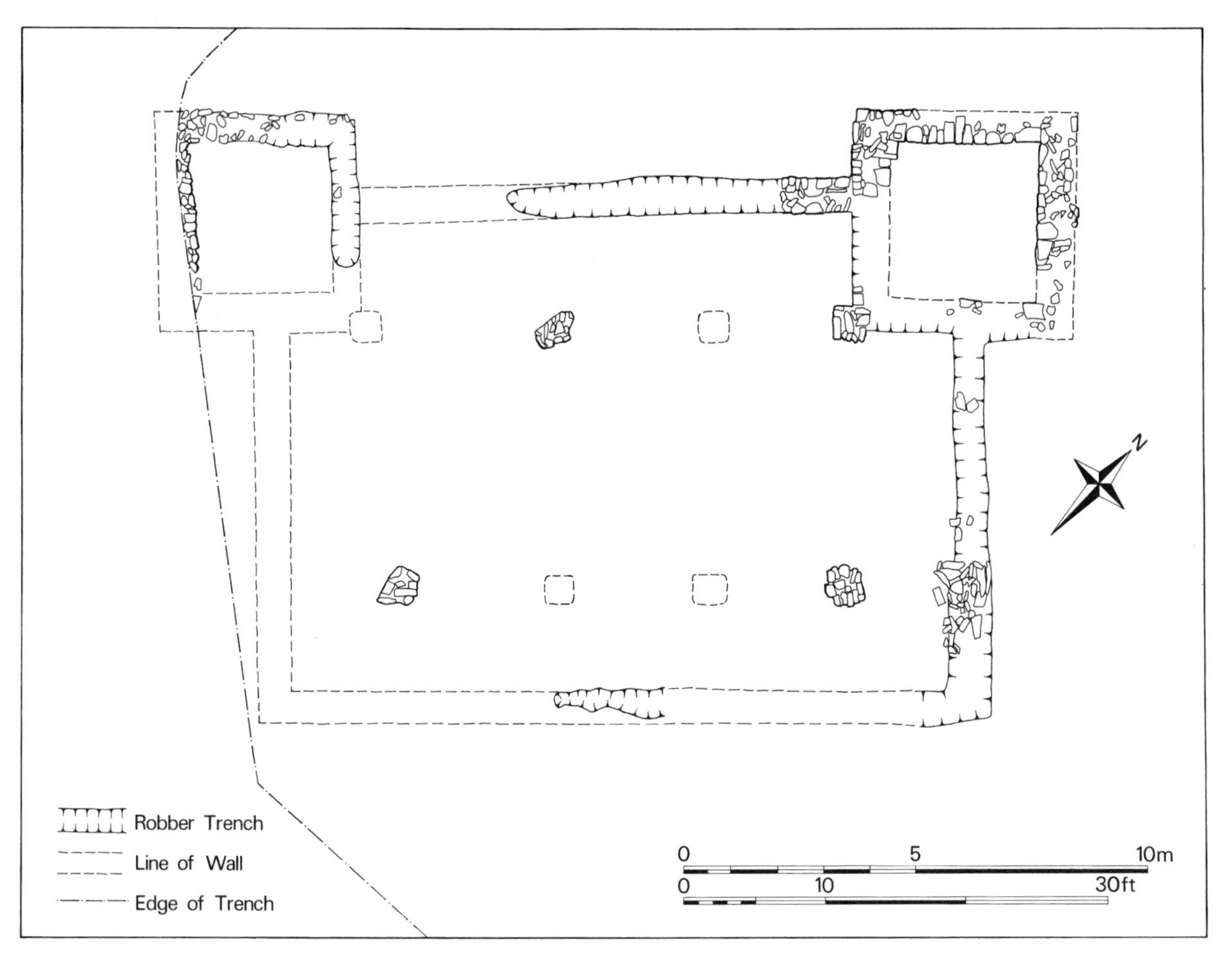

Fig. 4. Third/fourth-century stone [aisled] building, 1980–1 NFUMAI excavation.

On most of the excavated areas at Tiddington the occupation seemed just to die out after the end of the fourth century. The coin list from the site goes to Arcadius and Honorius, the latest piece dating to 402–6, just into the fifth century. A number of phases of late fourth-century activity were recorded on the 1980–1 NFUMAI site but how long into the fifth century the major occupation continued is uncertain, owing to a general absence of datable artefacts once the supply of Roman coins ceases. The site was not, however, absolutely deserted. Part of a single large enclosure, set at right angles to the Tiddington Road, whose ditches and some associated postholes contained Anglo-Saxon pottery dating probably to the late fifth to sixth centuries, was excavated in 1988 next to the 1982 Reading Court site.[30]

The presence of the Anglo-Saxon cemetery at Alveston Manor suggests that, following the decline of the settlement at Tiddington, the focus of activity shifted to the Bridgetown area on the south side of the *Streat*-ford (Fig. 5). The excavations by Wellstood and Ford in the cemetery revealed a total of eighty-three inhumations and thirty-eight cremations along with evidence for another four destroyed graves, dating from the fifth to the early seventh centuries.[31] Some of the graves contained Roman coins and one (no. 70) a late Roman buckle dated to the fourth to mid-fifth centuries.[32] These buckles were thought to be associated with late Roman Anglo-Saxon mercenaries and Slater and Wilson[33] suggested that a mercenary settlement may have been established to the south-west of the Tiddington settlement, co-existing with it before the Anglo-Saxons came eventually to dominate. They also noted a reference to Anglo-Saxon finds made in the 1930s at no. 77 Tiddington Road (Bradley Lodge), the site of the cemetery excavated in 1923–4 which suggested that this cemetery remained in use into the later period.[34]

While there may have been a degree of continuity with the Tiddington settlement this detailed scenario cannot really be sustained. The suggested association of the buckles and related metalwork with Anglo-Saxon mercenaries is no longer maintained. Apart from the coins and the buckle, the evidence from Alveston Manor is exclusively Anglo-Saxon; no significant quantity of Roman pottery has been found, and the buckle could belong to the late fifth century, or later, as they had long lives in use.[35] Furthermore, the evidence for Anglo-Saxon use of the 1923–4 Tiddington cemetery is probably spurious, as the alleged finds cannot be traced.[36] All this suggests that the sites were more successive than overlapping.

A more serious problem is the absence of any evidence for actual settlement at Alveston Manor by the cemetery. To the west of the burials, Ford excavated a series of palisaded boundaries, but apart from an undated posthole structure predating the graves there were no remains of a settlement associated with the cemetery. This settlement did not lie to the north. Trenching to the rear of nos 6–7 Tiddington Road in 1992 revealed only a single possible Romano-British field gully and a few Anglo-Saxon sherds,[37] and trenching and observation of foundations to the rear of nos 9–10 in 1974 and 1995–6 revealed little more.[38] Nor has it been found to the south. Other trenching and observation on a site south of the Banbury Road (adjacent to no. 2) opposite Alveston Manor in 1996 revealed no trace of settlement of any kind.[39] This is not to say that the settlement did not exist (although isolated cemeteries serving dispersed settlement, often lying close to parish boundaries, are common) as its natural position would have been west of the cemetery under Alveston Manor and close to the south side of the river crossing.[40]

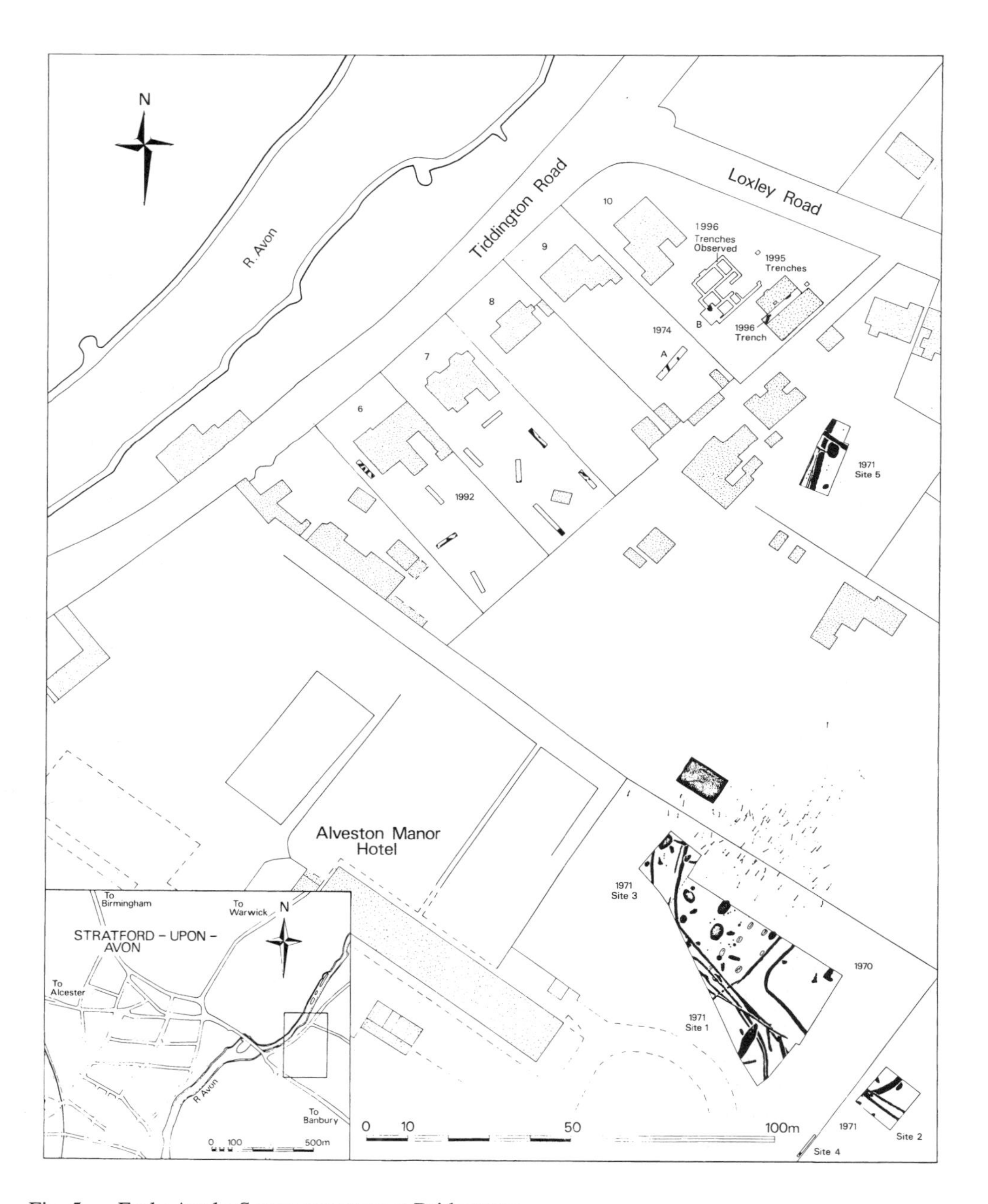

Fig. 5. Early Anglo-Saxon cemetery at Bridgetown.

A shift of settlement to this location would not be difficult to explain. The rise of Alcester as the main Roman town and commercial centre in the area would have skewed the trading patterns in the area towards it and, even in a period when the Roman pattern was breaking down, the *Streat*-ford, on the road to Alcester, would have retained its position as the most important crossing point in the vicinity. In the absence of any physical remains it is more difficult to assess the character and status of the putative Bridgetown settlement. It is impossible to be sure whether it would have inherited the predominant position of Tiddington and its minor market function. All one can point to is the absence of any competing settlement and the fact that the high quality of some of the grave goods from the cemetery shows the presence of people with considerable status.

The earliest documentary records for the area date to the mid-Saxon period. By this time much of the land on both sides of the river formed part of a large estate belonging to the church of Worcester, and apparently including most of the later manors of Stratford, Luddington, Clopton, Bishopton, Drayton, Milcote, Ruin Clifford, Alveston and Hampton Lucy. The earliest reference to this, apparently dated to 699/709 but now believed to be a later forgery, albeit incorporating genuine early information, refers to an estate at Shottery (1.75 km west of Stratford). However, the estate centre became fixed at Stratford, following the establishment of a minster at *Ufera Stretford*, probably by the late eighth century, although the first definite mention comes in 845 (and the last in 872 when it was granted the reversion of land at Nuthurst).[41]

This means that another shift of settlement had occurred as Upper Stratford is taken to be in the Old Town area around the parish church of Holy Trinity, the presumed site of the minster. The reasons for the decline of the settlement at Bridgetown are difficult to determine as the *Streat*-ford was still the preferred crossing place in the area throughout the period and, indeed, gave its name to the estate. It is possible that the reasons were ideological, the church deliberately choosing a new site, somewhat removed from the old and possibly tainted earlier one, for its new estate centre and minster. Alternatively it may have disappeared in some reorganization of the Alveston estate, possibly one involving the creation of the medieval villages at Alveston and Tiddington. The cemetery and any associated settlement had probably disappeared by the late tenth century as the boundary clause of a lease of Alveston of 985 follows the Roman road and the River Avon but makes no mention of any settlement at the junction.[42]

The parish church is set on an eminence above the river and it is likely that the settlement grew around it (Fig. 6). There has been relatively little archaeological investigation in the Old Town area and most of the evidence for the settlement is documentary or topographical. Apart from the church, a mill existed by the late Saxon period (recorded in Domesday) and possibly earlier, and this presumably lay on the site of the later Lucy's Mill.[43] At the south end of Mill Lane, adjacent to the mill, there was another ford which was in use in the medieval period and later, and whose presence must also have contributed to the siting of the settlement.[44] It is likely that the settlement extended along Old Town and Mill Lane, and also College (Sanctus) Lane and Southern (Southams) Lane. Its limits to the north and west are indicated in reverse by the boundary of the later borough.[45]

It is likely that occupation would have concentrated along the road frontages. Trial trenching east of New Street in 1992 revealed nothing in an area that would have been to the rear of the properties on Mill Lane.[46] Excavation in 1969 on the site of the vicarage on

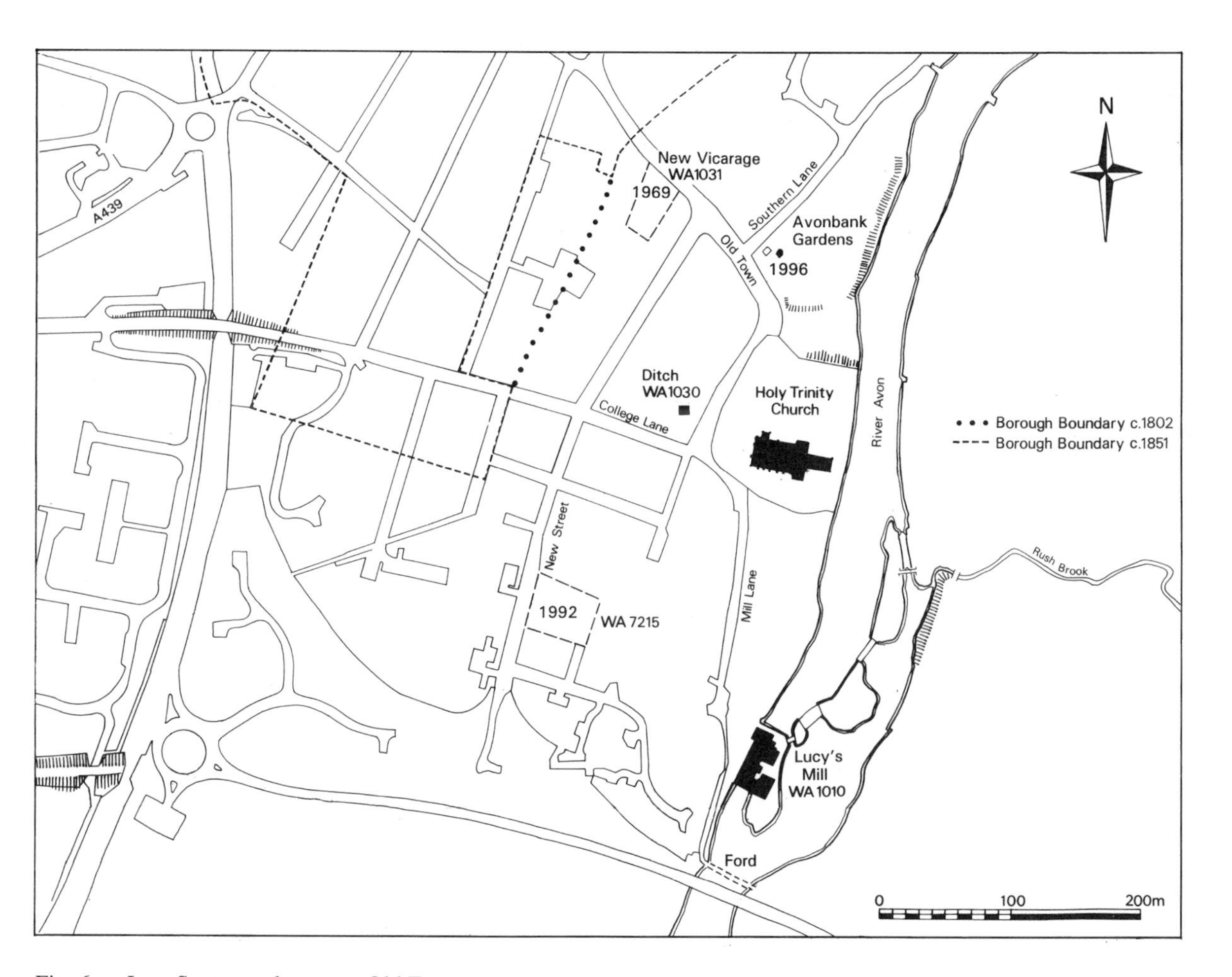

Fig. 6. Late Saxon settlement at Old Town.

the south side of Old Town revealed pits and postholes containing pottery which was identified as similar to St Neots Ware, a common Late Saxon type dating to *c*. 850–1100.[47] A recent re-examination of the material suggests it is actually Cotswold oolitic ware which dates to the eleventh/twelfth centuries, but here is likely to be post-1070.[48] Nonetheless, since this site lies close to the borough boundary it appears that this part of Old Town was densely settled by this date. Other excavations in this area have been inconclusive. Work on the site of the Methodist Church revealed a substantial but undated ditch, and observation in 1996 of construction of new public lavatories in Avonbank Gardens revealed nothing, although the work here was very small-scale.[49] Nonetheless this would have been the focus of the settlement and it is possible that an informal market may have developed here before the creation of the borough.

At Domesday the holdings of the Bishop of Worcester in the vicinity were divided into four manors: Hampton Lucy, Stratford, Alveston and Loxley.[50] In fact the manor of Stratford had a smaller population than that of Alveston, twenty-nine households as opposed to forty-four, although in both cases the population would have been divided between a number of settlements. Quite how dominant the settlement at Stratford would have been is difficult to say although it did contain the parish church on the former minster site, the administrative centre of the bishop's estate and possibly also an informal market.

In 1977 Slater and Wilson suggested that Upper Stratford may have been accompanied by a Lower Stratford and that the second settlement may have been at the northern end of the *Streat*-ford.[51] In fact there is no definite reference to a Lower Stratford and there are no relict topographical features here to suggest any settlement predating the establishment of the borough in 1196. Trial trenching in Cox's Timber Yard in 1996, albeit closer to the river than settlement would have extended, revealed nothing.[52]

The final shift of settlement was effected with the laying out of the borough of 1196. Apart from the Roman road running from the ford along Bridge Street, Wood Street and Greenhill Street, probably another road to the north-east along Henley Street and one or more running to Old Town from the main road, this was an empty site occupied only by the field system of the pre-existing settlement, some traces of which can be detected in the later property patterns.[53] Only a few unlocated or dubious chance finds are known: a Roman coin found at the Grammar School in 1843 which is more likely to have been part of some schoolboy's collection than a genuine loss at that location,[54] and another found in 1976 when the canal basin was drained which is also unlikely to be an *in situ* loss.[55]

The shifting pattern of early settlement at Stratford is fairly unusual and is probably to be explained by changes in the relative importance over time of the various roads and river crossings in the area, partly in response to strategic factors or trading patterns and possibly partly to changes in the river regime. The original Tiddington settlement may have reflected a north-west/south-east axis which was superseded by a more east-west axis established over the Roman period, directed towards Alcester and based on the *Streat*-ford. The Middle Saxon shift to the minster site at Old Town is more difficult to explain in these terms and may have had an ideological explanation. The creation of the borough of 1196 certainly reasserted the importance of the *Streat*-ford.

CHAPTER 3

Domesday Village to Medieval Town: the Topography of Medieval Stratford-upon-Avon

T.R. SLATER

This chapter examines the physical presence of the early medieval settlement at Stratford, its manorial context and the way it was transformed into a town at the end of the twelfth century. It is concerned with the topography of the town and therefore the underlying landscape is of significance, as are the streets, plots and buildings which formed the framework for people's lives in the past, and continue to form the framework for the lives of Stratford's citizens through to the present.

If we are properly to understand the town plan and buildings of medieval Stratford then we must begin with the rural settlement which preceded it. Medieval new towns such as Stratford were most certainly planned but that planning was an adaptive process taking cognizance of what was already there. Geographers call this pre-urban landscape the 'morphological frame' or the 'pre-urban cadastre'.[1] What then do we know about the landscape around Stratford-upon-Avon before 1196 and what can we reasonably infer?

First, we know that the Roman road from Alcester which crossed the Avon at this point was still in use. It is named in a number of Anglo-Saxon charters as the *straet, mycelan straete* (great road), or the *sealt straet*.[2] This word was used exclusively for paved Roman roads in Old English and we can be sure that it was the Roman road that is being referred to. It is clear, too, from other charter references that a number of routeways focused on this river crossing-point. The saltway from Droitwich continued eastwards across east Warwickshire; a *herpath*, or highway used by the army, ran along the south side of the Avon, and the Birmingham road was also already being used since it is referred to as the *Feldene stret* in another charter (Fig. 7). The *straet ford* gave name to the settlement of *Ufera Stretford*, Upper Stratford, though why 'upper' is not known.[3]

The Stratford ford was certainly not the only one in the vicinity. The River Avon is not an especially difficult river to ford and there were other crossing places at Tiddington, where a prehistoric ridgeway crossed the river and ran north to Pathlow, and at Hatton, where the *herpath* crossed at *Doddan-ford* according to the charters.[4] However, the ford at Stratford was more significant in terms of the number of roads focusing on it, perhaps because it had been paved by the Romans and was therefore a safer crossing than others. It therefore has a central-place functionality compared with others; in other words, more people were using it with the consequent opportunity for meeting one another.

We might guess that this was so in the late Roman period too, and it was for this reason that the very first pagan Anglo-Saxon settlers and soldiers are to be found living in the Bridgetown area on the southern side of the ford. Whether or not it was a strategic place because of its centrality on the route network and therefore needed to be secured in troubled times is uncertain but, by the eighth/ninth century, there was no strategic function here. The boundary between the kingdom of the Hwicce and Mercia was at Warwick,[5] while that between the English and the Danelaw was fixed along Watling Street. Consequently, Stratford did not acquire defensible earthworks of any kind in the early medieval period, though there is a possible motte at Welcombe.[6]

Next, we know that this was a prosperous agricultural area. It was long-settled. From Neolithic times onwards, the light gravel soils of the Avon terraces had provided good farming land which had been densely occupied by farming communities.[7] This was not land which was ever going to revert to scrub and woodland in times of population decline or in times of social and political change. It was too valuable for that and its value, in terms of its productivity, meant that it was always attractive to landholders and farmers. It had been granted, by the end of the seventh century at latest, to the church of Worcester for the support of the bishop. Christopher Dyer has shown how almost all the bishop's estates were based on earlier Roman settlements, suggesting something of this continuity of cultivation.[8] Each of the estates also acquired a proprietary minster church and, again, Stratford was no exception. The minster, it can reasonably be argued, was located in the settlement which was central to the bishop's extensive lands around Stratford and another central-place function was thus in place by the eighth century at the latest. The bishop's palace was probably at Hatton at this time,[9] midway between the adjoining episcopal estates of Stratford and Hampton Lucy.

The minster church was located on a site where the no. 2 gravel terrace of the Avon had been cut into by the river to produce a cliff 5 metres high so that the church was prominent from all directions, had direct access to the river, yet was safe from any danger of flooding.[10] The edge of this gravel terrace was subsequently to be of considerable importance in the laying out of the town, as we shall see. The churchyard around the minster was subcircular in form and from our knowledge of such minsters elsewhere we might speculate that it was surrounded by a bank and ditch and might have been a cruciform building well before the present building was constructed.[11] The clergy who served the minster probably lived to the west of the church in the area which was subsequently to become the site of the college of priests in the fourteenth century. The parish served by the minster was at first coincident with the estate and included the settlements at Shottery, Bishopton, Welcombe and Clopton to the north of the river, and Alveston, Tiddington and Ruin Clifford to the south (Fig. 1), together with the detached woodland estates of Lapworth and Bushwood in the Forest of Arden to the north. Parts of the estate were leased out to secular farmers and the boundary clauses of the leases have been used by Della Hooke to suggest something of the nature of the farming practices in this area of Warwickshire.[12]

The Domesday record of Stratford tells us that the bishop no longer possessed the estates at Lapworth, Clopton and Ruin Clifford – they were now in the hands of Hugh of Grandesmil and Robert of Stafford respectively – but the remainder of the episcopal estate within the parish was intact and flourishing.[13] There were mills at Hampton Lucy and Stratford, worth 6*s* 8*d* and 10*s* respectively, and Stratford mill also rendered 1,000 eels to the bishop.[14] Almost certainly it was located on the site which it was to continue to occupy for the next 900 years, a few hundred metres down river from the church. There was an even more valuable triple mill

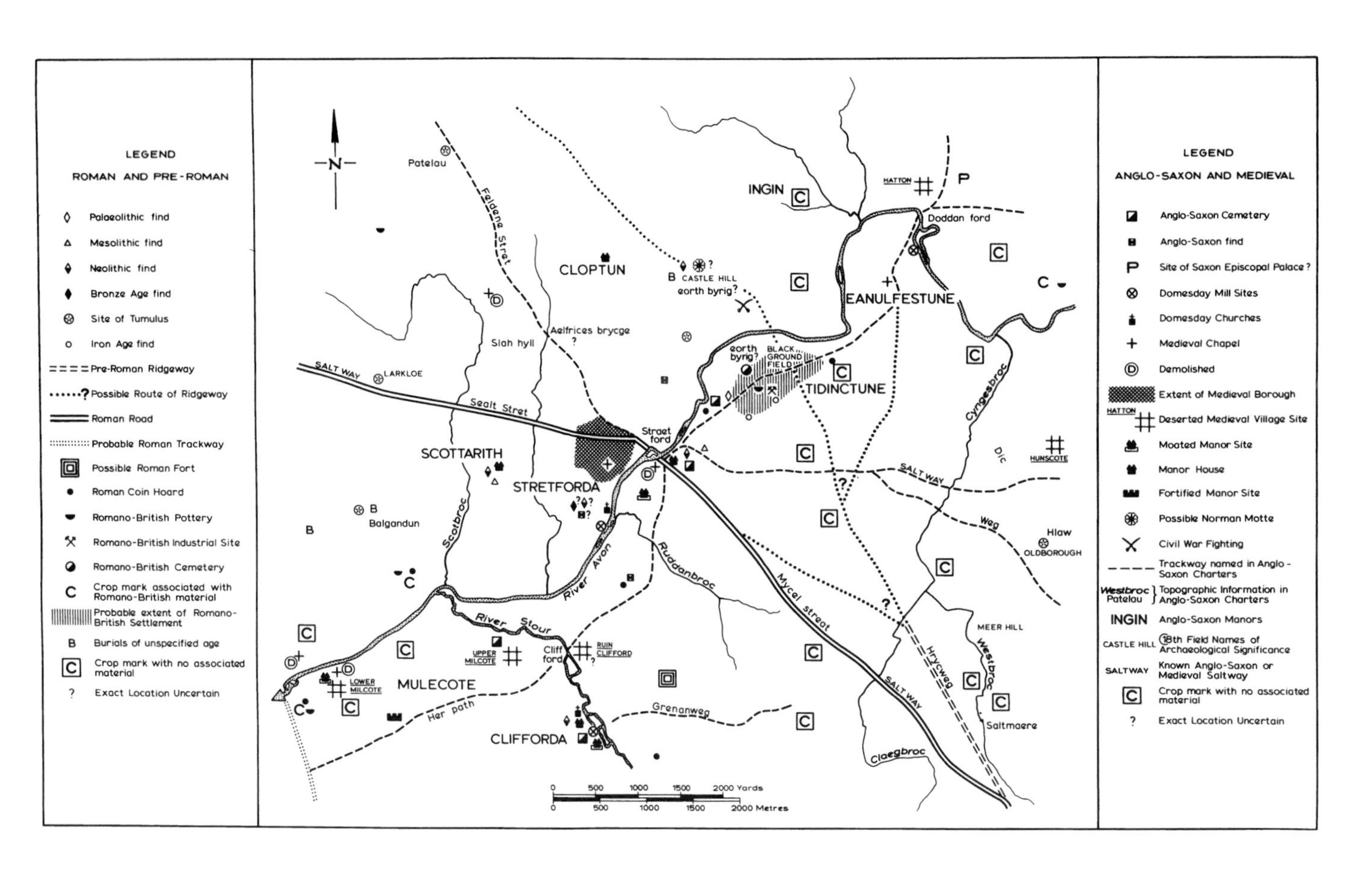

Fig. 7. Archaeological sites in the Stratford region. (Source: Slater and Wilson, 1977)

at Alveston worth 40*s* and rendering some 1,300 eels. The other feature of the estate recorded in some detail is the extensive and valuable meadows beside the Avon in Hampton, Alveston and Stratford. In Stratford they were five furlongs long and two furlongs wide.

The population of the estate was entirely agricultural, except for the priests at Hampton and Stratford. At Stratford twenty-one villeins and seven bordars are recorded, suggesting a population of about 140 people in Stratford, Shottery, Bishopton, and Welcombe. Each of these farming families had their own plough since the number of ploughs recorded equals the heads of household, and the bishop had another three ploughs for his demesne.[15] The most interesting thing about the Domesday record of Stratford, however, is that the value of the episcopal estate had increased enormously since the Conquest. Hampton had been worth £4 but by 1086 was worth £20; Alveston had risen in value from £8 to £15, and Stratford from £5 to £25. Clearly Wulfstan, the Bishop of Worcester, had set about reorganizing his estates so that they provided him with a greater income after the 1060s. It may be that this reorganization included some encouragement of marketing activities, either at the church gates on Sundays in the vicinity of the present street called Old Town (which was quite common elsewhere in the country), or at the hundred meeting place at Pathlow at monthly intervals. However, if this was so the documents and the landscape are silent on the matter. It is therefore not until the granting of the 1196 charter by Bishop John of Coutances that the trading community of the town comes properly into view.

Town-founding was already a profitable activity in the twelfth century on other estates, including, for example, those of the adjoining see of Lichfield, where Bishop Roger de

Plate 10. Aerial view of Stratford-upon-Avon, 1947. The grid, as laid out in 1196, is clearly visible in the centre, as is the flood-plain beyond. (Photo: Aerofilms)

Clinton had begun to develop the cathedral city in 1140,[16] and at Kenilworth, where his kinsman Geoffrey de Clinton had founded a borough before 1125.[17] Nonetheless, there were relatively few towns in Warwickshire before 1220[18] and one of the reasons for the success of the bishop's enterprise was certainly the fact that Stratford's foundation dates to the twelfth, not the thirteenth century. It is clear that the foundation was a success as Carus-Wilson's analysis of the episcopal survey of the 1251/2 has shown.[19] Fifty years after its foundation there were the equivalent of some 250 full burgages, many of which had been subdivided into halves and thirds. If each burgage contained only one family this would still imply a population of 1,250 or so, making the new borough a very respectable small town.

Burgages were physical entities of course; they were the plots of land granted to the in-migrants in free tenure in exchange for a yearly money rent of twelve pence. What is interesting about the Stratford charter is that it gives the dimensions of the plots which were granted. They were to be 3½ by 12 perches (18 m by 60 m), an area of somewhat under a quarter of an acre (0.1 ha). In some new-founded boroughs, burgages were combined with a strip of land in the fields but in the new borough of Stratford there was no field land; that was already being profitably cultivated by the bishop's rural tenants in what was soon to be known as the manor of Old Stratford. The residents in the new-founded borough were quite clearly intended to earn their living from trade and craft production, not from farming. There is no indication in the charter as to whether the first migrants to Stratford were helped to establish themselves by having a rent-free period of three, five or seven years, as happened in some other new towns, or whether the bishop assisted by providing building materials, as happened with the founding of St Albans, for example.[20] But knowing the size of the burgages granted does enable us to reconstruct the topography of the early borough and to say quite a lot about the thoughts of the people who planned it; it does not allow us to say who those people were, however. Later medieval documentation in Britain[21] and in Italy[22] suggests that there were men skilled in laying out towns and that they were not rural reeves, certainly not surveyors (who did not come into existence until the sixteenth century) but were rather most often 'architects' or masons, men who earned their living directing the building of castles, cathedrals and churches. Perhaps, therefore, it was the cathedral mason from Worcester who was sent for when the plan for a new town at Stratford was devised.

The 'ideal' plan of the town, the geometrical projection in the planner's head, is fairly clear.[23] It was conceived as a grid of intersecting streets; four or five east-west streets and three north-south. The street blocks so formed were surrounded by further blocks of plots around the outer edge on all sides but the river, the whole bounded by a back lane along which ran the borough boundary – the limits of burgage tenure (Fig. 8). It was clear to the planner that the road leading to the ford over the Avon would be the economic focus of the town and the provisions market is therefore a rectangular broadening of this street (the present Bridge Street). This was no mechanistic, geometrical plan, however; medieval planners took such ideal conceptions of the mind and adapted them to fit the site available.

The site's first problem was the gravel terrace beside the Avon on which the new town was to be established. The ideal plan had first to 'fit' this terrace since burgages established off the terrace, on the flood-plain of the river, would have been subject to inundation each winter. Though the squarish edge of the terrace was well-suited to the grid plan devised[24] there were two problems encountered. First, the Roman road crossed the terrace close to its northern edge and, secondly, the eastern edge of the terrace was not quite at right angles to the Roman road. Consequently, the grid plan was distorted to parallelogram form. The east-west roads were laid out parallel to the Roman road and the north-south roads parallel to the edge of the terrace. Secondly, the ideal plan would have been disposed equally on either side of the Roman road, so that the market place was central; but, because the road was so close to the northern edge of the terrace, all of the street blocks of the grid were to the south of the road (Fig. 8).[25]

Then, as we have seen, there was already a village at Stratford; it had a church, housing for the clergy, mill, and the cottages of the farmers gathered about. It, too, occupied the gravel terrace that was so crucial to Stratford's topography: indeed, it had occupied the best spot on the terrace where it was hard against the river. The new town was left with the area between the village and the road which was fronted with an area of water meadows, part of the flood plain of the river. This area, the Bancroft Gardens of today, was common grazing in the medieval period.[26] The area occupied by the tofts and crofts of the village of Old Stratford is carefully defined by the borough boundary. Whereas to the north, east and west the boundary runs straight and true, to the south-east it follows what was once the outer boundary of the crofts of the village (Fig. 8).[27] The street that links the new town to the church is called 'Old Town' in remembrance of this village. It remained outside the borough until the nineteenth century.

The earlier rural settlement affected the new town plan in other ways. Firstly it was linked to its neighbouring settlements on the bishop's estate by a network of paths and lanes since Stratford's parish church and mill was also the church and mill for Shottery, Welcombe and all the others. The paths and lanes therefore focused on the church and mill. Consequently, the east–west streets of the grid in the southern part of the borough were not re-aligned: they simply took the line of these earlier paths and lanes. Secondly, the road to Birmingham followed the northern edge of the gravel terrace as it departed from the Roman road so as to remain as dry and mud-free as possible. The planner kept this angled approach and, although there was a little dog-leg turn to enable a series of plots to be laid out to the north of the road, Henley Street, as a result, is not part of the grid and still approaches it at an acute angle, parallel to the edge of the terrace (Fig. 8). The edge, Guild Pits, was used as a sand and gravel quarry in the medieval period.

Finally, the village of Old Stratford was surrounded by its fields where the villeins and bordars recorded in Domesday Book ploughed, sowed and reaped their crops. It was over these fields that the surveyor had to lay out the new town. We know from the charter references that these fields were probably already farmed by open-field agricultural systems,[28] that the fields would have been divided up into furlongs and strips, and that the strips may well have been mounded up to provide better-drained soil. The fixed mould-board plough tended to lead to mounding anyway. To the surveyor of the town, levelling the land would probably have seemed an unnecessary trouble and expense so, again, some of these agricultural features were incorporated into the plan, most notably the gentle curves of the agricultural strips in the street block south of Wood Street. Of course, October would have been the best time to do this, when one crop had been gathered and the next had not yet been planted. None of these features are especially exceptional: they are characteristic of towns planned elsewhere in England at this time and throughout the thirteenth century.[29] It was only exceptionally that grid-planned towns were laid out in the way that they had been in Roman times and were to be again in the eighteenth and nineteenth centuries, that is with orthogonal grids of streets at right angles to each other. Indeed, grid plans were themselves exceptional despite their frequent reproduction in text books; the most typical new-planned town was the single-street town with a broadened lozenge-shaped market place such as is found in Chipping Campden (Gloucestershire) or Thame (Oxfordshire).[30]

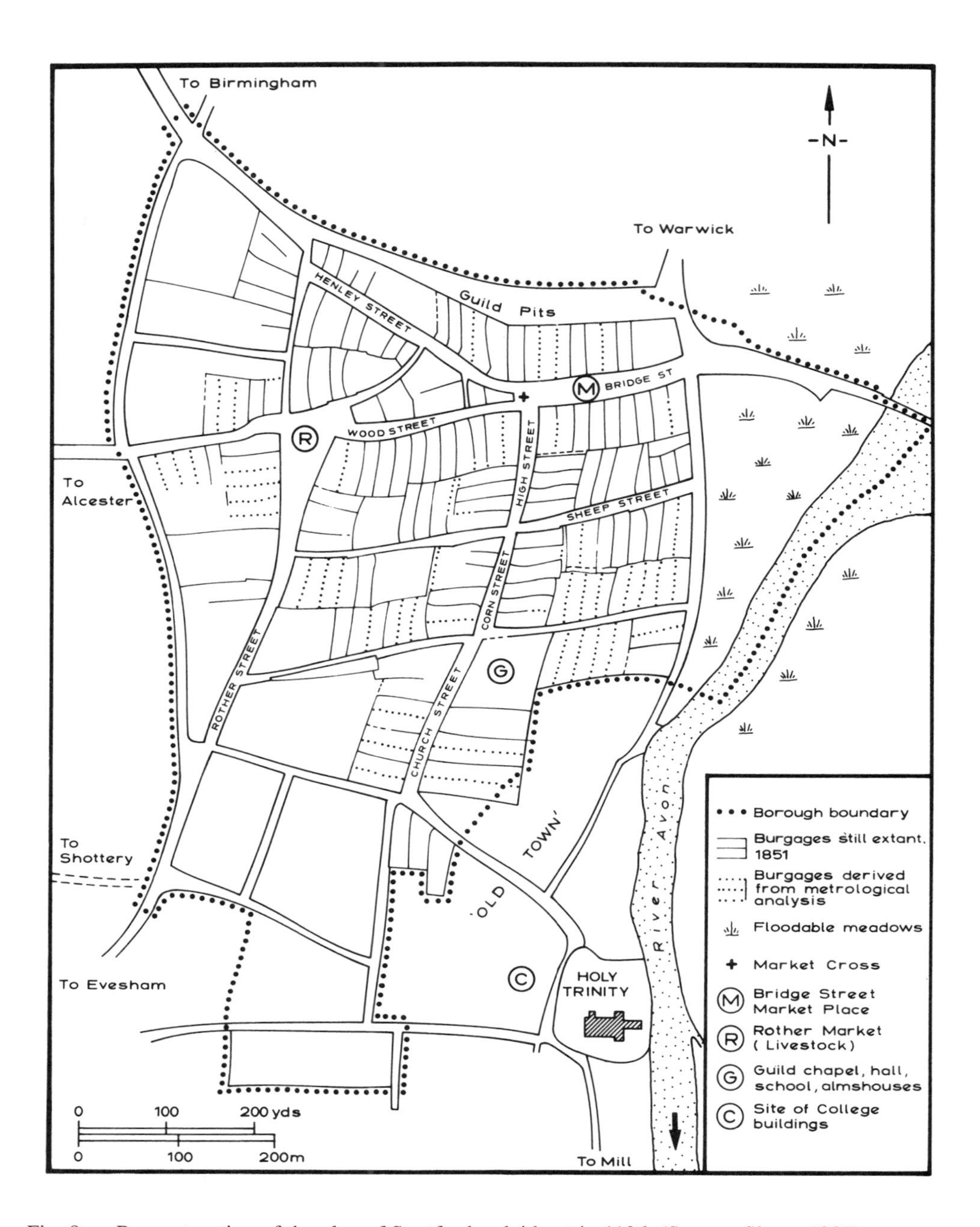

Fig. 8. Reconstruction of the plan of Stratford as laid out in 1196. (Source: Slater, 1987)

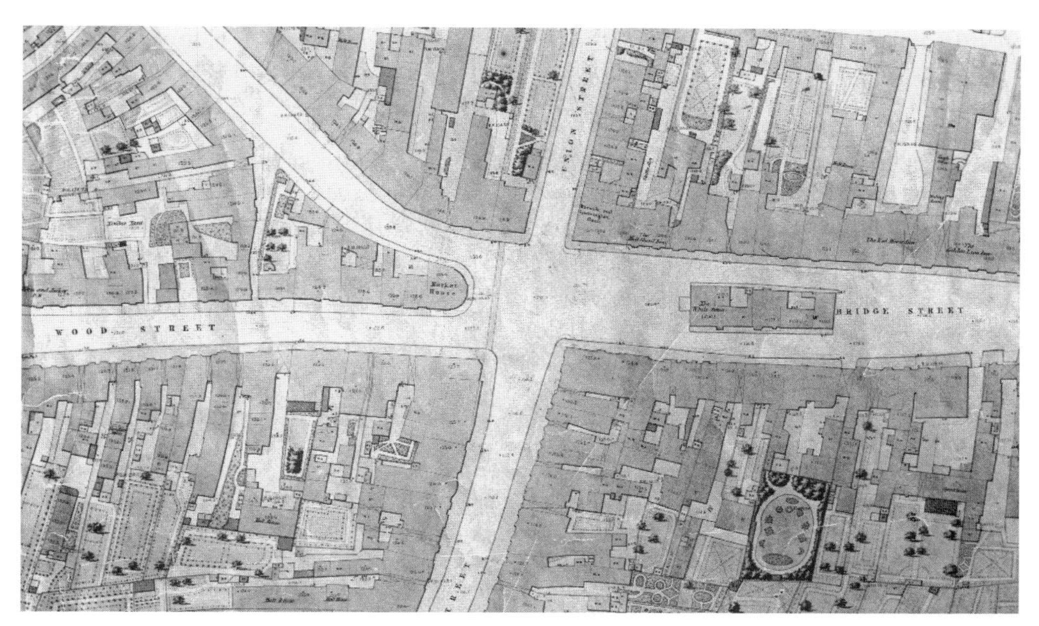

Plate 11. Part of the 1851 Board of Health plan for Stratford-upon-Avon, with the original burgage layout still clearly visible. Note also the last remaining portion of Middle Row in Bridge Street, which had evolved out of market stalls set out in the main market-place during the medieval period. (SBTRO, BRT 7/9)

We can now return to the 3½ by 12 perch plots specified in the foundation charter and ask whether such plots were in fact laid out on the ground. The answer is an emphatic yes; moreover, until very recently, these plot dimensions still gave character to the built form of Stratford.[31] It may at first seem surprising that building plots laid out in 1196 should survive through to 1996 but in fact this is again characteristic of many flourishing small towns in Europe.[32] Once laid out and developed with buildings of some permanence it becomes very difficult to change the boundaries of plots in an urban context. Only if a number of plots are cleared contemporaneously and are in the same ownership is this likely to happen, or if there is a particularly vigorous urban land market at some time with buildings being redeveloped under some powerful authority. Some of the urban fires of the early modern period would provide the first condition, though we can note that the late sixteenth-century fires in Stratford did not affect the property boundaries any more than did the Great Fire of London; buildings were simply reconstructed within existing patterns of property holding. The 1960s is an example of the second condition where a booming property market was allied with the compulsory purchase powers of local authorities. It was the 1960s which effectively removed so much of Stratford's historic plot pattern that had survived for nearly 800 years.

The plot dimensions laid down in the charter prove to have been employed throughout the town and used the statute rod, pole or perch of 16.5 feet. This can be confirmed both from the cartographic evidence of the large-scale 1:528 plan produced for the Board of Health in 1851 and from field measurement of plots undertaken in the 1970s.[33] The 18-

metre width of plots (57.75 feet) is found everywhere; the 60-metre depth of plots (198 feet) is rather more variable. Some of the plots in the blocks around the edge of the plan are both longer (in Rother Street) and shorter (in Henley Street) than this, and the plots on the east side of Church Street are also longer. However, it is possible to reconstruct the details of the plan as it was first laid out over much of the town and that exercise brings to light more features which tell us something of the planner's original intentions (Fig. 8).

First, he used the orientation of the plots to enhance the intended status of particular streets. It is clear that the central axis of the town – Church Street, Corn Street (now Chapel Street) and High Street – had plots facing onto it continuously from one end to the other except where it met Wood Street–Bridge Street (the Roman road). That east–west route was even more important (it had the market place) and so plots were oriented north–south along it and Henley Street. The other east–west roads of the grid were both narrower, and had plots oriented to them only away from the north–south axis. Almost no plots were oriented on the river along Waterside because there was no port function on the Avon.[34] Secondly, the analysis of the plan shows that there were narrow alley ways in some parts of the plan, now almost all gone, which provided rear access to the plots for their occupants. The indentations in the back fence lines are one indication of these alleys and the plots in the Sheep Street–Chapel Street block were serviced in this way. The entrance to what had once been an alley serving the rear of the Bridge Street plots is still preserved in a narrow building fronting High Street, as we shall demonstrate. Not all the series of plots needed such alleys of course, since some backed directly onto the borough boundary lane. The northern side of Bridge Street and Henley Street is the best example of this, rear access being gained from Guild Pits. It is no accident that the major chain stores have located here in the 1980s since it enables Guild Pits to continue this function for 40-ton lorries! Elsewhere in the town if vehicular access was required (whether by horse and cart, or by motor vehicle) it was necessary to use part of the plot frontage to gain access, as it still is.

Finally, we must note that the whole area of the borough was utilized. Though no plots are shown in the southern part on the reconstruction plan (Fig. 8), and we know that this area was occupied by pasture closes at least from the sixteenth to the nineteenth century, and probably from the late fourteenth century, the metrological analysis suggests that these areas were originally laid out with standard plots. The block of land to the south of College (formerly Sanctus) Lane, for example, is exactly 12 perches in depth, though the area is now occupied with an attractive estate of early nineteenth-century cottages. It may be that this was the result of an over-ambitious plan as others have suggested,[35] but the documentary evidence suggests otherwise. The 1251/2 survey of the bishop's new town[36] shows there to have been the equivalent of some 250 plots of the specified size (though many had been subdivided by then) as well as small areas of open land. The reconstruction plan accommodates only some 200 full plots, so many of the remaining fifty must have been in those areas which were open in the seventeenth and eighteenth centuries. Almost the last entry in the survey is for the holding of Richard of Bagendon which consisted of an unspecified number of burgages and land with an overall rent of 18*s*. He also held land in the rural manor. It may be that he deliberately rented a block of plots on the fringe of the town to use as pasture for animals which were ready for sale on market day, but this would have been an expensive way of doing this. More likely is that he was the largest investor in the developing new town. However, his holding was certainly substantial. Compared with the private landlords in Winchester in 1148,[37] for example, he would rank in the highest category since few landowners in Winchester held more than five or six properties. In that much larger city, however, the rents that could be derived from urban properties would have been much greater than in Stratford and presumably, therefore, the purchase price of properties was also much greater. On balance, it seems most probable that the fringe areas of Stratford were largely occupied with buildings in the twelfth and thirteenth centuries and were only abandoned in the post-plague decline of the late fourteenth century. Only archaeological excavations in the southern part of the borough will eventually resolve this question.

The 1251/2 survey also enables us to say something about what happened when the first migrant traders, and craftsmen and women moved to the new town. It tells us that many of the burgages had already been divided lengthways into halves and thirds by their occupants, while elsewhere, other occupants held two or three burgages. It is important to note that it was the initial or subsequent occupants who did the dividing, not the bishop's surveyor. In Stratford it seems that as the plot was subdivided so was the 12 pence annual rent to the bishop. A burgher holding one third of a burgage paid 4 pence, for example. This reduction in contribution might be sufficient reason for dividing the plot, but there were other reasons too. It was possible to divide the plot, for example, and charge a rent to occupants that quickly came to exceed the fixed rent to the bishop. This was quite typical in medieval towns large and small and was one way of making money in the town. It is also worth noting that in such instances the political franchise normally remained with the individual paying the 12 pence, the ground rent, as we might term it today, so that the number of voters was limited. This was the case in Henley-in-Arden, for example, where there were only sixty-nine burgages throughout the medieval period.[38]

The plot-holders who were likely to benefit most from dividing their plots were those who held them on the corners of the main street blocks since they had the advantage of two street frontages and it is clear that in some towns, founding lords ensured that such plots were in the hands of favoured estate officials. This enabled them to encourage the most rapid development possible, around market places, for example, in exchange for financial reward in the event of such successful development. It is not clear whether this was so in Stratford but the metrological analysis is so unambiguous that we are enabled to reconstruct the process of subdivision on some street corners.

The corner of Bridge Street and High Street is especially instructive in this respect. It has already been noted that the corner plots had originally been aligned on Bridge Street and were served by a rear alley (Fig. 9). It seems probable that the two burgages on the corner were originally held by one man because the pattern that ensued could not otherwise have been created. The eastern one was divided medially into thirds and the eastern two-thirds let as a single holding. The remaining land, equivalent to 1⅓ of an 'ideal' burgage,

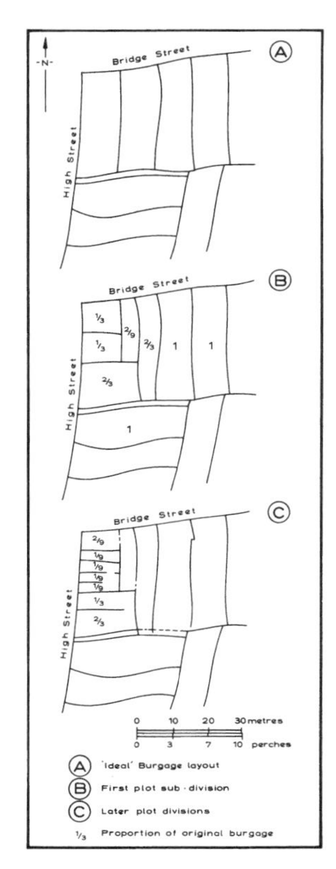

Fig. 9. The development of plot patterns at the junction of High Street and Bridge Street. (Source: Slater, 1987)

Plate 12. The Shakespeare Hotel before the renovations of 1920. The 'Five Gables' occupy the site of a burgage.

was subdivided in a way that related to the ideal dimensions in area, but not in length and breadth, so as to provide the maximum opportunity for subletting properties. The corner plot was divided crosswise into thirds and the southernmost portion included the rear of the ⅓ portion of the second Bridge Street plot. In this way plots equivalent in area to two × ⅓ and one × ⅔ of an ideal burgage were derived. The remnant ⅓ Bridge Street plot was 2⁄9 of an ideal burgage (Fig. 9). This might seem impossibly precise mathematically but it enabled the bishop's rent to be divided fairly between the holders of these plots.

The process of subdivision can be traced one stage further in this example since the plots now aligned on High Street were each subdivided into thirds once more, the northern and southern being occupied in ⅓ and ⅔ portions and the central plot in thirds. These little plots were equivalent in area to only 1⁄9 of an original burgage, but their street frontage of 22 feet (6.7 m), was more than sufficient for a dwelling, shop or workshop, with side-passage access to the rear of the plot if necessary (Fig. 9). This was only a little less than the 29 feet of frontage that was available on one half of a burgage, and more than the 19.25 feet available on one third of a burgage.[39]

This takes us to the question of buildings, since plot sizes and building forms have some relationship. Quite clearly, few buildings in medieval Stratford occupied the full frontage of a burgage. The five gables of the Shakespeare Hotel is the standard illustration of the scale of building that could be accommodated within such a plot width. Why then were not more of these broad plots subdivided immediately? And why were such broad plots laid out in the first place? One answer has already been provided, namely that there was no access for carts to the rear of these plots and that this had to be provided on the plot frontage. At first this would have led to a very open townscape of buildings separated from each other by access ways. Later, as the demand for town-centre plots increased, buildings could be built over the access way to give the covered passages that are so characteristic a part of the building fabric today.

Nonetheless, the pressure for plots to be subdivided so as to provide space for additional buildings seems never to have been especially great. This is not to say that some plots did not have more than one building on the frontage but that the ownership of the plot remained undivided. Even in the mid-nineteenth century, the 1851 Board of Health plan shows that plots with as many as four or five buildings on the frontage had not been subdivided outside the central area of High Street–Bridge Street. Even in the central streets plot subdivision rarely exceeded the halves and thirds which are recorded in the 1251/2 survey. Given the breadth of the plots, it seems likely that the majority of the houses in medieval Stratford would have been built with their long axes parallel to the street.

Recent archaeological work in larger towns, especially in London, has suggested that it was not until the later twelfth century that domestic buildings began to be constructed from materials which had any permanence.[40] Until then they were single story, wattle- or plank-built structures with thatch roofs with a lifespan of between twenty and forty years. Although more permanent timber-framed structures began to be built in larger towns from the end of the twelfth century, we might expect that the diffusion of these new techniques might take some time to reach a small town such as Stratford, and that for the first half-century of its existence the older type of urban dwelling predominated. However, Stratford's founder had frequent communication with London and other large cities and Stratford's position on the regional road network would have ensured that merchants and traders from a wide area would have passed through the town and enabled townspeople to have knowledge of the new building techniques. The other advantage of timber-framed buildings, besides their longevity when properly maintained, is that two or three storeys could be provided thereby doubling the accommodation available per unit area. This may be another explanation for the concentration of occupation in the northern half of the town and the virtual abandonment of the southern half.

There have been few archaeological excavations of plot frontages in Stratford and there has been no proper survey of Stratford's standing buildings, so it is difficult to confirm these hypotheses with local evidence. The two known late-medieval domestic buildings that are still standing, Mason's Court, built in Rother Street in the 1480s, and a building on the south side of Henley Street of similar age, are both variants of the typical hall-house plan with the hall parallel to the street as suggested. The present Falcon Hotel, in Chapel Street, is another early building of *c.* 1500 to which the upper storey was added in *c.* 1645, and the White Swan Hotel in Rother Market, probably built in the mid-fifteenth century, has a central hall and two projecting wings.[41] The excavation of a house in Rother Street by W.J. Ford in 1970 revealed a timber-framed 'long-house', the cesspits of which yielded twelfth-century pottery[42] which suggests that the earliest houses in the town might in fact have been timber-framed from the beginning, but the excavation remains unpublished. The majority of the other small-scale excavations in the town have been to the rear of frontages and they have confirmed that there were few structures on the rear of plots. These areas were used for the disposal of rubbish, for cesspits, and as garden and orchard ground. The Corporation surveys of the late sixteenth century are especially effective in painting a picture of the timber-framed houses, yards, gardens and orchards which constituted the majority of the town, the front houses having tiled roofs but the majority of the buildings around the yards still being thatched, hence the disastrous fires of the 1590s, 1614 and 1641.[43]

There were, of course, more than houses in the town. The 1251/2 survey notes that there were already a dozen stalls. These were the predecessors of the blocks of buildings that filled the centre of Bridge Street until the mid-nineteenth century. Again, these are typical of most medieval towns. Lords took the opportunity to increase their rents by allowing small timber booths to be constructed in the market place and charging a 2 or 4 pence rent for the privilege. There were in fact four market places in Stratford, three with market crosses. The Bridge Street market cross stood at the junction with High Street; a second cross, the White Cross, stood at the junction of Chapel Street and Church Street from at least 1275, where the butter and cheese market was held,[44] and a third cross stood in Rother Market where hides and cattle were traded. The fourth area was the site of the later Town Hall, where High Street became Chapel Street, where the corn market was located. Livestock other than cattle were traded in the middle east-west street: pigs in Ely Street (formerly Swine Street) and sheep in Sheep Street, presumably in relatively small numbers since these were streets of ordinary widths. Wood Street reflects the market for wood products from the Arden region to the north of Stratford. The market day specified in the 1196 charter was a Thursday.

To conclude, Stratford is an example of an early-founded, well-planned medieval new town. Its plan shows the thinking of the person who was responsible for its layout. The grid idea was applied pragmatically to the site available and existing landscape features were readily incorporated into the plan, distorting the ideal grid. The plot pattern was laid out using the dimensions of the charter with great subtlety and was emphatically not a hotchpotch of roughly measured and irregularly-bounded areas. Medieval masons were perfectly capable of measuring accurately and laying out set angles and, because burgages provided important legal rights, they were set out using the statute measures of perches and acres. Medieval new towns were not simply speculations for their founding lords but also for their occupants, especially the first burgage holders. The size of the first plot suggests that this was recognized by lords and that plots were deliberately designed so that they could be subdivided and sublet. Thereafter, however, there was comparatively little change in the plan of the town until the nineteenth century.

CHAPTER 4

Medieval Stratford: a Successful Small Town

CHRISTOPHER DYER

Stratford-upon-Avon is an ideal place to find answers to general questions about the development of medieval towns because it must rank among the twenty best-documented small towns in Britain.[1] It lacks a full series of borough court rolls, but the records produced for its lords, the Bishops of Worcester, can be used in conjunction with the archives of the fraternity of the Holy Cross. It has attracted the attention of a number of historians, who have identified some of the main characteristics of the society and institutions of the town.[2] The aim of this essay, observing Stratford as one of more than 600 small towns which existed in England at some time in the later Middle Ages, is to explain its relative success.[3] A few of the wave of new towns founded in the twelfth and thirteenth centuries, like Newcastle-upon-Tyne, grew far beyond the population limit of 2,000 which is customarily used to define a 'small town'; Stratford cannot be compared with these. But most towns had below a thousand inhabitants, and at one point Stratford's population may have reached double that figure. Dozens of new towns shrank in the fourteenth and fifteenth centuries until they ceased to be urban, but Stratford seems to have faced no danger of such terminal decline.

The first stage of the argument must be to justify the view that Stratford was a town which performed well, not just in the period of general urban growth between the late twelfth and mid-fourteenth century (using the Black Death epidemic of 1348–9 as a convenient end point) but also in the period of uncertainty and even decay in the two centuries between the Black Death and the Reformation. Then some reasons for the town's success will be suggested.

In a justly famous essay, Professor Carus-Wilson demonstrated how rapidly Stratford had grown in its first half century, and there is no need here to do more than to confirm her findings, and extend the picture by showing that the first phase of urban development was sustained for another hundred years.[4] Carus-Wilson's main source was the survey compiled for Bishop Walter Cantilupe in 1251/2, which survived as a nineteenth-century transcript.[5] She wondered if the original manuscript 'may even yet be traced'. Now it has been found, a document containing a survey of Stratford and of a number of Gloucestershire manors of the bishopric of Worcester, in Winchester Cathedral Library.[6] A comparison of the printed and manuscript texts, apart from revealing some small misreadings, confirms that the printed version is an essentially reliable source. Calculations based on the newly discovered manuscript are very similar to Carus-Wilson's: the survey lists 238 tenants, holding at least 245 burgages, about 60 plots, 14 selds (shops), 10 stalls, 2 ovens and 2 dyepans.

We naturally wish to know the size of Stratford's population, although the calculation is surrounded by many uncertainties. Not all of the burgages had houses built on them, and those on the fringes of the town may have been used as pasture closes. Some tenants were absentees, but their holdings could have been sublet. Subtenants are likely to have lived on some of the multiple holdings accumulated by people such as Richard Warner, who held five burgages and eight half-burgages. Legal disputes in the 1220s reveal the existence of subtenants, like Walter Troteman, a villein, who had bought a tenement in the town, and Nigel the Vintner who let out land for a rent of 3*d*.[7]

If the number of tenants in 1251/2 is multiplied by 4.5, the likely size of the average family, we arrive at a figure of 1,071, but the uncounted households of subtenants would swell the numbers considerably. The early fourteenth-century subsidy assessments for the borough of Stratford list between fifty-six and seventy-three tax payers, which, if we used the very fallible suggestion for rural settlements that 60 or 65 per cent of households were exempt, would lead to a population estimate of between 600 and 1,000.[8] But if the Stratford townspeople manipulated the tax system in the same fashion as their contemporaries in Coventry, who in 1327 contrived to omit four-fifths of households, then Stratford's total in that year could have been 1,300.[9] An even higher figure might receive some support from a rare piece of evidence found in an enquiry conducted by the Bishop of Worcester in 1336 into a proposal to enlarge Archbishop Stratford's chantry chapel by appropriating the rectory and creating a college of priests.[10] In his evidence the rector of Wilmcote reported that there were 3,000 people in the parish (which included a number of villages as well as the town), and was supported in this estimate by other local clergy. This could be dismissed as a typical example of medieval statistical imprecision, and it was in any case a piece of special pleading to justify the new college. However, in favour of taking the numbers seriously, clergy would have been in a position to know how many parishioners were making offerings at Easter or paying personal tithes.[11] If the parish total was 3,000, we can estimate the rural population at about 1,000 which would leave 2,000 in the town.[12]

The town's population between 1251 and 1336 is unlikely to have fallen below 1,000, and might have risen as high as 2,000. To put these figures in perspective, most market towns contained a few hundred inhabitants, and Stratford's modern population did not rise much above 2,000 until around 1750.[13]

Carus-Wilson's analysis of the surnames based on places of origin, like Robert de Kempsey, showed that by 1251/2 the town had attracted migrants largely from the surrounding villages, three-quarters of them within sixteen miles.[14] Additional locative names found in deeds and other sources of the thirteenth and early fourteenth centuries, before names became fixed and hereditary, support this generalization. No one in 1251/2 was called 'de Alcester' or 'de Warwick', because these nearby towns would themselves have been attracting migrants. However, both in Cantilupe's survey and other early sources, there are names showing that a significant minority came from towns – Birmingham, Chipping Campden, Evesham, Leicester, Nottingham, Stow-on-the-Wold and Worcester. Migrants had evidently left some small towns and also some relatively large and well-established places, presumably because Stratford as a growing urban community offered attractive opportunities. This movement must have brought useful experience and skills into the new town. Nonetheless, Carus-Wilson was quite right to emphasize that the majority of migrants were country people, willing to take a chance of making a new life.

Stratford rose to the top rank of market towns in the urban hierarchy of its region by 1300. In that year townspeople from Leicester paid money to juries in market centres in Warwickshire, apparently listing them in order of importance. They rated Stratford below Coventry and Warwick, but above Alcester, Kineton and Brailes.[15] A similar conclusion can be drawn from the tax assessments of 1327, when Stratford can be compared with other towns in Warwickshire and two adjoining counties.[16] Coventry, Gloucester and Worcester contained many more people and were assessed for greater amounts of tax, and Stratford was clearly ranked below Warwick. Birmingham contained more taxpayers, but Stratford paid more taxes than any other nearby market town (see Table 1).

Table 1: ***Tax assessments in 1327 for some West Midland towns (tax payers contributed a twentieth of the valuations of moveable goods)***

Town (County)	*No. of taxpayers*	*Total tax assessment*
Bristol (Glos. and Somerset)	347	£80 12*s* 0*d*
Coventry (Warw.)	200	£40 13*s* 6*d*
Gloucester	246	£28 4*s* 9*d*
Warwick	84	£13 5*s* 6*d*
Worcester	95	£10 8*s* 2*d*
Stratford (Warw.)	58	£10 2*s* 8*d*
Birmingham (Warw.)	75	£7 0*s* 6*d*
Alcester (Warw.)	55	£6 1*s* 11*d*
Evesham (Worcs.)	54	£5 3*s* 10*d*
Chipping Campden (Glos.)	27	£4 10*s* 10*d*
Pershore (Worcs.)	50	£4 0*s* 0*d*
Henley-in-Arden (Warw.)	24	£2 11*s* 4*d*

Sources: as cited in note 16, and in Hilton, *Medieval Society*, 200.

In its period of growth in population and wealth the town also developed distinctive institutions. It was governed by officials responsible to the bishop, described in the 1290s as the reeve and two catchpolls. Judging from the name of Walter Cachepol recorded in 1221, that office went back to the early years of the borough.[17] The borough court, if it resembled those of other towns for which early records survive, played an important role in making by-laws and hearing pleas of debt, and its jury and officials would, like the reeves and catchpolls, have been recruited from among the leading townsmen. The borough became increasingly independent. In 1299, when a new survey was made of the bishopric estates, the borough tenants and their rents were probably omitted. If a list was made, it was kept separately, and subsequently lost. At this time the bishops were continuing to make a reasonable profit from rents, tolls and payments in the borough courts, about £20 a year, but rents had ceased to increase.[18]

The townspeople were forming their own organizations, notably the fraternity of the Holy Cross, which was already in existence in the early thirteenth century, and was given formal recognition by Bishop Giffard in 1270. By that time it was associated with a hospital –

perhaps better described as an almshouse. By the 1290s the fraternity had built a chapel and a guildhall, in which an occasional *mornspeche* (business meeting) and an annual drinking were held. It looked after the poor and employed chaplains and probably a schoolmaster. The fraternity (commonly called a guild) was building up its estate of properties yielding rents in the town, and was beginning to keep an archive. The survival in that collection of tax lists from 1309, 1313 and 1332 suggests that the fraternity was performing administrative tasks on behalf of the whole town alongside its ostensibly religious and social functions. It was not the only body to represent the common interest, however, as in the 1330s the rector, Robert Stratford, applied to the king for permission to levy tolls to pave the streets on behalf of the bailiffs and the 'worthy men' of the town. There were other fraternities, like that of St Mary and St John, in existence by the 1260s.[19] The college, founded in the 1330s and combined with the parish church, could be seen as another institutional initiative by townspeople. Its founders, John Stratford, Bishop of Winchester and later Archbishop of Canterbury, and Ralph Stratford his nephew, Bishop of London, had been born into the Hatton family, who were prominent in the town as property holders and officials.[20]

The fully urban character of Stratford, using the generally accepted definition of a town that most of its inhabitants should make their living from a variety of non-agricultural occupations, was clear from the surnames deriving from twenty-five different trades and crafts in the 1251/2 survey. The layout of the market, with streets and buildings assigned to different commodities, such as meat, drapery, mercery, pigs, cattle, corn, hay, salt and honey, tells its own story of a busy trade in a high volume and wide range of goods. Carus-Wilson rightly emphasized the mundane nature of the Stratford crafts and trades, which satisfied the everyday needs of its region. But certainly in its formative years, in 1221, a townsman was called Robert the Vintner, and two others sold wine 'against the assize' (which meant at too high a price), so the town's customers must have included gentry and clergy buying a relatively luxurious commodity.[21]

Stratford was built in a form appropriate to a town, with stalls and shops, and two storey houses. Such was the competition for points of sale in the commercial heart of the town that stalls and shops were packed into restricted spaces, notably in the Middle Row in Bridge Street. They were rented as separate holdings, and could be as small as 14 feet by 5 feet, or 8 feet by 8 feet.[22] Holdings on the main streets commanded high rents – the chief tenants continued to pay to the bishop the annual 1*s* 0*d* rent fixed in 1196 (or often 6*d* or 4*d* because the plots had been split into halves or thirds), but their subtenants were expected to pay economic rents, as high as 10*s* 0*d* per annum for a shop, or 20*s* 0*d* for two houses. The growth of the town stimulated a land market, which lay behind the subdivision of plots, and was leading to disputes over title and succession from the 1220s. A house in Henley Street was sold in about 1294 for £13 6*s* 8*d*.[23] Property values reflected the high turnover and profits of urban traders. To provide a yardstick for measuring these sums of money, an unskilled labourer in full-time employment in the late thirteenth century could not have expected to earn more than 30*s* 0*d* to 40*s* 0*d* in a year. In addition to its intensive development at the centre, the town also acquired a suburb at an early date – the small settlement of Bridgetown across the river in the manor and parish of Alveston was surveyed in 1240, and one of its inhabitants worked as a fuller, participating no doubt in the town's cloth industry.[24]

In spite of the evidence for their varied occupations, commercial activities, and distinctive townscapes, doubts are still expressed about the urban character of small towns such as Stratford. It might be alleged that it had a rustic atmosphere: the burgage plots were bounded

Plate 13. Effigy of John Stratford, Archbishop of Canterbury, as drawn and engraved from his monument in Canterbury Cathedral by Charles A. Stodard, 1811.

by thorn hedges, elm trees served as landmarks around the streets, and the inhabitants cultivated gardens and kept pigs.[25] But the idea that such towns were semi-rural, or just villages with markets, ignores the fact that few town households possessed enough land for their subsistence, but made their living from crafts and trades. Horticulture and pig-keeping were intensive means of producing food appropriate to an urban economy, and indeed could be found in the largest cities, even in London. Stratford suffered from environmental problems, such as the smoke generated by a concentration of hearths, accumulations of refuse in great dung hills at the ends of the streets, and the danger of fires spreading among the high density of buildings.[26] The rapid expansion of the town, and its concentration of population, no doubt created social problems of vagrancy, unemployment and poverty. The sessions of the justices in eyre in 1221 offer a glimpse of an unruly place, with violent antagonisms between Welsh migrants and townspeople, themselves recent settlers.[27] The foundation of the hospital by 1270, and the charitable works of the fraternity, must have been a response to the insecurity and social deprivation inseparable from urbanization.

The townspeople's distinctive outlook and culture emerges even from their surnames. In 1251/2 while many of the peasants of Stratford manor were identified by a parent's name – 'son of Robert', or 'son of William' – the town dwellers were known by their place of origin, or their occupation, or by a nickname like that of Richard 'by-mi-stef', presumably after his favourite oath, 'by my staff'.[28] Guild feasts and drinkings were especially characteristic of urban society. Involvement in commerce gave women in towns a little more independence. Towns came into being through both geographical and social mobility, and their inhabitants expected to improve themselves. The members of the Hatton family provide a prime example of such advancement, firstly by moving into Stratford from the village of Hatton-on-Avon, where almost all of the tenants were serfs, and then establishing themselves as leading figures in the town between 1285 and 1318, acting as witnesses to deeds, and holding the office of reeve.[29] John de Hatton presumably attended the town school in the 1290s and, after a time at Oxford, went on to a brilliant career in the church under the name John Stratford, culminating in his election first as Bishop of Winchester and then Archbishop of Canterbury (1333–48). His nephew Ralph Stratford became Bishop of London, and his brother Robert, one time rector of Stratford, was elected Bishop of Chichester. Both John and Robert, as successive chancellors to Edward III, played a crucial role in national politics at the beginning of the Hundred Years' War. John helped the careers of a number of clergy from other Stratford families.[30] The town, by giving the Hattons the opportunity for acquiring some wealth and education, provided a stepping stone in their transformation over about four generations from peasant servility to the highest positions in church and state.

In its emergence as a populous bustling centre in the period 1196–1348, Stratford was participating in a Europe-wide growth of population, commerce and towns. Some historians would argue that the following two centuries saw an opposite tendency, in which reductions in the numbers of people were connected with economic recession and urban decline. Towns decayed physically with the fall in population and abandonment of houses; industry, and especially cloth-making, developed in the countryside; and patterns of trade shifted, notably with the shrinkage of the east coast ports and the rise of London. Townspeople were reluctant to take up office, and complained about taxes and civic expenditure.[31] Stratford is no exception in offering evidence both for decline and for prosperity. The negative tendencies will be examined first, and then the pointers to a more optimistic picture.

The population of the town diminished, though exact measurements are as elusive as in earlier centuries. The numbers of taxpayers in 1524 and 1525 (113 and 93) could be interpreted as pointing to a total population below 1,000, but this tax is very unreliable, and here the assessment seems to have been distorted by excluding the poorer wage-earners, as no one paid tax on goods worth 20*s*, the lowest tax band. This was a numerous category in other towns. The figure for communicants in 1546 implies a town population nearer to 1,650, but that could include an element of growth in the 1530s and 1540s.[32]

A more serious decline might be indicated by the drop in the Bishop of Worcester's revenues from the borough, from about £20 in the 1290s to £10 – £12 in the fifteenth and early sixteenth centuries.[33] The decay of rents recorded by the bishop's officials, which totalled £7 12*s* 5*d* in the accounting year 1506–7, were not just concentrated on the fringes in Rother Street or Greenhill Street, but were also found in the Middle Row in Bridge Street, implying a lack of tenants even in the town centre. The rent income of the fraternity of the Holy Cross was increasing for much of this time (Fig. 10), but this was achieved through the acquisition of houses, shops and land, which may have been aided by a slackening in demand. Like the bishop, the fraternity faced problems of decayed rents, especially between 1403 and 1408, in the 1450s and 1460s, and after 1490. Rents for individual properties often fell at some time in the fifteenth century. For example the payments for the house now known as no. 1 High Street declined in stages from 36*s* 8*d* in 1450 to 26*s* 8*d* in 1474.[34] The records of the fraternity refer to the physical decay of its buildings, or to plots which were 'not built on'. Clauses in leases requiring tenants to build anew and references to empty burgages appear in the period 1408–41, and as with the decays of the bishopric rents these apply to shops in the Middle Row as well as houses in Rother Street. Between 1473 and 1488 agreements to build reappear in the fraternity's leases.[35]

Cloth-making, one of the town's more important industries, must have been in decline in the fifteenth century, when the building called the 'Drapery' and used for cloth sales was converted into a private house. By 1537 the bishop's fulling mill was converted to grinding corn.[36] Frictions between townspeople are recorded periodically in the fifteenth century when the fraternity had to act as peacemaker, and a serious riot involving leading townsmen was provoked in 1504 by a deputy steward who chose unsuitable jurors, and ignored the normal procedure for electing a bailiff (the official previously known as the reeve).[37] This incident may have been part of some more profound crisis, as decayed rents of Guild properties reached their highest level in a century, more than £8, in the accounting year 1503–4, and the fraternity experienced a serious recruitment problem as numbers joining fell to a low point in 1499–1500, and the standard entry fine had to be reduced from 13*s* 4*d* to 6*s* 8*d*. An internal quarrel in the Guild seems to have arisen in 1500 when a master appointed a schoolmaster without consulting the aldermen, and two men served as masters of the Guild, possibly as rivals, in the year of office 1500–1. In that apparently troubled year John Elys, who as deputy steward was to provoke the riot of 1504, was acting as clerk of the Guild.[38]

All of these indicators of decline are capable of more positive interpretations, and Stratford people can be seen to have coped with the economic difficulties of the period. The fall in the numbers of inhabitants was probably not as great as the halving of the national total, and does not bear comparison with the collapse in the population of the south Warwickshire countryside, where a dozen villages were deserted within four miles of the town.[39] The difficulties of the bishopric officials in collecting rents could indicate inefficient management or a rise in evasion. Certainly court profits were affected by problems of

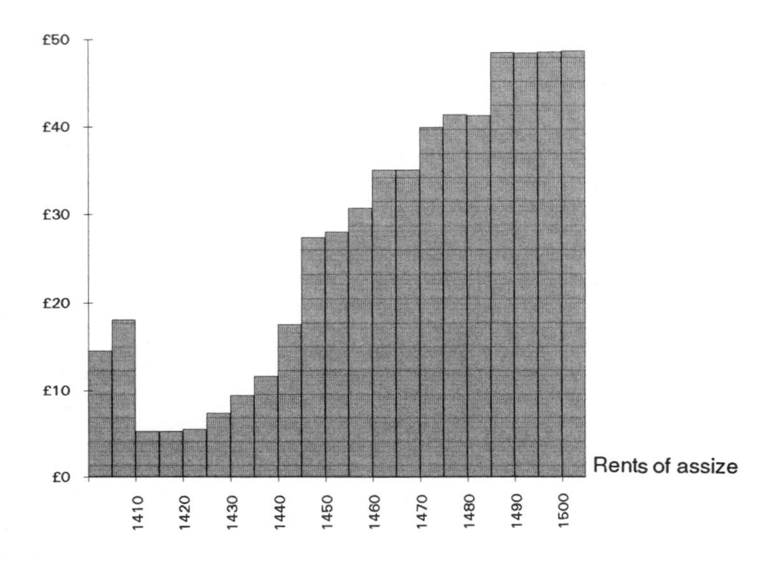

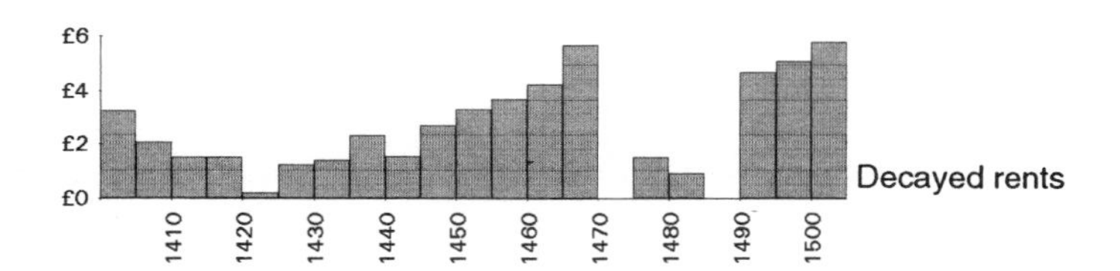

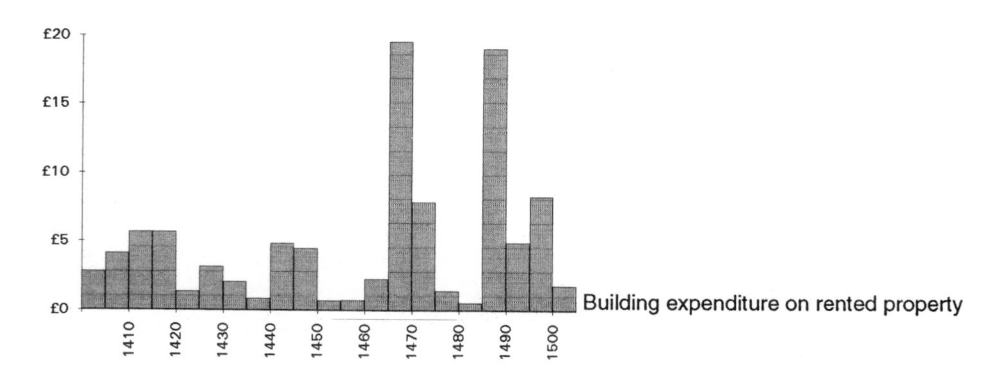

Fig. 10. Rents, decays of rent, and expenditure on property repairs, 1400–1505, from the records of the fraternity of the Holy Cross (proctors' accounts, masters' accounts, and rentals). The graphs show annual means, calculated for five-year periods. The fall in rents at the beginning of the fifteenth century was the result of changes in administration by which some rents were assigned to individual chaplains. The long-term increase reflects the growth in the number of properties, not property values. The fluctuations in decays and building expenditure are discussed in the text.

enforcement, such as the sum of 41*s* 10*d* in 1498 that 'could not be levied', and the farm of the tolls of the markets and fairs was deliberately withheld between 1501 and 1519.[40] Perhaps a better indicator of the prosperity of the town comes from the leasehold rent of £10 to £12 per annum paid to the bishop in the late fifteenth and early sixteenth centuries for the town mills, compared with £9 to £10 13*s* 4*d* in the 1290s.[41] Corn prices had fallen, so presumably the consumption of bread and ale in the town must have increased.

The officials of the Holy Cross Guild were quite assiduous rent collectors, serving as they were the interests of their own community rather than a remote landlord. They faced problems of rents which could not be collected, with decays standing at around £3 in the early fifteenth century when income from property was expected to bring in just under £15, and rose again to £4 or £5 in the early 1460s, and after a reduction in the 1470s and 1480s peaked at £8 in 1503–4 (see Fig. 10). Clearly rent collection was not an easy task, but the difficulties seem much less than those confronting the bishopric. While the bishop lost almost half of his rents, the Guild's decays rarely rose above 15 per cent of the total due. The records show that each property was carefully monitored, and losses were often caused by a house lying empty for a few months while a new tenant was found. The Guild may not have been a very harsh landlord, but defaulters were occasionally threatened with distraint. The rents paid to the Guild reflected demand, and property values were held up quite well. The series for individual houses show no very consistent patterns, but some rents rose during the fifteenth century. The

Plate 14. Mason's Court, Rother Street, a typical medieval burgess's home, dating from the 1480s. (Photo: Malcolm Davies)

property now known as no. 4 Chapel Street was charged with a rent of 6*s* 8*d* per annum from 1456 to 1463, and 13*s* 4*d* from 1464, while the rent of no. 32 High Street increased from 16*s* 0*d* in 1378–1450 to 20*s* 0*d* between 1469 and 1530.[42] The Guild contributed to maintaining its rent income by requiring its tenants to carry out repairs, or by spending money directly on building work (see Fig. 10). A vigorous campaign between 1394 and 1417, when decayed rents had been creeping up, absorbed in most recorded years between 12 per cent and 83 per cent of the rent income. A renewal of building in the 1440s did not prevent a rising trend of rent decays in the next fifteen years, and in 1465–75 and 1485–1500 expenditure rose to very high levels. In two accounting years, 1468–70, building costs equalled the whole of the income from rents. Against the references to disrepair must be set the 'new shop' in the Middle Row in 1431, a 'new house' in Wood Street in 1458, and two tenements 'newly built' in 1472, among many other rebuildings or extensive repairs.[43] We must conclude that active property development and management kept the Holy Cross fraternity's finances healthy, and helped the town by sustaining a sound fabric and providing employment for building workers. Perhaps other estates with holdings in the town, like the College, and private landlords, both gentry and wealthier townspeople, were stimulated to follow the Guild's example. The best known private addition to the housing stock towards the end of the fifteenth century was Hugh Clopton's New Place, and some timber-framed buildings survive from the same period, notably the Falcon Hotel in Chapel Street, and the White Swan and Mason's Court (both in Rother Street). Excavations in Meer Street have shown building and occupation at this time.[44]

Plate 15. The Guild buildings in Church Street, comprising, from right to left, early fifteenth-century almshouses, the Guildhall of similar date, and the tower of the chapel, rebuilt, with the nave, in the 1490s. (Photo: Malcolm Davies)

In addition to the Guild's investment in houses and shops, it also spent heavily on public buildings: the chapel, guildhall, school and almshouses all absorbed much money, especially between 1406 and 1428, and the High Cross was refurbished in 1431–2. Work on the parish church in the fifteenth century included such extensive projects as the rebuilding of the chancel, and the addition of the clerestory and porch. A major programme of construction on the bridge and on the nave of the Guild Chapel was funded by the bequests of High Clopton made mainly after 1496.[45] To some extent these projects reflect wealth generated in the town, as much of the income of the fraternity and the collegiate church came from rents, tithes and other payments collected in Stratford.[46] But the prestigious institutions of the town had the power to attract money from outside, in the hundreds of fines paid to enter the fraternity, and Clopton's bequests based on the profits of his London business. The renewal of the town's infrastructure in this period does not indicate any slackening in civic pride among the leading townsmen. Likewise the disturbance of 1504 showed that the right of the élite to fill important offices was jealously guarded.

There may have been a decline in cloth-making, but Stratford's inhabitants continued to pursue a wide range of crafts and trades, and indeed some new specialisms seem to have been added with the building of an oil mill in Swine Street (leading to its renaming as Ely Street), first recorded in the late fourteenth century, and the mining of gypsum near the town ('plaster pits' are mentioned in 1447) gave an opportunity for a 'plastermonger' to practise his trade.[47] Stratford kept its place in the regional urban hierarchy, and indeed improved its ranking. In 1404–5 the 'clerk of the market', attached to the royal household while it passed through the West Midlands, exercised his customary right to take fines on trade, mostly in food and drink – Warwick paid 30*s* 0*d*, and Stratford 20*s* 0*d*, while the other market towns such as Alcester, Rugby, Shipston, Solihull and Southam were each charged between 5*s* 0*d* and 15*s* 0*d*.[48] In the tax of 1524/5 Stratford paid more than Birmingham and Evesham, as in 1327, but now for the first time (but only in the short term) it overtook Warwick in taxable wealth.[49]

One of the weaknesses of the historical debate about 'urban decline' in the later Middle Ages has been the attempt to generalize about whole towns. Individuals or groups could well have been better off, even in a place that was showing signs of overall 'decline'. Stratford's building workers benefited from the universal rise in wages, so that skilled craftsmen such as carpenters were earning 4*d* per day in the 1350s and 5*d* to 6*d* by the 1490s. Unskilled workers' pay increased by a larger margin.[50] The food and drink allowances given to building workers in 1431 contained a high proportion of ale and fish (not meat, as the job was done in Lent) rather than the preponderance of bread found in lower-class diets before the Black Death.[51] The houses that they were building were solidly constructed from high quality materials, including tiled roofs. Urban expansion, as we have seen, was accompanied by some hardship, while the shrinking town might have afforded a better standard of living to its inhabitants.

While Stratford fared quite well in the two centuries after 1348, the period included short-term cycles of expansion and contraction. Two difficult patches stand out, one around 1400 and another around 1500, when some other towns were expanding.[52] Both episodes coincided with initiatives by the civic élite. They merged the fraternities in 1403, and obtained royal letters patent to approve the change, and Hugh Clopton funded the bridge and Guild Chapel after 1496. These may both have been attempts at rejuvenation during times of recession.

How can we explain Stratford's expansion in its first century and a half, and its resilience and capacity for renewal after 1348? Stratford could be seen as a 'primary town', of which Banbury has been quoted as an example, a place almost predestined to urbanization by its role as a pre-Conquest focus of government, religion and exchange. People visited such places to attend courts and religious services, and the gatherings became periodic markets, which encouraged artisans and traders to settle.[53] Stratford had some of the characteristics of a primary town because it served as the centre of a large estate, and it had a minster church; but it was not the centre of a hundred, and does not stand out before 1196 as being more important than nearby Bidford-on-Avon, Hampton Lucy, Tredington or Wootton Wawen. If a market was functioning beside the church, it does not seem to have attracted traders as permanent inhabitants, according to the survey of about 1166.

How do we explain the confidence with which the bishopric officials laid out the ambitious grid plan? Was it just a leap in the dark, inspired by hope rather than any firm expectations? If so, it was an inspired speculation, as the town grew very rapidly, not only in its first half-century, but in its first twenty-five years, because the records of the justices in eyre in 1221 show many Stratford families already established, and reflect the economic vitality and some of the turbulence of a new urban society.

One possibility is that before 1196 a periodic market was flourishing, and this was sufficient to indicate the commercial potential of the site. An unofficial settlement of traders near the river crossing may have been left out of the 1166 survey, or grown in the thirty years before John of Coutances's charter. The building of the bridge to replace the ford may have given the planners an assurance of success. The bridge is first documented in 1235, and we might speculate that it had been built in the late twelfth century, making the foundation of the town the next phase of development.[54] The planners presumed that Bridge Street would be the axis of the new town. Once the bridge was in place, it could be anticipated that a high proportion of the traffic of south Warwickshire would pass along Bridge Street, and guarantee the prosperity of the traders established there.

Setting aside any guesswork about the date of the bridge, there can be no doubt about the long-term importance of the river crossing for the prosperity of the town. The roads converging on the bridge served as funnels through which flowed the complementary trade of Warwickshire, with timber, fuel and cattle from the Arden to the north and west, being exchanged for the grain from the Feldon to the south and east. The specialisms of these two regions had developed long before 1196, and for centuries territorial connections, like that between Stratford and Bushwood in Lapworth, gave the corn-growers of the Feldon access to the woodlands and pastures of the Arden.[55] In the twelfth and thirteenth centuries the links were achieved increasingly through trade, and a number of markets developed on the frontier. Warwick and Coventry were already established by 1100, and were joined by Alcester and Stratford in the south, and Atherstone and Nuneaton in the north. The pace of commercial growth was increasing at the end of the twelfth century, when the bishopric officials saw a chance of founding a town in a strategic position which would benefit the estate directly in rents and tolls, and indirectly by stimulating production for exchange in the three nearby manors of Stratford, Hampton Lucy and Tredington. They may have noted that, compared with Worcestershire, where most of the bishop's land lay, south Warwickshire in the 1190s seemed undersupplied with towns.[56]

Clearly the imagination and foresight of the bishops and their officials played a decisive part in the town's origins, but did the lords of Stratford have a continuing influence? They seem to have intervened very little after the initial phase. They secured from the Crown a series of charters for fairs in 1214, 1239, 1269 and 1309.[57] Otherwise the bishops' main contribution was to leave the town to get on with its own business. The monastic lords of Shipston-on-Stour or Cirencester, who could not bear their tenants enjoying even the most elementary burghal privileges, may not have prevented the growth of those towns, but the discontent and occasional revolts cannot have helped.[58] The Bishops of Worcester instead tolerated the political role of the fraternity of the Holy Cross. Even Godfrey Giffard, a bishop temperamentally little inclined to make concessions to anybody, gave it formal recognition in 1270, perhaps in an attempt to exercise some control over it. In the long run, without showing any hostility towards the lord, the fraternity became 'the shadow government' of the town. The leading members discussed by-laws at their meetings, as notes on an *interlocutio* (council meeting) held in 1387 reveal, and a high proportion of the officials serving the bishop's administration – bailiffs (earlier called reeves) and under-bailiffs (catchpolls) – are also found among the leading figures of the fraternity, acting as masters, proctors and aldermen.[59] The bishops were content for their interests to be represented by members of the town's élite, and the only serious disturbance known in the town, in 1504, was caused by a temporary breakdown in the normally smooth cooperation between the lords and the leaders of the community.

Individual bishops made gestures of support for the town and its institutions, helping to found the College in the 1330s, making grants for the building of the parish church and the bridge, dining with the fraternity, and allowing (in 1517–18) the bailiff to spend some of the rent money collected in the town on two maces, so contributing to the civic regalia. They were remote lords, and the local gentry in the fifteenth century had more contacts with the townspeople, and probably more influence on their affairs (see Chapter 5). The bishop's courts in the 1450s were supervising transfers of burgage plots and new tenants were expected to do fealty to their lord, but the bishops turned a blind eye to the diminishing revenues from the borough, which were a financial symptom of independence.[60]

The town's trading prosperity was closely involved with its hinterland. Stratford's 'sphere of influence' was a rural area within which the inhabitants used the town as their main market. The borough court rolls of 1499–1507, in which the places of residence are sometimes recorded of people involved in pleas of debt, help to define its boundaries, as do the places from which the fraternity purchased food and building materials. Earlier and more complete series of records for Alcester and Shipston show how the marketing zones fitted together.[61] The area of Stratford's main commercial contacts seems to have had an elongated shape, so that it included places at a distance of eleven miles to the north-west and south-east, like Tanworth-in-Arden and Tysoe, but extended only five miles to the west (see Fig. 11).

If this territory had been much the same in the early fourteenth century, it would have included about sixty villages with a combined population in excess of 2,000 households. In 1327 1,000 contributors to the lay subsidy, many of them peasants with virgate (30-acre) holdings, would have been the people with a surplus of produce to exchange. They would also have had some cash, after paying their taxes and rents, to spend on goods manufactured and sold in towns. The borough court rolls mention the items traded – wheat, malt, sheep, cattle, sheepskins, straw and wax came in from the country, and the town could supply bread, ale, meat, fish, cloth (woollen and linen), iron, brass and

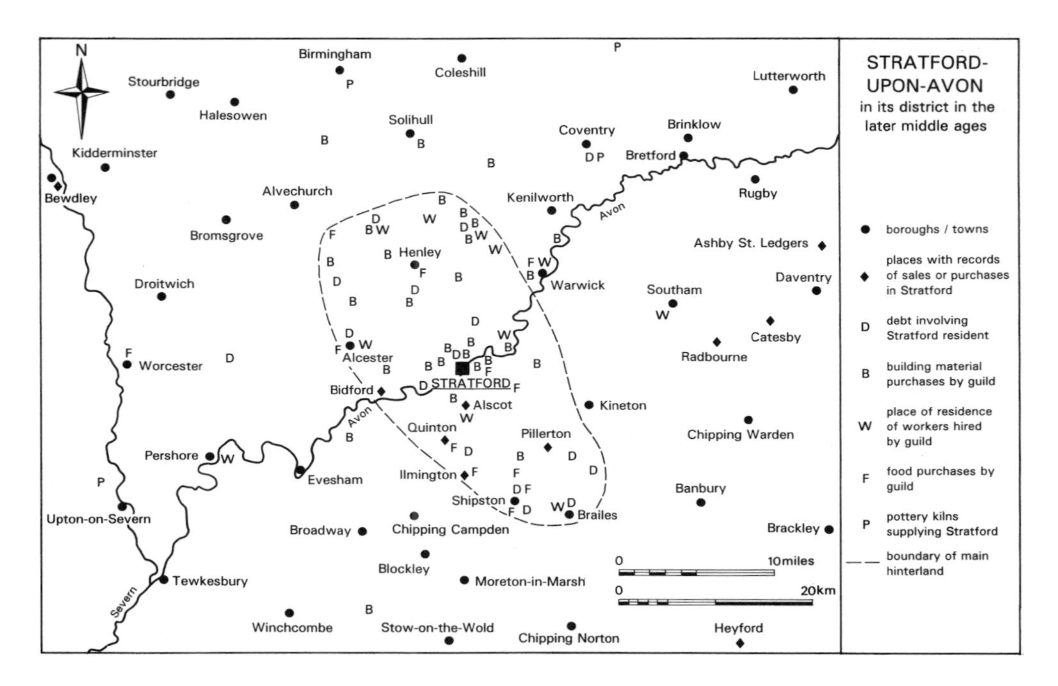

Fig. 11. Map of Stratford and its district in the later Middle Ages. The various records of debt, purchases, sales and employment define a 'main hinterland' which is indicated, but trade also extended over a much wider area. Sources include the records of the fraternity, manorial accounts, records of debt from other boroughs and the royal courts, and archaeology.

candles. The occupations in the town throughout the later Middle Ages show the range of activities appropriate to the everyday needs of the ordinary people of the district – preparation and sale of food and drink, manufacture of goods in wood, metal, textiles or leather, building, and the provision of services such as those of carters and inn-keepers. The average debt which litigants attempted to recover through the borough court amounted to a modest 5*s* 6*d*, but this gives a misleading impression because debts arising from numerous small-scale transactions worth only a few pence, involving, say, a pair of shoes or a few eggs, were not worth pursuing in the court. Market towns were also centres of sociability and entertainment, not just at grand occasions like the fraternity feast, but also more informally, especially when country people came in on market days and to the annual fairs; much ale was drunk (105 sellers of ale, almost all female, were named in 1452) and diversions could have been provided by a piper and juggler (recorded in 1251/2) and minstrels (in the 1450s and 1490s).[62]

Like most small towns, Stratford's local trade in ordinary commodities formed the basis of its economy. It enjoyed an advantage in its ability to attract business outside its immediate hinterland, involving large volumes of goods and high-status sellers and buyers. In the surrounding countryside landlords who cultivated their demesnes directly often sold in the best markets at some distance. To take an extreme case, the monks of Winchcombe Abbey, who held three manors within easy carting distance of Stratford, contracted to sell the wool of their whole estate in the early fourteenth century to Italian merchants.[63] A number of local lords, however, chose to use Stratford as their market, in preference to nearer points of sale. The Bordesley Abbey grange at Bidford, for example, which lay near to Alcester, sent rye to Stratford market and bought barley there in 1448–52. From his manor of Radbourne, which lay in the commercial orbit of Warwick and Banbury, William Catesby in the accounting year 1457–8 sold wool to a prominent Stratford trader, John Hannes, for £23 13*s* 4*d*. Even further afield, the nuns of Catesby over the border in Northamptonshire, also sold their wool in the 1450s to Hannes. The town had a sufficient trade in wool to attract the great William Grevil of Chipping Campden in 1384, when he was said to have bought ten sacks.[64]

Demesnes on many of the large estates in the Stratford district after about 1400 were leased to farmers who have left no accounts. But when we find among those joining the Holy Cross fraternity the farmers of demesnes some distance from the town, such as Blockley in the Cotswolds and Burton Dassett on the Northamptonshire border, it seems reasonable to infer that they had commercial as well as social and religious contacts with Stratford.[65] Indeed the farmers, who tended to hold only one or two pieces of land, were more likely to use local markets than the large estates with their centralized sales. The advent of the farmers was often also associated with a move towards pastoral farming. We find specialist livestock enterprises like that based at Alscot selling their sheep and sheepskins in the town in 1520, and pasture closes on the outskirts were used to keep stock on their way to market, like that held by Henry Warde, a grazier from Pillerton Priors, in 1493.[66] There must have been a general growth in the fifteenth and early sixteenth centuries in the prominence of animals and animal products in the town's market.

Stratford's position as a gateway market connecting different rural landscapes, which had contributed to its early success, made it a specialist centre by the later Middle Ages for the sale of timber and wooden implements. The manorial officials of Quinton (five miles to the south-west) acquired at Stratford in 1430–1 two wooden ploughs, a harrow, a dung cart and two gates; in the 1380s and 1420s boards and rafters for Heyford in Oxfordshire (at a distance of twenty-four miles) were bought in the town, and the nuns of Catesby purchased 2,000 laths at Stratford fair in 1454, and 2,000 laths and twelve wooden yokes on another occasion in the 1450s. One of the consignments of laths had been supplied by John Warrok from Bewdley in Worcestershire on the edge of the Wyre Forest.[67] Other products of woodland industries were travelling at least as far. Pottery found in excavations in Meer Street and Wood Street came from kilns at Hanley Castle in west Worcestershire, Chilvers Coton and Deritend in north Warwickshire, Brill in Buckinghamshire and an unknown site of manufacture to the east, probably in Northamptonshire. The iron goods bought in the town, such as plough fittings and iron tyres for cart wheels (and perhaps some of the leather goods such as horse collars and harness) came from northern Arden or south Staffordshire. An ironmonger from Walsall (Staffordshire) called Robert Shelfeld visited the town in 1406, and must have done good business, as he claimed that a sum of £5 16*s* 8*d* was stolen from his room in a Stratford inn.[68]

Stratford could occasionally supply luxury goods to the gentry, like the sweet wine bought for 16*s* 0*d* by the Catesby family from Ashby St Ledgers (Northamptonshire) in 1448–9, but much more typical was the barley sold to Sir William Mountford in 1433–4.[69] Mountford, and indeed the officials of Stratford's own fraternity, found their wine, spices and other luxuries in larger places – Worcester, Coventry and even London.[70]

If Stratford's main role was to deal in relatively cheap goods, we might expect that its volume of trade would have been adversely affected by the reduced number of people in its hinterland between 1348 and 1520. But the surviving population enjoyed increased resources, as peasants accumulated larger holdings and were often exploiting fifty or more acres of land. Wage earners, who had previously bought grain or bread and little else, were now able to afford more ale, meat and clothing supplied by Stratford traders. We have already noted that the new breed of farmer was inclined to sell in local markets. The flow of trade was helped by a growth in regional specialization. In the Arden, for example, the expansion of land used as pasture increased the inhabitants' dependence on grain from the Feldon.[71]

Stratford competed successfully with other trading places. Its rapid growth was helped by a lack of rivals as it took over the southern part of Warwick's commercial territory. The nearest towns in 1196, apart from Warwick, were Banbury, Chipping Campden and Evesham, and possibly Kineton and Alcester, although the precise time of their rise is not known (see Fig. 11). New commercial threats came in the thirteenth century with the foundation of Brailes, Broadway, Henley-in-Arden, Moreton-in-Marsh, Shipston, Solihull and Southam, all of them with burgage tenements, planned streets and market places. Villages developed a trading role, with or without the benefit of an official market charter, notably at Bidford, Burton Dassett, Snitterfield, Wellesbourne and Wootton Wawen.[72] These places were not all necessarily locked in competitive struggle. The minor markets could feed into the larger centres. And the general growth in population and commerce in the thirteenth century meant that more trading places were needed. But not all of them prospered, especially when the cold winds of recession were felt in the fourteenth century. If they had ever functioned as towns, Brailes and Broadway certainly reverted to villages, and many of the markets in villages disappeared.[73] Others remained small, and Stratford traders proved their superiority by moving into their markets, like Thomas Iremonger who was selling ale at Alcester in 1438, or seven people from Stratford who rented stalls in Shipston market place in 1509–10.[74] The town maintained its rank in the urban hierarchy, above Banbury, Campden and Evesham. It remained below Coventry, Worcester and Bristol in the pecking order, and recorded debts indicated the dependency of the Stratford traders on the merchants of the larger towns. The Holy Cross fraternity encouraged links by recruiting members in the larger places, and a prominent Stratfordian of the early fifteenth century, John Mayel, was enrolled in the Coventry Trinity Guild.[75]

The key to Stratford's expansion and renewal lay in its capacity to replenish its human resources by immigration. The initial flow of settlers was constantly supplemented by country people arriving as apprentices and servants, through marriages or by those seeking a new career. Members of the fraternity were sometimes said to have moved, for example from Quinton to Stratford, and families appear in deeds holding land and houses both in the town and in villages such as Charlecote or Tidmington.[76] Not everyone made their fortune. Agnes Jones of Compton Verney, whose first marriage was to Henry Wilkins of that village, by 1434 had married Thomas Baret of Stratford, and moved there with her son, John. He can probably be identified with the John Wilkins, described as a peddlar, who met a bad end leading a failed rebellion in Kent in 1452.[77]

Stratford also attracted talented newcomers who found a receptive and open society, judging from the experience of John Hannes (also known as Hannys or Hondyes). He was born in Idlicote, nine miles to the south-east, and first appears in Stratford in 1437–8 when he joined the fraternity with his wife, Alice. His prosperity is implied by his fine of 20*s*, higher than the usual entry fee.[78] He was probably then under thirty years old, but within five years he had become an alderman of the fraternity, and he was thought important enough, and his house sufficiently grand, to entertain a visiting dignitary, John Grevil, with wine. A year later he was elected master, and went on to hold that office another thirteen times in the next twenty-five years. He served in the bishop's administration as under-bailiff in 1446–7.[79] No doubt his success in business speeded his rise into the governing élite of the town. We have already seen that he was active in buying wool, he sold wax to the fraternity, and in 1452 he is recorded selling fish, and his second wife Agnes was among the numerous ale sellers.[80] He acquired houses in Henley Street and High Street, held land in Idlicote, and in 1464 took on the lease of a large pasture at Hatton-on-Avon.[81] His commercial contacts extended to Bristol: he encouraged a number of Bristol merchants to join the fraternity, and indeed he made his will in that town in 1473 (and probably died there). He was wealthy enough to bequeath 1,700 sheep and 16 cattle, and sums of money in excess of £380.

Major merchants like John Hannes are not found in any number in small towns, and it is perhaps not unexpected that his son Thomas went to London to become a mercer. Although Stratford lost its most ambitious sons through such emigration, it must have benefited the town to have personal contacts with the capital, especially when Hugh Clopton, Thomas Hannes and no doubt others gave money for charitable works in their home town. Hannes, by his will of 1502, intended to found new almshouses, though this scheme does not seem to have been implemented. But he left cash for the poor to be distributed by four 'honest and saddest men'.[82]

A final contribution to Stratford's success came from the Holy Cross fraternity. We have seen already that as a property holder it made a major contribution to renewing the physical fabric. By encouraging potential customers and suppliers to join, and to feel that they belonged to a worthwhile religious and social organization, commercial contacts were strengthened. In particular the local gentry were enrolled and then cultivated as a source of advice and patronage. The large country membership helped to bind the town to its hinterland.[83]

Among the townspeople the fraternity promoted harmony and held 'lovedays' to resolve disputes peacefully. The bishopric officials and the leaders of the fraternity together formed an oligarchy, which no doubt ruled the town for the benefit of the wealthier traders. They reacted strongly in 1504 when unworthy candidates were put into important offices. But the élite in a small town could not be too exclusive, as there were many positions, and not so many 'honest and saddest' men, as Thomas Hannes called them. And so we find filling the office of proctors of the fraternity not just drapers, mercers and ironmongers, but also bakers and shoemakers. The annual feast in particular expressed the unity of the body of the town, and reaffirmed its spirit of brotherhood, when social relationships were 'renegotiated' and potential frictions soothed and healed. Traders and artisans, debtors and creditors, clergy and laity, men and women were gathered in one hall to eat the same meal.[84] Membership of the fraternity gave some assurance of social security, through the almshouses, and the channel that it provided for donations to the poor.

Fraternities can be found in many small towns, but the Holy Cross Guild was especially wealthy and influential. Its buildings impressed visitors, and gave the town a distinctive character. How many other civic institutions in small towns could display a long range of timber framing like that in Church Street, or could boast two public clocks?[85] The

Plate 16. The Guildhall in 1894, the venue for the annual Guild feast in the fifteenth and early sixteenth centuries. It is now the library of King Edward's School. (Photo: John Valentine)

fraternity made Stratford famous throughout the Midlands and beyond – it was known in London, Salisbury and Exeter.[86] It brought splendour into people's lives, with the elaborate vestments, banners, statues and ornaments which made for colourful services and processions.

The annual feast must have caused a great stir, with lengthy preparations, the arrival of the animals and poultry from the countryside, and the gathering of the cooks from villages and towns. In the early fifteenth century between 108 and 160 people are known to have attended.[87] The occasion gained in solemnity because it was combined with religious rituals, as can be appreciated from the paintings of the patron saints still visible at the end of the hall. The meal resembled a grand aristocratic occasion in both quantity and quality. As they ate roast goose and veal, accompanied by sauces containing ginger and pepper, entertained by minstrels, sending out pots of ale and leftovers for the poor outside, shoemakers and ironmongers could imagine themselves rich for a day.

The College seems to have cooperated with the fraternity, apart from some friction in the 1420s, and the bridgewardens' main fund-raising celebration, the ale with a pageant of St George, would not have posed any threat to the Guild's activities.[88] The various organizations promoted a distinctive combination of religious cults, their unity being celebrated in the paintings in the Guild Chapel, which included the legend of the Holy Cross, the martyrdom of St Thomas (to whom the College chapel was dedicated), and St George (adopted by the bridgewardens).[89] The endowment of the schoolmastership in

1482 involved the bishop, the warden of the College, and the master of the fraternity, indicating the essential unity of the main town institutions.[90]

The fraternity occupies a prominent place in our view of medieval Stratford, partly because its archives and buildings still survive. We should be wary of exaggerating its importance, or idealizing its role. All that has been said about its unifying influence must be qualified by acknowledging that only a relatively wealthy minority could participate in its activities. Few of the building workers whom it employed, for example, could have afforded the entrance fine of 13*s* 4*d*, or the 6*d* charge for the feast.[91] Less than a fifth of the town's adult population were able to attend the feasts in the early fifteenth century, so unity and brotherhood were strictly limited. The fraternity did have a great reputation, which helped to raise Stratford's standing above its neighbouring towns, rather as the Shakespeare industry has done in more recent times.

The basis of Stratford's medieval success, and the main source of living for the bulk of its inhabitants, lay in its ability to serve the needs of its hinterland. It was planned to be larger and grander than the normal run of market towns, and for a number of reasons – among them the relatively early date of its foundation and its location in relation to roads and contrasting landscapes – Stratford was able to trade over a larger area, draw the custom of major producers, attract at least a few ambitious entrepreneurs, and occupy a superior rank among the market towns of its region.

CHAPTER 5

Town and 'Country': the Stratford Guild and Political Networks of Fifteenth-century Warwickshire

CHRISTINE CARPENTER

In the last decade or so the religious guilds, or fraternities, of late medieval England, have become a major focus of research, culminating in 1995–6 in the publication of no less than three books in which these guilds feature as an important element.[1] A certain amount of this work has been inspired by the growing interest in the internal economic and social history of the town,[2], but most has originated in the 'Catholic' re-evaluation of lay piety before the Reformation. Much of the original revisionary work was done on the beliefs of nobility and gentry but in recent years historians have begun to look seriously at the parochial level, tackling the much more elusive beliefs of the middling and lower orders.[3] Guilds in both town and country are being studied as manifestations of voluntary piety and communal activity, revealing the strength and vitality of orthodox beliefs at what could almost be called grass roots level.[4]

In all this work, illuminating as much of it is, one important element in several of these guilds has been largely neglected: the fact that they had nobility and gentry, usually from the surrounding region, among their members. This is symptomatic of the divide between historians of town and country which still exists in the study of the politics and political society of medieval England. The divide used to be almost universal in medieval English history but economic historians and historians of the lower orders are now beginning to produce exciting work on regions and on towns in their regional context.[5] Thus, the non-aristocratic membership of urban guilds from surrounding villages is beginning to get its due, and indeed Rodney Hilton, a pioneer in this, as in so much of medieval economic and social history, was giving the rural Stratford membership its due long before others began to think in these regional terms.[6] But historians are still puzzled as to what to do with the high-class members from outside the town and they are generally mentioned briefly or entirely ignored.[7] The only substantial work exploring links between towns and local landowners consists of two articles by Rosemary Horrox.[8]

And yet, even in the absence of serious research on these higher-ranking members, it is apparent that numbers of guilds had them. They included great guilds in large towns like St George's, Norwich, and Holy Trinity, Coventry, and lesser guilds in smaller towns, like the Guild of St Mary and St John the Baptist, Lichfield, the Palmers' Guild, Ludlow and, of course, the Guild of the Holy Cross, Stratford.[9] Except in the rare cases when they held guild office, we do not even know what kind of a role these men and women took in the ordinary affairs of the guild. In most guilds, members were expected to attend the patronal mass and take part in the procession and feast that accompanied it.[10] But, given that these events are interpreted by anthropologically-minded historians as occasions for displaying 'the hierarchy of power' and (depending on their ideological stance) revealing either the unity or the disunity of the town,[11] it seems doubtful that such rank outsiders, possessing no stake in the town's social structure, would have been involved. This point is nicely exemplified by the procession of the Norwich guild, in which the most prestigious position was given to the merchants, whom nearly all the landowning members would have considered far beneath them socially.[12] Perhaps some attended the service or the feast but one would presume that this was a voluntary rather than compulsory action.[13] It is still harder to imagine these status-conscious local worthies benefiting from the charitable side of a guild's activities, receiving alms or burial, for example. It is equally unlikely that the urban members, conscious of their own independence, would have given them much say in the choice of the chaplains whom so many religious guilds employed to say masses for them, except perhaps to offer the occasional piece of helpful informal advice.[14] And it is impossible to imagine the fifteenth-century kings who were enrolled in Holy Trinity Guild, Coventry, acting as ordinary guild members.[15]

So what were they doing in these guilds? Why did guilds want them as members and why did they wish to be members? Gervase Rosser has said perceptively that a voluntary association like a guild could change the boundaries of the institutionalized body to which it belonged. He was referring primarily to the way parish guilds could surmount parish boundaries, especially once they had become fixed, in about 1300, and thereafter in many cases out of date, demographically and geographically.[16] But the same point applies to the urban fraternity and the surrounding countryside. Assuming that the guild belonged to a town possessing some kind of independent government, town and country would each, to a greater or lesser extent, have its own discrete administration. Out of all the links that we are now beginning fully to appreciate between the political life of town and country,[17] there is no doubt that each was in many ways a separate social world.[18] However, the guild that recruited local landowners brought town and country together, and it is at this point that it is necessary to use quotation marks around 'country' and to explain why they are there.

In the later Middle Ages, the word 'country' had more than one meaning; one of these was a particular sphere of political influence, usually one associated with the dominance of a noble, or the region within which landowning families were particularly active. For example, in 1445 the Warwickshire landowner, John Throgmorton, referred in his will to his major sphere of activity as 'my countree'.[19] By a similar token, it could mean the public opinion of a region, an extrapolation of the phrase to 'place oneself upon the country', which meant to go before a local jury.[20] Thus, the landowning rural membership of an urban guild linked the town and the political life of its hinterland. The guild was buying into a political connection that was locally powerful, for in the later Middle Ages it was the gentry, often in clientage to the local nobility, that ran county administration, but it might be buying into one that was also a national force.[21] This was what the Norwich guild got when it recruited the Earl, later Duke, of Suffolk, who became the greatest power in the land in the 1440s, as the adult Henry VI's full vacuity was revealed.[22] Similarly, in 1486 the Lichfield guild appointed as master Humphrey Stanley, a collateral of the family of Henry VII's stepfather, and a member of a family that was at that time extremely powerful in the north Midlands in its own right.[23] We now need to ask what Stratford's guild expected to get out of the landowners when it made these connections with the 'country', and equally why landowners should have wished to have made such a connection.[24]

What formal function, as far as the records will tell us, did landowners have within the Guild of the Holy Cross? The Guild held its feast, and apparently its procession, on the Sunday after the Feast of the Ascension, which would be in May or early June, although there seems to have been more than one feast.[25] The accounts tell us that both male and female members from the landowning classes were given hoods by the Guild. These were penitential hoods, for wearing in procession, and would have been adorned with the Guild's livery, although whether this means they did process seems doubtful. It seems doubly doubtful that the womenfolk would have done so. It is indeed hard to tell why these hoods were given to the gentry at all. A livery would be worn to indicate a connection with a social superior, something which would not have been the case with the gentry and the Guild. We can only suppose that they stuffed them away in a chest like an unwanted wedding present and perhaps, again like a wedding present, pulled them out if a senior Guild official came to call. We know that large numbers of members attended the feasts but rarely do we know who these were.[26] There is incidental evidence suggesting that some, at least, of these were gentry. For example, the accounts record that in 1427–8 feasts were attended by two members of the local gentry.[27] In 1434–5 four gallons of wine were supplied for several local worthies at breakfast in the chapel on the day after the Guild's feast, so one surmises that they had been at the feast the previous evening, a sizeable hair of the dog which leaves one gasping at the alcohol capacity of our ancestors, who were presumably thoroughly hungover from the night before.[28] None of the references to the attendance of such people at feasts implies that it was either routine or universal.

The aristocratic members did have one very specific and important role in the Guild's governance. It was enacted that the Guild's officers, who were supposed to be changed by annual election, might stay in post for another year 'by advice and assent of the most worthy brethren, lords, knights, squires, if they will be present'. The consent of the officers themselves, apart from the master, had also to be sought but this was clearly a way of bringing in an outside opinion, divorced from the politics of the town, and powerful enough to make an impact on the membership, to prevent the officers re-electing themselves from year to year.[29] That in itself is striking evidence that these were *not* regarded as ordinary members. So perhaps is the voluntary nature of their attendance at the election meeting. The register of the Guild contains an entry showing that advice might be taken from gentry members on other occasions. In 1439 or 1440 four Warwickshire landowners were present in the Guildhall at a meeting when it was decided to rebuild one of the Guild's Stratford properties.[30] The fact that their presence was specially noted suggests that this may have been a relatively uncommon event but it does nevertheless show that gentry members did attend the Guild's deliberations outside the annual election meeting.

Plate 17. Clopton Bridge, built in the 1490s at the expense of Hugh Clopton; as drawn by Samuel Ireland for his *Picturesque Views on the Upper, or Warwickshire, Avon*, 1795.

One local gentry family was in fact intimately concerned with the affairs of the Guild but they are the exception to the rule. These were the Cloptons of Stratford itself, who supplied not just several Guild members but Guild officials throughout the century.[31] But, although they were undoubtedly gentle, the Cloptons were unusually bound up in the town's affairs and close to the Stratford mercantile world. Indeed, at the end of the century a younger son, Hugh, having made his pile as a merchant in London, came back to settle in Stratford and become a town worthy (he built New Place), Master of the Guild and a great benefactor of the town. Among other things, he 're-edified' the Guild Chapel and left the money to build the Clopton Bridge that still stands.[32] The other partial exception is Thomas Harewell, from a substantial gentry family, who was an alderman of the Guild in 1438–40. He too had a Stratford connection, for his family owned the manor of Shottery in Stratford, and the Harewells, as we shall see, were among those who had a particularly close affiliation with the Guild. But his involvement with the administration ended in 1440 and no one else of equivalent status held office during the fifteenth century.[33] We shall see later that gentry members did all sorts of things for the Guild but, on the evidence we have, it does not seem that they were directly concerned in its affairs as the urban members would have been.

What *was* the 'country' of the gentry and nobles who joined the Guild? Although it formed part of the estates of the Bishops of Worcester,[34] Stratford sat fairly well in the middle of the Warwickshire lands of the Earls of Warwick, which were themselves part of the heart of his power, stretching westwards and south-westwards from Warwick and into Worcestershire, where the centre of his estates was Elmley Castle. The acquisition of the lands of the Lords Berkeley in 1417 and of the Despensers in 1423 strengthened the earls' hold over the whole West Midland region, especially Worcestershire and Gloucestershire, but for much of the century their authority went further still. Undoubtedly if any one magnate family was going to take control of the whole of Warwickshire in the fifteenth century, it would be the Earls of Warwick. They did not always manage this, but Richard Beauchamp, Earl of Warwick from 1401 to 1439, was unchallengeable in Warwickshire for most of his time as earl. If none of his successors quite matched his achievement, none of them could be ignored. In 1478 George, Duke of Clarence, effectively the last of the medieval holders of the earldom, was executed for treason. At that point, in practice, if not yet officially, the Warwick estates came to the Crown, then represented by George's brother, Edward IV, to remain there into the next century. It was the Crown that dominated Warwickshire, especially the part from Coventry southwards, for the rest of the fifteenth century. In the fifteenth century the Warwick affinity, whether the Warwick lands were held by noble or Crown, was almost always pre-eminent in Warwickshire, especially in the west Warwickshire/Worcestershire region outlined above, and for most of Richard Beauchamp's adult life it was unstoppable.[35]

The most immediately obvious thing about the gentry members of Stratford's Guild is that they tended to come from a radius of manors and villages in and around the town: Clopton, Shottery, Luddington, Billesely, Binton, Milcote, Walton Deyville and then, moving a little further away, Wolverton, Wootton Wawen, Exhall, Wixford, Oversley, Coughton, Arrow, Lower Quinton, and Bidford-on-Avon.[36] Socially and (insofar as we can tell) economically, these local gentry members did not, generally speaking, belong to the highest échelons of Warwickshire gentry society. In the first part of the century there were three knights, Sir Thomas Burdet of Arrow, Sir William Bishopstone of Bishopton and Sir Ralph Neville of Oversley, the latter a younger son of the Earl of Westmorland.[37] However, the tax returns of 1436 tell us that even these knights were not among the wealthiest Warwickshire gentry: there were at least seven Warwickshire esquires who were recorded by the tax commissioners as richer than all three. Most of the local gentry members of the Guild were esquires of middling rank, who were nonetheless in many cases important members of Warwickshire society, like the Harewells of Wootton Wawen, Shottery and Bidford-on-Avon, or the Trussells of Billesley, or 'mere' gentlemen like the Cloptons and the Comptons of Lower Quinton.[38] To that extent Stratford was very much the local guild for the local gentry, a point emphasized by its immediate catchment area which was a semicircle, with a radius of about ten miles or so, to the south, west and north of the town. The size and shape of the catchment area can be attributed to the fact that to the north-east, between Stratford and Warwick, the Warwick lands were so dominant that there were few gentry,[39] that further to the north-west there was a guild at Knowle, which acted as the natural focus for the many small esquires and gentlemen in the west and north-west of the county,[40] and that further north and east the hugely powerful Guild of the Holy Trinity at Coventry pulled in gentry from much of central and northern Warwickshire.[41]

The localization of the Guild's gentry membership can be further illustrated by some of the members whose presence seems, on the face of it, surprising. A particularly good example is a group from the east and south-east Midlands: the Catesbys of Ashby St Ledgers, Northamptonshire, the Palmers of Holt, Leicestershire, and the Nevilles of Rolston, Nottinghamshire. Although the Catesbys had significant interests in east

Warwickshire as well, landowners from this part of the county were more likely to join the guild at Coventry, as indeed the Catesbys did. There seems to be no obvious reasons for any of these families joining the Stratford Guild, but there is a very simple answer which lies in the heirs of William Bishopstone, Stratford resident and loyal associate of the Guild.[42] His daughters and heiresses married respectively Thomas Palmer of Holt and William Catesby of Ashby St Ledgers, while William Neville married Palmer's daughter and heiress.[43] Thus, even though neither Palmers nor Nevilles, unlike the Catesbys, played any part in Warwickshire affairs, Thomas Palmer and his wife had property in Stratford, and in 1469–70 had dealings over some of it with the Guild. Beyond such practical reasons for Palmers and Nevilles to maintain the link with the Guild, which was the effective governing authority in the town, its continuance even after the end of the Palmer line must be some testament to the attachment to the fraternity of Bishopstone's descendants.[44] The strength of the tie can also be seen with respect to the Catesbys. In 1453–4, when William Catesby made his second marriage, the connection remained strong enough, even after the death of his Bishopstone wife and even though the new Lady Catesby did not come from Warwickshire, for Catesby to enrol his wife in the Guild and for the Guild to offer him wine in celebration of his wedding.[45]

Another local figure of considerable significance whom we would expect to find playing a large part in the Guild's affairs is the Bishop of Worcester. But perhaps surprisingly – or perhaps not, if the town wanted to keep its lord at arm's length – the bishop features rarely in Guild records. It could be that the small number of other eminent local clerics enrolled in the Guild in the fifteenth century – the treasurer of the abbot of Gloucester in 1469–70, the abbot of Bordesley in 1480–1, while the abbot of Pershore was entertained in 1427–8 – were honoured at the bishop's instigation, although it could as well have been at that of the Guild, since these were West Midland landowners with whom the burghers of Stratford were likely to have commercial dealings.[46] In 1463–4 the bishop was entertained at the Guild's expense, the only such reference to occur, and it may be significant that this particular bishop was John Carpenter, perhaps the only tenant of the see to be appointed to the bishopric, who was notable for residing within his see.[47] However, even a resident bishop might not have that much reason to come to Stratford since, although the bishop held the manor as well as the town of Stratford and the manor of Hampton Lucy close by, the real core of the estate was in Worcestershire. It is true that some of the Guild members were officials of the bishop. Notably, three of them were estate stewards: William Wollashull, enrolled in 1428–9, Thomas Throgmorton in 1469–70 (described as 'steward of the town of Stratford') and Humphrey Stafford of Grafton (Worcestershire) and Leamington Hastings in 1475–6. A fourth bishop's officer, John Wode of Worcestershire, was entertained at a feast in 1427–8, as 'receiver of the bishop's revenues', although he was in fact another steward.[48] It made eminently good sense to do well by the officials of the town's lord, especially if they came to Stratford on business, but we shall see shortly that there were other good reasons, apart from their employment by the bishop, to value them as connections for the town.

However, the Guild of the Holy Cross represented more than these highly local landowning interests. To understand why, while casting further light on the nature of local gentry membership, we need to examine the role of the political connection of the Earls of Warwick in the Guild constituency. Even if one does not wish to overplay it, the Warwick connection remains inescapable with respect to the landowning membership of the Guild.

There was in fact a guild at Warwick, the administrative capital of the county and the centre of the earldom, a town very much under the earl's command. Thomas Beauchamp, Earl of Warwick, Richard's father, and Thomas's brother, William, later Lord Bergavenny, had been involved in its foundation in 1383.[49] But, although there appears to be no surviving information on the membership of this guild, what we know of the Stratford Guild would suggest that it was the latter, rather than that at Warwick, which attracted the gentry linked to the earldom. For a start, the earls were territorially and politically so dominant around Stratford that, if one takes only the local gentry members, the number of Warwick men is already quite high: William Bishopstone, the Harewells of Bidford-on-Avon and Wootton Wawen, the Grevilles and Cokeseys of Milcote, the Lucys of Charlecote, the Burdets of Arrow, the Straunges and Middletons of Walton Deyville, Ailred Trussell of Billesley, the Throgmortons of Coughton, Thomas Crewe of Wixford and his stepson William Clopton of the same. Some of these were close servants of the holders of the Warwick lands and several of these families were linked to the earldom over more than one generation.[50] We shall see later how close the Burdets' personal tie to the Guild was, but in 1427–8 Thomas Burdet was entertained, not as the excellent servant of the Guild that he was, but as the Earl of Warwick's surveyor.[51]

The picture gets still more interesting if we look at some of the gentry members from outside the Stratford area. Between 1406 and 1408 the Guild gave a hood to John Weston of Coventry, and later of Weston under Wetherley, in east Warwickshire. He was a lawyer, recorder of Coventry from about 1415 to 1433 and clearly a useful man to know; but there were few Guild members from the other side of the county, rarely did anyone from Coventry join the Stratford Guild – not even the recorder – and there were plenty of other lawyers in the vicinity. Weston, however, was a close servant of Richard Beauchamp and he was given his hood at a time when they were also bestowed on no less than seven members of the gentry from around Stratford who were connected to the earl.[52] In 1428–9, when Richard Beauchamp had reached the height of his local power, new members included William Wollashull, a Worcestershire man, whom we have already met as the bishop's official but who was primarily a close associate of the earl; John Verney of Compton Murdack, later Compton Verney, in south Warwickshire, described in the register as 'provisor of the earl of Warwick', another intimate servant; Richard Curson, who served the earl over many years as soldier and household official, and Sir William Mountford. The latter is the most striking of all these, for he lived at Coleshill in the far north of the county and his neighbour and steward of his household, Richard Haversham, joined at the same time.[53] Mountford, the greatest member of the Warwickshire gentry, and Warwick's most notable local servant, as well as one of his most steadfast, should have joined the Holy Trinity Guild of Coventry, which served his part of the county and was a far grander affair than Stratford's, but there is no record of his membership there.[54] Why did he instead join Stratford? Part of the answer lies in the fact that William Mountford, the rector of the Mountford-owned benefice of Ilmington in south Warwickshire, joined at the same time.[55] The Mountfords had substantial property in south Warwickshire, of which Ilmington was the most significant, and the acceptance into the Guild of both these Mountfords may well indicate that Sir William was proposing to take a greater interest in his south Warwickshire estates than hitherto.[56] But those who joined the same year really leave very little doubt that Mountford had decided, perhaps because he was intending to visit Ilmington more frequently, that it would be a good idea to join a Guild which already had so many members from a political connection of which he was an integral part.

Another indicative collection of new members comes in 1475–6. In succession in the admission register are the names of Humphrey Stafford of Grafton and Leamington, John Hugford of Emscote near Warwick and of a non-gentry resident of Elmley, Worcestershire. The first was paid an annuity by Clarence, the second served him and came from a family closely linked to the holders of the Warwick lands throughout the century, while Elmley has already been mentioned as the centre of the Warwick estates in Worcestershire. This was two years before Clarence signed up his entire family and it occurred at a time when Clarence's power was faltering in the West Midlands and he was anxious to shore it up. Indeed his efforts to do so led to the show trial of his servant Ankarette Twynho at Warwick in 1477 which was one of the causes of his own downfall. It does not seem far-fetched, especially in the light of the numbers of jurors for the trial who came from Stratford or its surrounds, to conclude that he was positively encouraging his men to join the Guild so that he could exploit the links this gave him with Stratford and its hinterland for his own political purposes.[57]

Then there are the Guild's dealings with the earls themselves. Actual membership seems not to have been required by either Beauchamps or Nevilles. No earl is recorded as a member before the Duke of Clarence, who enrolled with his family in 1477, just before his fall.[58] Significantly, no sooner were the Warwick lands in royal hands than in 1478–9 there was a multiple wooing by the town of those around Edward IV's young son, the Prince of Wales, on the Council of the Marches. The Prince represented the royal interest which, with the power wielded by his Council along the Welsh border and the great West Midlands Warwick estate in his father's hands, was now the dominant power in the region. Accordingly, in that year, the Guild sent a representative to Shrewsbury to give membership to the Prince and to the main figures on his Council, Lord Rivers and John Alcock, Bishop of Worcester. In this instance

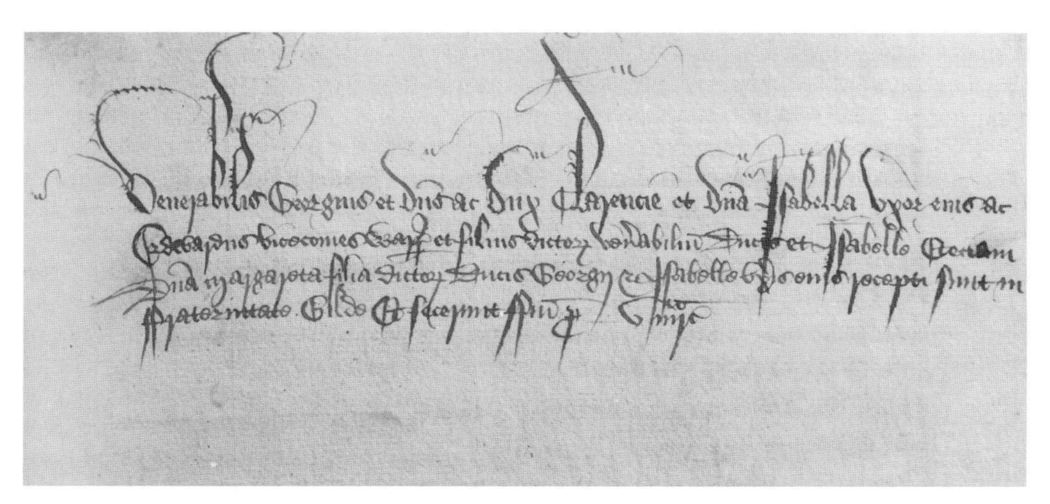

Plate 18. Entry in the register of the Stratford Guild, recording the enrolment of George, Duke of Clarence and his family as members, 1477–8. (SBTRO, BRT 1/1, fol. 106v)

the bishop was almost certainly being enrolled as the king's man rather than as bishop.[59] But long before this, the Guild was taking care to keep in with the earls. In 1416–17 it gave membership to Warwick's cook.[60] In 1450–1, not long after Richard Neville, 'the Kingmaker', had succeeded to the earldom, Neville's wife was entertained at the Guild's expense by Agnes Chacombe, wife – perhaps widow by now – of a former master of the Guild.[61] In 1453–4 the earl himself was given wine when he 'rode by this way towards Wales'. He was probably going south-west from Warwick, via his Worcestershire estates, to his lands in south Wales.[62] In 1454–5 a servant of the earl was admitted to the Guild free on the authority of the Guild's council.[63] Further evidence of the earls' interest in Stratford, if not in this case of support for the Guild, is that the arms of Richard Beauchamp's son and heir, briefly Duke of Warwick in 1445–6, were in the windows of the parish church of Stratford.[64]

A final gloss on the role of the Warwick affinity within the Guild is provided by the relations of Stratford's lords, the Bishops of Worcester, with the Earls of Warwick. By the later Middle Ages, the church was tending to rely on local landowners and local political connections to defend its interests when they were challenged by its landowning neighbours. This was the logical outcome of the devolution to local gentry of so much of the king's administration during the course of the thirteenth and fourteenth centuries and of ecclesiastical lords' – especially bishops' – frequent absenteeism and increasing concentration on other realms of jurisdiction and administration: papal, diocesan, governmental and estate. Ecclesiastical institutions would often employ local gentry as officers or sometimes just pay them retaining fees. The gentry might derive other benefits from the lord, including access to leasehold land.[65] For much of the fifteenth century, in both Warwickshire and Worcestershire, it seems that the bishops were sensibly putting their trust in men from the Warwick affinity. William Wollashull, Thomas Throgmorton, Humphrey Stafford of Grafton and John Wode have already been mentioned as men associated with the Guild who served the bishop; indeed the Throgmortons were tenants of the bishop at their principal Worcestershire residence of Throckmorton in Fladbury. But all of them, even the Throgmortons, were much more closely linked to the house of Warwick, and the dates of their enrolment in the Guild by no means coincide with the start of their service to the bishop.[66] Philip Morgan, bishop from 1419 to 1426, was in fact godfather to Richard Beauchamp's son and heir Henry. He was also an associate of another of Henry's godparents, Beauchamp's aunt, Joan Lady Bergavenny, even before he became bishop.[67]

It would be wrong to imply that the Warwick connection was the only one linked to the Guild; after all, it was very much in the Guild's interest to make sure it was in with all the potential powers in its hinterland. Thus, in 1439–40, Ralph Boteller, soon to be created Lord Sudeley, lord of Henley-in-Arden and Beaudesert Castle, became a member, along with his son and son-in-law. In 1442–3 he was entertained in a member's house in Stratford, where three tenches and three eels were served up to him 'for the profit of the gild'. The reason for cultivating him at this time was that early in 1439 Richard Beauchamp died, leaving an under age heir, that Boteller was one of the keepers of part of the Warwick lands, and was increasingly becoming a force in the king's household and, in the 1440s, was one of the nobles who took part in the struggle for power in Warwickshire caused by the ten-year Warwick 'interregnum', the period of minorities from 1439 to 1449.[68] Earlier, in the 1420s, when Joan Beauchamp Lady Bergavenny had made a play for some of the authority in and around Warwickshire of her nephew, Richard Beauchamp, while he was fighting in France, two of her officials, neither of them Warwickshire men, had been enrolled in the Guild, specifically as receiver and steward of Lady Bergavenny.[69]

If the noble and gentry membership of the Guild reflected not just the society of landowners around Stratford but also to some extent the political configuration of that part of Warwickshire and the West Midlands, one can see that that was all to the Guild's advantage, but what did the nobles and gentry themselves expect to get out of it? In fact, the noble/gentry side of the problem is much the harder to deal with, as the profit they might derive from membership is generally less tangible than the benefits of their membership to the town. There were some obvious advantages. As Professor Dyer has pointed out, many of the local gentry traded their goods to Stratford. Since the Guild was also to all intents and purposes the ruling authority of the town, it made excellent sense to join and to get all the trading benefits that might accrue. These, of course, included the informal ones of access to the Stratford Guild members who might be interested in buying landowners' agricultural wares. Any of the gentry who owned property in the town would equally find that it made good sense to be involved with the authority that made the town's by-laws, and they might also rent property from the Guild, as Elizabeth Palmer was doing in 1477–8 and William Catesby in 1456–7; in both cases one assumes that these were rents that had once been held by Bishopstone.[70]

But in the last analysis most of the advantages to the gentry cannot be computed. Can we get any further by analysing the reasons for the particularly close connection to the Guild of certain individuals and families? These were William Bishopstone, Sir Ralph Neville, John Hubaud or Hyband, a minor esquire of Ipsley, the Cloptons, the Harewells, the Burdets and the Lucys of Charlecote.[71] The Cloptons have already been dealt with and Bishopstone can be almost as quickly disposed of. At a time when, in the hope of a quick passage through purgatory, the gentry were lavishing their generosity on their local church, Bishopstone, effectively a Stratford man, was likely to choose a Stratford church for his patronage.[72] But the parish church of Stratford was so much on the fringes of the town that the much more central Guild Chapel tended, in parishioners' minds, to assume the status of a parish church.[73] Moreover, we have just seen that he almost certainly rented property from the Guild.[74] These are perhaps sufficient explanations for Bishopstone's decision to make the Guild rather than the parish church the object of his devotions, and, as guilds acted as chantries, saying prayers for the souls of their departed members, that saved him costly expenditure on a personal chantry.[75] Bishopstone was in fact rare among the gentry in having an *obit* instituted for him with the Guild. He also gave a bell to the chapel.[76] However, if Bishopstone's enthusiasm for the Guild seems easy to explain, we should note that one of his ancestors had given an advowson to a religious institution in Warwick in the fourteenth century,[77] so William's devotion to the Guild shows how far Stratford had superseded the county's political and administrative capital in the family's estimation.

Sir Ralph Neville is a more problematic and most interesting case. As already mentioned, he was a cadet of the house of Westmorland. He came to Warwickshire by marrying the daughter and coheiress of Robert Ferrers, Lord Wemme, and took over the Ferrers seat of Oversley.[78] After joining the Guild in 1435–6, between 1439–40 and 1451 he became one of its principal gentry supporters, offering advice, receiving entertainment, putting his name to Guild deeds[79] and even nominating a chaplain, a privilege which the Guild would surely have guarded jealously.[80] The reasons for his close relationship with the Guild are obscure. The owners of Oversley had a tie with Alcester Abbey going back several hundred years and it was usual for newcomers to an estate to stress their links with the focus of their predecessors' religious interests; but it seems that Neville and his family did nothing for Alcester at all, although it was badly in need of further endowment and in fact was to be absorbed by Evesham Abbey in 1465. Neither did he apparently take any interest in the chantry of St Mary in the parish church, although the chantry's advowson was owned by the Lords of Oversley. Indeed, it seems that Alcester Abbey's parlous situation, which led to its being taken into Crown hands under Henry VI, may well be one of the keys to the participation of Neville and of one or two others in the Guild's affairs.[81] If Alcester was an unsuitable religious centre for anyone living in its vicinity who was not wealthy enough to refound it – a project that only someone with the lands and income of a great noble could contemplate – then the Stratford Guild was the closest substantial religious institution which was not in danger of dissolution. In taking his religious patronage to Stratford, Neville must also have chosen to abandon his interest in the parochial church at Alcester. Moreover, there was an added benefit for him. Despite his background and fortunate marriage, he never became the power that he should have been in Warwickshire. That his income was not as high as one might have expected has been noted. His only periods of local office were in the 1440s, during the Warwick interregnum,[82] and he seems not to have been a particularly attractive prospect to the Warwickshire nobility. Although he was at his most active in the Guild just when he was at his most prominent in local affairs, he did not at any time maintain the political profile in his 'country' to be expected of someone of his background, while at Stratford he could cut a much greater figure, even among the other local gentry who patronized the Guild. Indeed, in this instance, 'patronizing' is the key word, for, as the younger son of an earl and the husband of the co-heiress to what had once been a barony, it must have pleased him immensely that within the Guild he was called, quite improperly, 'baron of Oversley'.[83] However, his initial interest in the Guild may have been purely accidental: in the 1420s he was on service in France with a group of men who included William Bishopstone and Nicholas, son of Thomas Burdet, the Guild's most faithful gentry supporter, and it may be their enthusiasm which led him to join after he returned to England.[84]

Neville's involvement with the Guild in the Warwick interregnum coincides with that of John Hyband, and behind both may also lie a political explanation. Hyband's participation is rather baffling on the face of it: he resided at Ipsley, certainly not a place within the normal Guild radius, and had no particular links otherwise with the town nor with the Warwick political connection. However, it was during this period that both he and Neville became linked to John Beauchamp of Powick, created Lord Beauchamp in 1447. Beauchamp was a long-time associate of Ralph Boteller, and, like Boteller, had done extensive war service in France. Both were responsible for the custody of parts of the Warwick lands, and both were now becoming significant figures in the king's household. The two worked together to take over much of the Warwick power in the West Midlands during the interregnum, recruiting numbers of local gentry, some of whom, like Hyband and Neville, had not previously served any local lord. If Ipsley was some way from Stratford, it was not very far from Alcester, which was not only close to Neville's residence but was Beauchamp's base in Warwickshire. Beauchamp, like Ralph Neville, should have acted as patron to Alcester parish church, for his family had anciently had the advowson of the other chantry in the church,[85] but it may well be that the decay of the abbey, as well as discouraging him from any connection with the abbey itself, deterred him from putting any energy into the church.[86] Since some of the men who moved into the Beauchamp-Sudeley sphere at this time were already affiliated to the Stratford Guild, it was probably seen as a natural place for other clients who had no strong religious affiliation to take their religious patronage, even for someone like Hyband for whom it was by no means an obvious one geographically. Although Beauchamp, unlike Sudeley, is not known to have joined the Guild, the appearance among its foremost gentry supporters in this period of two men linked to Beauchamp, both of whom lived within easy reach of Alcester, may well indicate the Guild's growing interest in Beauchamp's entourage. Hyband, like Neville, held his only Warwickshire office in this period – in 1445–6 – and so it was well worth the Guild's while to cultivate him at this stage.[87]

The Harewells, who had branches at Shottery, Wootton Wawen (their principal manor) and Bidford-on-Avon,[88] joined and served the Guild throughout the century. Why they did so is not entirely clear, as there is no evidence in their wills or other religious dispositions of any particular desire to remember the Guild. The Shottery connection must be the main link, and Richard Harewell, a younger son who resided at Shottery and died in about 1435–6, was buried in Stratford parish church, although none of the rest of the family is known to have been interred there.[89] However, the family seems to have been at its most energetic within and on behalf of the Guild at times when it was providing active members of the Warwick affinity. This applies to various Harewells under Richard Beauchamp, culminating in Thomas's election to the office of alderman right at the end of the regime, and to William Harewell in the early 1450s when the new Earl of Warwick was flexing his muscles in the county.[90] In fact, when William was fed by the Guild at this time, at Epiphany in 1454, he had come in the company of servants of the earl.[91]

Apart from the Burdets, the Lucys were the most eminent local family to have extensive and extended dealings with the Guild. Members of the family joined the Guild and at times put their names to its property transactions during much of the century, but what is most unusual for a prominent gentry family is that the William Lucy who died in 1492 and his wife were buried in the Guild Chapel.[92] What makes this all the more remarkable is that this family already had a long-established religious centre at Thelsford Priory, near Charlecote, which was where nearly all the other members of the family were buried, including William's own son and heir only three years later.[93] Given Charlecote's proximity to Stratford, it is more than likely that the Lucys were often in Stratford, but it is not at all clear why William should have chosen the Guild Chapel as his last resting place. One possible reason for the fairly close family link is that the Bishops of Worcester owned Hampton Lucy,[94], which was very close to Charlecote, although no other evidence of family ties to the bishopric has been found.

The Burdets of Arrow fall into a class of their own among the greater local families in their closeness to the Guild. Sir Thomas Burdet features on a high proportion of the Guild accounts up to his death in 1442 and his grandson and heir, another Thomas, although less active, is found in Guild accounts and on their deeds until the early 1450s.[95] Rather touchingly, Richard, the second Thomas's son by his first marriage, whom he had tried to disinherit in favour of the sons of his second marriage, celebrated his first successes in reclaiming his estate in 1479–80 by immediately joining the Guild.[96] The almost complete absence of Richard's father from Guild records from 1451 until his death (for treason) in 1477 may be explained by the fact that during the early 1450s he began to take steps to obtain an annulment of his first marriage, on the grounds of consanguinity. It was later said that this annulment was come by in exceedingly dubious circumstances and it was implied that the real reason was that Burdet already had an eye on a replacement, so his disappearance from the records may well reflect the burghers' moral outrage at his behaviour.[97] On the other hand, when he does resurface briefly in the Guild records, in 1463–4, he is found supping wine in company with the Bishop of Worcester;[98] maybe the bishop could condone what the respectable Stratfordians could not. Unfortunately, evidence for the religious dispositions of the Burdets is more than inadequate: not only are there no surviving wills but we do not even know where they chose to be buried. One would have expected them to make Arrow, where they owned the advowson,[99] the centre of their religious patronage, or, if they wanted to be linked to an institution, the nearby Alcester Abbey: the abbot of Alcester was Richard Burdet's godfather and – according to the story – helped in the rescue of the boy when his father sought to have him murdered after failing in his initial attempts to rid himself of Richard's mother.[100] This may therefore be another case of a family, for which Alcester was the obvious religious focus, being deterred by its parlous state. This hypothesis is supported by the fact that, although the Guild celebrated Thomas Burdet's *obit* in 1443, the year after his death, it was actually performed at Alcester. This suggests that he had been buried in Alcester but, even so, had no faith in the ability of the institutions there to perform the remembrance ceremony for him a year later.[101] It was the Stratford Guild to which the Burdets seem to have made their only known religious grant during the entire century, when Thomas Burdet I granted a family property in Stratford to fund a schoolmaster appointed by the Guild.[102]

One thing made clear by these individual stories is that, with the exception of Bishopstone and possibly the Burdets, the more substantial gentry families did not regard the Guild as a significant object of religious patronage. They did not, as far as we can tell, grant it money or land and most gentry families of any social pretension at all would expect to have their own religious focus, usually by now in the parish church, less often in a neighbouring religious institution. The prayers of the Guild's chaplains would help speed all its members through purgatory, but landowners, who, as the richer element in society, had both more sins and more money to buy their way out, usually expected to have their own chantries and were certainly unlikely to rely on an urban Guild for the worldly status that religious endowment brought.[103] For the less wealthy gentry, especially for those from smaller and less wealthy parishes, the Guild had the advantage that it was the chantries in such parishes that were less likely to survive for any length of time;[104] membership of a large corporate body, with an apparently guaranteed existence, was insurance for their souls against the demise of their private *post mortem* arrangements. But that seems insufficient explanation of the breadth and degree of support for the Guild found among the Warwickshire landowners. What then were the more general grounds, beyond the purely practical, for the gentry to join the Guild? Much of the answer, as far as the gentry from around Stratford are concerned, may lie in the case histories of Ralph Neville and John Hyband. If it was understood that *noblesse oblige*, it was clearly understood, at least by the *noblesse*, down to almost the least gentleman, that those who were not part of the world of lords of manors, while they were owed the protection and assistance of their superiors, were in a firmly subordinate position and should be grateful for what was done for them.[105] It must have been very pleasant for these gentry from around Stratford, few of them possessing any real stature, and several of them no more than parish gentry, to assist the local Guild in matters where political influence beyond the town was necessary, and to experience the Guild's humble gratitude in return.

They would not only be invited to feasts but, as we have already seen, specially entertained, sometimes in members' houses. In 1431–2 a breakfast was given in the Guild Chapel to Thomas Burdet and William Bishopstone, while in 1421–2 it had been offered to Burdet and his wife in the Guildhall.[106] Some time between 1411 and 1417, a harper was hired in Burdet's honour.[107] In 1442–3 wine was given to John Hyband on various occasions 'for the profit of the Gild': there can have been few other occasions in Hyband's life when anyone wealthy enough to give him wine would see this as profitable to the donor rather than to the receiver.[108] In 1448–9 the Guild helped celebrate the marriage of the children of Thomas Middleton of Walton Deyville, a member since 1439–40, and of John Wode, the man who was at the Guild's feast as the bishop's receiver.[109] The Guild contributed a wedding present, entertained both Wode and Thomas Burdet as they passed through on their return from Walton and, it appears, paid for a minstrel at the wedding. Neither Middleton nor Wode were negligible men in local terms but neither could have expected this level of respect from the landowning society in which they normally moved.[110] That the Stratford Guild was *not* directly under the patronage of the Earls of Warwick must have made it doubly attractive to the middling and lesser gentry: to those who were not part of the Warwick affinity, it gave some political status which they would otherwise rather lack in this part of the county. To those who were, it gave both a reflected glory and the chance to experience it without the earl's presence; also without the presence of some of his wealthiest gentry followers, many of whom, like the Mountfords, resided in the north of the county. But the Guild also knew how to honour those in the front ranks of the Warwickshire gentry: in 1473–4 it sent a representative to the funeral of the mother of Sir John Greville of Milcote. John's mother had enrolled herself and her two sons as far back as 1443–4 and since then a fortunate marriage and the death of a long-lived dowager had placed the family among the foremost in the county.[111]

But the less tangible benefits were not all a matter of lording it over perceived inferiors. Among the gentry themselves the Guild could play an important role. Historians of late medieval England are beginning to realize the enormous importance to lesser landowners of 'horizontal relationships': ties of friendship and mutual respect among people of roughly equal status. It was these connections which enabled the gentry to build up the networks of mutual trust which would allow them to make use of each other in dealing with their prime business, the preservation and extension of their lands. From their pool of trusted associates would come the men who would act as feoffees, or trustees, for their estates, and witnesses to all their land transactions, from sales and feoffments to marriage settlements and wills. The same group might well produce marriage partners for members of their families. As with all social groups, informal gatherings were essential to the development of a sense of mutual solidarity, all the more important when trust was so essential to their dealings with each other. Once a strong network was established, such gatherings could be the occasion for the transactions themselves.[112] If enough of them were to meet with sufficient regularity, they would usually have to do so in places which they would visit reasonably often. Obviously, in areas where a lord's affinity was dominant, there was the residence of the lord. Then there were the homes of the greater gentry, and, for those involved in the administration of the shire, there were the county's administrative centres. But what could be a better meeting place than the local market town, where most of the local gentry were likely to go anyway, to buy and sell, on a fairly regular basis? If it had a Guild which encouraged gentry membership, then joining it was an obvious thing to do, for in the Guildhall, or in the houses of the urban members, they could see each other, be entertained without the necessity to visit a tavern and have privacy for any business they wished to do.

If we examine some of the groups of local gentry brought together by the hospitality of the Guild or found together on Guild deeds, or just those that belonged to the Guild at the same time, they replicate to a greater or lesser degree the groups found on the men's own deeds: Burdet, Bishopstone, Harewell, Hyband, Neville, Lucy, Throgmorton, Trussell, to name just some.[113] Stratford's role in providing opportunities for landowners to 'bond' was a particularly important one because, unlike, say, Norfolk, where Norwich was both the administrative and commercial capital, Warwick, over-supervised by its earls, and unable to compete with Coventry and Stratford to its north and south, had failed to thrive.[114] If it had the additional attraction of being the centre of the earldom, the earldom had other West Midland centres, at Elmley, at Berkeley for a while, and later at the Despenser seats of Hanley and Tewkesbury, not to mention the Warwick residences closer to London and the fact that the Beauchamp Earls were not infrequently in London or in France.[115] Later, under the Kingmaker, Clarence and the Crown, the territorial responsibilities of the earls were still more diverse.[116] Accordingly, the earl might be at Warwick at only infrequent intervals and so, given its lack of local importance as a town, only the regular county officers would have regular cause to go there.[117]

Because several members of the Warwick affinity were already members of the Guild, simply because they lived close to Stratford, there was therefore good reason for others to join it, especially if, like John Hugford, they did not live all that far from Stratford or, like William Mountford, might well need to go to Stratford themselves. It was doubly attractive if the Guild provided hospitality for those who lived a fair way away. Thus, it is not just familiar groups of names from Stratford's immediate locality that we find linked with the Guild, but familiar clusters from a whole region whose primary link was often their connection with the house of Warwick. For, if horizontal linkages were crucial to the gentry, horizontal ties were more often than not confirmed and cemented, even created, where nobles were locally dominant, by the 'vertical' ties of lordship.[118] Of the local grouping listed above,[119] the first six were all Warwick men under Richard Beauchamp and to these we should add other Guild members who belonged to the Warwick affinity, either then or later: for example, Mountford, Mollesley of north Warwickshire,[120] Hugford, Greville, Middleton, Verney, Wollashull, Wode. The Middleton-Wode marriage on which the Guild lavished so much attention brought together the daughter of one follower of Richard Beauchamp, Earl of Warwick with the son of another,[121] who was also stepson to a future follower of Richard Neville, Earl of Warwick.[122] And for those not yet within the magic circle but who wished to be so, the Guild could be seen as a possible entreé to the Warwick affinity.

Thus, the Stratford Guild was performing a particular social function within its locality, but also one which was given a broader dimension by the local dominance of the Earls of Warwick. However, it was by no means the only Guild in the county which performed this function, even if its particularly strong political dimension probably was unique. Warwickshire was in fact a county which was economically, geographically and politically so disjointed that it had to have a number of social foci for its gentry.[123] It is a reflection of Warwickshire's lack of county identity that, even though Stratford took members from a long way away and Coventry's membership was startling in both social and geographic terms, membership of those guilds for which registers survive still tended to be largely localized: there was no major guild, as at Norwich, which served the whole county. The different regions of Warwickshire, which were the real location of identity within the county, and which often included part of a neighbouring county, were served by several guilds, which acted as focal points for their particular part of the county: for instance, Coventry for the central and northern parts, Stratford for the west to south-west, Knowle for the west to north-west.[124]

The benefits to the town of gentry members are much easier to see and implicit in what has already been said. There was a certain amount of material benefit to the Guild: some benefactions have already been mentioned but we must not forget what was perhaps the major one from a landowner in the fifteenth century. This was the advowson of Wilmcote in Aston Cantlow, given by Henry Lisle in 1481, in return for prayers for himself and his wife. Lisle is another unexpected name in the Guild's annals, as his main residence was at Moxhull in north Warwickshire. Presumably visits to Wilmcote had made him acquainted with Stratford and its Guild, although he made no mention of either in his will of 1504 and was buried in his own chapel in Wishaw in the parish of Moxhull.[125] As has been observed, most of the gentry were very ungenerous to the Guild; even William Lucy and his wife, who were buried in the Guild's chapel, made no known bequest to it. They must have assumed that paying their dues was enough to participate in the prayers of the Guild to extricate all its members from purgatory.

The chief benefits to the Guild of its gentry and noble members were less concrete than this. As Rosemary Horrox has shown, what medieval urban authorities needed was assistance in managing the wider world of governance and politics. As the Guild of the Holy Cross was the effective town authority in Stratford, it was through the Guild that 'urban patronage' was managed on Stratford's behalf.[126] What these gentry members – and occasionally the noble members – did above all was to provide the Guild with authority: the authority of England's ruling class who collectively knew their way round politics and administration, locally and nationally. That was why they could have a special role in the Guild's elections, why they were used in the Guild's transactions; they would be respected as feoffees and witnesses. They might act as agents for the Guild on other occasions. For example, John Campion, a lawyer and minor gentleman of Gaydon, much used in various capacities by the gentry of southern Warwickshire, joined the Guild in 1424–5 without fee, in return for acting for it in legal affairs.[127] Thomas Burdet and Ailred Trussell were in the Hall with the Master and Aldermen some time in 1414–15 'when they were arranging about the land of Studley'.[128] In 1453–4 a man was hired to ride to Warwick with William Harewell on the Guild's business.[129] In 1450–1 John Hyband was given money for 'divers evidences belonging to the Gild' which he had presumably had copied, and in the same year the Guild showed its appreciation by giving him a pair of gloves.[130]

Influence could be used in more formal spheres. The wisdom of having William Mountford on the books was apparent in 1445–6 when there were dealings with him at Coventry while he was there as a royal commissioner. He was indeed a major local officer almost throughout his adult life and consequently a most valuable Guild member.[131] The same year there were expenses at Henley in relation to the escheator who, most fortunately for the Guild, was none other than their own John Hyband.[132] In 1448–9 payments were made to Thomas Bate, specifically as justice of the peace and escheator, *pro proficuo gilde* and in the same year to William Bermingham, who was at Stratford *pro mensura burgi*, probably a reference to the assessment for a loan commission for the French war, on which Bermingham was placed in 1449.[133] Both of these men were prominent and well-connected local officials from the north of the county, neither had any direct tie with the Guild but both were linked to the Guild in one way or another.[134] In fact, if one looks at the Warwickshire officers, one can see how many possible venues of influence the Guild had. Dr Horrox has noted how helpful gentry Members of Parliament could be to towns they represented.[135] As medieval Stratford, unlike Warwick, did not have its own Member, the town had no one specifically charged with defending or pursuing its interests in Parliament, but numbers of Warwickshire Members of Parliament did belong to the Guild. This is most striking in the early part of the century, when Richard Beauchamp's power was less extended through the whole county than it was later to be, and so more officers came from the area west and south-west of Warwick. Between 1401 and 1421 the vast majority of the Members were from south Warwickshire, many from the area of Beauchamp dominance. They present a familiar gathering: Burdet, Trussell, Lucy, Crewe, Harewell. Of thirty-one known Warwickshire Members in that period, eleven belonged to the Guild, a high strike rate for a Guild and town not in the big league.[136] There were also sheriffs, Justices of the Peace and other commissioners throughout the century who were Guild members – and of course Members of Parliament – and we have seen already how the Guild was able to exploit its link with John Hyband, the escheator in 1445–6; he was one of several Guild members who held that position.[137]

If these were avenues to the official channels of power in Warwickshire, the links with the dominant magnate connections opened the way to the unofficial channels which underpinned the whole process of governance.[138] It may have suited the holders of the Warwick lands and some of their followers to congregate around the Guild, and equally suited Lady Bergavenny in the early 1420s, Ralph Boteller in 1439–40 and John Beauchamp of Powick in the 1440s, but it was still more helpful to the Guild. One reason for the arrival of more north Warwickshire members in the 1420s may well have been that the Guild wanted to make sure it had a toe-hold in Richard Beauchamp's widening sphere of influence within the county. This was particularly important when the enlargement of his power brought more officers from parts of the county beyond the reach of the Guild's membership: it might recruit the occasional northerner like Mountford but it was never going to be a mecca for gentry outside its immediate region and may well not have wished to be so.[139] The entertainment of the Earl of Warwick in 1453–4, reciprocated by his sending two deer to the Guild, may have been provoked by the fact that, after Warwick's rather clumsy and mostly inadequate attempts to reconstruct the Warwick affinity in the wake of the ten-year interregnum, he began to do rather better from late 1453.[140]

The political antennae of the Guild can be seen at their most acute on two occasions of local and national crisis. One, already mentioned, was the rush to seek the favour of the new royal holders of the Warwick lands after Clarence's fall. This may have been considered all the more urgent because of the embarrassing role played by jurors from Stratford and its surrounds in the judicial murder of Ankarette Twynho, a significant factor in Clarence's disgrace.[141] The other is from 1460–1, the year when a series of battles produced enormous see-saws of power between York and Lancaster, a particularly urgent matter for a town in such close geographical and political proximity to Warwick the Kingmaker, the leading supporter of York, and to the temporary seat of Lancastrian power at Coventry.[142] In that year – unfortunately we do not know when, so are ignorant of who was actually in power in England at the time – the Guild entertained Richard Verney of Compton Murdack to breakfast. He was nominally a Warwick man but had proved extremely adept at trimming for most of the 1450s and took a significant part in certain transactions of 1460–1 which were clearly a means for some Warwickshire gentry to give a gentle adjustment to their political position. At breakfast with Verney were two other Warwick clients, who would have been almost as useful to the Guild. One, Thomas Middleton of Walton Deyville, we have met already. He was a Guild member, a neighbour and associate of Verney. The other, John Hugford, was much more closely linked than either of these to the earl but all three contrived to avoid repercussions from the Yorkist disasters of 1459–60 and 1460–1.[143] If Warwick were to come back in triumph with the victorious Yorkists, these would be good people to know; if Warwick's lands were confiscated and ended up in a newcomer's hands, Verney and Hugford would be necessary supporters for the interloper in constructing a local power base, and Verney's cross-factional connections would make him especially valuable.

Dr Horrox has suggested that 'most major towns' had a guild with extensive membership among the local nobility and gentry.[144] As has already been pointed out, there is just too little information and too little work on the subject to be sure that this is the case, although her evidence argues persuasively for it. But an alternative hypothesis can be put forward which might allow for the curious fact that the towns known to have valued these members were not of uniform size and importance. Is it possible that the common factor among urban guilds of this sort was often the absence of a single source of corporate authority within the town?[145] This might mean, as at both Stratford and its much bigger sister Coventry,[146] that the guild became a substitute for the town government. It could also mean that as, again, at Stratford, at Lichfield and at Ludlow, the guild was the principal buffer between a potentially intrusive overlord, usually but not invariably ecclesiastical, and the town.[147] Norwich is a peculiar case, for it was a heavily-divided town politically when the 'country' members of the Guild of St George were at their most influential, and it has been argued that the settlement of 1452, which made the Guild the town's authority, was designed to mitigate this external influence.[148] What is suggested here is that towns would seek out and then cultivate noble and gentry members if there was a particular reason for wanting to have access to the greater power wielded in the 'country' that lay beyond the administrative and political urban boundaries.

One historian has argued that, because the religious guilds represented a communal religious and social endeavour, to some extent they cut across the social and economic divisions of the members even though they clearly preserved hierarchy in much of their formal proceedings. That might work in a town or a parish, delineated by administrative boundaries of some sort, but what happened when members came from outside the administrative unit and from a very different political and social world, one educated to denigrate those who did not own estates with lordship? Is the essence of this kind of relationship that the landowning members *were* quite other and that was why they were valued, as indeed much of this chapter has suggested? Or was there still a communalism and mutuality of the sort that apologists for the late-medieval church would have us see running through all these voluntary parochial associations?[149] This is a question which cannot be answered here, but it is an appropriate place to leave this investigation of the mutual needs of two very different worlds, the urban guild and its circumambient 'country'.

CHAPTER 6

Crisis and Resolution: Government and Society in Stratford, 1540–1640

ALAN DYER

The people of Stratford could well have met the arrival of the sixteenth century with feelings of modest pride in the success of their town. As far as we can tell it was quite prosperous and had avoided the worst experiences of some towns in the fifteenth century – depression, violence, insecurity – and could reasonably look forward to a stable future under the joint rule of its landlord bishop and the Guild of the Holy Cross. The townsmen could see physical evidence of the late medieval achievement of the community in two great building projects, the reconstruction of the Guild Chapel in stone, begun in 1496, and the replacement of the inadequate wooden bridge over the Avon by a durable stone one in about 1490, both the generous gifts of the locally-born, wealthy London merchant, Hugh Clopton. Yet the middle years of the sixteenth century were to witness an acute phase of administrative uncertainty when the Bishop of Worcester lost possession of the town which his predecessors had founded and the Guild was destroyed: the resultant vacuum had to be filled. Meanwhile, the whole century from 1540 to 1640 was marked by rising social and economic stress caused by an expanding population and price inflation, coupled with rapid economic change. In Stratford these broad pressures were accompanied by a series of disasters – famine, fire and epidemic. It is the purpose of this essay to examine the nature of these stresses, and to see how the town coped with them.

An administrative crisis began when the Guild of the Holy Cross, which had been a dominant influence in the town throughout its history, was dissolved in 1547, along with the hundreds of similar organizations in other English towns and villages, part of that greedy assault on religious property which was an integral part of the protestant Reformation. What provision was made for the continuation of the Guild's main contribution to the welfare of the town, that is the maintenance of the school, almshouses and bridge, is not known, but since the Guild represented, as it were, 'the leading townsmen at prayer', the civic élite presumably cobbled together some sort of ad hoc arrangements to keep things going.

However, in 1549 that other pillar of authority in the town, the Bishop of Worcester, gave up his ownership of the manor, which had been the basis of the town's government since its foundation in 1196. We might assume that there had been some potential for conflict between the bishop and the townsmen during the later Middle Ages, as in many other towns ruled by the clergy, for we should expect a collision between the natural

Plate 19. John Dudley, Duke of Northumberland and Earl of Warwick, lord of the manor of Stratford-upon-Avon from 1549 to 1553; after a painting by Holbein.

aspirations for self-government of increasingly prosperous and self-confident townsmen and the equally natural wish of the church to retain control of its revenue-producing estates. Some indication of possible conflict is indicated by an incident in 1504 when what was claimed to be a riot took place at the election of the new bailiff in the manorial court: apparently it was customary for the jury which directed the court's activities to be drawn from the leading townsmen but on this occasion the deputy steward, John Elys, had packed it with poorer citizens, 'simplest persons', a piece of 'misdealing contrary to their laudable customs' which could have been part of an attempt by the bishop's officials to gain more power, or might have had purely local and personal origins.[1] Whether the bishop was himself involved in all this we do not know, but it seems likely that the affair was a brief interruption in a comfortable coexistence between bishop and town élite, in which the townsmen in practice managed their own affairs within the traditional framework of the manorial court and the Guild, with the bishop content to draw his revenues (the very useful sum of £54 by the 1530s[2]) and retain the nominal lordship of the borough, which must have carried with it some indefinable social and political advantages.

The ending of the episcopal link did not precipitate the same sort of hiatus that the dissolution of the Guild created, since the manorial structure continued, but it is likely that a secular manorial lord would be less indulgent than the bishop had been, and the bishop had also functioned as a powerful protective patron, able to act as a shield against hostile interests both in the capital and in the county; the town was entering an unfamiliar and potentially hostile environment. The circumstances in which the bishop lost control are not at all clear. What we do know is that in July 1549 the royal administration registered an exchange of lands between the bishop and John Dudley, Earl of Warwick, in which the manor and borough of Stratford formed part of a parcel of episcopal properties which look to be considerably more valuable than the lands and rights handed over by the earl in response; we must assume here that the bishop had been bullied by the earl, exploiting his very powerful position in the aristocratic clique which had taken over the government of the state during the minority of the boy-king Edward VI.[3] If Dudley had been building up his power base in the Midlands, centred on his castle at nearby Warwick, control of Stratford would have made very good political sense, as well as representing a lucrative addition to his estates.

The issue is complicated by the suggestion made in February 1549 that Thomas Seymour, the powerful brother of the then Protector Somerset and rival of Dudley, had claimed that the manor of Stratford was his, that Dudley had tried to get it from him but that Seymour had refused to exchange it, despite its 'beggarly houses', because it 'would make many men'.[4] Since this was stated in the context of alleging that Seymour had been building up a potentially treasonable power base in the country, these words were meant to suggest that he saw Stratford as a source of military forces, and in Dudley's home territory too. There is no supporting evidence that the town passed in some way from the bishop to Seymour and then to Dudley, but the fact that Seymour was executed in March 1549 would have cleared the way for Dudley to be granted the manor four months later: to see themselves as the helpless pawns in ruthless games of high politics could not have added to the townsmen's peace of mind.

The first four years (1549–53) under the lordship of Dudley (who had in the interim disposed of Protector Somerset and become the effective ruler of England as Duke of Northumberland) have left little mark on the town records, so we do not know how the administration of the town and its charities was managed. What is very clear is that in 1553 the town was given a royal charter which set up its government on a new and regular footing and cleared up most of the problems created by the changes of the previous decade or more. This took place six years after the dissolution of the Guild and we do not know why there was such a long delay in regularizing the situation. Other towns, of course, had been placed in a situation similar to Stratford's, but had secured chartered reorganizations more quickly: Lichfield had been hit hard by the loss of its guilds in 1547, but had acquired a new charter in the following year, while Maidstone had lost its dominant bishop and been chartered in 1549 too, while Stafford had secured the re-endowment of its school in 1550.[5] In these cases, powerful local patrons had worked to speed up the legal solution, so we must assume that similar forces were delaying the resolution of Stratford's problems.

Perhaps Dudley saw a self-governing Stratford as a threat to his local power, and used his authority in London to frustrate any unrecorded moves made by the townsmen to acquire greater independence; certainly his willing assent would have been essential for the borough's petition to the Privy Council to be approved in February of 1553, a formality which led to the issuing of the requested charter in June.[6] It is not easy to explain Dudley's motives behind this change of policy, if we are right, that is, in assuming that he had discouraged such a move until this point.[7] Remarkably few charters were granted during Edward's six-year reign, despite the pressing need for them in a goodly number of towns. Dudley may well have considered that the town was worth more to him politically if chartered, and, as we shall see, he ensured that the charter preserved some authority for himself. He may well have calculated that the king might die in the near future and that in the ensuing power struggle, his hold over south Warwickshire might be usefully strengthened. Whatever the truth of all this, the charter was granted on 28 June and the king died a week later; Dudley tried to avert the accession of Mary by placing Lady Jane Grey on the throne, failed, and paid the price of treason with his life; had there been a delay in granting the charter by another few days, the history of Stratford might have been rather different.

The charter of 1553 is rightly seen as a major milestone in the town's history.[8] The medieval political history of Stratford had ended, and the borough was placed on an administrative footing which has lasted, with modifications in the nineteenth and twentieth centuries, until the present day. The most basic act of the charter was to create an incorporation, a permanent body which could act legally as if it were the townsmen as a whole, which could hold property, make by-laws and generally act as the town government. The structure of the new Corporation consisted of an upper body of fourteen named aldermen, of whom one was to be elected annually as bailiff, and a lower body, also of fourteen, who were left to the aldermen to appoint. The choice of fourteen, rather than the more usual twelve, was probably due to a need to satisfy the ambitions of that number of leading townsmen who formed the natural ruling élite at that moment. The stated purpose of the charter was to create a permanent body which could continue the work of the Guild, so the new Corporation received the property of that body which the Crown had confiscated in 1547, plus most of the tithe revenues which had belonged to the College, the association of priests which had staffed the parish church until its dissolution as a quasi-monastic institution in 1539. The Corporation took over the Guild Chapel and associated buildings, which became the centre of municipal administration, besides accommodating the re-founded grammar school. In return it undertook to pay and house the schoolmaster, to care for the poor housed in the almshouses and to shoulder the burden of maintaining the bridge; it also was to pay the wages of the vicar and his assistant chaplain, and house him. The income provided amounted to £80 per year and the outgoings to £67, which left a reasonable margin and the potential for increasing revenue from the estate.

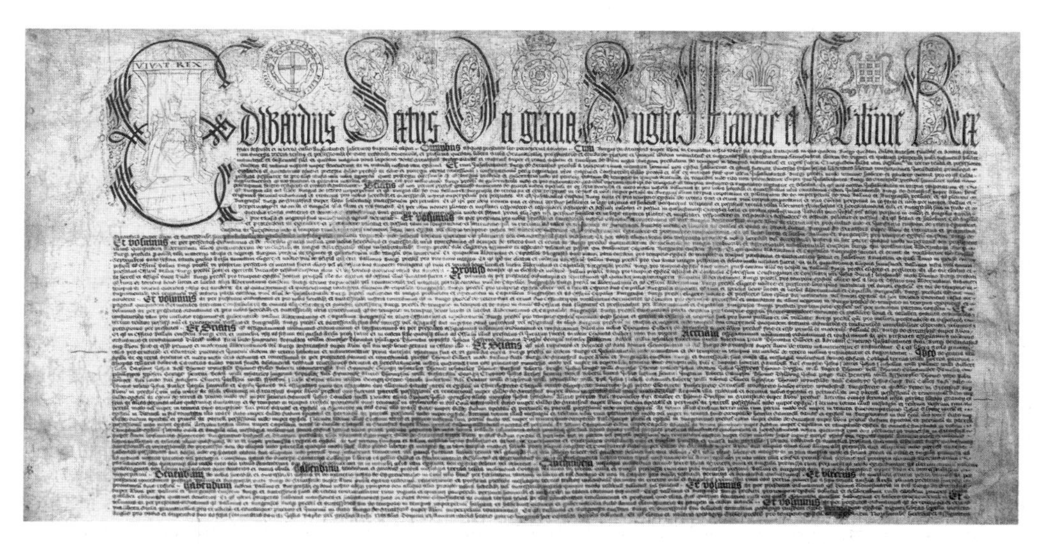

Plate 20. Charter of Edward VI incorporating the borough of Stratford-upon-Avon, 28 June 1553. (SBTRO, BRU 1/1)

Thus far the town seemed to have solved its crisis of governance, but the charter contained inbuilt problems which were to dog the new Corporation during the first decades of its existence. Dudley ensured that he retained some formal control over the town by reserving to himself the right to approve the name of the bailiff between his election by the council and the swearing-in; he also retained the right to nominate the vicar and the schoolmaster, which would presumably produce an income. When Dudley fell from power and lost his estates, these rights passed to the Crown, and then to local landowners and onwards to speculators intent only on recovering the value of their investment. Along with them went the bishop's manorial rights which included the holding of a manorial court with jurisdiction over various petty matters, and, more seriously, the right to levy some tolls in the market. Rights of patronage to the school and vicarage were still being exercised in the 1630s, an irritation to the council.

This problem of a self-government which was in fact to be shared with a manorial lord was a common enough problem, and one replicated in Evesham where even a chartered incorporation was delayed until 1604/5.[9] But Stratford's charter was also technically deficient to an extent which might suggest poor legal advice, or excessive haste, at the time of its drafting. It received the powers of Justices of the Peace, but not the right to hold quarter sessions which would have made much more of this authority; it had the right to make by-laws but not the power to fine or imprison those who broke them, and its authority was restricted to the geographical limits of the medieval borough, which meant that the Old Town, including the parish church, was outside the Corporation's control. To some extent these rights could be assumed, using the traditional customary principle that powers which were exercised without challenge became legal rights, but this could lead to endless complications in the courts, and from at least the 1590s onwards the Corporation tried to secure a new charter. The fact that it was not granted until 1610 would suggest that either the town was remarkably inept at working the system, or that powerful interests at court, presumably local landowners, pulled more influential strings than the town could afford to counter. From 1610 onwards, only the appointment of vicar and schoolmaster remained as an irritant, but it nevertheless remains the case that for much of the period under review the Corporation was not master in its own house, and that throughout these years the powers granted to a town council of this sort were scarcely adequate to cope with the problems which faced it; in particular, the new authority found itself in great difficulty when attempting to control the immigrant poor and in compelling the abandonment of thatch as an inflammable roofing material.

The other great class of challenge, apart from governance, which faced Stratford in this century was a series of linked issues – the consequences of rapid social and economic change on a national scale, and their regional manifestation in terms of widespread poverty and migration, coupled with peculiarly Stratfordian problems associated with a series of local disasters, fires, epidemics and famines. We should begin with the general situation. The population of England rose rapidly after more than a century of stagnation or decline, increasing by over 80 per cent between 1540 and 1640.[10] Warwickshire had at least its fair share of this rapid growth, and with it the stresses which overpopulation brought in its trail. The general economic effect of population growth was firstly to stimulate prices (though other factors played their part) which rose by six or seven times by 1640, with most of this very great increase being concentrated in the sixteenth century. Wages increased too, but the extent of population growth provided a surplus of labour which kept down wage increases so that the standard of living of manual workers must have fallen substantially in these years, even when employment could be found.

The effect of all this was to accelerate the importance of production for the market, especially in agriculture, where an insatiable appetite for foodstuffs, even at their inflated levels, could be guaranteed. Agriculture became rapidly commercialized and so more hazardous for the weak or inefficient, and in any case the numbers of landless cottagers in the countryside grew as its population outstripped the supply of available land. So many were squeezed from the village community altogether to migrate to less overcrowded areas, or to the towns or to take to the roads as vagrants. The open-field, corn-growing villages of the Avon valley grew as fast as any, and must have contributed generously to the migrant flow, while the marked prevalence of deserted or shrunken village settlements in south Warwickshire, where large-scale sheep farming was creating more migrants, must have added to the misery of the poor. All of these trends contributed to economic growth, but they all created instability and problems of dispossession and poverty which had to be addressed. Unfortunately, Stratford received more than its fair share of migrant poor, while itself being badly placed to cope with them at the best of times, and least of all when suffering its own peculiar problems.

At this point we should consider the economic condition of Stratford in our period, but this task is a surprisingly difficult one. The town does seem to have had a textile industry in the later Middle Ages, as one might expect in a place near to wool supplies and to major clothmaking centres in Coventry and Worcester; this is shown by the high proportion of trades connected with cloth which are mentioned in the Guild's membership register. But there is no very striking number of references to clothmaking trades in the surviving Stratford records after 1570, though perhaps a few more than one would have expected in an average Midland town.[11] When this lucrative group of trades declined is not documented, but it may well have followed the collapse of the Coventry industry, to which it was probably linked, in the later fifteenth and earlier sixteenth centuries. Certainly the Corporation was claiming in 1590 that the town was 'now fallen much into decay for want of such trade as heretofore they had by clothing and making of yarn, employing and maintaining a number of poor people by the same, which now lives in great penury and misery'.[12] This must refer to the last tatters of the trade, for there is no reference to the better off, self-employed tradesmen whose troubles would have been the most conspicuous feature of the process at its start. The decline of the clothing trades might well have had an effect on the prosperity of the town at an earlier date, and some confirmation of the thesis of a depressed town at some stage during the first half of the sixteenth century might be derived from a comment by the Bishop of Worcester in 1537 that its 'houses are toward ruin, and the whole town far out of frame for lack of residence', coupled with Seymour's remark about 'beggarly houses' in 1549 already quoted.[13] By the 1560s this phase was probably over: the crucial issue is the success of the town in adjusting to these changed circumstances.

Stratford was essentially a market town, and it is this function which lies at the heart of its economic role in our period. At this date there were over 500 of these towns distributed at fairly even intervals over the English countryside. Their task was to provide a centre for the marketing of agricultural produce and for the retailing of urban goods and services to rural dwellers who had no other source for them. So farmers came every Thursday to Stratford's market places to sell their corn and cheese, deal in cattle, sheep and pigs and then to buy cloth, sugar, shoes, tools or services such as those provided by the tailor or barber, inn or alehouse. On this exchange between town and country rested the prosperity of most towns, and more particularly Stratford, for lists of traders present in the town[14] reveal no particular specialism with the exception of glove-making, though this common Midland's trade seems to be in decline by the seventeenth century. There is not even that scattering of less common trades which distinguishes the larger Midland's market centres like Tewkesbury. It did show some signs of a concentration of professionals serving the gentry, such as lawyers and physicians (like Dr John Hall, Shakespeare's son-in-law), but this was to be Warwick's forte, and Stratford could not compete with it.

Stratford's only distinguishing feature was a concentration on making and dealing in malt. Beer and ale were basic items of diet for everyone, and their most important component was the roasted and ground barley which is malt. Since grain was bulky and heavy, and so expensive to transport, the malting process was best carried out near to the origin of the grain, which in this case lay in the arable lands to the south of the town. However, malting deployed capital rather than skill or labour, so that it was often carried on as a second or third occupation by traders whose main concern lay elsewhere, and even as an investment by local gentry. It required spare money, but only outbuildings and minimal, cheap labour: indeed we find by-laws discouraging the use of children and blind people as malt-kiln attendants.[15] Thus this activity strengthened the commercial role of the town and enriched many of its wealthier citizens but provided the least possible employment for the rural dispossessed: indeed it diverted investment away from other manufacturing activities such as leather or metal-working which could have created more employment.

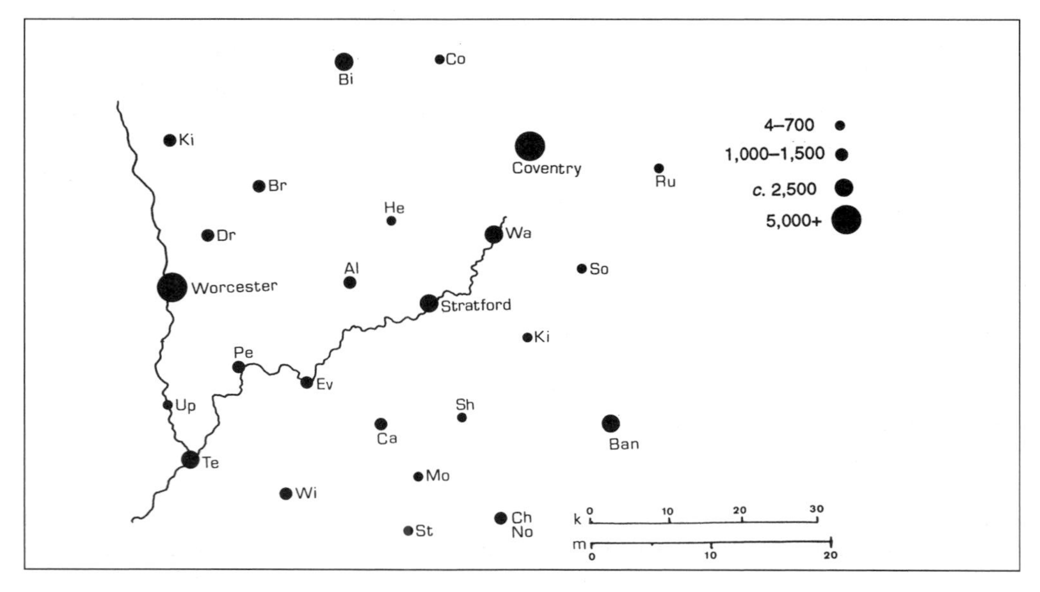

Fig. 12. Towns in Stratford's region, 1540–1640.

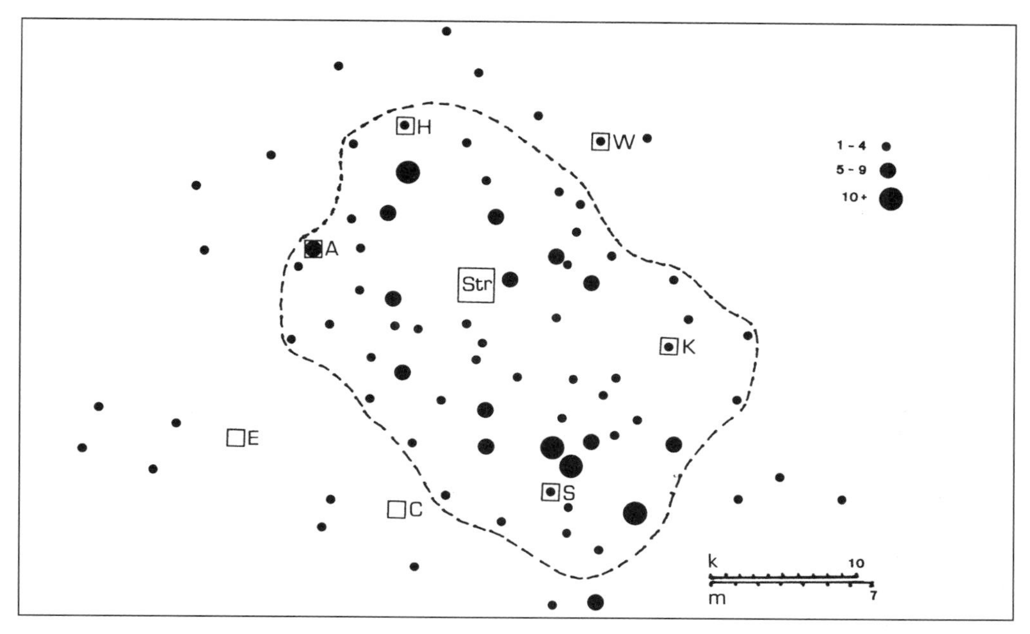

Fig. 13 Stratford's region: the origins of marriage partners listed in Stratford parish register, 1653–8.

The town's prosperity, then, rested on supplying basic goods and services to the country people who attended its markets and fairs, and its fate was thus shaped by the nature and development of the region in which it lay: if the hinterland prospered, so would the town. Here there is a complex and contradictory situation to unravel. In many ways Stratford was advantageously situated. It lay far enough away from major towns – Coventry, Worcester, Oxford and the growing industrial area centred on Birmingham – to benefit from their trade without suffering from their competition (see Fig. 12). In its immediate hinterland, Alcester and Warwick were relatively weak trading centres while Evesham and Banbury, which were stronger, lay further away. In particular, it lay on the edge of the Midland urban network, for a system of vigorous and interdependent towns lay to the north, north-west and north-east, while to the south lay an under-urbanized no man's land before the Oxford-centred network, which was really part of the outer limits of London's commercial region, was reached. Symptomatic of this area's lack of urban strength was the poverty and small size of Shipston and Kineton (perhaps 500 people each by 1640); they evidently lacked a commercial role and good marketing potential which would have been derived from a key position in a strong urban network – they lay between, and isolated from the two systems. This allowed Stratford to extend its zone of commercial influence, which one would normally have expected to extend only to the half-way point between itself and its neighbouring market towns; here it stretched further to the south-east to overlap the hinterlands of Kineton and Shipston, mopping up the customers left unserved by the modest urban facilities available in these two weak competitors, a fact which one could guess from the relative sizes of the towns shown in Fig. 12, but which is illustrated more clearly in the personal links reflected in the patterns plotted in Fig. 13.[16]

Thus Stratford's market region was larger than average, which should have enriched it. It also enjoyed a position guaranteed to favour any market town of the time, that is, between contrasting agricultural regions. To the south and south-west lay the corn-growing lands of the Feldon, producing a surplus of cereals which had to be marketed, while to the north lay the Arden, a formerly forested area which specialized in dairying and stock-raising and which needed in its turn to import the corn it lacked and to export its cheese, skins and other pastoral products to regions which required them. Such a basic exchange trade was just what had grown up with the increasing commercialization of agriculture during this period; it enriched not only well-positioned marketing centres, but also fostered a long-range, inter-regional commerce which must have been one of the major growth points in the sixteenth-century economy. We can see this in the destination of Stratford's malt, which the Corporation claimed in 1598 passed through Birmingham and onwards to supply Wales, Shropshire, Staffordshire, Cheshire and Lancashire.[17] Much the same pattern still prevailed in 1818, when Stratford market was said to funnel corn and seed from Gloucestershire and Oxfordshire on its way to Birmingham and the Black Country.[18] In the opposite direction, cheese flowed from northern Warwickshire via Stratford to London by road and down river towards Bristol.[19] The town must have profited in many ways, direct and indirect, from this class of trade, as we can see in the number of Stratford traders who acted as middlemen in the exchange of agricultural produce, not just the maltmen but dealers in corn, wool and cattle.

However, there were weaknesses and problems lurking in this generally favourable picture. If Stratford's market region was large and productive, it was also relatively thinly populated. Deserted medieval settlements lay immediately around the town, at Milcote and Billesley for instance, and wider areas of these thinly populated landscapes lay to the south-east (see Fig. 14) where population densities in 1563 were half the levels achieved in the lower Avon valley around Evesham.[20] Such low levels of settlement could only be reflected in fewer customers for Stratford traders, although one should not draw this conclusion automatically, since large numbers of impoverished landless labourers would provide few shop customers either. Another problem lay in the forested landscapes to the north which do not seem to have been very reliant on market towns. One of the few forest towns, Henley-in-Arden, was very small and for a time operated its market fortnightly rather than weekly, a rare sign of commercial weakness,[21] while the forest parishes contained a high proportion of tradesmen, which made them more independent of urban businesses.

The Corporation in 1598 complained that a major problem lay in the fact that the town was not a thoroughfare, that is, that it did not lie on a well-frequented road. If this were true, and protestations of difficulty addressed to the central government in this period were frequently exaggerated, then the route from London through Oxford to Birmingham, which was to be the main coaching line through Stratford, was not yet well used.[22] This opens up the whole question of communications and Midland towns, for it was well known at the time that distance from navigable rivers and the sea was a guarantee of commercial stagnation in an age when it was much cheaper to convey heavy or bulky goods by water than by land. The opening up of the Avon navigation as far as the Severn at Tewkesbury, which began in the 1630s, brought renewed prosperity to the town, and one could argue that this shows that it was the land-locked character of the area which was holding it back before this development: the cheapness of the local

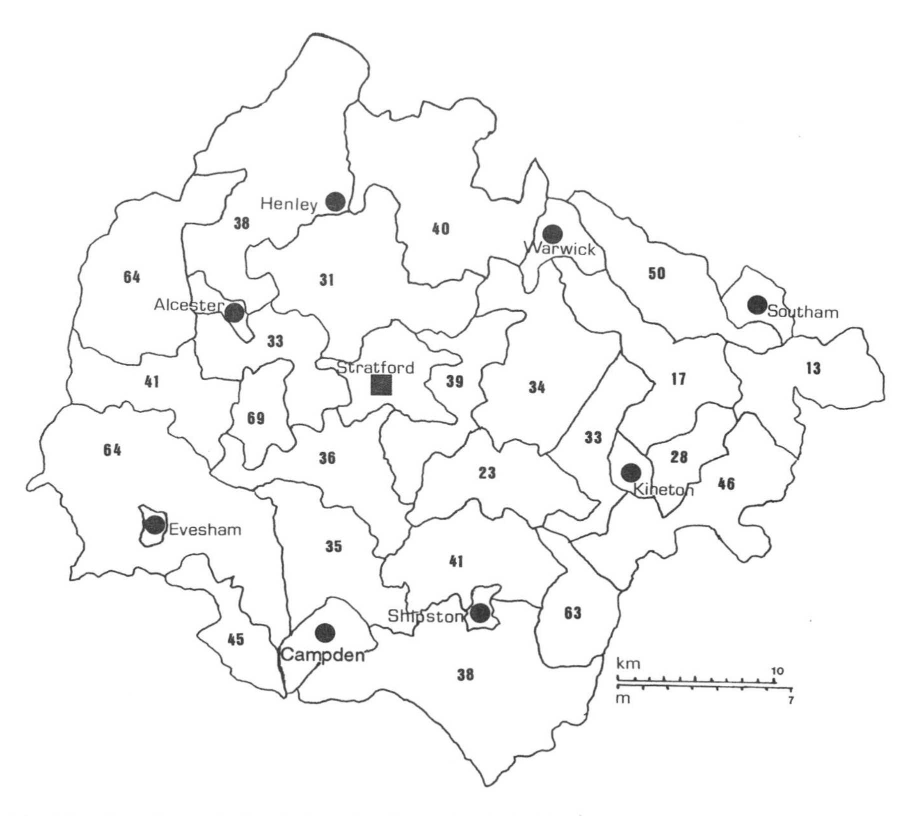

Fig. 14 Density of population in Stratford's region: inhabitants per square mile, 1563.

corn, which eventually attracted the navigation speculators, is a clear indication that its markets were too inaccessible for local resources to be fully exploited.[23] Yarranton in the later seventeenth century called the area 'locked up in the inlands'.[24] The Avon opened up a cheap export route for corn, malt and cheese, and allowed Bristol imports and heavy raw materials such as coal and iron to be brought up at reasonable cost, thus strengthening the town's role as a commercial, shopping and industrial centre; the cutting of the Birmingham canal and the turnpiked Oxford road gave further injections of economic vitality later on. So we can use the prosperity created by improved communications later on to suggest that the town was being held back by poor transport links before 1640.

The economic fortunes of Stratford ought to be reflected in the size of its population, but it is not easy to extract from the limited source material any very firm information. The earliest possibility of assessing urban population in the sixteenth century is often provided by the subsidy records of 1524–5, but the total number of taxpayers in Stratford is so unrealistically low that it must be used with great caution, though this might be taken as an indication that the town was informally under-assessed because of poverty. We have no direct information on the size of the total population before the eighteenth century, and must rely on estimates derived from indirect evidence. This would suggest the following totals for the town:

1546	–	1,650
1563	–	1,450
1570s	–	1,540
1580s	–	1,970
1591	–	2,500
1598	–	2,500[25]

If it is true that the town had grown from under 1,500 in the early 1560s to approaching 2,500 by 1600, then up to 1,000 extra people had been acquired quite rapidly, an expansion of over 60 per cent; but there must remain some uncertainty about the reliability of these figures, though perhaps not about the trend which they indicate. Whether this growth continued far into the next century is hard to say.[26] However, most of the expansion had disappeared by the 1670s when the hearth tax records point to a total population of 1,700–1,800 in the town, a level confirmed by a count of houses in 1730.[27] Expansion had resumed by 1765, when an exact census of the town gives us 2,287 inhabitants, but this was still below the estimated level reached in 1600.[28]

It is frustrating not to know if the population actually fell in the middle years of the sixteenth century between 1546 and 1563, and whether the town continued to grow in the earlier seventeenth century before being cut back; but the striking feature of the picture is of relative long-term stability – or stagnation, it is hard to know which term might be more appropriate – despite the apparent phase of growth by several hundreds under Elizabeth. Either Stratford could not, or would not, grow in the long term and this needs to be set against a general pattern of solid growth in population through most of the surrounding countryside and in most towns. The demographic pattern seems perverse when seen against the economic background, which appears to be indifferent when population growth takes place in the later sixteenth century yet improving when the population was static or falling in the seventeenth century – though one might argue that growth caused poverty and contraction led to prosperity.[29] This is clearly something which needs to be explained. But we do have here a basis for understanding the Corporation's concern at the growth of poverty in the town in the later sixteenth and earlier seventeenth centuries and in particular its concern at the immigration of impoverished people from the countryside: the later loss of most of the Elizabethan growth would suggest that the town's economy was indeed incapable of supporting such an expanded population.

Discussion of the social and economic circumstances of any town in this period benefits greatly from an analysis of the parish register, and in the case of Stratford we are fortunate that we have a generally well-kept and well-preserved register beginning in 1558.[30] The most basic lesson to be learnt from an analysis of its entries (see Fig. 15) is that the sixteenth-century growth suggested above could not have been derived from the natural growth of the indigenous inhabitants, for the balance between baptisms and burials in the period 1558–99 shows a deficit, with about forty more people buried than baptized. This is not quite such a bleak picture as at first appears, for there was in fact a

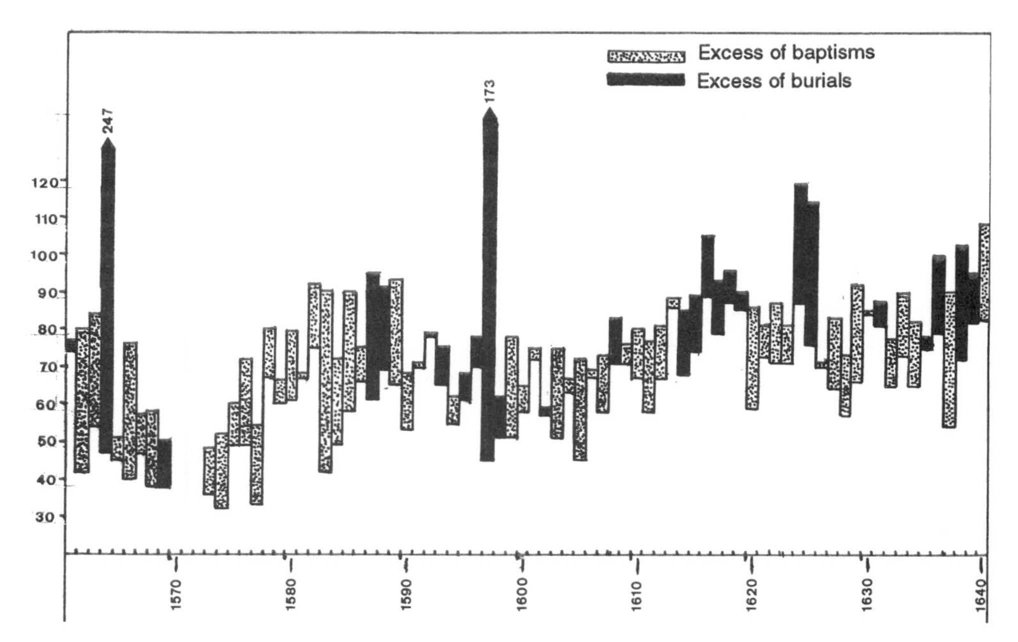

Fig. 15. Stratford parish register: annual totals of events.

small surplus of baptisms in a majority of years – twenty-eight out of forty-two.[31] The years 1565 to 1586 show a particularly consistent pattern of growth. However, the surplus is always a modest one, amounting to only about 360 in these two favoured decades; virtually all of this was counterbalanced in a mere two disastrous years, 1564 and 1597, when there was a total deficit of 328 people. The closing years of the century, from 1587 to 1599, were particularly bleak, with eight years in deficit and only five with a modest surplus of baptisms. The pattern in the seventeenth century shows an improvement for a time, with almost every year in surplus until 1614 ushers in a period of deficit. But there were no striking disasters on the sixteenth-century pattern and there was an overall surplus of 132. The whole period 1558–1640 shows a surplus of under one hundred, and if we had entries for the disastrous months between 1556 and March 1558, not covered in the register, they would almost certainly remove this surplus. We must conclude, therefore, that there is no evidence here for any natural growth at all, and strong *prima facie* indications of a relatively sickly and disaster-prone community, since many English towns appear to have achieved a surplus of baptisms before the seventeenth century, even when towns are quite large and so more liable to epidemic damage.

If we are right about a growth of several hundreds in the total number of Stratford's inhabitants in these years, then most of this growth must have been due to migration from the countryside. This reliance on immigration will take on an extra relevance when we come to note the anxiety of the authorities about the inward movement of the poor; it would also help to explain how the town contracted again by the later seventeenth century, for the absence of population surplus in the countryside, which was a general phenomenon by the middle years of the seventeenth century, would have cut off the migrant flow on which the town depended to maintain its size in adverse circumstances: here we have one explanation of the curious drop in the town's size during the course of the seventeenth century.

Table 2: ***Child Mortality in Stratford, 1560–1639***

	1 *Average annual baptisms*	2 *Average annual child burials*	3 *Average annual difference 1–2*	4 *Child burials as a percentage of baptisms*
1560–9	62.8	42.8	20.0	68.2
1570–9	61.7	23.0	38.7	37.3
1580–9	78.9	34.6	44.3	43.9
1590–9	64.9	39.1	25.8	60.2
1600–9	70.0	32.1	37.9	45.9
1610–9	80.8	37.8	43.0	46.8
1620–9	81.7	38.4	43.3	47.0
1630–9	81.3	42.4	38.9	52.2

Further conclusions can be squeezed from the analysis of the register. The summary contained in Table 2 shows that the level of baptisms rose until the 1580s, which would be consistent with a rising population, fell in the troubled 1590s but again reached a level of about eighty a year between 1610 and 1640. Since the accepted view of national birth rates was that they were dropping slowly by the early decades of the seventeenth century, this would suggest that Stratford kept its late Elizabethan increased population until 1640 at least, and that the decline which had taken place by the 1670s was a relatively recent one, perhaps beginning in the disturbed Civil War years. These figures also compare the recorded burials of children over our period, and these make chilling reading.[32] Burials of children amount to a reasonably stable 45–50 per cent of the total number of baptisms. This is not quite the child mortality rate of more elaborate demographic studies, but it is quite close to it, and indicates that mortality among Stratford's young people was very high when compared with other market towns which have been studied, such as nearby Banbury.[33] Here we have one reason for the lack of natural growth, though relatively low birth rates and high adult mortality may also be involved. High child mortality may well point to serious problems of poverty, and perhaps relatively low standards of living, especially of feeding and housing, among the poorer townspeople. They also reveal a pall of grief and loss hanging over most of the town's families at one time or another; behind these dry statistics lie untold private tragedies.

The general situation revealed by the register is of an adverse level of mortality in the town, but we may learn more of the diseases which were killing so many of the inhabitants of Stratford, young and old, by looking at the pattern of epidemics revealed

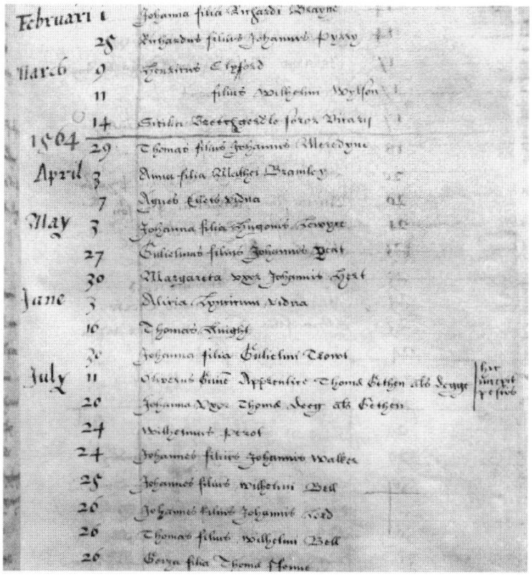

Plate 21. The burial register for Holy Trinity Church, Stratford-upon-Avon, with the vicar's marginal note against the entry of 11 July 1564: 'hic incipit pestis' (here begins the plague). (SBTRO, DR 243/1)

by the burial entries. Most towns were attacked by at least one epidemic of bubonic plague during this period, so Stratford's disastrous experience of 1564 is not exceptional. There is no problem of identification since there was a nationwide outbreak in this year, spread from the major London epidemic of 1563, and the disease is specifically identified in the parish register when the epidemic began with the burial of the apprentice Oliver Gunne on 11 July.[34] Typical of plague was the way deaths tended to be concentrated in family groups, reflecting the fact that once the rats resident in a particular building were infected, then all the people sharing that shelter were highly likely to catch the disease: so we read of the burial of William Pynson on 12 August, his wife Margaret on the 20th and his daughters Alice and Anne on the 20th and 24th. The corollary of this concentration of multiple deaths in a limited number of households is that many families must have been unaffected, despite the fact that the disease killed about 200 people, or about 13 per cent of the population, a blow which needs to be considered with the likely impact of the recent heavy mortality of the years around 1558.

No other epidemic year is as easy to identify, for though there were other outbreaks of bubonic plague in the town they did not give rise to such serious mortality: the epidemic of 1645 lasted from May to September but killed scarcely more than the forty people who are marked in the register as dying from 'pest'. Although those who lived in poorer quality housing were more likely to catch plague, it is not easy to suggest that there was a strong necessary connection between social conditions and plague deaths, since there was a strong element of luck in the arrival of the disease in any particular place. But we may draw stronger conclusions from Stratford's other great sixteenth-century epidemic disaster which took place in 1597 when over one hundred people died in excess of the normal total. To appreciate what happened here we need to consider the broader picture again. The years 1594 and 1597 were characterized nationally by a series of four consecutive harvest failures, with the harvest year 1596–7 showing the highest food shortages, all the result of cold, wet summers. Shakespeare, whether thinking of Warwickshire or London, writes around this time, in *A Midsummer Night's Dream*:

> The oxe hath therefore stretch'd his yoake in vaine,
> The ploughman lost his sweat, and the greene corne
> Hath rotted, ere his youth attain'd a beard.

Two successive harvest failures had a serious impact at this time, but the cumulative effects of four years of dearth were disastrous. Grain prices doubled and trebled, putting the usual staple diet of the poor, bread, beyond their reach, while the whole economy was depressed by the diversion of all available money into acquiring food supplies. Some starved, many died of famine-related diseases and the hungry took to the roads, spreading disease as they went.

The royal government did what it could to keep down food prices and guarantee an even distribution of what was available. The town government was placed in an awkward quandary by this, for among the central government's policies was a discouragement of malt-making, which was seen as a diversion of bread-corn into the production of beer which was over-strong and consumed to excess. But many people in Stratford, and

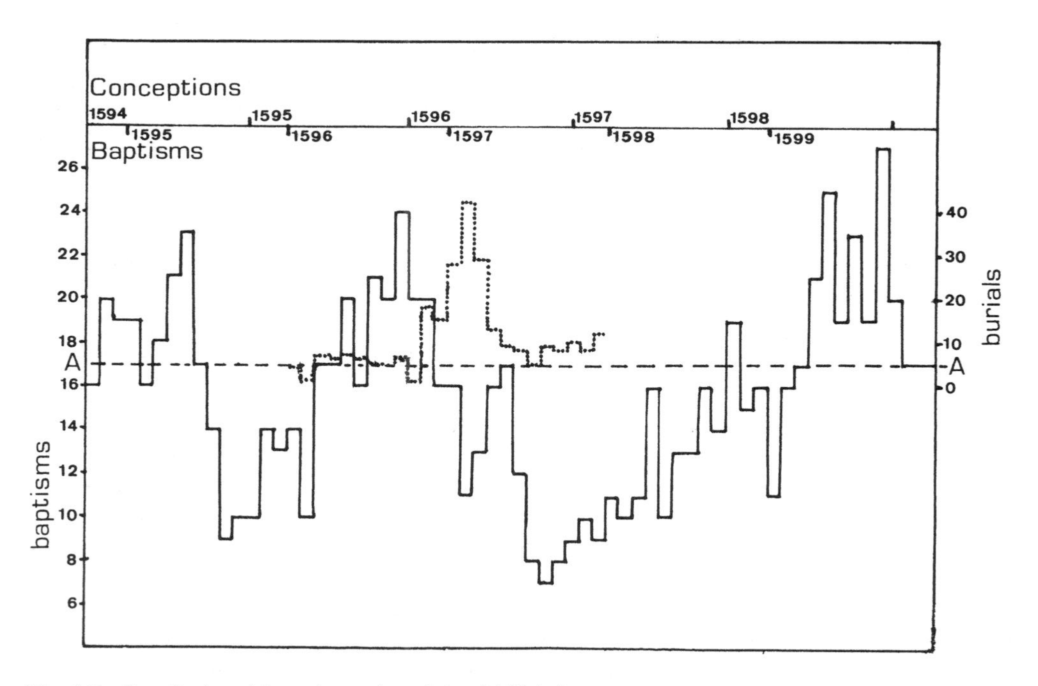

Fig. 16. Stratford parish register: the crisis of 1594–9.
AA = Approximate normal level

especially the élite represented on the Corporation, were deeply involved in the trade and reluctant to damage it. In 1595 the Privy Council ordered the town magistrates to act, and by January 1598 local feeling against the maltsters, who were clearly seen as scapegoats, was running high, with some wanting to see the maltsters 'hanged on gibbets at their own doors'.[35] This popular resentment led to attempts to bring in Warwickshire magistrates and the central government to force sterner action on the town council, which in turn pointed out that the loss of the malt trade would impoverish the town in general.

The nearest we can get to reconstructing the impact of the famine years is through the parish register. The record of baptisms (see Fig. 16) can be regarded as reflecting the conceptions of nine months previously, and analysed in this way we can see a trough in conceptions beginning in November 1594, when the first harvest failure was evident, and stretching through to May 1595. Another deeper trough extends from September 1596 to October 1598, when the first normal harvest had been gathered. The way in which famine reduced the birth rate is not clearly understood, but must reflect both the physiological effect of malnutrition on the human body, and, probably more importantly – since the timing is so closely related to the gathering of the harvest – a realization by many couples that they could not afford to risk a pregnancy at such an inappropriate time. These patterns are a more revealing indication of the stress caused by food shortage than raised mortality, for an increase in deaths requires the accident of disease organisms being introduced from outside, which might not occur. In Stratford the mortality crisis came in November 1596 and lasted until the spring of 1597, with a peak in February when forty-two people were buried, close to the annual total in a normal year. The diseases involved must remain a matter of speculation, but the fact that all ages were involved but adults rather more so, and that the deaths were concentrated in winter would point to typhus and dysentry, the classic famine-related infections, with the possible addition of poisoning from tainted cereals. Death visited the poor more frequently than the better off, for of the eighty-five adult deaths between November 1596 and the following May, as many as thirty-five are described as poor, widowed or from the almshouses, and more were presumably poor without meriting the formal description 'pauper'. This would point to malnutrition as a major factor in causing these deaths, rather than just the accident of infection. However, compared with some places, the Stratford register records few vagrants, so that the town's problems lay with its resident and local poor. There was nothing basically unusual about Stratford's experience in these months, which fits in neatly with the national pattern, but it should be considered in the context of the town's multiple problems in these years.[36]

The troubles caused by famine were but part of the tribulations which afflicted the town in the closing years of the sixteenth century. Major fires were a not uncommon feature of the history of many towns which were constructed of half-timbering and thatch, but Stratford seems to have been especially unfortunate in this respect. Serious fires caused extensive damage in 1594 and again in 1595, both fires, it was said, occurring on a Sunday: moralists saw in this the hand of God, punishing sin in general and lack of sabbath observance in particular. It was claimed that over 200 houses were destroyed and that the total damage amounted to the then huge sum of £12,000.[37] Despite the organization of charitable collections through neighbouring counties which must have been of some help, the financial damage to the town was very considerable, and must help to explain its impoverished state in ensuing years. Some houses were rebuilt rapidly, but the 1598 rent roll of the Corporation reveals that much remained to be done. In time, the rebuilt town presented an improved front to the visitor which would have helped its economy, but in the short term the fire damage could only have worsened the strain of poverty. A petition of 1601 refers to 700 poor, and, though we cannot tell what this means in detail, in general it would suggest that Stratford was in more serious difficulty than most towns of its kind. Further fires in 1614 and 1641 point to the inability of the Corporation, even with its new charter, to exterminate the use of thatch, but the absence of pleas of poverty in their wake might suggest that by this point the town was better able to take such accidents in its stride, and the fact that the harvest failures of the earlier seventeenth century were not followed by major mortalities in the town might suggest that here, too, Stratford was less vulnerable to such stresses than it had been.

The political, social and economic difficulties of this period were clearly serious challenges to the town. One must, however, not exaggerate their significance. Bad news tends to be recorded, and good taken for granted, and Stratford emerged from its difficulties in a strengthened form, rebuilt and with the Avon navigation on the horizon as a solution to the worst of its economic problems. The underlying strength of the town was reappearing from what was after all a temporary series of crises, to see it through to a modest and more stable prosperity.

CHAPTER 7

Building a Godly Town: Religious and Cultural Divisions in Stratford-upon-Avon, 1560–1640

ANN HUGHES

In January 1564, John Shakespeare, the father of William, noted in his accounts as chamberlain, the disbursement of two shillings, 'payd for defasying ymages in ye Chappell'.[1] Hitherto Stratford townsmen and women had been entertained and instructed by a typical late medieval collection of narrative paintings recounting the martyrdom of Becket, the struggle of St George and the Dragon, the meeting of Solomon and the Queen of Sheba and the life of Empress Helena, the mother of Constantine, as well as images of the passion and death of Christ and, over the great arch leading to the chancel, a representation of the day of judgement.[2] Henceforth the Guild Chapel became a whitewashed auditorium for the preaching and hearing of the word of God, maintained by the town's Corporation who had taken over many of the functions of the dissolved Guild.

The defacing of images has a fine Protestant ring to it; the authorities of a small Warwickshire town removed distracting, superstitious objects of veneration and made the transmission and understanding of true doctrine their religious priority. The event is more ambiguous than it at first appears, however, and highlights the complex cultural impact and reception of Protestantism in England. As Patrick Collinson has recently pointed out, Stratford was rather late in eliminating its images: most towns in the south-east of England had destroyed them in 1560, as the central government had ordered.[3] In any case, covering the pictures with whitewash was perhaps a rather half-hearted response compared to scraping them off completely, although the crosses, regarded by zealous Protestants as especially sacrilegious, had been attacked with sharp instruments. Did the authorities envisage a time when the pictures could be revealed again? By 1564, of course, the people of Stratford had experienced some bewildering changes of political and religious policy. During the zealously Protestant Edwardian regime the town's Guild had been dissolved and, at the last minute, a charter had been granted establishing a corporate authority.[4] The brief return to Catholicism under Mary was halted with Elizabeth's succession in 1558; henceforth there were to be longer lasting and more consistent attempts to make England, for the first time, a country of Protestants.

The earlier Henrician Reformation had made the English church independent of the papacy but had had a limited impact on the doctrine and worship of the church and its

Plate 22. Part of the 'Day of Judgement' wall painting in the Guild Chapel, whitewashed over in the 1560s; drawn by Thomas Fisher in 1804, when the painting was uncovered.

parishioners. The ambitious Edwardian reforms had been short-lived. Under Elizabeth, however, zealous Protestant clergy and lay-people attempted massive cultural changes. The Protestant Reformation aimed not only at theological changes but also sought a dramatic reorientation of what it meant to be a Christian. The most committed Protestants worked to create a godly society through reformation of the moral and social behaviour of the population as well as through changing religious beliefs more narrowly defined. As might be expected, such a transformation was not easily achieved and met with much resistance, covert and stubborn more often than reckless and open. Stratford-upon-Avon, like many other communities, demonstrates how the highest hopes of the godly foundered in the face of evasion, ridicule, and defiance.[5]

Within the medieval Catholic church people gained religious understanding and sought salvation in a variety of ways, many of them collective or communal. Gazing at images, visiting shrines, going on pilgrimages, joining in pageants and processions, as well as the more obvious giving of alms or paying for and hearing masses, were among the religious 'works' that comforted people in this world and offered the prospect of heaven thereafter. The stress was on what people did, often with their neighbours. To Protestants, however, the concentration on works was an affront to God's authority; only God's divine will, not human effort, could gain salvation for sinners. A religion based on heedless repetitive rituals and the worship of images was too easy, it pandered to the sensual weaknesses of humanity. Protestantism thus focused on the individual's faith or understanding of doctrine as written in the Bible or preached in the sermons of a godly minister. For some this was a liberating and exciting prospect, but for others, probably a majority, it was alarming and over-demanding. Works could not earn salvation; by the 1560s most 'advanced' English Protestants were Calvinists with a predestinarian theology, arguing that God had chosen or elected, out of his own inscrutable wisdom, a minority of 'saints' for salvation. For many this suggested a depressing and not very useful connection between religious teachings and the experience of everyday life. For a crucial minority, however, who held Calvinist Protestant ideas with a particularly practical zeal, this view provided the basis for an activist programme of reform. Such people, increasingly denounced as 'Puritans' by their opponents, sought assurance or confidence in their own election to salvation by leading self-consciously godly lives themselves and by seeking to improve the morality and behaviour of their neighbours. Such godly activity could not earn salvation, but it was a clear sign of election as one of God's saints. Indeed the fact that one could never be absolutely sure of election gave a particular edge to this active quest for assurance, and encouraged the godly to gather together to clarify their own identity and to further God's work of reformation.[6]

An example of the creative integration between church and broader social life in the later medieval period can be found in the arrangements for the repair of the great bridge over the Avon. In the fifteenth century, bridge wardens organized a pageant on Ascension Day when the drama of St George and the Dragon was performed. The money raised then contributed to the upkeep of St George's altar in the parish church, and the candles sold and burnt there in turn paid for the upkeep of the bridge. This arrangement was ended in Edward's reign and after a brief revival under Mary, bridge repairs became, from 1562, the responsibility of the Corporation who raised rates for the purpose. This was no doubt a more orderly arrangement and one which avoided an unseemly mixture of the religious and the worldly. But it was not necessarily more efficient and it was certainly less entertaining.[7]

Parallel examples of the relationship between church and society in Protestant Stratford are rather more gloomy, as will be shown later in the account of the workings of the town's local ecclesiastical court. More specifically there was the zealous Protestant view that misfortune was a judgement of God on human sinfulness. It was reported that the town's minister, John Bramhall, attributed the fires of 1594 and 1595, both of which providentially occurred on Sundays, to the inhabitants' profanation of the Sabbath Day. Lewis Bayly, in his *The Practice of Piety*, one of the most popular manuals of devotion in the early seventeenth century, wrote that Stratford's fires were a punishment, 'chiefly for prophaning the Lords Sabbath and for contemning his word in the mouth of his faithfull Ministers'. Such providentialism offered committed Protestants a convincing framework for understanding their world, but it was not much of a comfort to most of the victims of Stratford's fires.[8]

It is too simple to suggest that Protestantism was attractive only to the educated or to the literate; in a society where most people could not read fluently, religious ideas could be spread by visual or oral means. The memory was much more effectively used than in more print-focused recent times; the formally illiterate might know by heart extensive sections of the Bible or Foxe's *Book of Martyrs*.[9] Nonetheless, the understanding of Scripture was crucial to Protestantism and it was harder for those without the skills, time and money to acquire and read books to participate fully in the faith. In mid-sixteenth-century Stratford most of the population would thereby be excluded, while only four of the sixteenth-century local wills and inventories analysed in Jeanne Jones's recent study mention books.[10]

By the end of the period discussed here Stratford was undeniably a Protestant town but it was by no means the wholly reformed godly community that the most zealous Protestants or Puritans aimed at. By the mid-seventeenth century also, resistance to thoroughgoing reform came mainly from other Protestants who regarded Puritans as extreme and divisive, rather than from Catholics. In the 1560s, however, and throughout the sixteenth century, there was clearly a significant Catholic presence in the town. In 1569/70, after the failure of the Catholic 'Northern Rising', both the vicar and the schoolmaster fell under suspicion and were replaced by genuine Protestants. A later schoolmaster, who probably taught William Shakespeare, left a few years later and had become a Jesuit by 1578.[11] Lay Catholic sympathizers are found throughout our period. John Shakespeare's retirement from the Corporation in 1577 was most likely prompted by Catholic beliefs while several other Shakespeare kin, notably the Ardens, were Catholics. A cousin of Shakespeare's, John Somerville, was arrested in 1583 on his way to assassinate the Queen.[12] In 1592 an investigation of 'recusants', as Catholics who refused to come to church were now defined, named several Stratford families, especially the women among them, as suspect; Cloptons, Lanes, Cawdreys and Reynolds are examples. The investigation produced several promises to conform but Frances, the wife of John Jeffreys, the town clerk, 'continueth still a willful recusant'.[13] Among aldermen and burgesses, George Badger was a Catholic. He was expelled from the Corporation in 1598 after several years of trouble – quarrels with fellow burgesses, and wilful non-attendance, culminating in a refusal of the office of bailiff.[14] The alarm in Stratford and neighbouring towns during the Gunpowder Plot, and the rigorous measures taken by the authorities, had some foundation.[15]

By the seventeenth century, however, religious and cultural divisions were more commonly found within Protestantism, rather than between Catholics and Protestants. For Puritans, the Elizabethan church was but 'halfly-reformed'. There was too little encouragement for preaching of the word by a godly ministry, and too much survived that

Plate 23. Ambrose Dudley, Earl of Warwick and lord of the manor of Stratford from 1562 until his death in 1590; a drawing by William Hilton, taken in 1820 from a painting at Hatfield House.

smacked of superstition and popery, rituals such as the making of the sign of the cross in baptism, elaborate clerical vestments, regular festivals through the year and set prayers. The episcopal government of the church was hierarchical and ineffective as a means of eliminating abuses or of raising the standards of lay and clerical behaviour. Following the defeat of the Catholic northern rising of 1569, signs of more committed Protestant reform are visible in Stratford. The stained glass in the Guild Chapel was removed in January 1571 while in September of the same year the Council agreed that Bailiff Adrian Quyney could sell the velvet and damask copes and other vestments in the Corporation's possession. In 1587 the pulpit in the Guild Chapel was improved with the addition of a sounding board.[16] In the earlier part of Elizabeth's reign, the lord of the manor of Stratford was Ambrose Dudley, Earl of Warwick, who with his brother Robert, Earl of Leicester was a major patron of advanced Protestant beliefs. One of Leicester's most important clerical associates, Thomas Cartwright, a leading campaigner for a Presbyterian alternative to episcopacy, became master of Leicester's hospital in Warwick in 1585 and preached in Stratford on two occasions at least in the following years. On one occasion he was accompanied by Job Throckmorton of Haseley, a radical Protestant plausibly suspected of a major role in writing scurrilous propaganda against the bishops under the name of Martin Marprelate.[17] Leicester died in 1588, Warwick the following year and without such powerful backing the more conformist elements in the church were able to defeat Presbyterian/Puritan campaigns to transform the government of the church. Cartwright himself spent over a year in prison in the early 1590s and attacks on episcopacy disappeared until the 1640s.

The broader moves for zealous Protestant reform, and for the development of a godly town continued. In 1586 a Puritan survey of the ministry in Warwickshire (part of a nationwide attempt to transform the clergy) had denounced 120 out of 186 incumbents as 'dumbe', inadequate preachers; only thirty were acceptable resident preachers. Among those approved, however, was Richard Barton of Stratford, 'a precher, learned, zealous and godlie, and fit for the ministrie. A happie age yf o^r^ Church were fraight [provided] with manie such.' In nearby Snitterfield, in contrast, the curate was 'dumbe and unlearned, yet thought to be honest, but far unfit for the ministerie'; he augmented his salary through teaching music and drawing. Several ministers in the county including those at St Nicholas, Warwick, and Bidford, were denounced as 'subject to the vice of good fellowshippe'.[18] The defining of good fellowship as a vice offers a useful insight into what Puritans demanded of the parish clergy. Despite the Protestant doctrine of the priesthood of all believers, the ideal godly minister was a skilled and learned expounder of the scriptures, distanced from most of his parishioners by intellectual training and moral discipline. He was emphatically not an easy-going participant in local social life. From the 1580s until the later 1630s most Stratford ministers seem to have approached this ideal, being zealous Protestant, even Puritan, preachers.[19] The Corporation collectively encouraged this, urging in a 1591 petition that the vicar, whose stipend was small, be freed from paying first fruits so that able and learned ministers were not discouraged from taking the living.[20]

A godly preaching ministry was not an end in itself but part of the Puritan drive for a disciplined and purified society, a drive that had broad social and cultural implications. As has often been noted, in Shakespeare's Stratford there was increasingly suspicion of dramatic performances, as likely to provoke disorder but also as an inappropriate and corrupting means of conveying ideas. In the 1580s, promotion of plays was clearly compatible with advanced Protestantism. Stratford chamberlains paid players from the Earl of Leicester's company as well as players sponsored by the Earls of Worcester, Essex, Berkeley and Derby. There was nothing apparently incompatible about paying Cartwright to preach and paying actors in the same accounts.[21] In 1602, while the Puritan Daniel Baker was bailiff, a 10*s* fine was imposed on any member of the Corporation who allowed any plays or interludes to be performed on Corporation property.[22] In February 1612 this fine was raised to a prohibitive £10 in a more sweeping order: 'the inconvenience of plaies beinge verie seriouslie considered of with the unlawfullnes, and howe contrarie the sufferance of them is againste the orders hearetofore made, and againste the examples of other well governed Citties and Burrowes'.[23] This attempt to exclude players from the town, like other 'Puritan' initiatives, was controversial and it was not consistently adhered to. The chamberlains' accounts for 1618 record payments to 'a company that came with a shew to the town' and to 'a company of players'.[24] It was perhaps such laxity that prompted elements in the town to seek a more zealous minister, a move that was to spark off serious conflict in Stratford, as we shall see.

Stratford's local ecclesiastical court was a potent weapon in the hands of Puritan reformers, especially when the minister and leading members of the Corporation were working together. Stratford had a 'peculiar court' whereby ecclesiastical jurisdiction was exercised by the vicar independently of the Bishop of Worcester in two years out of three. It could be used as an energetic, collective instrument for reform, offering some of the advantages of a Presbyterian framework whereby a committee of laity and clergy supervised religious and moral behaviour in a parish. For much of the period between the 1580s and the 1630s, the Corporation seems to have been anxious to support the work of the court. The delivery of the register book to the new godly minister Richard Barton, along with a gift of £4, is recorded in the Corporation minutes for 1584.[25] There do not seem to be records surviving for Barton's incumbency, but from 1590 to 1608 and again, more fully, in the 1620s and 1630s, there is considerable evidence for the work of the court. Religious and secular authority in Stratford cooperated to enforce church attendance, Sabbath observance, and to punish drunkenness and sexual offences. In the 1590s, predictably, the greatest concern was with the profanation of the Sabbath Day. In 1590 Bramhall ordered the churchwardens with the help of the constable to check who was 'in any alehouses or innes or other suspected places in gaminge or typlinge, or otherwyse', during the time of divine service or sermon and to present the names of householders and offenders to the next court. They were also to 'diligentlye vew and see whatt persones doe use to bowle or playe att anye games att tymes aforesaid and to presente the same'.[26] In October 1592 thirty-seven people were accused of opening their shops on Sabbath and holy days. This can be compared with seven accusations of fornication or adultery, one presentment for receiving 'evill companye and suspected persones into his house' and one for a public rumour that he was 'a maker of slaunderous libells', something that was to become a very contentious issue fifteen years later.[27] Behaviour in church was also a concern as in the case of Joan Tawnte who admitted, 'going oute of the churche with beckininge with hir fynger and laughinge, also for sweringe by the name of God'. For such an offence she was allowed to acknowledge her fault before the congregation in 'hir accustomed clothine' whereas a pregnant stranger, Joan Dutton, had to perform public penance 'clad in a sheet'.[28]

For Stratford's Corporation as a collective body, zealous Protestantism had much to recommend it, for a variety of social, political, and cultural motives. In the 1590s Stratford's governors, as elsewhere in England, were dealing with the potential social disorder brought by poor harvests, disease and high mortality. In this troubled decade a strict social and religious discipline was attempted through the ecclesiastical court, and also through the orders of the Corporation itself. There was strict supervision of alehouses and heavy penalties for the harbouring of strangers. Tradesmen were to be sorted into companies and apprenticeships restricted.[29] At the same time the Corporation was much less concerned about the hoarding of scarce corn and malt by prosperous townswomen than were external authorities such as the Warwickshire Justices of the Privy Coucil.[30]

Furthermore, reformation was at the heart of Stratford's corporate and urban identity. It was only through the Protestant Reformation that the Corporation acquired a formal identity through the dissolution of the Guild and the transfer of many of its functions by charter to the aldermen and burgesses. An elevated notion of the religious responsibilities of the Council – promoting godly preaching and moral reformation – added status and purpose to a body whose authority was less secure and more contested than in larger cities. Stratford was a manor and a parish as well as a borough; overlapping jurisdictions and uncertain boundaries undermined the power of the Corporation. An annual sermon established by the will of Robert Perrot was arranged for the borough's perambulation day in Whitsun week. Although very zealous Protestants were sometimes suspicious of the ritualistic sociability of parochial perambulations, here a necessary demonstration of urban identity was reinforced by godly preaching.[31] The Corporation paid the vicar's salary, but the right to present to the living lay with the lord of the manor while the parish church itself was outside the town's boundaries. Though cooperating with the minister in the proceedings of his ecclesiastical court, Stratford aldermen could develop some influence in the whole parish of Stratford, including the 'rural' townships whose inhabitants had an uneasy relationship with the town.[32]

From the 1590s to the 1630s the Corporation's relationship with the lord of the manor was difficult, particularly when, as with Sir Edward Greville of Milcote in the 1590s or Lionel Cranfield, Earl of Middlesex, in the 1620s, a new lord sought to assert his authority over the town. The Corporation trod carefully with Greville at first, sending him their nominations for bailiff in 1593, 'nott doubtinge butt we shall finde as good dealinge from you as ever we did from the late Earle of Warw[ick]', but over the next ten years there were repeated struggles over the town's choice of bailiff and the rights to market tolls. In 1619 the Corporation managed to circumvent the lord of the manor's rights of presentation and in effect made their own choice of minister. In the ensuing quarrels between the Corporation and the vicar, Thomas Wilson, Middlesex was able to extend his influence in Stratford.[33] Ideally, however, active cooperation between lay and clerical reformers in the town reinforced urban as opposed to manorial authority.

But attempts to build a godly town were hindered by the fact that the collective urge towards reformation coexisted uneasily with many individual differences over religion. Furthermore religion was clearly an issue in many conflicts in the town whose origins may well have been personal or practical. Among the aldermen and burgesses themselves, disaffection provoked by religious change seems to have exacerbated personal tensions and to have reinforced the reluctance of some leading men to play a role in the Corporation. The case of George Badger has already been mentioned; Ralph Lord, a capital burgess, was also frequently at odds with the Corporation and in trouble with the ecclesiastical court. Between 1592 and 1608 he was presented in the latter for keeping his shop open on the Sabbath, 'for encouraging in his house in time of divine prayer and sermon time certain persons eating and drinking', for selling meat on Sunday in sermon time and for drinking on the Sabbath in prayer time.[34] Lord only took office as chamberlain of the borough in 1597 after being threatened with a fine; he was fined again for his refusal to become an alderman and for non-attendance in September 1600 and yet again three years later when he submitted reluctantly to the 'orders lately made' for the good government of the borough.[35]

Lord's strategy when in trouble at the vicar's court was to submit fairly quickly and quietly and pay his fine, but others were less cooperative. In 1595, when Elizabeth Wheeler, accused of brawling, abusing and not attending church, appeared, 'in the court itself she brawled', saying, 'Goodes woondes, a plague a God on you all, a fart of ons ars for you'.[36] This was not necessarily, of course, a clearly thought out rejection of ecclesiastical discipline, but it shows that ordinary men and women of Stratford were not always grateful or even passive recipients of reformation. By the early seventeenth century Stratford had experienced some twenty years of zealous Protestant preaching and teaching. There are, as Jeanne Jones has shown, signs of increasing literacy and book ownership, which may have made conscientious Puritanism an option for a broader element amongst the townspeople.[37] But if godliness increased, so it would appear did anti-Puritanism. A hostile stereotype of the Puritan, as a deceitful and hypocritical troublemaker, hiding all sorts of immorality, but especially sexual misbehaviour, behind a smooth godly veneer, was a powerful presence in late Elizabethan and early Stuart culture, seen in the plays of Shakespeare and Jonson, for example.[38] Anti-Puritanism was equally important in the life of small towns like Stratford, provoking and complicating conflicts both intimate and generalized. It was very likely a motive for some of the accusations of immorality levied against the apparently respectable such as the notorious accusation made in 1613 by John Lane, a local gentleman with Catholic connections, that Shakespeare's daughter Susanna, the wife of the godly Dr John Hall, had been intimate with Ralph Smith.[39] One of the most prominent Puritans in the town, Daniel Baker, was presented in the local Stratford court for incontinence with Anne Ward in 1606. She claimed that he was the father of her unborn child; he denied the charge but admitted that a 'fame' or rumour to that effect was circulating in Stratford.[40]

But it was the choice of Thomas Wilson as vicar that unleashed years of pent-up resentment at Puritan attempts to impose their styles of divinity and morality on the townspeople and parishioners of Stratford. In 1619 elements on the Corporation took advantage of the unwise acceptance of an additional living by John Rogers and obtained a declaration that the Stratford living was vacant. Patronage thereby lapsed in theory to the Crown but the new vicar, a godly learned minister from nearby Evesham, Thomas Wilson, was clearly chosen by Stratford men who had managed to bypass the lord of the manor's rights of presentation.[41] On 31 May, when Wilson took possession of the living, he was riotously opposed by a group of craftsmen, yeomen and local gentlemen including John Lane, armed with swords and stones. According to testimony later given in Star Chamber, Wilson was attacked because the 'confederates . . . understood that if he should be their vicar there, he would by his sermons reprove their great vices and disorders'. The new vicar's character was defamed with 'vaunting and boasting speeches . . . that the said

Thomas Wilson was an ill-liver, and incontinent person, that he had the French pox, and was burnt by means of his incontinency with lewd women'. Wilson and his allies locked themselves in the church for their own safety but were 'in a very dreadfull manner, astonished, affrighted and amazed' as walls were damaged and windows smashed.[42]

Wilson retaliated by presenting John Lane and other opponents in his church court, but the 'confederates' in their turn adopted a common tactic of anti-Puritan campaigners, the circulation of derisory libels.[43] 'Several false, scandalous, infamous and wicked libels in rhymes, verses and prose . . . maliciously and slanderously defaming and disparaging' the minister and his allies in the Corporation were spread throughout Warwickshire especially in taverns and alehouses. As in similar clashes elsewhere, Puritans were denounced as sowers of division and disorder, hypocrites whose zealous prying hid their own covetousness and immorality.

> These men seeme of a puer faction,
> But like the devill in dissemblacon,
> As smooth as oyle outward, in words,
> But within they are full of dissension and discords.

They were 'deepe, dissemblinge hypocrites/That in good workes have no delite'; an attitude attributed to their adherence to the predestinarian ideas of Calvinists like the Cambridge theologian William Perkins: 'One of the chiefest hath red far in Perkins' workes.'

Specific accusations were made against Wilson's allies, the lawyer Thomas Lucas along with William Smith, Henry Smith, Richard Castle and Daniel Baker from the Corporation. A prose libel highlighted the confederates' support for a lively festive culture against Puritan discipline. Directed to 'any honest Puritan where yow finde him,' it came from 'Romanye, this merry moneth of Maye' and claimed the vicar and his friends, 'have sett all the towne together by the eares, which is the true office of a Puritant'. Indeed, conflicts over traditional festivities were tangled up with Wilson's intrusion into the town in May. For opponents of Wilson, communal festivities symbolized the nostalgic social unity they believed was threatened by Puritanism. John Nash, another gentleman supporter of Rogers, erected a maypole near the site of the horse fair; this remained in place until the eve of the autumn fair. When Bailiff John Woolmer and Alderman Henry Smith removed it, Nash and his supporters staged another riot and put it back again.

The outcome of these interconnected disputes is unclear and for much of the 1620s, Wilson, in cooperation with the majority of the Corporation, led an energetic campaign of religious and moral reformation. The minister was paid £40 a year and then £60, rather than the £20 established by charter, significant sums of money were repeatedly levied for the repair of the parish church, a weekday lecture was regularly preached in the Guild Chapel, which was again refurbished and, most notably, the peculiar court operated systematically to reform backsliders among the population.[44] Between 1619 and 1624, for which there are extensive surviving records, churchwardens presented some eight to ten offenders at approximately six-weekly intervals. Wilson conducted a systematic visitation in the spring of 'his' years and there were usually more cases before the court in the weeks immediately afterwards. The busiest period of all was in May 1622 when the court considered forty-seven cases. Five of these concerned procedural issues or outstanding fees, six dealt with excommunicated persons, probably recusants, and a further accusation was made against someone who had associated with an excommunicated person. Six people were presented for not coming to church or receiving the sacrament, seven for profaning the Sabbath (two had gone fishing, one had been playing ball). Four people had refused to be catechized; there were two common swearers and one man accused of 'scandalous speeches and slaundering'. Two men were presented for brawling in church; they were let off lightly when they explained they were chastizing young boys whose noise drowned out the preacher's words. Eight people stood accused of a range of sexual offences, while another glimpse of the festive culture that challenged Puritan discipline is revealed in the prosecution of five men 'for dauncing the morris in evening prayer tyme on the feast day of Phillip and Jacob'.[45] A similar mixture of sexual, religious and disorderly offences is found throughout the 1620s. The churchwardens who made the presentments were often leading members of the Corporation and offenders performed penance before the bailiff and aldermen as well as in church, in a very visible blending of secular and religious authority.[46]

In the 1620s the Corporation regarded the peculiar court as an 'ancient privilege', part of 'our liberties' and spent considerable time and money on defending Wilson when his energetic use of ecclesiastical jurisdiction brought him into conflict with the Bishop of Worcester.[47] One recalcitrant burgess was expelled from the Corporation for not accepting the jurisdiction of the peculiar court. As the Council minutes declared in September 1625:

> At this hall the company, taking into consideration, that Christopher Smith hath much wronged this company and disgraced them, not only by his heinous offence in committing adultery but also in that he hath refused to be censured by the judge of our peculiar jurisdiction appealinge to the court of Worcester, thereby weakening our liberties of this borough, as we conceive it, contrary to his duty.

Here it is not clear whether it was the adultery (involving presentations in three successive months with three different women) or the appeal to a rival jurisdiction that most annoyed his fellow burgesses.[48]

Within a decade of Wilson's arrival in the town, however, his alliance with leading lay figures had broken down. This does not seem to be because Wilson or his former allies such as Daniel Baker, Richard Castle or Henry Smith had changed their religious views or had become somehow less Puritan. Rather the troubles of the 1630s in Stratford reveal further religious fragmentation arising from the complexities within Puritanism itself. Zealous Protestantism or Puritanism might have different implications for different people – particular tensions might arise between laity and clergy. As we saw in the survey of the 1580s, Puritans had an elevated notion of the functions and character of the ministry, condemning the simple, the dumb and the 'good-fellows'. But Puritanism also stimulated lay activism and stressed the importance of godly magistracy in reforming society. Throughout their bitter disputes with Wilson the leaders of the Corporation remained committed in theory to godly ministry, if no longer enamoured of their individual minister. When Wilson ceased preaching the Wednesday lecture in 1629 and caused 'suits and troubles' for the company, they appointed the Oxfordshire Puritan Robert Harris in his place. They were to try hard to obtain Harris as Wilson's replacement on the latter's death in 1638.[49] Within limits, too, the Corporation remained committed to godly reformation as we can see in the record of summary fines levied by Bailiff Anthony Smith during his year 1630–1. Smith punished forty-six swearers, thirty-one drunks, and twenty-four Sabbath breakers, compared with only ten offenders against weights and measures regulations.[50]

The origins of the quarrel between minister and Corporation are unclear but they came to a head in 1633 when Wilson, tiring of inconsistency over the payment of additions to his stipend, brought a Chancery case against the Corporation for a salary of at least £60 a year as of right. Associated with Wilson in this case was the physician John Hall, who had been at odds with the Corporation for many years, two educated professional men against the tradesmen of the council.[51] Wilson's argument by the end of the case was that, as in 1553, the minister and his assistant, the schoolmaster and the almspeople had received almost all the Corporation's revenue from the tithes of the former collegiate church, so they should in the 1630s receive the bulk of the much increased revenue. Tithes were the 'dower of the Church' and to spend them on the Corporation's 'vaine affectations' of feastings and excessive numbers of offices was intolerable.[52] Of course, if this argument was accepted Stratford's whole existence as a Corporation would be untenable. In any case, precisely because it was, as Wilson jeered, 'soe small a corporation', a certain level of pomp and ceremony was all the more important: aldermen and burgesses were required to wear fine gowns, they were attended with fine maces, and they sponsored regular feasting of local gentry.[53] In retaliation, Henry Smith, a prominent and particularly alienated alderman, denounced Wilson for nonconformity in the High Commission; more generally, the Corporation that had defended Wilson against the bishop's accusations of nonconformity in the 1620s and early 1630s, now queued up to denounce him.[54]

Most of the Corporation had supported Wilson in the reforming drives of the 1620s. There were, as we have seen, many advantages in having a conscientious minister who would discipline mostly poorer townspeople along with the occasional notorious deviant amongst the borough élite like Christopher Smith. The Wilson of the 1630s, however, was a rather different matter. He appeared to many former allies as arrogant and quarrelsome, and he was seeking an independent role for the ministry. Along with his attempt to obtain financial independence for the ministry it is clear he was also claiming the right to denounce any behaviour of which he disapproved. During the metropolitical visitation of 1635 conducted for Archbishop Laud, Wilson was accused of 'grossly particularing in his sermons' while the Corporation's witnesses in the Chancery case were asked 'in what manner the said Mr Wilson from time to time abused and disgraced the magistrates of the said borough in his sermons and otherwise by particularizing and taxing them unjustly'.[55] Henry Smith was perhaps singled out. He complained in High Commission that he had been 'scandalized' by Wilson while it was alleged at the 1635 visitation that the vicar 'refused to give waye to Mr Trapp his assistant minister to preach the funerall sermon of Mrs Smyth, late wyfe of Mr Henry Smyth an Alderman . . . but sate himself on the pulpitt stayres and forbad Mr Trapp to preach'.[56] While Wilson denounced the élite from the pulpit it seems that he may in other ways have taken a narrower view of reformation by the later 1620s. Prosecutions in the peculiar court increasingly focused on failure to pay church dues or on misbehaviour in church rather than on broader social offences.[57]

The majority of the Corporation opposed the vicar in the 1630s but he kept some allies, notably Alderman William Smith, haberdasher, a 1619 supporter of the vicar who, unusually, remained loyal, and chief burgess John Eston. From 1632 to 1636 Corporation business was disrupted by quarrels among the members, where attitudes to Wilson were a crucial issue. One arena for undignified brawling was the parish church where disputes over seating reflected arguments about status in the town. When Richard Castle was preferred to Smith as bailiff in 1632/3 there were scuffles in church as Smith tried to maintain his place above Castle in the Corporation's pew. To add insult to injury, Smith appealed to Wilson for support, stressing that the parish church was beyond the borough limits and so subject to parochial not urban authority.[58] Eston had been expelled from the Corporation in December 1634 because of his support for Wilson but he was still using the burgesses' pew in January 1635. When his former brethren tried to eject him his response was a vigorous, 'Who will keep me forth?'.[59]

Puritanism has sometimes been described as a culture of discipline or as a means of enforcing order.[60] Perhaps for brief periods in the 1590s and early 1620s it worked as such in Stratford-upon-Avon. But zealous attempts at Puritan reform could as easily provoke disorder and conflict, sometimes on a small scale, as with the recidivist morris dancers of July 1622, or the resentment of adults who were subjected to catechizing like the man who shouted 'Shyte uppon the court' on his appearance in May 1624.[61] On occasions, as in the 1619 riots or the burgesses' brawling of 1633–4, the troubles could be more dramatic. In a small town like Stratford, beset by complex rival jurisdictions and uncertain boundaries, lay and clerical aspects of the Puritan impulse could fracture, causing yet more conflict. In these circumstances, and in a social atmosphere more tranquil than that of the 1590s, even former adherents of godly zeal might come to believe the risks outweighed the benefits. It is significant that Wilson's ultimate successor Henry Twitchett was expelled for royalism during the Civil War but managed to keep a Huntingdonshire living until the 1650s. He seems to have been a mainstream Protestant, but not Puritan, minister, ideal for a town that had tired of excessive godliness.[62]

In any case it seems that the impact of Puritan reformation was often temporary and limited. In 1628 and again in 1633 Augustine Boyce was presented by the churchwardens. On the first occasion he had purloined the communion wine, on the second he was accused of 'tipplinge and suffering the bell ringers to tiple and drink at the communion table in the chancel and for slobbering and fowling the same'.[63] Yet Boyce was employed by the parish to take care of the church fabric and to supervise the behaviour of the scholars in service time. With such a failure close to home, it is no wonder that the broader project of building a godly town foundered.[64]

CHAPTER 8

Stratford-upon-Avon in the Civil War

PHILIP TENNANT

In the preceding essays increasing emphasis has been placed on the tensions and crises which beset Stratford's small but quarrelsome community in Tudor and Stuart times. In 1646 Stratford was emerging from arguably the most stressful period of all in its long history, that of the central, most intense phase of the English Civil War. That the stresses, this time, were not peculiar to Stratford but were shared by countless other communities made them no less real or painful. In this essay we consider the nature and scale of the burdens suffered by the town during the unprecedented drama of 1642–6 and try to assess, as far as the evidence permits, how its people had been affected by events over which they had little or no control.[1]

By October 1646 peace was slowly spreading across the country as people everywhere breathed a collective sigh of relief that the soldiers were at long last gone, or, to be more precise, going. Locally as nationally, the war was in effect over. The Royalists at Banbury had finally surrendered after many desperate weeks of siege, Parliamentary soldiers were vacating requisitioned mansions like Compton Wynyates, the last battle had been fought, at Stow-on-the-Wold, and the two last remaining loyal cities, Oxford and Worcester, had capitulated to the New Model Army. The King himself had surrendered, and the victorious Parliamentary army was under orders to disband, apart from small garrisons to be kept at Warwick and Coventry. Those leading citizens who had thought it best to evacuate themselves from Stratford during the war were drifting back, among them the austere schoolmaster John Trapp from his lodging under the castle walls in Warwick. Plans were afoot to patch up the town bridge, wrecked only the previous year, pending proper repairs at some later date. How had Stratford fared over the last four or five years?

It is now recognized that, quite apart from the actual battles which have been given perhaps undue prominence in the past, the Civil War caused substantial destruction to property, heavy loss of life and material and acute personal suffering in hundreds of towns and villages throughout the country. The more sensational aspects of the war, however – death, devastation and horror – were not, on the whole, Stratford's own experience. In retrospect, with that most valuable quality historians possess, hindsight, its citizens had much to be thankful for. After four long years of conflict which had ebbed and flowed across Warwickshire, Stratford remained physically intact. There had been no further outbreak of fire since 1641, civic government had not been seriously interfered with, as it had at Worcester, new Corporation officials had just been sworn in, and a new vicar was on the way. The taverns were as thriving as ever, last year's outbreak of plague had mercifully not returned, and the recent horse-fair – one indicator of economic prosperity – had, perhaps surprisingly, been exceptionally profitable. Those among the town's citizens who travelled abroad must have been aware that Stratford had been fortunate. It had not seen the wholesale devastation that Banbury had experienced, been damaged by the building of defence fortifications, as Warwick had, seen street barricades erected, as Alcester had, never suffered the indignity of martial law under a permanent garrison, as Banbury and Warwick had. Admittedly, the vicar had disappeared and regular Bible lectures been suspended, but the people had not been spiritually starved, since the curate had proved an excellent substitute, regularly preaching and reading from the pulpit and having been warmly thanked for doing so. Unlike so many others, the church had not been damaged or desecrated. There had been anger and unpleasantness, but that was nothing new, and at least there had been no public pillory punishment, as at Warwick, or public hanging, as at Banbury. Above all, the town had been spared the full-scale sieges of both Banbury and Worcester. Things might so easily have turned ugly on a number of occasions, but one is forced to recognize an apparent paradox: that although the Midlands was almost unique among the English regions in the sheer volume of military traffic it endured, Stratford, at its very heart, survived relatively unscathed, with its physical environment virtually unchanged since Tudor times.[2]

Reasons for this may be found in a combination of historical accidents. In the first place, Stratford was military indefensible, situated in a wide plain open to the fields on all sides, surrounded by low hills useful to any attacker and with no ancient walls or fortress to protect it. One Parliamentarian report did in fact accuse the Royalists of dragooning inhabitants into constructing defences, but, significantly, not one citizen mentioned this in his list of grievances submitted after the war. It was also a valuable regional market, and although many markets did indeed suffer, attacking them was never official policy and both sides recognized increasingly that such action was simply counter-productive in further alienating the local community and impoverishing its economy. Stratford's very proximity to Warwick was also to its advantage since it was, in theory at least, firmly within its castle's protective orbit; Parliament had neither the resources nor indeed the need for another costly garrison in the district. Above all, however, Stratford's allegiance – insofar as it is possible to pin down a communal loyalty anywhere and accepting that it was certainly divided here – was if anything probably largely Parliamentarian.[3] In spite of strong local pockets of Catholicism and, as war came, a Royalist bailiff, John Woolmer, the town had a long and active Puritan tradition, and early in the war any potential Royalist faction must have been seriously depleted when several conservative elders like Thomas Dighton, Nathaniel Duppa and Thomas Hitchcock promptly fled, along with the new vicar, Henry Twitchett – an act which looks suspiciously like that of an apprehensive minority. This left effectively in control the curate William Hawling, the radical schoolmaster John Trapp, the town's two wealthiest residents Thomas Nash and Lord Brooke's deputy as lord lieutenant, William Combe, and various merchants like John Brooks – all staunch Puritans – in alliance with Stratford's recorder and, as it were, spiritual guide, Lord Brooke himself. In this context the report of a Stratford contingent of volunteers enlisting at Warwick in late July, the gift of a generous £100 voted by the Corporation to Lord Brooke on 29 August 1642 and the names of several residents recorded by the chamberlain as enlisting in Parliamentary armies rather than the Royalists' all look significant.[4] Also suggestive is the fact that the Puritan curate remained on

Plate 24. John Trapp, aged fifty-three, headmaster of Stratford's grammer school from 1624 to 1651, and a leading Protestant figure in the town; from an engraving of 1654.

excellent terms with the Corporation throughout the war, the only slight friction being caused by his evident reluctance to leave his post when a new vicar was eventually appointed.[5] At the beginning of the war the influx of high-ranking Parliamentary officers lodging at Thomas Nash's New Place, surely by prior arrangement, must have been intimidating to any potential Royalists,[6] while soon after, the armed force from Warwick which collected the town's weapons, followed by Lord Brooke's own rout of demoralized Royalists outside the town in February 1643, must have seemed the last straw to them.[7] With all this, Brooke could reasonably conclude that Stratford posed no serious threat. Once he was killed, at Lichfield, John Bridges, his trusty governor at Warwick Castle, through his intimacy with Nash and Combe (who as members of the Parliamentary county committee were frequently at Warwick) was able to keep Stratford under surveillance: his 'watchfulnesse [there] is much to be commended', one Parliamentary supporter enthused.[8] As long as Stratford dutifully paid its 'contributions' to maintain the garrison at Warwick, the town was left alone by the authorities – if not by the soldiers.

If, then, a combination of such factors ensured that Stratford was outwardly less affected by the war than other Midland towns, can it be concluded that the war passed it by? That indeed seems to be the traditional assumption judging from the sparseness of references to it in the standard histories.[9] Such an assumption would certainly have astonished a contemporary who had spent the war in Stratford and chronicled events. Converted into modern tabloid-speak, his news headlines might have read as follows: 'King Declares War – Royal Cannons Blast Warwick and Coventry'; 'Late Playwright's Home Becomes Army High Command Planning Major Offensive'; 'Church Bells Warn of Soldiers Ransack Mission – Widespread Theft'; 'Leading Catholics Targeted in Witch Hunt'; 'King's Men Flee as Lord Brooke Routs Royalists Outside Town'; 'Vicar and Councillors Missing – New Town Hall Wrecked in Brooke Assassination Attempt'; 'Prince Rupert in Town Preparing Northern Offensive'; 'Royal Visit – Queen Feted at Public Banquet as King Expected – Schoolmaster Disappears'; 'Historic Milcote Mansion Gutted by Army Arson'; 'Benefactor's Bridge Sabotaged to Prevent Royal Counter-Offensive'; 'Acting Minister Refuses to Quit Vicarage – Corporation Emergency Session Debates Cash Inducement'.

Allowance made for journalistic hyperbole, such news items, each broadly substantiated by reliable contemporary evidence, suggest not some rural backwater oblivious to national events but a community fully implicated in them and for whom they remained unforgettable. Long after, Stratford's citizens dated their recollections from 'the same day yt Kineton fight was', 'the morning the towne hall was blowne up', 'when they disarmed the towne', 'when Lord Brooke was in towne and drove away ye Kings force', or 'when Sir Tho. Fearfaxe past by'. If these dramatic events are not further developed here it is for reasons of space and because they are described in some detail elsewhere.[10] But there is a further reason: memorable though such events were, they scarcely do justice to Stratford's experience of the war, which was at once more, and less, than a series of disconnected highlights. The English Civil War cannot be equated with sensational headlines or even periodic fighting, any more than the Second World War can be reduced to the Blitz, Monty at Alamein, Stalingrad and D-Day. What happened at Stratford as elsewhere and what the war 'meant' to everyone, was a less conspicuous and more humdrum, demoralizing, bleak and above all more continuous process which disrupted daily life at every level. The full impact of the war came essentially in the form of two burdens from which there was literally no escape day or night: permanent fiscal and military oppression – exorbitant taxation which ate at the people's very livelihood and the almost continuous military harassment to which everyone was subjected. Before considering briefly each in turn, however, it is important to remember Stratford's recent social and economic profile.

The war which finally came alight in the summer of 1642 hit not a well-balanced, prosperous and harmonious community but one already deeply divided, strained almost to breaking point not only by the protracted religious feuds analysed by Ann Hughes but by severe economic and social pressures of the kind detailed by Alan Dyer: inflation outstripping wages throughout the pre-war period, steeply rising food prices, and deep unease over unsustainable population growth since at least the 1560s. By 1590 Stratford was a town 'fallen into much decay' and facing the problem of 'maynteyninge a number of poor people', specified ten years later as 700, or virtually one-third of its population. Housed in shoddy, hastily-erected thatched 'poore Tenements and Cottages . . . very many lately erected', the near-destitute remained there up to and throughout the war years: in 1614 and again in 1649 came other official warnings that 'the number of extreme poor people is so great that the rest are not able to relieve them'. Even among 800 Stratford residents respectable and affluent enough to leave wills and inventoried goods between 1570 and 1630, over thirty ended their days in the almshouse. Successive natural disasters like bad harvests, fires and plague had taken an additional toll, and by 1640, before yet another fire which caused an estimated £20,000 worth of damage, a local farmer could complain that 'the times are so ill and things so unsettled that I cannot sell any land except for an extreme under value'.[11] Even more alarming were hints of social unrest: ugly scenes near Stratford in the summer of 1640 over army recruiting involving fatalities among some 500 soldiers and civilians, a disturbance serious enough to provoke a royal rebuke, national hysteria over the Irish crisis of 1641 and a local offshoot, a supposed papist plot implicating Old Stratford's bankrupt lord, Sir Charles Smith. Reactions included the doubling of the night watch throughout the county, the distribution of ammunition among Stratford's leading residents, the replenishment of the town's stock of gunpowder, the refurbishment of weapons and repairs to 'the Armer howse'. Like a comet, the Civil War cast a long, ominous shadow before it.[12]

As events escalated, mansions were being fortified, more rioting was reported, recruitment was beginning in earnest and military rallies were being held in towns across the country and on nearby gentry estates. At Stratford itself, on 30 June, Lord Brooke, after making fiery speeches, laid on lavish entertainment in the taverns to conclude a day of musters. A month later, hundreds of aspiring Royalists were seen parading 'in a warlike posture in a meadow beyond Stratford', as one observer put it.[13] But the prevailing civilian mood was not eager militarism or even crusading idealism but bewilderment, dismay and open fear of complete social breakdown. In a rainy July local brickmakers were exploiting the situation by being obstructive, 'so loytring that they will worke noe longer than followed', while 'tenantts complaine they cannot sell any thinge to pay their rents'. People rushed into making inflammatory judgements: 'every one as his fancy leads him takes upon him with open invectives to censure his Majestie or Parliament'. Apprehension was the keynote in letters between friends: 'here in Warwicke Shire wee are like to fall into great calamities', wrote Thomas Johnson from Sambourne, near Alcester, on 4 August, 'here is nothing but providing of armes . . . I am afraid wee shall have a wofull time of it'.[14] By September soldiers were everywhere, often indistinguishable from common thieves and causing consternation to Robert Fawdon, a local estate manager across the river at Milcote: 'heere the times are verie dangerous, for this cuntrie is full of scattered troupes which doe pillage in manie places, as also of vagrant persons which waite for mischeife, soe that we are full of feares'. Among those anxious to save their skins was the crafty William Combe, who advised Puritan colleagues against provocative measures 'least the Kinge should take them for Enymyes'.[15] It is, then, against such a background of fear, despondency and economic hardship that the two major burdens of the war for ordinary people, already mentioned, must now be considered.

If it is true that it was ultimately lack of money which cost the King victory because of the greater efficiency of Parliament's tax machinery eventually set up in 1643, Stratford was peculiarly unfortunate.[16] Not only was it situated at the heart of a county considered by Parliament as a relatively rich one and therefore taxed accordingly at a punitive rate which the county bitterly resented,[17] but the town's proximity to Warwick and Coventry meant that, unlike more far-flung parishes, tax evasion was not an option: the area was dominated by Puritan zealots, like William Purefoy and John Barker at Coventry and Lord Brooke's protégés John Bridges and Joseph Hawksworth at Warwick who evidently kept the collection machine well oiled. Whereas local Royalists were forced to rely on raiding, intercepting convoys, highway theft and irregular collection on supposedly friendly territory whenever enemy forces were temporarily engaged elsewhere, Parliament would have at its disposal from February 1643 a formidable and largely efficient collection system. Military taxation was in fact nothing new; it had already been a sore point when it escalated before the war, and Stratford had quibbled over paying both Ship Money and Coat and Conduct Money.[18] This controversy was immediately followed by new tax impositions in 1641 to pay for the unpopular Scottish war and, more generously received, charity demands to help Protestant refugees from Ireland. Stratford grudgingly paid the former, including £55 for a poll tax, much more willingly the latter – again a hint of the town's political alignment as being generally more Parliamentarian than Royalist.[19]

When the political climate darkened further during 1642, amid a widespread perception that a national emergency was at hand, the prevailing fear was of what a contemporary catch-phrase termed 'a world turned upside-down'. Like towns everywhere, Stratford was primarily concerned to avoid bloodshed; hence the anger, no doubt, expressed by some members of the Corporation early in June in accusing the vicar and bailiff of 'betrayal' in approving the billetting of soldiers in the town.[20] The townsfolk therefore dug deep into their pockets, at first willingly, soon under compulsion, to lend or give money, household plate and horses to the person most able to safeguard the neighbourhood from disorder; and that person – in his own estimation as well, probably, as that of a majority of Stratford's leading residents – was clearly Lord Brooke, acting, as the deliberately ambiguous phrases went, 'for King and Parliament' and 'for the safety of the county'. The names of those contributing, not to wage war but to keep the fragile peace, included therefore men who would shortly be supporting opposite sides: the new conservative vicar Henry Twitchett side by side with the rebel scholar John Trapp, the royalist bailiff John Woolmer (soon offering his home to the Earl of Northampton and Lord Dunsmore while they organized the Stratford Royalist rally) next to the staunch Puritan Thomas Nash (shortly to be proud host at New Place to the Parliamentary military high command on the eve of Edgehill) and so on. The Corporation sent money for Lord Brooke's military feasting in the town's taverns and voted him a further generous £100 in August. The result

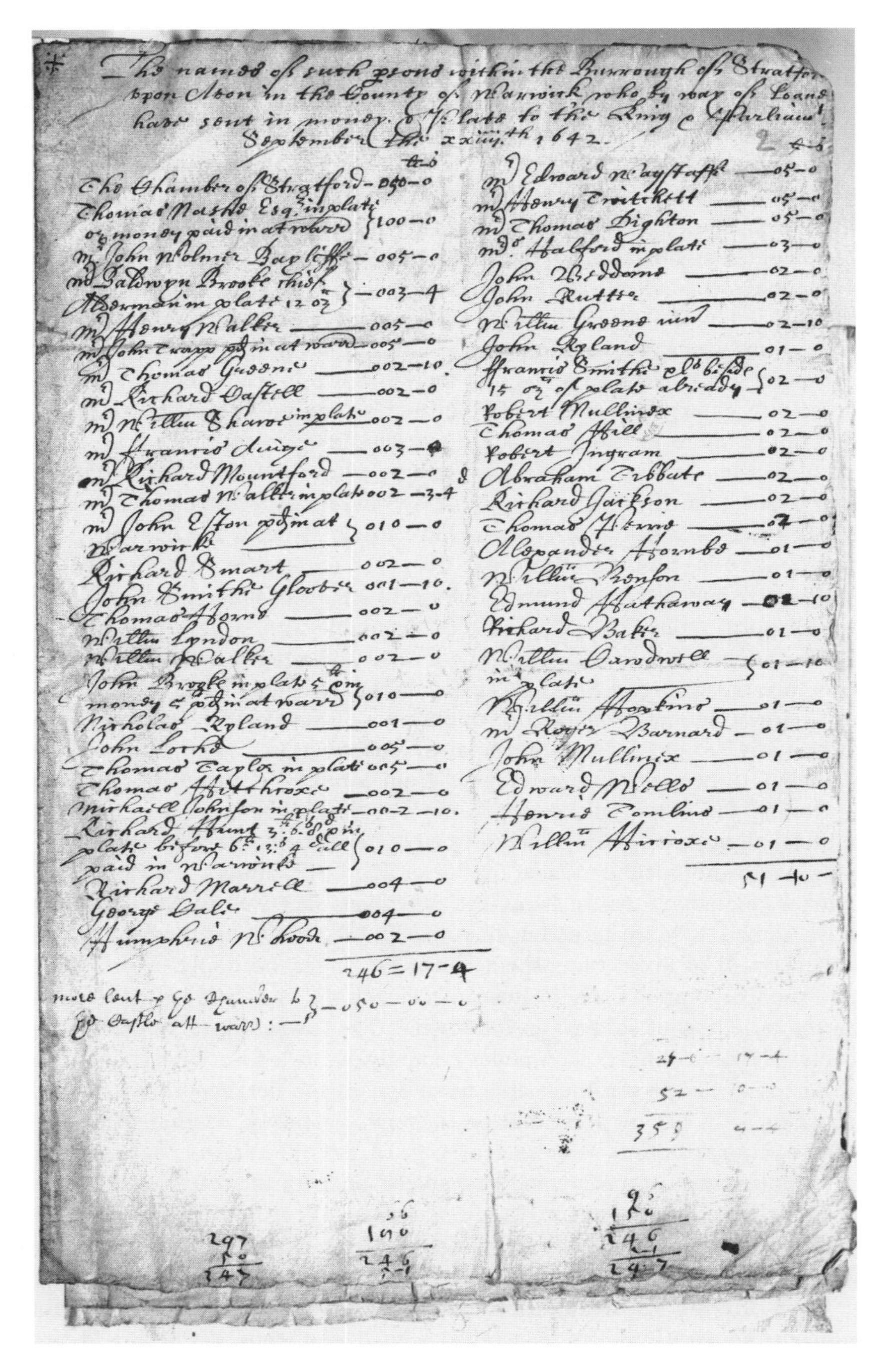

The names of such persons within the Burrough of Stratford upon Avon in the County of Warwick who by way of Loane have sent in money & plate to the King & Parliamt September the xxiiijth 1642.

The Chamber of Stratford	050–0
Thomas Nashe Esq. in plate or money paid in at Warwick	100–0
Mr John Woolmer Bayliffe	005–0
Mr Baldwyn Brooke this yr Alderman in plate 12 oz	003–4
Mr Henry Walker	005–0
Mr John Trapp pd in at warwick	005–0
Mr Thomas Greene	002–10
Mr Richard Castell	002–0
Mr Willm Sharpe in plate	002–0
Mr Francis Ange	003–4
Mr Richard Mountford	002–0
Mr Thomas Walker in plate	002–3–4
Mr John Elton pd in at Warwick	010–0
Richard Smart	002–0
John Smith Glover	001–10
Thomas Horne	002–0
Willm London	002–0
Willm Walker	002–0
John Brooke in plate & money & pd in at warwick	010–0
Nicholas Ryland	001–0
John Lorke	005–0
Thomas Taylor in plate	005–0
Thomas Holthroxe	002–0
Michaell Johnson in plate	002–10
Richard Hunt 3li 6s 8d in plate before 6li 13s 4d all paid in Warwick	010–0
Richard Marrell	004–0
George Hale	004–0
Humphrie Woode	002–0
	246=17–4
more lent p ye Aunciente ... at Warwick	050–00–0

Mr Edward Waystaffe	05–0
Mr Henry Crutchett	05–0
Mr Thomas Dighton	05–0
Mr Halford in plate	03–0
John Widdowes	02–0
John Rutter	02–0
Willm Greene iun	02–10
John Ryland	01–0
Francis Smith elder besides 15 oz of plate already	02–0
Robert Mullinex	02–0
Thomas Hill	02–0
Robert Ingram	02–0
Abraham Tibbats	02–0
Richard Jackson	02–0
Thomas Horne	02–0
Alexander Hornby	01–0
Willm Bonson	01–0
Edmund Hathaway	02–10
Richard Baker	01–0
Willm Cardwell in plate	01–10
Willm Hoskins	01–0
Mr Roger Barnard	01–0
John Mullinex	01–0
Edward Wells	01–0
Henrie Tomlins	01–0
Willm Hiccoxe	01–0
	51–10

Plate 25. Loans in money and plate by Stratford's leading burgesses in 1642, ostensibly 'to the King and Parliamt' but in fact to finance the Parliamentary army. The first two contributions are by far the largest: £50 from the Corporation and £100 from Thomas Nash. (SBTRO, BRU 15/17/2)

was that, in addition to the large sums already paid over the last two years, by 24 September 1642, a full month before Edgehill, Stratford had raised almost £400 which went (whether the donors intended this or not) directly into Parliament's war coffers at Warwick and Coventry. At this point, as Ronald Hutton has pointed out, 'local communities do not appear to have been dividing. On the contrary, they were closing ranks.'[21]

However, following the stalemate at Edgehill and failure of peace negotiations, both sides recognized that, as no quick solution was in sight, costly garrisons needed to be established and maintained, and that the voluntary contributions they had relied on so far were totally inadequate to sustain a lengthy conflict. Parliament led the way in establishing a national machinery to assess and collect large sums of money from every county and parish in the land according to estimated wealth, leaving local county committees to work out the proportion due from each parish and individual. As assessments were unprecedentedly high – ten or a dozen times pre-war levels – how to meet these bills and not fall into arrears and have goods confiscated for doing so was a permanent nightmare for countless small communities and individuals, without taking into account other heavy burdens to be discussed later. The Coventry authorities were strict but tried to be fair, and Stratford's initial assessment of £20 per week was by degrees drastically reduced to less than half that sum after what looks like special pleading by members of the Corporation who travelled to Warwick and Coventry on several occasions to see John Bridges and William Purefoy. Clearly it is impossible to quantify precisely the degree of hardship such taxes inflicted, since figures are incomplete and reflect inconsistent and hastily improvized accounting methods. At a time-remove of three and a half centuries the surviving figures are also virtually impossible to convert into meaningful modern equivalents anyway. But at the end of the war Stratford's tax bill for Parliament alone of £1,686 (adding £158 for pre-war military taxes to the £1,528 for maintaining the Warwick garrison over the thirty-three months to Janary 1646) and collected week by week by soldiers escorting constables in case of trouble, was a heavy one.[22] The successive reductions in the assessment look like significant recognition of Stratford's economic plight, particularly when coupled with the fact that arrears of Corporation rents doubled during the war and that after it, Warwickshire's Justices of the Peace handled nearly three times as many poor relief cases as pre-war.[23] As assessments were proportionate to estimated wealth the taxes hit everyone. The conspicuously affluent were particularly soft targets, especially if they were politically unreliable, like Stratford's lord, the elderly Earl of Middlesex, or actually Catholics, like Old Stratford's lord, the already bankrupt Sir Charles Smith. These would watch their estate revenues dwindle to a fraction of their pre-war value when impoverished tenants surrendered leases they could no longer afford, or have their lands actually confiscated. The losing struggle which Robert Fawdon, the Earl of Middlesex's loyal bailiff at Milcote, fought month by month to save his master from total ruin is well chronicled and at times moving. Collection could at times be ruthless: not content, for example, with wanton destruction of the great Milcote house in December 1644, the Coventry authorities continued to pour forth tax demands and threats of punishment as before to the shocked bailiff. In such cases sheer vindictiveness is suspected: where Stratford's own tax was more than halved, Milcote's was at one point doubled overnight without explanation.[24] Civilians were at the mercy of sometimes arbitrary rulings from local officers not sanctioned by the authorities. Residents with land outside town were naturally taxed on that too: John Bromley's in Old Stratford, Nicholas Atwood's at Tamworth, Francis Ainge's at Halford, William Shaw's at Clopton and Welcombe. Those with estates farther afield, over the county border, found themselves paying to several counties simultaneously: William Green and Thomas Nash, for example, to Gloucester as well as Coventry. Perhaps most graphic of all, again, was the case of the Earl of Middlesex. With estates straddling the Warwickshire-Gloucestershire border, his bailiff found himself not only paying taxes to both Gloucester and Coventry but harassed simultaneously by Royalist demands from their garrisons at Worcester and Chipping Campden. 'The demaunds on both sides . . . were never soe vyolent as now,' he reported despairingly in February 1645, 'and to add to those great Taxes everie high constable, by Authoritie from the Comaunders, rates those great somes as they please, and no remeddie, for the Soldier cares not who paies soe they may have it.'[25] After the war tales of hardship were common even among the normally comfortably off. The prominent Richard Tyler of Shottery, an almost permanent Corporation office-holder, was still owing Stratford £136 for tithes in May 1647, a sum amicably reduced by his colleagues on the Corporation after taking into account 'his great losses by reason of the badenesse of the tymes'. Even the wily and influential William Combe, emerging from the war on the supposedly winning side, could not escape unscathed, being reported by a relative as late as 1650 to be 'farr in debt, and all the land he hath about Stratford is sould or now upon sale'.[26]

The foregoing relates to taxation by the Parliamentary side only. How much Stratford's residents also contributed to the Royalist cause (and to what extent willingly or under compulsion) is altogether more obscure. In general Stratford escaped the scandal of double taxation about which other local communities bitterly complained. But the Earl of Northampton's Royalists, who certainly inflicted 'very great taxes for weekely Contribution' on nearby villages like Packwood and Tachbrook Mallory, were reported in January 1643 to be 'raysing money upon [Stratford] to the great impoverishment of the Inhabitants', and after the war the Corporation did acknowledge some Royalist taxation, eventually compensating fifteen or sixteen claimants over £40 as 'monys laid out in the middest of the wars'. Baldwin Brooks, for example, claimed he had paid almost as much in weekly tax to the Royalists (£9) as to the Parliamentarians (£13). As late as 1653–4 Stratford was still seeking large repayments from Coventry, though with what ultimate success is unknown.[27]

The main Parliamentary taxes soon brought other demands in their wake. These included regularly raising funds to buy horses and to equip local forces for a variety of initiatives like the assaults on Compton Wynyates and Banbury, to maintain an army in Ireland, to relieve maimed soldiers, to help fortify Warwick or Kenilworth, to meet occasional smaller levies by dictatorial commanders whenever they thought fit, like the extra £10 suddenly 'demanded by Colonel Purefoy' (in Stephen Edkins's words), and even to pay officers' wages. Particularly notorious was an excise duty 'for 2 yeares wanting a month', according to Thomas Scriven, payable on basic commodities like food and beer, enforceable by officers with powers to search cellars and storehouses. This tax, particularly resented, hit some twenty of Stratford's brewers and innkeepers and brought in at least a further £60, adding £7 more to Elizabeth Wheeler's bill and £6 each to Thomas Horne's and John Rutter's.[28] And not only the affluent were affected by the spiralling burden of this legalized robbery. The wealthy William Lindon in the High Street could doubtless spare his £33 share of Stratford's tax bill more than could Jane Norman,

Alexander Price, Robert Whittle and others their modest £1 – interesting confirmation of Stratford's huge gap between rich and poor.[29] But what of the abject poor, the silent many simply absent from the records? As the military regime at Warwick seized at least £60 of Stratford's tithes collected for charity purposes and the out-towns repeatedly refused to fulfill their obligations to contribute to Stratford's poor relief fund, their suffering may only be imagined. Cases like that of widow Isobel Briscoe of nearby Tanworth, left destitute when her charity pittance dried up in 1643, were all too common.[30] Finally, the heavy taxation continued at only a slightly reduced rate after the war, when what one historian has termed the 'fiscal oppression' of a 'Roundhead tyranny' fuelled anti-Parliament feeling under the Commonwealth, contributed to general unrest and ultimately helped bring about the Restoration.[31] Over this long period the burden of taxation is ultimately unquantifiable. The least that can be assumed is that the wealth of the community was significantly impoverished by the diversion of large sums of money away from the fragile local economy, and that money which would otherwise have been spent on trade, job creation, family comforts, charitable giving or, in the case of the near-destitute, on the barest essentials, went on maintaining soldiers whom everyone would have preferred to do without altogether. It is to the additional burden of the soldiers themselves that we now turn.

It may seem obvious to point out that the militarization of the district spelt trouble but the enormity of this additional burden on the people needs particular emphasis. The presence of soldiers was not limited to officially designated, clear-cut 'campaigns' ending in the odd battle in some suitably remote place after which they all dispersed. Soldiers were everywhere, for much of the time, a permanent nuisance, uniformly unpopular yet impossible to ignore. Since there were no barracks to confine them to, they roamed freely, all the more so because their garrisons were cramped, disease-ridden and foodless, and their commanders' policy, understandably, was to dispatch them to live off the land, scavenge and bring back the spoils. The lucky frequently found luxury accommodation for a time in the great houses of the neighbourhood, like Milcote, Coughton, Baddesley Clinton, were in no hurry to leave, and could not, of course, be easily recalled to base. The sheer volume of military traffic across the Midlands during 1642–6 has never been recognized in its two major aspects: the transits of the field armies, or portions of them assigned to specific missions (see Fig. 17); and the simultaneous presence of numerous garrisons, both temporary and permanent (see Fig. 18). On Fig. 17 each arrow represents the passage of usually large numbers of men, including those accompanying the King and Queen; in the country as a whole some 60,000 to 80,000 men were constantly on the move. There were, therefore, about four or five marches across Warwickshire for each year of the war, many passing through or near Stratford. Even then the picture is incomplete, since to avoid confusion the number shown has been limited to twenty, and return routes are not shown either (some units retraced their steps barely weeks later, sometimes meeting colleagues or enemy forces coming from the opposite direction). The limitations of arrows as a representational device are also misleading in giving the impression of a neat and direct progress across the country which is far from the case. On march no. 3, from Worcester east to Edgehill, for example, while the commander Essex was himself passing through Stratford, some of his units quartered in Studley while others were busy stealing in Ilmington, fifteen miles to the south. It was these loiterers who caused particular trouble, 'souldiers as lye stragling behynde the troupes who putt us in

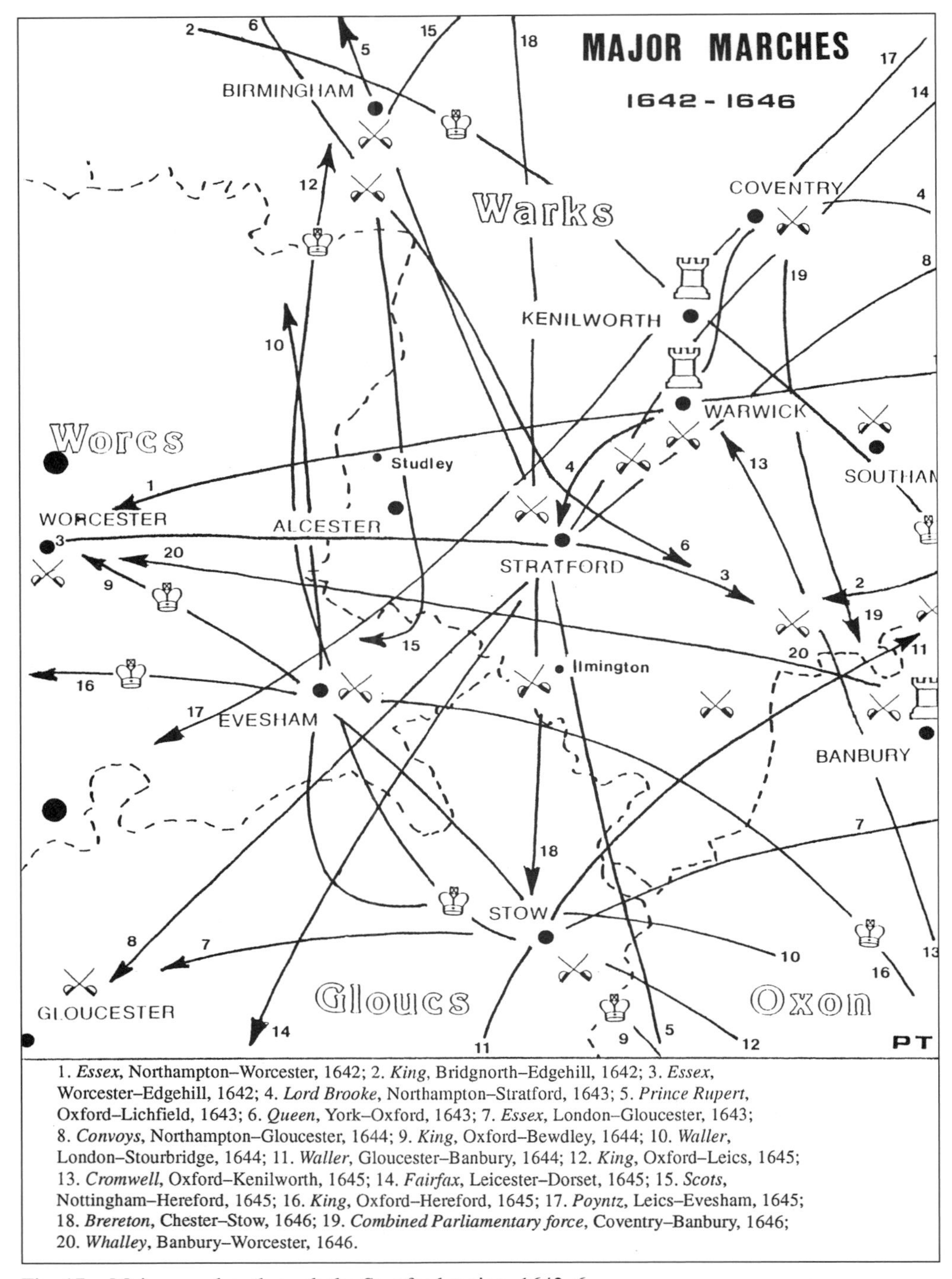

Fig. 17. Major marches through the Stratford region, 1642–6.

great frightes, soe that wee are contynuallie in feare of the losse of our goods & lives', as the Milcote bailiff explained. No one, of course, knew that he was marching to Edgehill, or even if or when a battle would eventually take place, and, as is well known, some Parliamentarian units failed to arrive on the actual day of battle. Other defensive units were deliberately left behind to their own devices in Stratford, so also missed the encounter near Kineton.[32]

Again, armies were usually accompanied by numbers of women too; how many is not known, since neither side wished to publicize this, but the presence of camp followers is well attested on a number of occasions. If the Royalists are to be believed (though their figures were doubtless wildly inflated for propaganda purposes), 3,000 women and children trailed through Birmingham on their way towards Stratford following the Scots in July 1645 (Fig. 17, march no. 15).[33] There are few reliable reports of women from the Stratford district, but a prostitute had the temerity to follow the psalm-singing Parliamentarians into Coventry on their way to Stratford, an 'Irish-Whoore furnished with a strong-water bottle' enlivened Prince Rupert's ragged company in Shipston-on-Stour before arriving next day in Stratford. Thomas Toone reported lodging 'a Dutch man and woman' in his home in Wasperton, a Warwick blacksmith lodged a wounded Cavalier, his wife and two sisters for a time and, pointedly, Parliament issued a stern warning against would-be feminine infiltrators into the army that 'no woman presume to Counterfeite her sex by wearing mans apparell under payne of the Severest punishment'.[34] As for the sick and wounded, a nearby battle like Edgehill or the two sieges of Banbury increased the burden: some are reported being cared for in Stratford homes, often for long periods – fifteen weeks at John Hunt's, twenty at Richard Morrell's – some dying in the town for whom shrouds were purchased before being buried, presumably (the burial register is missing for the war years) in Stratford churchyard. A few repaid their host's care by not paying for nursing board and lodging when they were well enough to leave. The clear-cut arrows beloved of military historians give no hint of such repercussions across the country in terms of care, anguish, provision of shelter and food, not to mention the widespread harassment, damage and theft which accompanied the soldiers everywhere.[35]

The militarization of the district is further confirmed by adding the details shown on Fig. 18, indicating the widespread presence of garrisons. The more of these there were, the more civilian life would be disrupted and the more the people would feel they were living under martial law. Garrisons were supposed to protect the area from the enemy by consolidating territory but the immediate practical purpose was more aggressive: to raid enemy quarters, locate (and suitably punish) potential civilian enemies and intercept useful cargoes venturing on the roads. Above all, they would ensure the collection of the vital taxes already discussed. All of these functions were clearly open to abuse, and the parish records everywhere are full of examples of kidnapping for ransom, extortion by threats, attacks on property and, above all, constant theft – though actual physical brutality is rare in the Stratford district. Whenever necessary, garrison soldiers would also escort military cargoes, supplement passing regiments, assist friendly forces outside the county and contribute to major local initiatives like the seizure of Compton Wynyates, the sieges at Banbury, or indeed Lord Brooke's rout of the Stratford Royalists in February 1643. Stratford's parish accounts are full of details of such events.

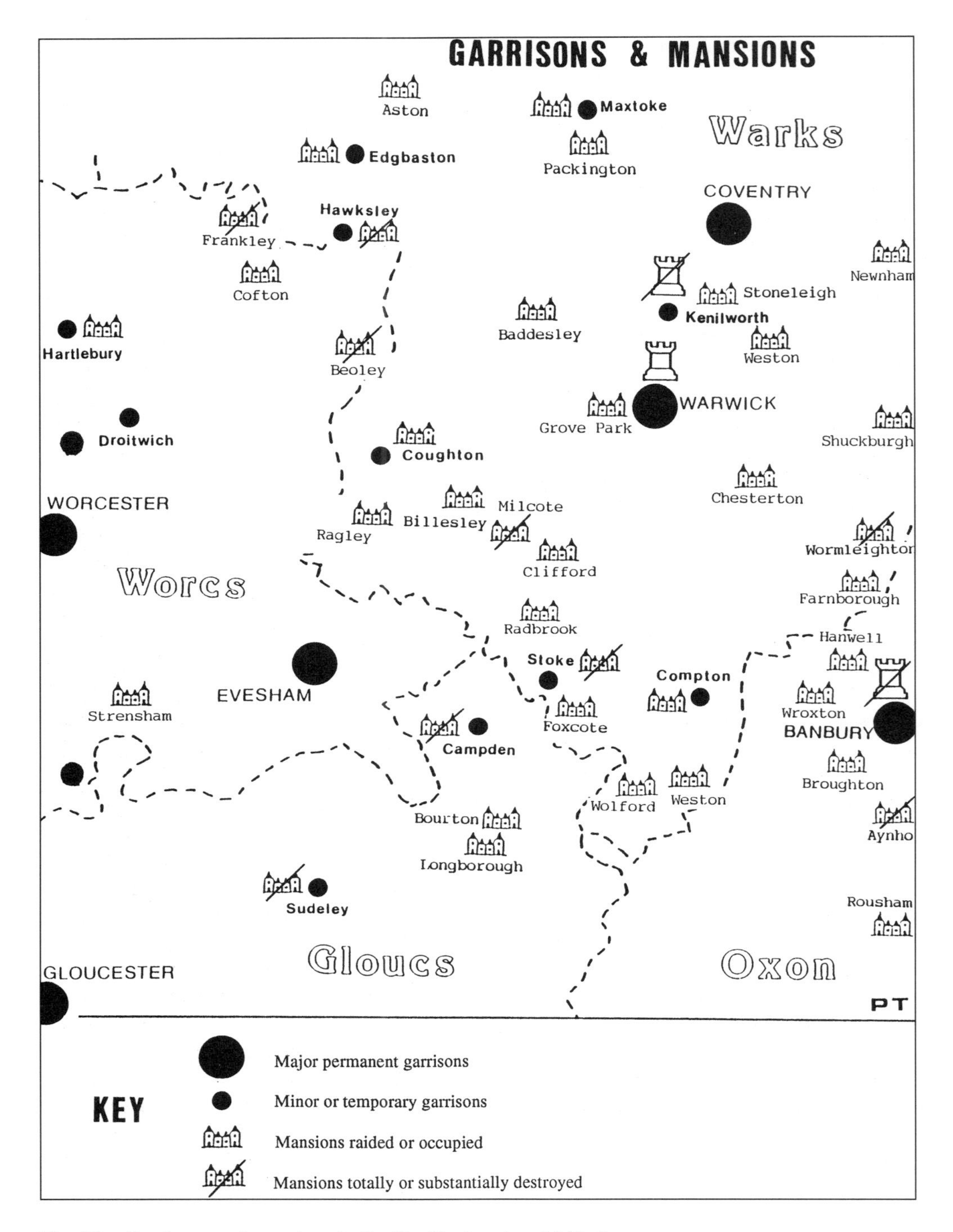

Fig. 18. Garrisons and mansions in the Stratford region, 1642–6.

The presence of large numbers of scavenging soldiers in and around Stratford for much of the war is not, therefore, in doubt, as is evident if Figs 17 and 18 are superimposed. On several occasions (before Edgehill, during the passage of the convoys to Gloucester, on the Queen's visit, before and after Naseby) one can go further and claim that the district was saturated with soldiers: in 1642, 'My Lord of Essex is heare with great forces'; in 1643, 'all the Towns about us [are] full of soldiers'; in 1644, 'there is about 1,000 horse and dragoones now at Stratford-upon-Avon'; in 1645, 'this great Armie part whereof is every day amongst us' or, in a soldier's own pointed comment, 'I feare the way is something dangerous from Warwick to Glocester'.[36] Many small communities were therefore regularly dwarfed by the huge influx of men and horses, straining meagre resources to the limits as all available accommodation was seized on and makeshift quarters were improvised in barns and outhouses using stolen straw for bedding. From Binton alone came reports at different times of 120 men under Major Moore at one house, 50 Aylesbury men at another, 50 of Cromwell's at another, over 120 Scots, and so on.[37] The population of Stratford itself must have seemed at times to double overnight as seventeen arrived at William Walker's, thirty at Nicholas Ryland's (mercifully, only 'for a night & breakfast in the morning'), thirty-seven at Edward Wells's. Alice Halford had somehow to accommodate fifty men and horses at her house in Wood Street, William Abbott in Church Street lodged a whole troop of one hundred or so with their horses, while Henry Bacon at Charlecote, evidently with room to spare, received no less than 300 of Sir Thomas Fairfax's cavalry after Naseby.[38]

All complained of hay stolen, crops ruined, sheep and cattle slaughtered, lush meadows trampled, gates and palings burnt as firewood, barrels of beer emptied, valuable articles of clothing which disappeared: Thomas Nash reported that the soldiers had taken even the scarlet pettitcoat and lacework of his wife Elizabeth, Shakespeare's granddaughter. The poor were no more immune than the wealthy: the Earl of Denbigh, a humane Parliamentarian commander, condemned a subordinate, Colonel Hans Behr (prominent in and around Stratford in 1643–4), for 'the insolent behaviour and plunderings' of his men, 'their unjust taxes of horse, money and provisions, and for the unequal distribution of his men in their quarters, sometimes 20 or 30 of them having defrayed themselves for diet and provender at the charge of one poor family'.[39] The comfortably off complained too; Richard Tyler at Shottery of having to provide for Behr 'and divers Comaunders att Dinner' for a week at a time and Thomas Nash likewise for 'keepeing a Constant table with extraordinary fireinge'. Catholics and sympathizers were perhaps the worst hit: Margaret Sheldon at Temple Grafton had her home stripped of £400 worth of household goods on one occasion, while Thomas Peers, or Pierce, at Alveston was looted, his cattle driven off and himself thrown into the dungeons at Warwick Castle.[40] The details vary according to status and, no doubt, the whim of the moment, but the impact was the same as the soldiers meddled everywhere; threatening to wreck William Higgins's home unless he gave money, breaking into Edward Cook's and Richard Sturley's shops and stealing their wares, emptying Robert Simcock's Luddington barn of its carefully stored apples, absconding with silver spoons and salt cellars from Shakespeare's old home in Henley Street, shooting William Green's mare, even taking two hives of bees from John Tewe's at Charlecote. Edmund Hathaway complained of 'money which Behr's soldiers forced from me at 2 severall tymes', Thomas Walton's wife at Alveston was similarly maltreated, while both Edward Wells's physical and spiritual health were jeopardized by soldiers who

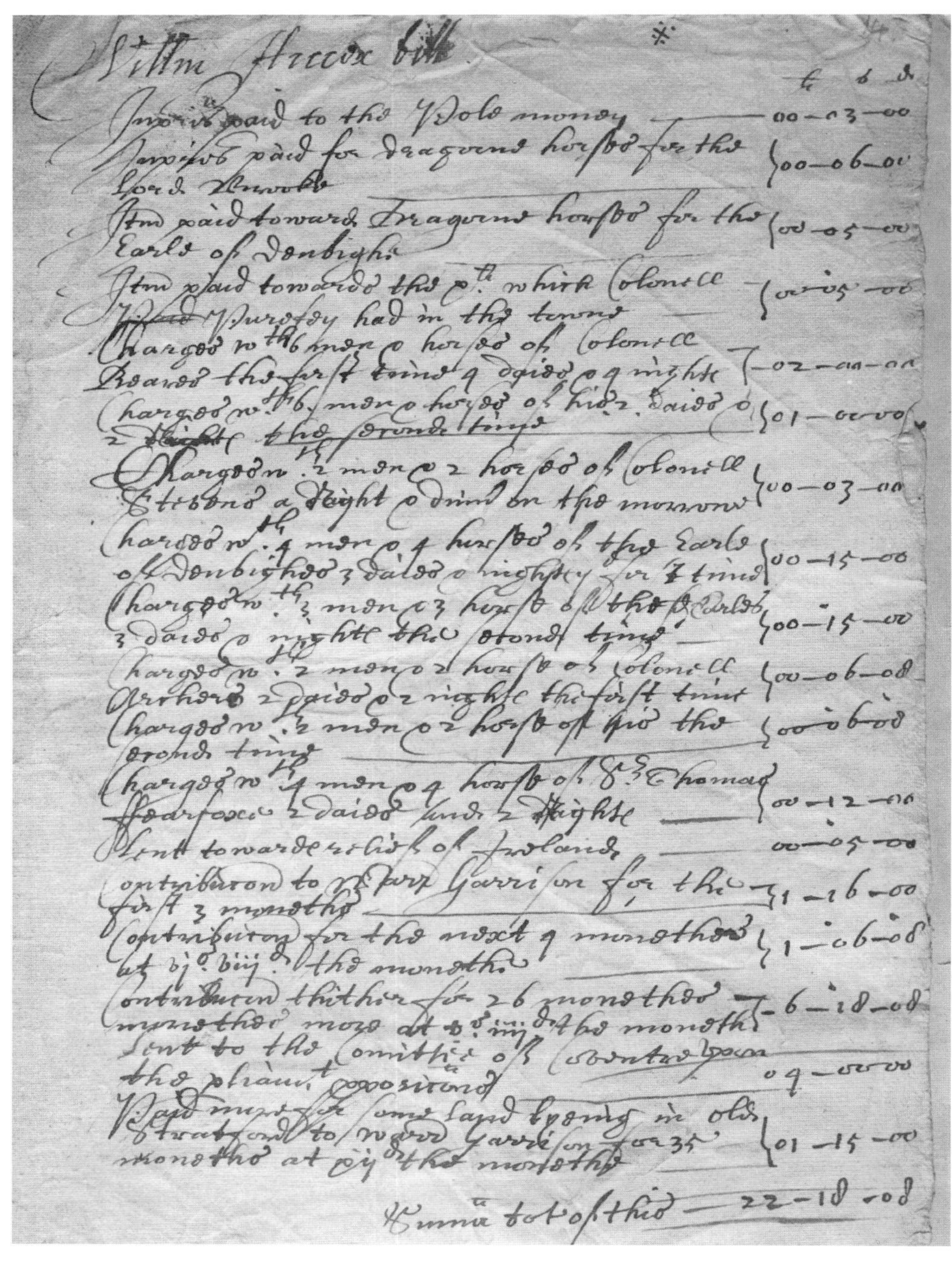

Willm Hiccox bill

	li s d
Imprimis paid to the Whole money	00–03–00
Item paid for dragoons horses for the Lord Brooke	00–06–00
Item paid toward Dragoons horses for the Earle of Denbighe	00–05–00
Item paid towards the [illegible] which Colonell Purefoy had in the towne	00–05–00
Charged wth 6 men & horses of Colonell Beard the first time 4 dayes & 4 nights	02–00–00
Charged wth 6 men & horses of his 2 dayes & 2 nights the second time	01–00–00
Charged wth 2 men & 2 horses of Colonell Stevens a night & dinner on the morrowe	00–03–00
Charged wth 4 men & 4 horses of the Earle of Denbighes 3 dayes & nights for 1 time	00–15–00
Charged wth 3 men & 3 horses of the Earles 3 dayes & nights the second time	00–15–00
Charged wth 2 men & 2 horses of Colonell Archers 2 dayes & 2 nights the first time	00–06–08
Charged wth 2 men & 2 horses of his the second time	00–06–08
Charged wth 4 men & 4 horses of Sr Thomas ffearfaxe 2 dayes and 2 nights	00–12–00
Sent towards releife of Ireland	00–05–00
Contribucon to Warwick Garrison for the first 3 monthes	1–16–00
Contribucon for the next 4 monthes at vjs viijd the moneth	1–06–08
Contribucon thither for 26 monethes more at [illegible] the moneth	6–18–08
Sent to the Comittee of Coventry upon the [illegible] propositions	04–00–00
Paid more for some land lying in old Stratford to Warwick Garrison for 35 monethes at xijd the moneth	01–15–00
Summa tot of this	22–18–08

Plate 26. William Hiccox's claim for compensation for losses suffered at the hands of the Parliamentary forces, amounting to £22 18*s* 8*d*. He details at least eight occasions on which troops were billetted on him. (SBTRO, BRU 15/17/14)

threatened to take his Bible and did take his two chamber-pots. Servants were seized for forced labour, or even to go into battle, teams of valuable horses were constantly requisitioned for long-distance haulage, houses were converted into temporary guard posts, and even the important Thomas Nash was required at one point to waste valuable time 'drying up the fords about Binton', on the main Stratford–Evesham road, to allow carriages to pass. Little wonder, when even a friendly report confessed that 'the Yorkshire horse behaved verie ill at Warwickshire', that appalled citizens could fear the 'verie great Armie . . . eating up all where they come, without respecting Persons or protection'.[41]

The combination of relentless billetting at the householder's expense, often in large numbers, and the inevitable accompanying theft, made 'free quarter' the most bitterly resented imposition of all – besides adding almost as much again, a further £1,100 or more, to Stratford's heavy tax bill. Although figures must remain approximate, the town's total war bill including all the above and adding Royalist charges for which no data exist, was well in excess of £3,000 and perhaps nearer £4,000, a large sum for a town which seems to have remained largely impassive, and even cooperative to both sides in turn – besides benefitting from the substantial reduction already mentioned.[42] How quickly it recovered from such losses and from the unquantifiable emotional scars the war inflicted can only be speculated. Outwardly Stratford doubtless soon regained its composure: a local observer in October 1647 could find no more dramatic news to report from the district than that of a Warwick yeoman who sold his wife to a friend for £5 (less than the price of a good horse, incidentally) and then regretted it, and of a Stratford youth who had been drinking and whose spurs got entangled as he peered over Clopton Bridge and was drowned when he fell into the Avon.[43] Yet the legacy of war is not so easily effaced. Not all sons and husbands had returned; the market hall stood roofless and the bridge unsafe; the mills on the river were silent; the once-stately Milcote house across the Avon remained a charred and plundered ruin; a plethora of lawsuits between late enemies was pending.[44] Some individuals, like the Puritan cloth merchant John Brooks who had profited from supplying local garrisons as well as the New England colonies, had done well, but the majority had not and one correspondent could report to a friend in May 1646 that 'friends about Stratford have beene wofully plundered, and soe have most parts of the land', and even William Combe was heavily in debt.[45] The enterprising Andrew Yarranton, as a captain in the Parliamentarian forces, had been prevented from pursuing exciting projects to exploit the river commercially and so bring much-needed relief to the faltering economy. If Stratford had escaped the worst, it had been at a price, a material price but one also paid in the breakdown of neighbourly trust. 'These tymes will make any man dishonest', one local commentator despaired, while immediately after the war an anonymous official hinted gloomily at unusual lawlessness in the town: 'For wach and ward the times have bin troublesome, and we cannot tell what hath bin dun in it'. Above all, perhaps, was the sense of some huge, bewildering communal folly: 'I have lent money to both sydes, bene plundred by both sydes, bene imprisoned by both sydes. A mad world!'[46]

CHAPTER 9

'A Little Purging and Bleeding': Poverty and Disease in Eighteenth-century Stratford

JOAN LANE

In considering the health and disease, the poverty and prosperity of any Georgian community, the numbers of inhabitants and the numbers of medical practitioners are crucial. However, in the first half of the eighteenth century it is difficult to estimate how many people lived in Stratford-upon-Avon and what medical personnel were practising there to attend them. From the Hearth Tax Returns of the 1670s there appear to have been around 400 householders which, multiplied by 4.25 (the accepted average size of a contemporary household) would give a population of 1,700.[1] Curiously, this figure was to change only slowly throughout the eighteenth century, in spite of local economic and demographic pressures. By 1730 it was estimated that there were about 420 houses in the borough and a further thirty-seven in Old Stratford.[2] The town's layout can be clearly seen in a map of 1759 (Plate 27). From it, the Reverend Joseph Greene noted 552 houses and calculated 2,760 inhabitants,[3] while the first national census of 1801 cited a population of 2,418, of whom seventy-four were regular paupers.[4] There seem always to have been four qualified surgeon-apothecaries (the equivalent of the modern general practitioner) in eighteenth-century Stratford to care for this population. For the year 1765 a unique borough population survey also exists, made specifically to discover who had had smallpox, who had not and where pauper inhabitants could claim their settlement rights under the Old Poor Law. This survey listed 2,287 residents in some 500 households, as well as those living in institutions (Plate 29).[5]

Other facilities in the town for the relief of poverty and often to aid the sick were those widely found in eighteenth-century England – a workhouse, almshouses, various welfare charities and four friendly societies. The old workhouse, established in 1725, on the corner of Henley Street and Windsor Street,[6] had thirty inhabitants in the 1765 survey, of whom only nine had not had smallpox. The medieval almshouses, granted to the Corporation in 1553, were for twenty-four elderly townspeople.[7] By 1794 Stratford had twenty-six public houses (one for every 109 inhabitants), whereas Warwick had thirty-one (1:180) and Rugby only seven (1:212).[8] There were three friendly societies for men, which met at the Garrick, the Red Lion and the Falcon (the oldest, founded in 1780), where the sole women's society also met.[9]

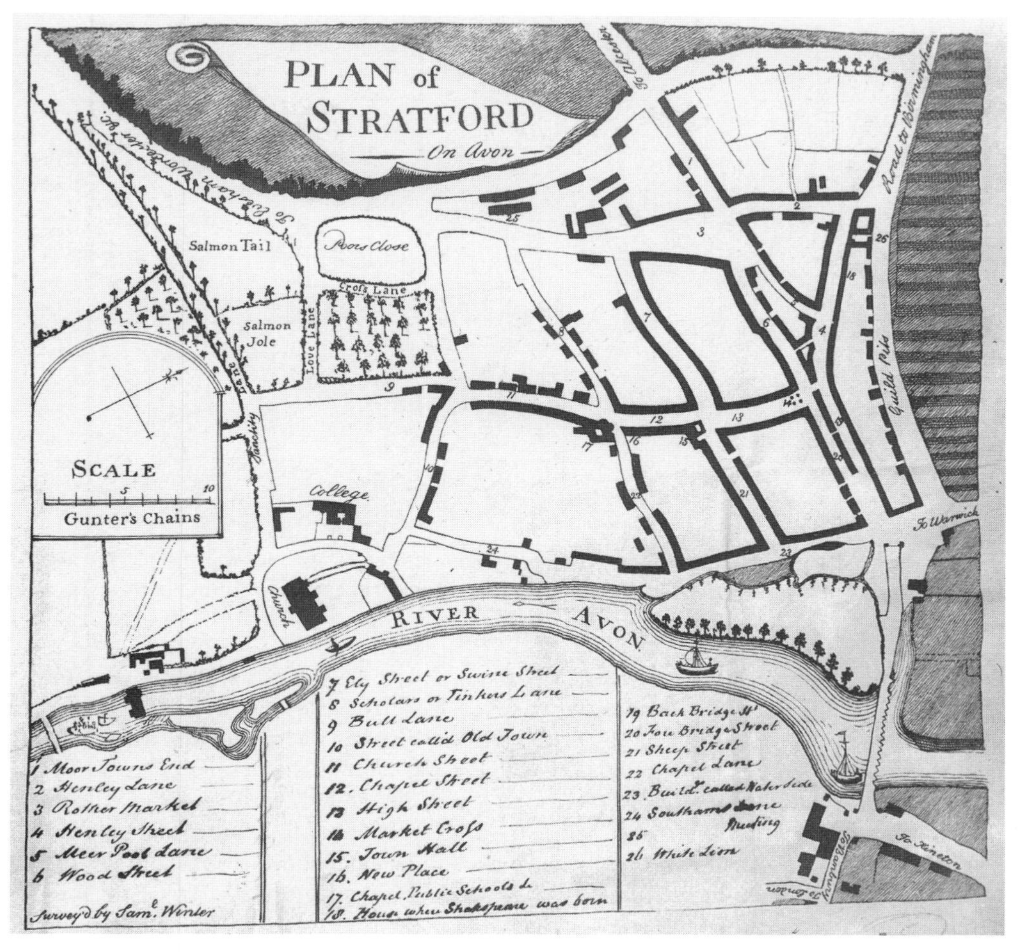

Plate 27. Map of Stratford-upon-Avon by Samuel Winter, 1759. Among the features shown is 'The house where Shakespeare was born'. (see page 163)

Most usual original sources for investigating the health of a town are extant for Stratford, namely parish registers of baptism, marriage and burial (with bishops' transcripts), trade and other directories, personal papers, diaries and correspondence. Unfortunately, Stratford did not have local newspapers until relatively late (1860), although in the eighteenth century the town was occasionally mentioned in the neighbouring county's newspaper, *Berrow's Worcester Journal*. Medical registers were not published until the third quarter of the eighteenth century[10] and thus information about Stratford practitioners is very erratic. The greatest loss, however, for the history of the population is the absence of accounts of the overseers of the poor: only the volumes after 1792 have survived to give a rich picture of town life, disease, medicine and practitioners for the nineteenth century.[11] The 1765 survey, however, clearly indicates that parochial

Plate 28. Henley Street, looking south-east, from a watercolour by Celina Flower, 1835. The borough workhouse is the first building on the right-hand side. (Shakespeare Birthplace Trust)

administration was actively concerned at the possible risk and costs of smallpox in the community, and overseers' accounts for several parishes nearby show that Stratford practitioners were regularly employed to treat the poor in these smaller neighbouring communities and similar services would have been available in the borough itself.

By the eighteenth century Stratford was fairly well linked to other towns and villages; it was the regional market and, after the 1769 Shakespeare Jubilee, an expanding tourist centre. Better transport, turnpikes and canals meant that infections spread more easily, but other factors were significant. Some diseases changed their virulence, some inhabitants acquired greater natural immunity, while other diseases were virtually unknown or presented strikingly new strains. Crop failures were a constant fear, especially in the early eighteenth century, resulting in high food prices and a diminished level of nutrition for the poorest in Stratford. The only organized socio-medical response was inoculation, and later vaccination, against smallpox. However, while a single bad harvest, as in 1718, 1728 or 1740, could be endured in a series of otherwise adequate or abundant years, when there was a combination of adverse factors, of poor harvests with epidemics for a decade, as in the period 1720–9, then an increasingly weakened population faced near catastrophe (Fig. 19).

The second half of the 1720s was the worst period of the whole century, nationally as well as locally, dramatically reflected in Stratford's burials:[12]

year	*burials*	*year*	*burials*
1720	65	1725	142
1721	68	1726	67
1722	59	1727	155
1723	64	1728	132
1724	94	1729	180

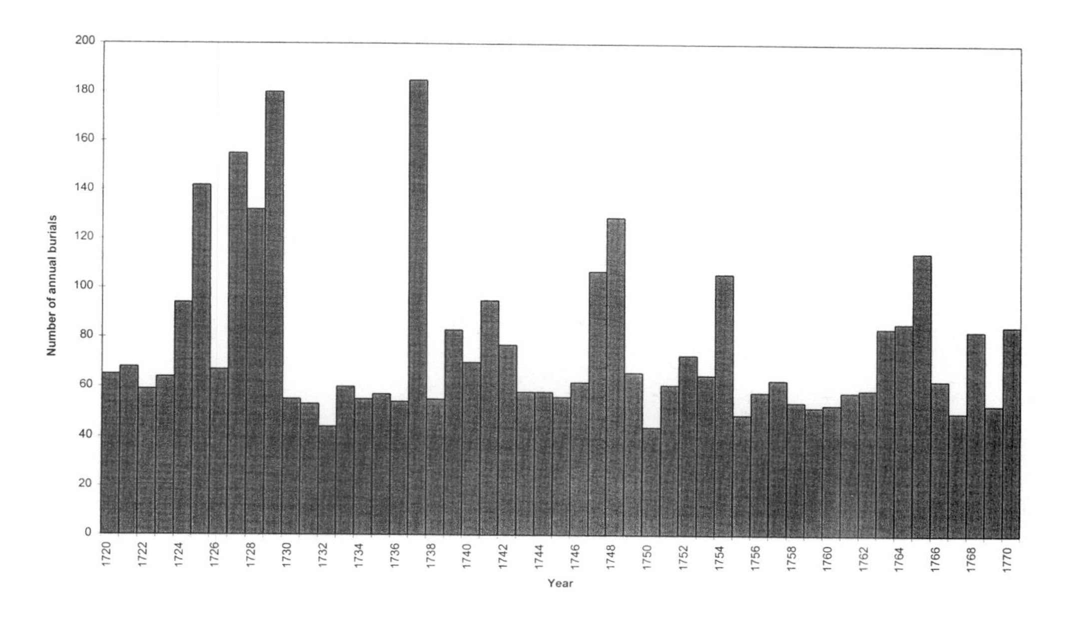

Fig. 19. Burials in Stratford-upon-Avon, 1720–70.

Unusually, the incumbent noted on 24 October 1724 that, 'The smallpox began about this time and was very fatal throughout the year', and on 31 July 1727, 'The fever began and was very fatal'. A stranger was noted among the burials on 5 July 1727 and two months later, in the peak for deaths, a town surgeon's son was buried. The year 1728 showed a slight reduction in mortality, only to be followed by the 180 deaths of 1729, including Richard Willis, a Stratford apothecary. The mortality of the period 1727–30 is considered to be the last great epidemic of pre-industrial England, with older people especially affected. The fact that mortality was heaviest in the summer and autumn suggests that the epidemic was most likely to have been typhus. However, an epidemic often disguised an outbreak of other equally fatal infections, especially in August and September, but all bear the hallmarks of a local crisis – of short duration, with a rapid onset and ending.

In other decades Stratford also suffered severe epidemics of smallpox, in 1737 (with 185 burials), in 1747–8 (107 and 129) and in 1765 (115). However, by the 1770s, the effects of inoculation, reduced virulence and natural immunity were reflected in only three erratic epidemics, with lower burial rates, in 1770 (85 burials), 1772 (65) and 1774 (90). Sometimes, children comprised a substantial number of the burials, as in 1737 (56 per cent), 1748 (58 per cent) and 1754 (38.6 per cent), clearly with a limiting effect on future population size. For the most part, however, we cannot state with confidence why so many died or the nature of most epidemics, for eighteenth-century burial register notes, as in Stratford's for 1724 and 1727, are extremely rare. A known epidemic in an adjacent community cannot be presumed to have infected Stratford.

Henley Street Ward

	No. 1.	2.	3.	4.	5.	6.	7.	8.	9
	Brought forward	2192	974		591	189	113	425	207.
	William Mayne	5	3	Great Orton Northamptonshire	—	—	—	5	3
	Mary Canning	1	1						
	Richard Harman	3	—	Alverton Warwickshire	—	—	—	3	—
	Harris, Widow	8	7	Campden Gloucestershire	—	—	—	8	7
	Joseph Jobson	3	—	Query?					
	Mrs Aston & her Daughter	2	1	Alcester Warwickshire	—	—	—	2	1
Bricklayer	Joseph Mosely	6	4	Borough of Stratford	4	—	—	—	—
	John Lord	6	3	Do	3	—	—	—	—
Bricklayer	James Guest	7	4	Do	4	—	—	—	—
	Dutton, Widow.	3	3	Old Stratford	—	3	3	—	—
	Thomas Wheeler	7	4	Kings Norton	—	—	—	7	4
	Robert Walker	3	1	Borough of Stratford	1	—	—	—	—
	James Cooper	3	1	Do	1	—	—	—	—
	Mrs White	2	-	Do		—	—	—	—
	Rhodes, Widow	2	1	Do	1	—	—	—	—
	William Jordan	6	1	Tiddington, Warwickshire	—	—	—	6	1
	Elizabeth Davis	2	—	Borough of Stratford	—	—	—	—	—
	Do a Lodger	1	—						
	Thomas Woodward	5	5	Clifford Chambers Glostershire	—	—	—	5	5
	William Mills	6	4	Borough of Stratford	4	—	—	—	—
Currier	Mr. Lench	9	6	Do	6	—	—	—	—
	Mr. Wayham	5	4	Do	4	—	—	—	—
	Total	2287.	1027.		619.	192	116.	461.	228

It appears from the foregoing Account, that the whole Number of the Inhabitants of the Borough of Stratford upon Avon, on April 19th 1765, (the Day on which they were taken,) was 2287, of which 1027 had not had the small Pox.

That of the 1027 who had not had that Distemper 619 were Parishioners of the Borough.

That the number of Persons belonging to the Parish of Old Stratford permitted to reside in the Borough in Virtue of their Certificates was 192, of which 116 had not had the ~~[illegible]~~ Small Pox.

That the number of persons permitted to reside in the Borough in Virtue of their Certificates, & whose places of their legal Settlement were known anywhere (except Old Stratford) was 461, of whom 228 had not had the small Pox.—

Plate 29. The final page of the Stratford-upon-Avon census of 1765, as copied by R.B. Wheler, *c.* 1800, from the lost original. (SBTRO, ER1/8)

The 1765 survey was carried out in Stratford on 19 April and of the total population of 2,287 it was found that there were 1,027 (44.9 per cent) who had not had smallpox. Of these, at least seventy-two families came from thirty-five other communities in Warwickshire and a further forty-nine from thirty-seven places beyond the county. Altogether, 114 places of origin were given for recent immigrants, a total of 461 persons, of whom 228 had not had smallpox. The list was compiled by George Beauchamp (d. 1768), one of the town's four ironmongers, who lived in Church Street, with John Baylis, a surgeon-apothecary, as a neighbour. The survey shows 512 households, as well as twenty-one inhabitants in the almshouses and thirty in the workhouse (of whom nine had not had smallpox); there were also thirty-nine residents in the White Lion inn. The largest households had eleven inhabitants each (a baker, butcher and blacksmith), as well as eight households of ten. The High Street ward was the most prosperous, with merchants and tradesmen as heads of households; it primarily consisted of the middle-aged and elderly, with few young children. There were also fifty-one households in single occupancy, while three persons per household were the commonest, with ninety-three of these. Men were stated to be the heads of 274 households, women of forty-five (including sixteen single occupancy) and widows of fifty-one, of whom eleven lived on their own. There were only a small number of gentlemen, Sir Henry Parker and three esquires, as well as four medical practitioners (none a physician) and an attorney (the town clerk). The usual range of market town trades was represented (Table 3).

Table 3: Household sizes and occupations in 1765

number in household	*number of households*	*occupations of heads of household (where known)*
11	3	baker, blacksmith, butcher
10	8	barber, brazier, joiner, tailor, town clerk, victuallers (2)
9	16	bakers (2), carpenter, clockmaker, curriers (2), distiller, dyer, glazier, grocer, plumber, shoemaker, tailor, victualler
8	22	carpenter, gardener, ironmonger, joiner, mercer, saddler, vicar, victualler
7	40	barber, blacksmith, bookseller, collarmaker, exciseman, flaxdresser, hatter, ironmonger, maltster, mercer, silversmith, surgeon-apothecary, tailor, victualler, woolcomber
6	44	blacksmith, bricklayer, butchers (2), carrier, coachmaker, cooper, glover, ironmonger, shoemaker, silversmith, supervisor, tailor
5	69	baker, baronet, breechesmaker, carrier, collarmaker, confectioner, dyer, esquire, fishmongers (2), flaxdresser, glover, joiners (2), milliners (2), staymaker, victuallers (2)
4	84	barber, bookseller, brazier, bricklayer, butcher, chandler, esquire, exciseman, innkeeper, joiners (2), maltster, mercer, saddler, surgeon-apothecaries (2), tailor, tobacconist, victuallers (2)
3	93	barber, blacksmiths (2), bricklayer, confectioner, cooper, currier, flaxdresser, grocer, maltster, supervisor, surgeon-apothecary, town crier, writing master

number in household	*number of households*	*occupations of heads of household (where known)*
2	84	carpenter, chandler, cooper, currier, esquire, gardener, grocer, ironmonger, maltster, organist, victualler
1	51	carver, collarmaker, cooper, maltster

A month after the 1765 household survey was made, smallpox was recorded in the Stratford burial register on 17 May, when an inoculated boy was buried, followed a day later by the death of Sarah Westbury from smallpox. There was then a lull in burials for ten days until 28 May, after which forty-seven smallpox funerals were noted (42.6 per cent of the total), the last on 23 August, as well as nineteen townspeople who did not die of smallpox. In all, in 1765 115 burials were recorded for the town, a figure which reverted to the normal levels of sixty-three in 1766 and fifty in 1767.

Table 4: Burials by month in 1765

month	*total*	*men*	*women*	*children*	*smallpox deaths*
January	6	2	3	1	
February	7	3	1	3	
March	5	3	2	–	
April	7	1	1	5	
May	10	2	7	1	2
June	36	14	21	1	31
July	19	7	12	–	13
August	8	4	4	–	3
September	4	2	2	–	
October	6	4	2	–	
November	3	1	2	–	
December	4	4	–	–	
	115	47	57	11	49

Unfortunately there is no evidence of how many inoculations were carried out on those inhabitants in the third and seventh columns of the survey (Plate 29), but a striking number of smallpox burials were of those who resided in the town's poorest Wood Street ward.

We know something of the effects of epidemics from Joseph Greene, who had earlier written, on 14 July 1737 (the year of 185 burials), that: 'The smallpox is ruining my School as fast as it can'.[13] The dramatic effect of many deaths can be clearly seen in the burial register for the summer and autumn of that year, although smallpox deaths are this time not differentiated; in September two strangers were among the deaths.

Table 5: Burials by month, June to November 1737

month	*total*	*boys*	*girls*	*men*	*women*	*infants*
June	7	1	2	2	2	–
July	13	7	3	1	2	
August	18	7	4	1	6	
September	34	8	9	6	10	1
October	55	15	19	10	11	
November	22	8	6	5	3	

Plate 30. The Reverend Joseph Greene, headmaster of the grammar school, aged seventy-two, from an oil painting by Edward Grubb, 1784. (Shakespeare Birthplace Trust)

Greene later recalled that, in 1768–9, when 'every Inn, House and Hovel . . . swarms with Company', smallpox had reduced his twenty scholars to fifteen or sixteen.[14] The most revealing of his accounts, however, was to his brother, Richard, a Lichfield apothecary, in a letter of 17 July 1780: 'Stratford has for two months past been miserable harrass'd with y[e] smallpox and I wish they may get rid of it before Michaelmas: Great fault is found with the Inoculators: for though many of y[e] patients have been blameable for their want of caution, it is said y[e] Gentlemen of y[e] Faculty themselves are not wholly undeserving of their share of Censure.'[15] In some years the population at large, and no doubt Stratford too, suffered more than one major epidemic, with a second overlapping fatal infection having its effect; thus in 1727 there were deaths from both typhus and influenza, while in 1737 deaths from influenza were added to those from smallpox. Indeed, influenza is noticeably less acute after the 1788 outbreak and seems to have developed its modern pattern as endemic but, less virulent, with increased natural immunity among the population. Childhood diseases were not necessarily fatal and evidence is therefore very sparse. However, Greene noted measles was widespread, including in his own family, in November 1758, a year of low mortality figures.[16]

Smallpox, in spite of fairly widespread inoculation for all classes, including the poor, by the 1760s remained a terrifying infection for society. Apart from death rates, smallpox could leave survivors blind and facially scarred (pockmarked), as well as causing sterility in adult males. For the parish overseers, an outbreak of smallpox was invariably an enormous drain on the ratepayers, obliged to pay relief in aid of wages, nursing expenses, food and fuel costs, as well as the surgeon-apothecary's fees and medicines. Burial charges alone were often considerable, as well as future expenses for maintaining widows and orphans. However, smallpox was not exclusively a disease of poverty and deprivation, but attacked all levels of society, spread by human contact (rather than contaminated water supplies or vectors such as lice), while natural and maternal immunity were recognized in both folk and professional medicine.

Lady Mary Wortley Montagu (1689–1762) was responsible for bringing the technique of inoculation or variolation to England in 1717 from her time spent in Constantinople as the wife of the British ambassador. After George I's grandchildren had been safely inoculated, the technique was very widely used. It was, however, a hazardous procedure for, unlike vaccination (when cowpox virus is used to protect humans), inoculation involved applying infectious matter from a smallpox sufferer's pustules into the skin of a healthy patient, who would then develop a mild case of smallpox in the hope of lifelong immunity. As burial registers show, including Stratford's, inoculation could prove fatal. At first it was a costly and time-consuming procedure, involving three weeks' preparation and isolation, with a 'low' diet (little red meat, no alcohol) under medical supervision. There was also the constant risk that the patient might develop a fatal attack of smallpox or infect others. However, the preparation and isolation technique was soon abandoned as inoculation became more widely available.

From its early days, inoculation was quickly and universally adopted, especially in rural areas and country towns, and by the mid-eighteenth century parish inoculating was quite commonplace across Warwickshire. Sir Charles Shuckburgh MD (1722–73) wrote a substantial pamphlet stoutly defending inoculation,[17] presumably from his own professional practice experience in Warwickshire. In some parishes, Astley, for example, money was given by a local gentleman for inoculating the poor of the parish, an obvious way of preventing the disease from spreading through the whole community. In Shipston-on-Stour, which had endured two serious epidemics in 1731 and 1744, the overseers of the poor signed a contract in 1772 with a town surgeon-apothecary, William Horniblow, to inoculate paupers who were willing. A total of 157 parishioners were inoculated under the contract for 6*s* a head (a total cost of £47),[18] whereas more prosperous patients would pay a guinea or more for the same procedure. Deaths from inoculation were occasionally noted in parish registers, as, for example, at Offchurch in a smallpox epidemic of 1792, when Maria Cox and Lydia Taylor died, 'the first by inoculation, the second in the natural way'.[19]

Smallpox and other epidemics can be discerned from the monthly mortality figures throughout the century, sometimes with a hint from the register of 'fever' or '*de peste*' in an earlier period. When burials, for whatever reason, reached very high rates in certain months of the year the implications for the parish and poor law officials must have been dramatic. Funeral charges, nursing and medical treatment were an immediate demand on the poor rate, widows and orphans a long-term expense. Little wonder, then, that inoculation of paupers was undertaken whenever possible as a short-term expense with future financial and health benefits for the community at large.

Without epidemics, the death rate of children in Stratford could still be extremely high, even for a prosperous family like the Masons, whose monuments in Holy Trinity Church indicate how precarious a hold on life many had. Ten children of Nathaniel Mason, born in the period 1699–1717, died between 1706 and 1718, aged from fifteen days to seventeen years. Their mother, Anne, the daughter of John Bartlett, died in childbirth aged only thirty-nine in 1717; their father was not buried until 1734 at the age of sixty-three.[20] For the years 1714–37 nearly half of all children died as infants, especially those born early in the year (January to April). The later children in a family seem to have been always more at risk of early death. The reduction in child deaths in Stratford was considerable, from 42 per cent in 1730–49, to 33 per cent in 1750–9 and to 24 per cent by 1813–19.[21] All such reductions in the death rate would produce a population rise by the later part of the eighteenth century, even if the adult death rate remained unchanged. In 1994 the British infant mortality rate was 0.3 per thousand of the population.

An unqualified but essential medical assistant for the poor in the eighteenth century was the midwife. Earlier, local women had been licensed by the Bishop of Worcester as fit and proper to practise their skills in the town but such registration was dying out by 1700. In Stratford in the last decade of the eighteenth century the overseers' accounts record two women being regularly paid for delivering babies in the town, Mrs Elizabeth Niblett and Mrs Harris. Mrs Niblett attended women outside Stratford, for in the years 1776–81 she acted as midwife in Clifford Chambers.[22] However, for the Stratford overseers she attended twenty-six women in five years (1792–7), mostly poor labourers' wives but also two paupers at local farms when they lay in. Mrs Harris delivered twenty-eight poor women in the years 1792–1800, including the occasional spinster. She may have been the inhabitant listed in the 1765 survey as a widow, with eight in her household, living in Henley Street ward but with her place of legal settlement given as Campden (Glos). Both women were paid for delivering a baby the standard fee of 5*s*, unchanged across a quarter of a century but half the surgeon-apothecary's charge.

Much eighteenth-century debate centred on the question of whether a large total population meant greater national wealth in what was undoubtedly a period of great prosperity and growth, of unprecedented economic expansion and personal fortunes. Whatever the variations of disease and death, the century witnessed a higher overall standard of living, raised wages and better food supplies, alongside improved medical facilities and an expanding medical profession. The population everywhere certainly grew because of earlier marriages (crucial for females) and because greater geographical mobility, with a wider range of potential marriage partners, enhanced fertility generally. In 1753 Parliament tried unsuccessfully to take a national census. Contemporary interest in the causes of death can be seen in the weekly mortality figures printed not only in many national but also in regional newspapers of the period; for example, in *Aris's Birmingham Gazette*, even though the diagnosis and medical terminology may be unconvincing after over two centuries.

Although the population question was of widespread concern in the eighteenth century, the topic of greatest anxiety was the poor, whose numbers, many felt, were growing disproportionately. The parish, of course, was legally responsible for its own paupers, but all ratepayers showed a marked reluctance to pay an increased poor rate on their farms and other properties, especially in an unprofitable year, for the 'undeserving poor'. The deserving were clearly understood to be widows, orphans, the elderly and the sick, not necessarily those 'overburdened with children', and certainly not those who did not work or whose income would not support their dependents. In 1754 *Aris's Gazette* ran a typical leader on the great increase in the poor and how the problem might be tackled, while eighteenth-century publications, from pamphlets to three-volume works such as F.M. Eden's *State of the Poor*, regularly aired the problem. It was widely accepted that poverty could not be cured and was, in biblical terms, 'ever with us', but that somehow it had to be managed and controlled. Medical attention, although not specified in the various acts dealing with the Poor Law, was universally provided by the overseers, either on a *per capita* basis for individuals treated or by paying the surgeon an annual contract fee.

There were some ten Stratford medical practitioners acting as parish surgeons to adjacent communities throughout the eighteenth century, and the range of their duties was considerable. Thus, at Welford-on-Avon in 1778 Thomas Nott was paid £5 15*s* 8*d* for attending and opening a large abscess on Lewis Harrison's wife,[23] while at Whitchurch in 1782 Charles Pestell's bill for £3 17*s* 3*d* was for attending and dressing William Huckfield's arms and also treating Thomas Wollerson.[24] In 1794 John Preston inoculated the parish poor of Claverdon.[25] Even fetching medicines was charged to the overseers, so that, for example, Clifford Chambers officials paid a shilling for 'going for medicines to Dr Preston at Stratford',[26] the standard cost of fetching a surgeon-apothecary to a domiciliary visit in a neighbouring south Warwickshire parish.

From 1792 surviving overseers' accounts for Stratford reveal the usual range of illnesses and afflictions treated by the parish surgeon.[27] It cost 5*s* to treat two boys with 'scald heads' (ringworm), 5*s* to inoculate a single child and 5*s* or 10*s* 6*d* to deliver a poor woman, presumably depending on the difficulty of the case and the surgeon's time. Attending fractures and providing medication, including leeches (six for 2*s*), were all the surgeon's responsibility. Other entries are often uninformative and payments for ague, fever, lameness and illness all too frequent. Occasionally, the Stratford practitioners were paid for unusual tasks, as in 1797 when £6 13*s* 6*d* was given to Mr Nott 'for cure of Persons wounded at the time Jos Pinfield was murder'd' in a street *fracas* with the Fifth Regiment of Dragoons. Occupational accidents were also a charge on the poor rate; for example, Thomas Cooke of Evesham received a guinea when he was 'lame with timber falling on him'. Parish surgeons also attended inquests, certified the insane and examined apprentices before they entered factories. However, in some cases hospital facilities were required for the Stratford poor and, although the borough did not become an institutional subscriber to Birmingham hospital until 1810, in 1794 the overseers' accounts noted that John Edwards was sent to Birmingham as an in-patient, to be attended by Mr John Freer, a leading surgeon there, apparently for a venereal complaint. By the turn of the century, the overseers had standardized medical expenditure by engaging the parish surgeon on a contract basis, no longer *per capita*, under which arrangement John Gamble was paid five guineas a year. The parish also gave elderly poor women small sums, pennies only, for nursing (really nothing more than attendance) and for laying out the dead.

Several of these practitioners played leading roles in the town's activities, especially in their tenure of public office. Five eighteenth-century mayors in Stratford were medical practitioners. All were qualified men and most took apprentices. Thus, John Baylis was apprenticed to a town practitioner, John Bott, in 1749,[28] treated paupers in Quinton and Clifford Chambers,[29] served as an alderman and was Mayor of Stratford in 1763; he was noted as an inhabitant in the 1765 survey and appeared in the first *Medical Register* of 1779. Although John Meacham attended the poor in Quinton and Whitchurch[30] and was master to three apprentices,[31] there is no evidence that he worked for the Stratford overseers, although he provided embrocations and liniment for Joseph Greene.[32] He was listed as an inhabitant in the 1765 survey and served as both alderman and mayor (in 1768) before moving to Tamworth. His only son died in 1784. John Gamble treated the poor in Stratford for at least forty years (1792–1833), but also in six other south Warwickshire parishes. We know that in 1801 he carried out a *post mortem* examination on the body of William Palmer's sister, sentenced to death and to be anatomized as an accessory in the murder of his wife. A contemporary noted in his memorandum book that 'Gamble had the girl & Desected her in a place in his Close near the Warwick Road.'[33] Charles Pestell, apprenticed to John Power of Polesworth in 1779 for five years,[34] was in Stratford by the 1780s, married a local girl and became an alderman and mayor. He advised Joseph Greene about his hernia[35] and was wealthy enough at his death to bequeath to his five nephews £150 each.[36] Thomas Nott, born about 1739, was apprenticed to Thomas Bott in Stratford in 1753[37] and practised in the town until his death in 1802. However, until the arrival of John Bree in the early 1790s, no university-educated physician practised in Stratford in the eighteenth century. Indeed, in 1783 there were only nine physicians in the whole of the county – two at Warwick, two at Coventry, one at Atherstone and four at Birmingham.[38] In neighbouring Worcestershire there were only five, of whom four practised in the city.[39] John Bree MD (1752–1823) belonged to a considerable Warwickshire medical dynasty, but there is no evidence that he was ever consulted by the Stratford poor law officers.

Although medical attention might seem today to have achieved little for the poor of Georgian Stratford, and age at death has generally been regarded as class specific, a town listing of 1801 shows a good cross-section of the inhabitants living well beyond the age of seventy, some with remarkable longevity.[40] Many of these had humble occupations, some were labourers, and yet of the 454 names listed at least five lived into their nineties, and thirty-five into their eighties (a total of 8.8 per cent). A further fifteen lived to be 75–79 and twenty-six to 70–75:

Table 6: Longevity from 1801 listing

age	*occupations*
92	weaver
91	milliner
90	blacksmith, publican, tailor
89	labourer
88	labourer, saddler
85	labourer, mason, organist, ostler, printer
84	baker, butcher, carpenter, grocer, labourers (2), publican, shoemaker
83	butcher, farmer
82	collarmaker, labourer, publican
81	upholsterer, widow
80	butcher, cooper, flaxdresser, gardener, labourers (3), tanner

Perhaps the most appropriate assessment of a medical practitioner in the town in the eighteenth century is provided at the death of Richard Bartlett (1683–1750). He was Joseph Greene's unwilling father-in-law and endured the deaths of four of his own young children in seven years. However, his monument in Holy Trinity described him as 'skilful in his profession and of a friendly disposition; of exemplary piety, strict integrity and an unblemished character. He dy'd greatly lamented.'[41]

CHAPTER 10

'Tracts and Bills Galore': Political Processes in Victorian Stratford

NICHOLAS FOGG

What gives the character to an era and what prompts change? Certain it is that eras have character. To discern this we need look no further than the contrast between the dynamic energy of the Victorian Age and the apathy and slothfulness of the eighteenth century, when the phrase 'No business could be conducted for want of a forum' appears against around one third of all meetings of the Stratford Corporation, one-tenth of the town's houses were empty and, in 1777, the grammar school contained but one boy.[1] It is unlikely that the government of the day had any interest in such issues, but if it did, it could at least have claimed to have done wonders for pupil/teacher ratios in Stratford.

One of the themes of this essay is the strong relationship between religion and politics in the Victorian era. While there may have been many causes behind the institutional revival which undoubtedly occurred in Stratford and elsewhere, there can be little doubt that religion was a powerful motivating factor. In the period before Victoria ascended the throne, two great religious movements had swept the nation. The evangelical revival was typified by the Clapham Sect, of which the adherent best known to us was the great reformer, William Wilberforce. It owed much to the fervent preaching of John Wesley a generation before. The revival sought to express a forgotten Christian truth: that Jesus is a personal saviour. It seems astonishing that this seemed a thoroughly revolutionary message in the eighteenth century. Its corollary is that all men are of value, even equal value. This simple thought has obvious political implications and we can see within it the seed of Wilberforce's lifelong fight against slavery. The second great revival was that of the Tractarians, who perceived Christ as not only a personal saviour, but as a sacramental presence in the world. This too has clear political implications.

Even before the Victorian era began, we can see men of Stratford seeking to enhance these propositions. John Conolly, a devout churchman, came to Stratford as a young physician in 1823. He remained for just six years, although in that time he became its mayor. He also established a public dispensary for the sick poor, organized mass vaccinations against smallpox and founded a public library. His immense moral energy was later demonstrated in his work as resident physician to the Middlesex Asylum, where he effected a revolution in the treatment of the mentally ill. As 'friend and guide to the crazy' he abolished the prevailing system of restraint.[2] In his field, he ranks with great reformers like Elizabeth Fry and Florence Nightingale. It is to be regretted that his achievements are not more celebrated.

Plate 31. Dr John Conolly, founder of the Stratford-upon-Avon Dispensary; lithograph by T.M. Baynes from a painting by Thomas Kirby.

The Reverend Francis Fortescue Knottesford of Alveston Manor, who was to found a church in Wilmcote, was a kind of pre-Tractarian Tractarian. He was highly active in the anti-slavery movement and was local correspondent of the National Committee for Abolishing Climbing Boys. It says little for the Stratfordians that his efforts were depressingly sterile, although in the best Victorian tradition, they included a strong practical element. The local committee attempted to gain apprenticeships for the boy sweeps in other trades and bought a machine that could sweep chimneys mechanically. When these tactics did not prove a success, the Reverend Knottesford wrote to the Committee in London: 'Our greatest hope lies with the passing of the bill to be brought forward next session.'[3] This is fascinating for it represents an early recognition that the great Victorian theme of 'self-help' was insufficient, that only corrective intervention in society could fully achieve social objectives.

Both Conolly and Knottesford were churchmen. At the start of Victoria's reign, the Church of England was in a state of deep crisis. In his *Principles of Church Reform*, published in 1833, Thomas Arnold propounded, or rather, re-propounded, the idea of a national church to which Anglicans and Dissenters could belong (he conceded that Roman Catholics, Unitarians and Quakers would not be interested), which would be based on mutually acceptable basic formulas and diversity of worship in an atmosphere of tolerance. 'The Church,' he said notably, 'as it now stands, no human power can save.'

In this Arnold was undoubtedly right. The Church as he knew it did not survive, although it retained its historic ascendency over virtually every aspect of national life, based on the supposition that every Englishman was an Anglican and that the sects were irrelevant, or non-existent. The Church was in at birth – the only official registers were the Church baptismal ones – and at marriage – the only legal marriage was in the Church of England, although the sects often conducted their own services. In death, the churchyard belonged to the Church of England and only the Anglican liturgy could be employed. There were many other privileges. The Church-controlled National Schools were the dominant force in primary education. Until 1829, Oxford and Cambridge were the only universities – and only Anglicans could graduate from them. Only in that year did qualified non-Anglicans gain the vote. The Church Vestry could even levy its own rates to pay for the upkeep of the parish church. Such an Establishment cannot be diluted and therefore it was protected by the fact that the key offices in the land – those that exercised patronage – were open only to Anglicans, including the Colonial Secretaryship, which had a role in colonial ecclesiastical appointments.

Yet, clear as it may have been to Arnold, not everyone perceived the impending erosion of the privileges of the Established Church. The process of pluralization was fought all the way, both in the civil and ecclesiastical spheres. John Keble's Assize Sermon, which Newman regarded as vital to the formation of the Oxford Movement, concerned the reform of the Church of Ireland bishoprics. The necessity or otherwise of the measure was no concern of Keble's. The question was whether the Whig Government had the *right* to do it. Newman's friend, Hurrell Froude, recognized the political paradoxes in the Oxford Movement. In its earliest days it gained the support of contradictory factions that he classified as 'aposticals and conservatives, or X's and Y's'. Owen Chadwick explains what he meant by this: 'The Xs were high churchmen who now cared nothing for the establishment and wanted to recover the spiritual authority of the Church apart from the

Plate 32. The Reverend James Davenport, vicar of Stratford-upon-Avon from 1787 until his death in 1841; from a lithograph, *c.* 1825, by C.F. Green.

State. The Ys were conservatives who believed that no good could come out of abandoning establishment or endowment, and that the only consequence would be harm to the Christianity of the country.'

As surely as Knottesford was an X, the vicar of Stratford for the first four decades of the nineteenth century, the Reverend Dr James Davenport, was a Y. He had been the only man in Stratford to sign the petition against the Great Reform Act of 1832. In common with other Ys, he was to help bring about a noted political institution, the Conservative Party.

Maude Royden's famous axiom that the Church of England is 'the Conservative Party at prayer' may have had some accuracy as a statement of voting intentions. It had become evident to most Tories by the 1830s, however, that this was not enough. The old bi-partisanship of Whig and Tory regarding the Established Church was doomed. Hence the formation of Conservative Associations during the 1830s. This was partly in opposition to the new Liberal Associations pledged to the reform of Church and State, but it was in itself a concession to pluralism. The Church now needed its own faction, albeit an important one, to defend it. On 9 May 1835, the inaugural meeting of the Conservative Association for the Southern Division of Warwickshire was held at Warwick. The cry of 'The Church in Danger' brought strong clerical backing. Dr Davenport was among the 'nobility, gentry and farmers' in the audience and seconded the motion to establish the Association. The chairman, Mr Evelyn John Shirley of Ettington Park, declared that he was sure that anyone who had any feeling of loyalty in his heart, love to the King, attachment to the Protestant religion (of which everyone present was a member) would enroll his name.[5] Mr Shirley was doubtless engaged by the issue of the Irish bishoprics. The family had ancestral estates in County Monaghan, so it is no surprise that he regarded the main threat to the nation as its infiltration by Roman Catholics, particularly those of the radical Irish variety. His remarks brought many cheers and it was decided to incorporate the aims of the Association in a Loyal Address. The liberal *Warwick Advertiser* unprophetically considered it unlikely that the new Association would succeed, but it changed its tune as the patrician power of organized Toryism became apparent. Mr Shirley put his name forward in a subsequent parliamentary by-election. On the Sunday before polling, almost all the local clergy 'devoted the usual and useful length of their moral and instructive sermons for the purpose of canvassing their parishioners'.[6] The Conservative ascendancy over the semi-feudal world that surrounded Stratford was established. Until after the First World War, south Warwickshire by and large returned what we would now call 'Knights of the Shires', decent and limited men to whom no vestige of 'sleaze' is known to cling. Mr Shirley's vision was of one Church, contained within a unitary state. Circumstances did not make it, politically at least, a very practical one, as may be seen in an examination of municipal affairs in Stratford during the 1830s.

The self-appointing oligarchies which had controlled the boroughs for centuries were terminated by the Corporation Act of 1835. At Stratford, 304 ratepayers now had their first chance to choose their representatives, but most of the old councillors were re-elected. A letter to the *Warwick Advertiser*, signed 'Justice', alleged that threats 'were made, promises were held out. . . . They took advantage of the poor, ignorant, newly-made burgesses, and defrauded them of their votes by all sorts of false pretences'.[7] Yet it is a measure of the strong underlying urge for change that the old tradition of holding meetings *in camera* was causing outrage. Even worse, the borough had established a four-man police force 'to strut about the streets, insinuating that the people are becoming thieves and pickpockets'. 'Justice' regarded the old town watch as 'not a tenth part as odious as these Peel's police are become; and they are annoying the inhabitants with a code of by-laws, so ridiculous as to excite one universal feeling of contempt'.

There were thirty-four of these by-laws. The first thirty-three were generally ignored, especially by the councillors, 'yet our one-eyed police, acting under their directions of course, have not been able to discover but one infringement'. It was the thirty-fourth, forbidding the Sunday opening of shops, which provoked great outrage. As the only free day for working people, it was the only time when many could shop. Over sixty shops opened on Sunday mornings, some openly, others when the back door was knocked. Great resentment was caused when five shopkeepers were prosecuted. 'It is only those who are honest enough to open their fronts that commit sin,' roared 'Justice', 'just as if God could not see them up their back yards! Oh! what a nation of hypocrites we are becoming!' One case was dismissed, four were convicted, but refused to pay the fines, although that of Henry Baldwin, the butcher was paid anonymously. The goods of the others were sequestrated. They demanded a public sale of their property, but it was refused, 'such was the magistrate's dread of public opinion'. A valuer was appointed, but no one would buy the goods, so he was obliged to have them himself. George Compton, the ironmonger, had nothing that the valuer wanted, so 'our *liberal* Mayor' (Mr David Rice, the surgeon) committed him for fourteen days hard labour. The police hired a gig at the Shakespeare Hotel to convey him to Warwick, but when he learnt why it was required, the proprietor ordered its return.[8]

'Justice' considered that the by-laws had caused the 'demon of party spirit' to take root in Stratford. This was much in evidence in October 1836, when four councillors (one third of the body) came up for re-election. The factions were associated with public houses: the Tories at the Falcon and the Liberals at the Golden Lion. The Liberals were first into action, having selected their candidates two months before. The Tory four were supported by a handbill signed by twenty-six 'leading men', although they were so pushed for friends after the 'Sabbath-opening' affair that not all were voters. In an attempt to gain popularity, they dropped one of their candidates and added the popular Liberal, Charles Lucy, to their list, canvassing for 'Mr Lucy and party'. They also put forward a dissenter, although they were half-hearted in their support for him. They justified the 'foolish and vexacious by-laws' and the 'useless and odious police force' by the extraordinary claim that the Reform Act had obligated their establishment. Joseph Price was paid 6*s* to canvass on the Sunday before the election. Presumably the righteousness of the cause obviated the sin of Sabbath-breaking.

The tenuous position of employees under the open voting system is revealed by an affidavit from Matthew Hirons. Timothy Smith, junior, the son of Hirons's employer, said to him, ' "Matthew, Mr Horton and me shall want your vote again this year." I said I had promised my vote to the Golden Lion Party. He said "*Damn that – we must and will have it.*" On Saturday evening he again tried to persuade me not to vote, saying that if I did vote, it would be the worse for me.' He voted as he intended. Soon after the son arrived and ordered him to go to his father to be paid off. Mr Smith, senior, told him he was a great fool for voting against their instructions. At the Golden Lion a spontaneous collection raised a small compensation for his loss of earnings.[9]

The election was a triumph for the Liberals. Charles Lucy topped the poll with 254 votes and the other three candidates were not far behind. For the Tories it was a disaster. Their best candidate secured a mere 48 votes and poor William Bolton, the only councillor to seek re-election, secured an unenviable record by achieving just one vote, perhaps his own.

Public opinion had prevailed. The next meeting of the Council resolved to open all meetings to the public and to instruct the police to take no further action on the by-laws. The *Warwick Advertiser* was jubilantly free in its advice to the vanquished, urging the Tories to 'learn wisdom' from their defeat, and 'instead of trying to influence the people of this town against their party, weak as it is in number, in influence and wealth – let them endeavour to atone for their past conduct and rashness, by vieing with the Reformers in studying the interests of the people at large, and not sacrifice the public good to promote the interests of the few; but should they let this opportunity slip, their power is gone for ever – the people now know their strength, and never again will be Tory slaves.'

The Tories took this advice and learned to look beyond the days of oligarchy. Their performance improved in the following year when five vacancies occurred on the Borough Council. A contemporary account gives an insight into the class base of the political system. Of the 386 local voters 70 were Tories, 100 Whigs: there were 197 working men and 19 in 'the middle class' who would ally with the working men. Ten of the sixteen councillors were Whigs or Tories, but there were no working men, although it was freely pointed out that to be proportionately represented, they should have had nine; so they ran four candidates. Three were elected and the fourth exerted himself to prevent his election, 'so this was a contest between the Whigs and the Tories against the working men; and although they made use of their influence, still the working men beat the combined parties'.[10]

In this context, of course, 'working men' means 'men who work', that is, the class of shopkeepers and artisans; 'middle-class' means the professional classes, but it is interesting to note that the very survival of the Tory Party was in doubt in the 1830s. That it did survive was due to its metamorphosis into the Conservative Party, under its most brilliant leader, Robert Peel, who allied it with the concept of moderate reform – it was he who brought in Catholic Emancipation, repealed many of the Corn Laws and created a grand coalition that could include Mr Shirley, although his political instinct was similar to that of Mr Thorne in *Barchester Towers* who 'looked on those fifty-three Trojans . . . who had censured free trade in November 1852, as the only patriots left among the public men of England'.[11]

Perhaps Mr Shirley's heir, Evelyn Philip Shirley was one of them. He represented Monaghan in the House of Commons from 1841 to 1847 and South Warwickshire from 1853 to 1865. Although he rarely participated in debates, he became a friend of the great Conservative leader, Benjamin Disraeli, who was a visitor to Ettington. Indeed, he introduced Mr Shirley into his novel *Lothair* as Mr Ardenne, 'a man of ancient pedigree himself who knew everybody else's'.[12] Disraeli saw romantically the necessity for the party to build a patrician alliance between the old landed aristocracy and the working man, against the kind of new wealth created by the Industrial Revolution. In so doing he ensured the political influence of Mr Shirley and his ilk, who became slow converts to the concept that, if reform was to come about, it was better to control it themselves – the foundation of the historic Conservative Party. It is worth mentioning in passing that there were exceptions to this alliance with progress in Victorian Stratford. One example is a Guardian of the Poor, the Reverend Oswald Mordaunt, who in 1899 successfully moved the abolition of outdoor relief for the able-bodied – a reversion to the system which Dickens had attacked in *Oliver Twist* sixty years before.[13]

The major manifestation of the 'pub parties' came with the publication, in May 1849, of the report into Stratford's sanitation to the General Board of Health, which proposed stringent measures to clear the Augean deposits of the centuries. Although Stratford's was one of the first corporations to ask to adopt the Public Health of Towns Act of 1848 the borough's name was inadvertently omitted from the enabling statute, leaving implementation to local initiative rather than governmental decree. There were strong differences between those who wanted full implementation of the Report, based around the Falcon, and 'The Economists', based at the Seven Stars, who were cautious about costs. The Falcon party was led by two wealthy men, Edward Flower and Charles Lucy, the latter commenting that he would participate in none of the advantages of the scheme, 'but it will be for the benefit of the poor. I shall advocate it.'[14]

The sanitation battle went on for nine years and was won by those in favour of implementation, with the resultant huge improvement in public health. This was to be the last of the single issues around which parties formed. Stratford's local politics were to be dominated by 'Independents' for over a century. After the first flourish of local democracy, it became the custom to select councillors at the annual town meeting in November. An election would only occur if more than the requisite number of candidates came forward.[15]

Two Anglican citadels which were stormed electorally during the Victorian era were those of church rates and education. Because church rates were levied by the vestry, of which every ratepayer was a member, it was a manifestation of the Establishment that nonconformists could resist. The first place to do so was Birmingham, where the Liberals had formed the first political association in 1832. Through organization within the vestry, the reformers postponed the levying of a rate from meeting to meeting, until on 2 October 1832, they finally refused to pay. The movement spread. In some places the rate was overthrown – Owen Chadwick calculates that there were 622 of these 'tea-cup squabbles' – of which the Establishment won some two-thirds, but even where they won there were still problems, because many dissenters refused to pay. The most celebrated of these was William Baines of Leicester, who in 1840 was elected unanimously to the City Council, while serving seven months imprisonment for non-payment.[16]

Often the vestry tried to avert the issue by not ordering a rate, but even there they faced a problem. At Stratford in 1835, Holy Trinity Church was in a ruinous state. Despite energetic efforts to raise funds, there was still a shortfall. The vestry was legally obliged to maintain the building in good repair, but the only way in which it could make up the deficit was to impose a church rate, which would be generally unpopular, and an issue of principle to dissenters. As was feared, many refused to pay and in July 1837 four dissenters were summoned, giving them ample opportunity to air their grievances. James Cox, a prominent local Baptist, put the basic argument of dissenters when he objected to being compelled to support a church he did not use. He paid a voluntary subscription to his own place of worship. The supporters of the Church were wealthy enough to support their own services. Compulsory payments were contrary to all true principles of religion. After a long consultation, the magistrates decided that the rate must be paid. The dissenting four declared that they would pay nothing and eleven days later their goods were sequestrated.[17]

The 'anti-raters' had a great success on 6 April 1838, when an amendment to adjourn the meeting was carried by a considerable majority at a crowded vestry. An attempt to convene a poll on the issue failed because the meeting was closed, and so the rate was defeated. The issue was revived in August at what was probably the best attended vestry ever held in the parish. A rate of 2*d* in the £1 was moved, but the ancient vicar refused an amendment calling for the adjournment of the issue for a year. The only question, he said, was whether there should be a rate or not. After great confusion, a show of hands resulted in 105 votes for the rate and 103 against. The opponents demanded a poll, which started immediately at the Town Hall, continued for two evenings and resulted in a victory for the 'pro-raters' by 410 votes to 310. The 'anti-raters' were swift to deny anything other than a tactical victory for the church party. There had been multiple voting according to rateable value and those overdue with their poor rates had been disenfranchized: 224 people voted for the rate and 294 against. The other 582 electors were 'afraid to vote, or their poor rates were not paid'. The *Warwick Advertiser* reckoned that, had they voted, about 500 would have polled against the rate. Among the successful minority, 62 people, mostly living outside the borough, polled 248 votes. 'The only supporters the Church had in this contest were the interested parties, the time-servers and the slaves.'

The issue subsided with the completion of the restoration at Holy Trinity, but resurfaced during the next incumbency. John Greves, a young radical lawyer, denied the validity of the rate in 1844. After lengthy litigation, he obtained a protection order from process in the Birmingham Bankruptcy Court. Another twenty-two people refused payment on the grounds that Greves was not paying and this effectively blocked payment for four years. The churchwardens took the issue to the Consistory Court and obtained judgement that Greves and others were not exempt from payment. The vestry resolved to enforce payment and costs, but Greves was told by the churchwardens that they had no desire to injure him, implying that they merely wanted him to acknowledge the validity of the rate. This he did at the next vestry, while maintaining his personal opposition to the principle. Nevertheless, Mr Lane, the legal adviser to the parish, recommended that proceedings must be taken, or any future rate could be invalid. Given the labyrinth of ecclesiastical law, this was a mistake. Greves won an appeal in the Court of Arches on the grounds that he had never been charged with contempt. In victory, he mocked the churchwardens: 'this petty, insignificant impotency of those barking poodles is to be pitied and not feared'. Yet the action against him, in the perverse spirit of contemporary justice, had enabled the imposition of another rate.[18] The next incumbent, the Reverend George Granville, took a conciliatory line, expressing his personal opposition to church rates, while asserting that it was the churchwardens' duty to collect them. This satisfied the honour of all parties and the rate continued to be collected until its abolition in 1868.[19]

It is interesting to speculate whether or not the origins of political parties in the religious questions of the day was instrumental in giving Victorian political values that air of highmindedness that characterizes the age. Victorian political speeches rarely deal with materialism. They are usually about the great principles of Unity (Tory) or Tolerance and Justice (Liberal) in relation to the issues of the day. The ultimate collapse of Victorian Liberalism reflects its success – its values gained the day – and its weakness, its optimistic view of human nature and of progress. Gladstone's belief that 'the leading and determining considerations that ought to lead to a conclusion are truth, justice and humanity' contrasted with the cruel realities and there were the problems of the masses for which its patrician style could not be perceived as providing an answer.

The third great strand, the Radical movement, often allied to Liberalism, but never fully absorbed by it, also had its foundation in religious feeling. In 1837, a recession combined with agricultural depression to produce the re-emergence of the wild talk and action of the 1820s – the 'Swing' era – a situation aggravated by the Poor Law Amendment Act of 1834, which severely curtailed outdoor relief for the able-bodied and gave the under-employed the choice between destitution and the workhouse. The need for more spacious premises led the Stratford Union to construct a large new workhouse in Arden Street, where those unable to support themselves lived under a regime of increasing utilitarian severity. A Stratfordian signing himself 'A Lover of Justice' wrote an open letter to local farmers in 1838. The first sentence reveals the religious nature of contemporary radicalism with a quotation from St James: 'Behold the hire of the labourers who have reaped your fields, which you have kept back by *fraud*, crieth: and the cries of them which have reaped are entered into the ears of the Lord of Sabaoth.'[20]

There is a local personification of this religiously-based rural radicalism in the farm-workers' champion, Joseph Arch, a hedger in the employ of Mr Angell James at Bridgetown. His parents had been employed by the Earl of Warwick, which enabled his father to buy a cottage at Barford and, later, to work as an itinerant artisan. The father was a man of courage. He refused to sign a petition organized by local landowners against the repeal of the Corn Laws and so faced years of persecution and poverty.[21]

When Joseph Arch was born in 1826, rural England was in deep crisis. Enclosures had largely driven out the old peasant-freeholders and substituted a new labouring class. At the same time, the growth of manufactures had destroyed the cottage industries at which wife and children had worked to bring in extra income. His parents were Anglican, but Joseph Arch developed a contempt for the Established Church. 'People wondered,' he recalled, 'why the Church had lost and continued to lose its hold on labourers in the country districts. It never had any hold on me . . . I never took communion in the parish church in my life.' He related this antipathy to an incident in Barford Church when he was seven. One Sunday his father stayed after Matins to take communion. Young Joseph had to wait outside, but could not resist observing the service through the keyhole.

> What I saw will be engraved on my mind until the last days of my life. That sight caused a wound which has never been healed. My proud little spirit smarted and burned when I saw what happened at that communion service. First, up walked the squire to the communion rails; the farmers went up next; then up went the tradesmen, the shopkeepers, the wheelwright, and the blacksmith; and then, the very last of all, went the poor agricultural labourers in their smock frocks. They walked up by themselves; nobody else knelt with them; it was as if they were unclean – and at that sight the iron entered straight into my poor little heart and remained fast embedded there. I said to myself, 'If that's what goes on – never for me!'[22]

After acquiring a rudimentary education, Arch became a Methodist local preacher and used his itinerant trade to spread his social gospel. 'I would preach in chapels . . . and more than once I have "held forth" in my everyday clothes.' The chapel is seen as 'the most potent influence making for independent action by the country poor'. There the labourers learnt 'self-respect, self-government, self-reliance and organisation; men learned to speak, to write, to lead their fellows'.[23]

Plate 33. Joseph Arch, in the 1880s, President of the National Agricultural Labourers' Union. (Photo: Getty Images)

The biblical language of rural radicalism stems from the chapel, for it was the only public means of expression the labourers knew. Joseph Arch's own account of the nocturnal open-air meeting at Wellesbourne in 1872 which led to the formation of the first constituted trades union – the Warwickshire Agricultural Labourers' Union – is so permeated. A letter to the *Royal Leamington Chronicle* from some local farmworkers had called for a minimum wage of 2*s* 6*d* a day. Eleven Charlecote labourers called a meeting at Wellesbourne on 14 February. Labourers came tramping in from miles around. The room booked at the Stag's Head was inadequate, so it was decided to move to the village green. Someone at the local gasworks had cut off the street lamps, so lanterns were hung on bean poles, before the chairman called on Arch to speak.

> I mounted an old pig-stool and in the flickering light of the lanterns I saw the earnest upturned faces of those poor brothers of mine – faces gaunt with hunger and pinched with want – all looking towards me and ready to listen to the words that would fall from my lips. These white slaves of England stood there with darkness all about them, like the children of Israel waiting for someone to lead them out of the land of Egypt. I said to myself, 'Joseph Arch, you have not lived in vain, and of a surety the Lord God of Hosts is with us this day.'[24]

The formation of the Union was followed by an extensive strike of local farmworkers and a lock-out by the employees, in which Stratford became the rallying centre with a number of public meetings held in the Rother Market. On 11 June 1873, 2,000 people heard the Wilmcote brass band before Arch proposed 'that the borough franchise should be extended to the counties'.[25]

The Union faced huge organizational problems. Its disparate membership combined with a mechanical revolution in the countryside to make emigration the most realistic option for many labourers. 'There is no hope of escape,' wrote a clergyman, 'for a reckless and degraded peasantry except by emigration to foreign lands or manufacturing districts, which will take away the strong, the healthy and the brave and leave us the cripple, the drunkard and the beggar.'[26] The Agents-General of the Canadian and Australian colonies became regular visitors to Stratford where they lectured on the opportunities represented in their far-flung lands.[27]

In *Lark Rise to Candleford*, Flora Thompson recalled her village pub where:

> questions of the moment were thrashed out and settled . . . 'Three Acres and a Cow', 'The Secret Ballot', 'The Parnell Commission and Crime', 'Disestablishment of the Church'. . . . Sometimes a speech by Gladstone, or some other leader would be read aloud from a newspaper and punctuated by the fervent 'Hear, Hear' of the company. Or Sam, the man with advanced opinions, would relate with reverent pride the story of his meeting and shaking hands with Joseph Arch, the farmworkers' champion. 'Joseph Arch!' he would cry. 'Joseph Arch is the man for the farm labourer!' and knock on the table and wave aloft his pewter mug very carefully, for every drop was precious.[28]

The conversation is set in 1885, the year that Joseph Arch became the first working man to be elected to Parliament, as Member for north-west Norfolk, a decade before Keir Hardie was presented in his cloth cap. More flamboyantly, Arch appeared in his farmworker's bonnet and tweeds and formed an incongruous figure as he stomped forward between Joseph Chamberlain and A.J. Mundella. The *Stratford Herald*, which had once dubbed Joseph Arch 'The Warwickshire Agitator' came to regard him as a quaint homely figure of the 'jog-trot, solid responsible order'. New radical forces were at work in the latter part of Victoria's reign. The word 'Socialism' was much mooted. Even the vicar declared himself a supporter, although he remained a Tory voter. The Methodist minister defined an ideology that was a curious mixture of the homespun and theoretical. Society, he considered, was founded on clothing. Socialism would abolish fustian, corduroy and moleskin and dress the people in broadcloth – it was widely believed that fabrics other than wool were bad for the skin. Equality would follow through a modest programme of manhood suffrage, free, compulsory, non-sectarian education, adequate housing and worker shareholding. The railways might be nationalized with adequate compensation, and also the land, under the slogan, 'The Land for the People, the People for the Land'. Industrial disputes would be settled by arbitration. The keynote was 'the gradual evolution of the people through the influence of moral education into a christian brotherhood'.[29]

More analytic and radical forces were abroad. The 'Red Van' of the 'English Land Restoration League' travelled the area, proclaiming the 'abolition of landlordism'. Among those speaking from its platform were Dr Edward Aveling, who wrote a column of London tittle-tattle for the *Herald* under a pseudonym, and his common-law wife Eleanor, daughter of Karl Marx. 'Discontent is your duty,' she told her audiences. 'The workers of England are poor not because they are idle, but because they are robbed.'[30]

Thus far we have gained an impression that Stratfordians in the Victorian era showed deep interest in the political processes and an optimistic faith that the system could deliver what was required. Yet to look back on the age with undiluted admiration and nostalgia would be to miss a fourth dimension: the one that was frequently referred to as 'the submerged one-tenth'. In April 1831, in the midst of the crisis surrounding the passage of the Parliamentary Reform Act, Sir Gray Skipwith of Alveston House, the Recorder of Stratford, was elected a county Member. Stratford Corporation asked him to give the people the 'pleasure' of escorting him into the town. On 13 May a huge crowd, accompanied by a band, greeted his carriage on the borough boundary. At the Town Hall the Mayor declared 'that we are trusting our interests in the care of a gentleman well worthy of our entire confidence'. Sir Gray's reply was a model of moderation. 'Many excellent men he knew admitted the need for some reform, but thought that the bill went too far. They think it will make the House of Commons too democratic and thereby incur the danger of a revolution. I have no fear of that kind. I have too high an opinion of the strong sense of Englishmen.'[31]

The reverse of this coin was revealed in December 1832, when the borough franchise of ninety-nine electors had its first experience of local balloting in a contest for two places between Sir Gray and his fellow Whig, Sir George Phillips and the Tory, Evelyn John Shirley. The unfranchised took a Hogarthian view of the proceedings. While there was no interference at either polling booth, it was popularly believed that an election was a time for mayhem. On the first morning of the three-day poll, disorderly groups roamed the town. By 2 p.m., the constables were powerless to disperse a crowd which had assembled in Ely Street. George Cope rushed from his house in Windsor Street brandishing a poker and shouting, 'Damn me if I don't murder someone with this before I have done with it.'

At four o'clock the mob, now exceeding 500 and armed with bludgeons and staves, marched to the Tory headquarters at the White Lion and smashed the windows with pitching broken from the street. The constables tried to arrest the ringleaders but were forced to retreat. After the mob had performed the same service for the George and Dragon up the street, a party of gentlemen rode to Coventry for the military. At the Shakespeare, the constables grouped to bar the entrance. Cope raised his poker to one and threatened to split his skull. When the military arrived at 10 p.m. the Riot Act was read, several rioters were arrested and the mob was dispersed. Constable John Ashford spotted Frederick Lewis in the Bricklayer's Arms with a bludgeon concealed under his coat. When he tried to take it from him he was knocked to the ground. At the Quarter Sessions, Lewis, Cope and nine others were gaoled for riotous behaviour.[32]

In 1865, Lord Duncan put up for the Liberals, favouring the abolition of church rates and a modest extension of the franchise, to bring about the first local parliamentary contest in thirty years. An election was a novelty to most people, who were astonished at the placard-covered vehicles tearing about the streets. Perhaps it was this unfamiliarity which ensured that 'scarcely a black eye was given all day'.[33] Although the *Stratford Herald* had declared that Lord Duncan's election would reflect honour on any constituency, the local voters failed narrowly to distinguish themselves and opted for the Tories, Sir Charles Mordaunt and Mr Wise.[34] After extending the franchise and abolishing church rates, the Tories returned to the hustings in 1868 to recommend the policies that they had previously opposed. This time Mr Wise put up with Mr John Hardy and the Liberals fielded Lord Hyde and Sir Robert Hamilton of Alveston. Election morning was quiet. The only disturbance came from a few small and very dirty boys, who sported blue Liberal favours and cheered all those voting. With the arrival of some grammar school boys and a few non-voting shop-assistants, blazing with orange Tory rosettes, groaning and howling started. This brought out some 'unwashed hobble-de-hoys and roughs of a maturer age' who chased the Tory supporters off the streets and then amused themselves by groaning or cheering each voter as he made his declaration. Anyone interfering with them became a marked man and some people were roughly handled. That evening the mob, which had considerably increased in numbers and noise, paraded the streets. At the Tory committee rooms in the Shakespeare, someone rashly made a provocative gesture out of a window. An assault was made on the building and several windows were broken. Curiously, the Liberals accused their opponents of intimidating the electors. Despite winning a majority in Stratford, they lost the division. The *Stratford Herald* considered that this reflected the influence of 'the old maids of Leamington, duly organised to do battle with the Pope'.[35]

The introduction of the secret ballot in 1872 made elections less riotous affairs. Not everyone approved of the reform. Years later the *Statford Herald* published 'The Lament of an Old Voter', which revealed the attraction of the old system for those with a vote:

> Tis true that tracts and bills galore are now before me set,
> And lots of talk to keep us straight – but how can I forget?
> For oh! There are so many things that recall the past to me;
> Plum puddings hot, prime roast beef, with plenty of gravee . . .
> They tell me to be happy now, the gayest of the gay,
> But little will they think of me after the polling day.

Given the religious basis of much Victorian political ideology and the contrasting mob-element that generally put a tinge on its practical manifestations, it is appropriate that there was an event which encapsulated both strands. School attendance was made compulsory in 1880 which placed a great strain on Stratford's denominationally-based system. Two years later the powers of the Education Department were stiffened to enable the withdrawal of grants from inadequate schools and Stratford's nonconformist-controlled British School lost its funding. Since the voluntary societies could then be said to be no longer providing sufficient school places, Stratford was legally compelled to elect a School Board in 1881. It was dominated by the 'Church Party', which feared that any new Board School with a heavy governmental subsidy would threaten the status of their own National School. The main factor in the election, however, was the fear that the provision of a Board School would be a costly burden on the rates. As a temporary measure, the British School was reopened as the Board School. The Board offered to extend it, but the Department threatened to use its powers of dismissal if a new school for at least 400 children was not built. The blood of the local ratepayers was up. Leaflets circulated containing spurious claims about the cost of the new building. At a public meeting in the Town Hall the few speakers in favour of the scheme were shouted down. Steam was let off, but nothing was achieved against the inexorable demands of the Department. The Board School opened in 1883 in Broad Street and continues in use today.[36]

The School Board elections presented the riotous with a new opportunity for uproarious assemblies. At a turbulent meeting of candidates at the Town Hall in March 1884, two-thirds of the packed audience were under voting age. They were very disorderly, but impartial, cheering and hissing indiscriminately. When they tired of this, they threw chairs about.[37] The Church party again won a majority at the subsequent election, demonstrating an impressive power to turn out its vote.[38]

Educational issues were polarizing the town on denominational lines. The headstrong vicar, the Reverend George Arbuthnot, even used his influence to prevent nonconformist ministers from visiting patients at the hospital. An Anglican lady decided not to take up lodgings which overlooked the Methodist church. When a nonconformist lady engaged a maidservant from an outlying village, the family was visited by their vicar, who tried to dissuade her from taking up the situation. A leading Congregationalist, Fred Winter, complained that he frequently heard of cases of distress where assistance was refused 'because the parents happen to send their children to the Board School'.[39]

Yet, after the early School Board elections, the denominations, realizing that there was little to be gained from such raucous affairs, established a *modus vivendi*. The Church of England filled four of the seven seats, the nonconformists two and the Roman Catholics one. The arrangement was uneasy. The nonconformists suspected that the Anglicans were in league with the Roman Catholics to underfund the Board School and so make their own denominational schools more attractive. Open conflict came in 1896 when the Anglican majority refused to endorse the appointment of a Unitarian, Miss Gold, as a teacher at the Board School. A national storm ensued. The Board, said the *Stratford Herald*, had made itself notorious from Land's End to John O'Groats. The Liberal Unionist leader, Joseph Chamberlain, expressed sorrow that such bigotry still existed, while at Stratford there was a stormy public meeting.[40]

The Anglican majority was undaunted by such protests and decided that the Apostles' Creed should be taught in the Board School to children whose parents did not object. This was to be decided by asking the children. 'Among people who are not priest-ridden,' wrote a protester, 'to ask babies whether they or their parents object to the Apostles' Creed is sheer imbecility'.[41] Despite their objections to Anglican catechetics in a maintained school, the nonconformists considered it in their interest to maintain the pact at the next School Board election in 1899, fearing that their representation might be obliterated. But Mr Francis Talbot, a Unitarian, was not bound by any such caution and his nomination ensured a contest. The fact that public personalities like Father Thomas, the Catholic priest, and George Arbuthnot, the controversial vicar, were standing increased excitement. The degree of the decline of institutional religion represented an uncertain factor. Many voters went to neither church nor chapel and their influence might prove decisive. Numerous canvassers pounded the doorsteps. The Anglican clergy, unlike their nonconformist equivalents, campaigned hard. On polling day, carriages, mostly Anglican, ferried voters to the polls ensuring a very high turnout. The issue was further complicated by a complex voting system which enabled the distribution of seven votes as the elector chose. Father Thomas was expected to do well. As well as the votes of his own flock, he could expect to pick up Anglican votes for not being a nonconformist and vice-versa.

The news that John Smallwood, a popular nonconformist, had topped the poll with 1,542 votes was greeted with huge cheers by a large crowd outside the Town Hall. The biggest cheer, however, came for Francis Talbot's 1,289 votes. The vicar's name, twenty votes behind, provoked loud hooting, mingled with cheers, which was repeated for the other three church candidates, including Mr Ashwin, who failed to get elected. When Mr Smallwood tried to say a few words, there was a surge forwards and the candidates fled for home. The crowd continued its frivolities by kicking a policeman unconscious before dispersing.[42]

There were agonized post mortems in church circles. The vicar had instructed his supporters to plump for him, rather than distributing their votes, so he appeared to have few friends apart from his faithful. The regular cry of defeated candidates was raised: scores of people had failed to deliver votes they had promised. The *Stratford Herald* was not surprised. If an elector would not promise a vote, canvassers assumed that he intended to support the opposition.

> This suspicion finds its way to the committee room and if he be a poor man the order goes forth that he must in future be struck off the charity list; or if the elector be in a good position, patronage from his business must be withdrawn. This is a very common thing, and to prevent this kind of intimidation being exerted, canvassing should be an offence, disqualifying the candidate resorting to it.

The nonconformists were elated. In the same issue, the Reverend J.J. Pugh, the former Methodist minister, wrote to congratulate 'lovers of civil and religious liberty' on the result. 'All parties are now represented as in justice should be the case in a community holding diverse opinions. The day of "family government" is over. No clerical corner or party should be in possession in Stratford again.'[43]

In fact the Anglicans maintained control of the School Board through their alliance with Father Thomas. Yet Pugh was right. The election reflected the decline in that hegemony of the Church over social policy which had formed the programme of Mr Shirley some sixty years before. Doubtless the vicar would have gone down with all guns firing, but in 1902, the powers of the Board were transferred to the newly formed Warwickshire Education Committee. Not that this reform was hailed by nonconformists, for it enabled denominational schools to receive extended public subsidies. A passive resistance movement had manifestations in Stratford. In 1904, nine men were summoned for non-payment of rates. In court, J.J. Asquith of Rother Street declared that they had deducted the portion that would go to denominational education. No doctrinal tests should be applied to state employees. A sequestration order was made. Two weeks later an auction raised £4 18*s* 9*d* amidst great hilarity. The proceedings closed with the hymn, 'Dare to be a Daniel'. Honour was satisfied and the denominational issue in education gradually faded.[44]

The greatest of all Stratford's political riots came in the Boer War, when passions were riding high. On 30 January 1900, news of the relief of Ladysmith brought unbounded joy. That night a 200-strong mob (a shift of allegiance appears to have taken place from the Liberals to the Tories) gathered outside the Conservative Club in Rother Street and marched through the streets, bawling patriotic ditties and visiting the premises of 'pro-Boers'. In Sheep Street, Mr Wyatt's shop window was splintered by a heavy stone and coal was thrown through his bedroom window. The mob moved on to the antique shop of the Quaker Bullard brothers in Chapel Street. It was rumoured that they hoped that the British Army would be annihilated and that they had flown a Boer flag, which had been removed on police advice. The mob battered down the shop door. The Bullard brothers and their young lodger were met by a hail of missiles. An appeal to a nearby policeman proved fruitless, so the three, with great bravado, drove the rioters out. Several of the crowd were hurt in the mêlée. Mr W.P. Bullard then began, with amazing sang-froid, to explain his views to the crowd. Surprisingly he got a hearing, until someone shouted, 'Don't listen to his soft soap' and a stone was hurled through his window. Shortly after midnight, the mob moved off. Rumours had been circulating that the sons of a man called Flint were helping the Boers. In fact his one son in South Africa had taken no part in the war, but his repudiation of such 'odious insinuations' did not save his windows from destruction.[45]

It was common knowledge that the mob would rendezvous again next evening. The superior courage of the Bullards rankled the malignant. Reinforced by local roughs, they went straight to Chapel Street, where a mere half-dozen policemen waited. Such a feeble force was no deterrent. The gas lamp opposite was extinguished and the front windows smashed to loud cheers. The Bullard children, asleep in the front bedrooms, were endangered by falling debris. The mob dragged furniture from the shop window and set it alight. The bombardment continued for over two hours. Mr T.R. Elleker found it remarkable that none of the crowd appeared worse for drink. Around midnight, Councillor E. Deer persuaded the mob to disperse after calling for three cheers for the Queen and the soldiers at the front. Part of the crowd was to smash into the Bullards' workshop on the Banbury Road and their auction rooms in Guild Street.

Next evening 500 rioters were heavily outnumbered by spectators hoping to see more fun. Some rushes at the 'kopjes of the pro-Boers' were easily checked by the large police presence drafted into town. Bullards' shop had been so boarded up as to look a 'miniature Ladysmith'. The disappointed mob trekked towards Tiddington, where a prominent resident had come under its suspicion. They were met by police with drawn truncheons and fled back to Stratford. Numerous names were taken through the evening and, after

PRO-BRITON
or
PRO-BOER?

THAT IS THE QUESTION

Your country calls for answer true,
Make answer true and say,
Are you for Britain through and through,
Or for the Boers to-day?
For God and right
Respond in might,
Be men from skin to core,
The issue note,
You'll have to vote
Pro-Briton or Pro-Boer.

Are other countries always right,
Your country always wrong?
Are English Statesmen blackguards quite,
And Boers an Angel throng?
The answer give,
If you would live
As men from skin to core,
The issue note,
You'll have to vote
Pro-Briton or Pro-Boer.

Shall we patch up a Majuba peace,
Or Boer and Bond let see
Intrigues to oust us now must cease,
And Britons e'er be free.
For every white
An equal right,
OUR flag, THE flag once more;
For gain or loss,
Go place your cross,
Pro-Briton or Pro-Boer.

VOTE FOR FOSTER!

The Empire for all,
But all must be for the Empire!

Printed and Published by Edward Fox, 1, High Street, Stratford-on-Avon.

Plates 34 a & b. Rival candidates' election posters for the south-west Warwickshire parliamentary by-election in 1901. A vote for Bolton King was interpreted by his opponents as a vote in favour of the Boers. (SBTRO, DR 375/6)

four men were arrested, the town was quiet. Two weeks later, the news of the fall of Bloemfontein brought a huge crowd onto the streets, but no damage was done.

Henry Bullard announced his intention to claim compensation for the riot damage. Many people had communicated their sympathy, but most did so secretly for fear of reprisals. Edward Fox, son of a local printer, wrote an arrogant letter to the *Stratford Herald*, implying that he had been a ringleader and concluding that England was 'too free for those who are not loyal to her'. Mr Wyatt replied scathingly that his idea of patriotism was 'something higher than terrifying helpless women and young children, and coming to demonstrate and destroy in the darkness . . . as Mr Fox and his sympathisers seem so brimful of it there is a splendid opportunity for them to show it by joining some branch of the military service . . . instead of enjoying the luxury of a feather bed and home comforts while others do the hard and dangerous work, and they the talking and shouting.'

The ripples from the riots went a long way. 'Who would think', asked the *New York Herald*, 'that dear, sleepy old Stratford-upon-Avon could get so excited as to break windows and smash warehouses?' The Home Secretary was questioned in Parliament. The theme was taken up by the vicar in a splendid sermon. 'I for one rather admire a man who is not afraid to give vent to views which he knows are unpopular . . . I am annoyed at the indifference with which many regard what has occurred. . . . It has been publically stated that men occupying good positions were in the crowd encouraging them to violence.' He called for an official enquiry. 'If Stratford with its population of 8,000 can produce an uncontrollable mob, what could Birmingham do if they were similarly stirred?'

When the four 'ringleaders' appeared in Court, one was recategorized as drunk and disorderly, while three others were imprisoned for a month. A subscription was opened in the town for the only 'prominent' individual who had been sentenced. Stratfordians were in no doubt as to why the real ringleaders had escaped punishment: 'It was their cloth as saved 'em.'[46]

Edward Fox took the advice and embarked for South Africa with the Warwickshire Yeomanry in February 1901. He proved a point by his absence, for violence flared again in Stratford, during a by-election caused by the death of the sitting Member, Colonel Victor Milward. The Liberals had wisely decided not to test local passions during the General Election in 1900, but now they had little choice. Their candidate was the local radical idealist, Bolton King, whose aim was 'to carry the principles of Christianity into political and social life'. In ordinary times he would have been a splendid choice, but these were not ordinary times. His adoption meeting at the Corn Exchange was turned into a farce by the same well-dressed camaraderie that had orchestrated the riots. Speeches were interrupted by the inebriate singing of patriotic songs, chairs were overturned and fighting broke out. On the following evening, the Tory candidate, Philip Foster of Ingon Grange, issued an appeal for tolerance. This went unheeded. Two more Liberal meetings at the Corn Exchange were broken up. At the eve-of-poll rally, the first speaker, a Welsh Member of Parliament, William Jones, was interrupted by shouts of 'Get your hair cut', 'You're no Englishman' and 'Go home'. 'I do not reason with beer,' he retorted, 'I reason with men.' Fighting broke out and a number of people were knocked about. One speaker, Mr A.M. Scott, was dragged into the street, knocked down and trampled in the gutter. The police arrested the man who kicked him, but also took Mr Scott's name, as it was alleged that he had struck the first blow.[47]

Outside a large excited crowd had gathered. When Mr and Mrs Bolton King arrived, the struggle was so fierce that they were not noticed until they mounted the platform. The police ejected a number of brawlers, but the Liberals complained that these included some of their stewards who were trying to keep order. When William Jones threatened to report the matter to the Home Secretary, the Police Superintendent replied that he had no power to interfere unless there was a breach of the peace. At that moment Mr Scott reappeared with blood streaming down his face to demand if his condition was not sufficient evidence. When he tried to speak again he was greeted with cries of 'Traitor'. 'The traitors are the men,' he replied, 'who have sent our soldiers to one of the greatest campaigns in which England has been engaged without first providing them with the means of defending themselves.' Mr Bolton King tried to say a few words but could hardly be heard. The last speaker, Miss Marshall of the Women's Liberal League, at least got a better response, the crowd singing 'I'll be your Sweetheart'. As Mrs Bolton King left, coarse expressions were flung at her. Given the prevailing hysteria, her husband did better than he probably expected, losing by 2,977 votes to 4,755. During the election he had learned that he beat his wife, farmed 2,000 acres but employed no local labour and that anyone voting Liberal would have to pay towards his election expenses. For the second time in a year, there were questions in Parliament about disturbances in Stratford.

In 1908, Mr J.C. Huckvale, 'not himself a Socialist', attended an Independent Labour Party rally at the Fountain in Rother Street and felt ashamed of some of his fellow townsmen. 'The senseless and witless exclamations of the half-drunken and thriftless part of the crowd, together with the sheer inability to frame the semblance of an intelligent question, would have disgraced a horde of primitive savages.'[48] A further manifestation of this mob came on 16 July 1913 when fifty-six supporters of women's suffrage, marching to London, held a public meeting at the Fountain. After the first speaker had welcomed the 'jolly sporting ladies', unruly elements began a continuous barrage of organized heckling. The mob surged towards the platform and several ladies were jostled. Arrests were made, but the cacophony was irresistible. The meeting was abandoned, but from another platform the formidable Mrs Despard, sister of Sir John French, awed the remnant of the crowd into silence. The Very Reverend George Arbuthnot, now Archdeacon of Coventry, took up his pen to express his shame at the 'violence shown by some contemptible rascals to ladies, who whether we agree with their views or not, are peaceable citizens and entitled to that free speech, which . . . is the birthright of every Briton'.[49]

The 'Suffragist Riot' was the last manifestation of the Stratford mob. To say that it was swept aside in the changed world that followed the First World War would in part be true, but it would also undervalue the achievements of Stratford's Borough fathers. The town was fortunate in the nineteenth century to be served by a number of men whose talents graced stages beyond the parochial: mayors like John Conolly, Charles Lucy, Edward and Charles Flower, the two James Cox's, Sir Arthur Hodgson (a former Premier of Queensland) and many others, as well as talented and dedicated ministers of religion of all denominations. By the end of Victoria's reign, the place that David Garrick had described as the most 'wretched-looking Town in all Britain' had been transformed into a place of hygiene and sanitation. The foundations had been laid of education and public housing systems that would go a long way towards anaesthetizing Stratford's colourful, but dangerous mob. 'The duties of the Bench are light and becoming lighter,' commented Councillor John Smallwood in 1887, on the occasion of the Queen's Golden Jubilee. 'People are becoming better and I think the schoolmaster has not been abroad to no purpose.'[50]

CHAPTER 11

The Rise of Stratford as Shakespeare's Town

ROGER PRINGLE

When did visitors start coming to Stratford because it was Shakespeare's birthplace? How did they come? What did they expect to see? And how did the locals and others respond to this interest? This essay offers a few of the answers, but by no means all, to these questions, concentrating on the story up to the beginning of the twentieth century.

Stratford appears to have remained largely unaffected by its association with Shakespeare until well over a hundred years after his death. It was only from around the mid-eighteenth century that visitors started to arrive in any appreciable numbers and local people began to be aware of the value, cultural and financial, of living in the town in which the dramatist was born, grew up, retired and died. Why was there such a delay before the first stirrings of tourism showed themselves? Clearly Stratford's emergence as a place of Shakespearian pilgrimage was a process rather than an event that happened at a point in time, and it was a process which depended on a number of cultural, social and technological developments that did not occur until long after the dramatist was laid to rest in Holy Trinity Church in 1616.

What components had to be in place before Stratford was established as a literary shrine? First and foremost was a widespread recognition of Shakespeare's genius; second, information about his many links with Stratford needed to be known and disseminated; third, ease of travel to the town was a prerequisite, together with the creation of a social climate in which the enjoyment of visiting historical sites was an acknowledged leisure pursuit. To consider Shakespeare and Stratford in a seventeenth-century context is to realize how little the necessary conditions existed to establish the town as a visitor attraction.

Shakespeare was not then the dominating cultural figure which he subsequently became. Although highly successful and much admired by many of his contemporaries, the image of him as the 'Immortal Bard' had yet to be formed. During the seventeenth century Shakespeare was often talked of as being on a par with Ben Jonson, Francis Beaumont and John Fletcher. Among some literati, indeed, Jonson's reputation was judged to be the higher and during the two decades after Shakespeare's death, the 1620s and 1630s, and later in the years immediately following the restoration of the monarchy in 1660, the plays of Beaumont and Fletcher challenged Shakespeare's for popularity on the stage.[1] It was not until John Dryden published his *Essay of Dramatic Poesy* in 1668 that Shakespeare began in any way to be the subject of literary criticism, let alone the centre of an academic industry. By the end of the seventeenth century his collected plays had been issued four times since his death, in 1623, 1632, 1663 and 1685. These editions, without any commentary, were relatively expensive folio-size volumes that could not be read without difficulty outside a library or away from a desk. This also applied to Jonson, and to Beaumont and Fletcher, the only other dramatists to enjoy having their works appear in folio. In the case of all four playwrights, the potential size of their readership was limited not only by cost and the relatively modest number of their works available in print, but also by literacy levels and an educational system that did not embrace 'modern' literature.[2] Shakespeare was probably best known during the seventeenth century through performances of his plays but, like all dramatists, his stage reputation suffered an eclipse for twenty years as a consequence of the Civil War and Interregnum, during which the public theatres closed their doors and many were destroyed.

Furthermore, by the end of the century there was still little known about Shakespeare, even among the well educated. Only a few brief references to his life were to be found in books, such as a short passage in Edward Phillips's *Theatrum Poetarum*, an alphabetical dictionary of poets, published in 1675, which included the comment: 'William Shakespear, the Glory of the English Stage; whose nativity Stratford upon Avon is the highest honour that Town can boast of.'[3] Although the antiquary John Aubrey penned some more substantial, albeit random notes and stories about Shakespeare in about 1681, they remained in manuscript form. No biography, not even a short memoir, was available in print to give an account of the dramatist's career and his family background, and thereby generate among some of its readers a curiosity to visit the places connected with him. Travel, in any case, was arduous and slow, with roads often in poor condition. People travelled for business, in search of jobs, or for other necessities, rather than for pleasure. The Civil War disrupted patterns of life, and not until the end of the century did there begin to develop a fashion and taste on any scale for sightseeing for its own sake.

It is in no way surprising, therefore, that Stratford did not become established as a destination for visitors during the seventeenth century. This is not to say there were no pilgrims at all. The fragmentary evidence points to a slow build-up of interest. In 1634 a Lieutenant Hammond made a tour of various counties with two companions. On reaching Stratford they went to view the church and took particular notice of 'A neat Monument of that famous English Poet, Mr William Shakespeere; who was borne heere'.[4] Twenty years on, in 1653, Sir William Dugdale, the Warwickshire antiquary, also made a note about the monument and three years later included the first illustration of it, albeit an inaccurate engraving, in his history of the county.[5] A few years after this, in the early 1660s, the vicar of Stratford, John Ward, may have been having difficulty in answering visitors' questions about the town's distinguished inhabitant, as he wrote in his diary: 'Remember to peruse Shakespear's plays, and bee versd in them, yt I may not bee ignorant in yt matter.'[6] Ten years later, in 1673, there is another record of a visit to Holy Trinity Church, by one Robert Dobyns, who transcribed the four-line verse epitaph on Shakespeare's grave. In the final decade of the century two fuller descriptions survive recording visits to the church and focusing on the dramatist's monument and gravestone. In one case, dating from 1693, a Mr Dowdall was shown round the building by an octogenarian 'clarke', who imparted to him some biographical information about Shakespeare.[7] This would appear to be the first record of a guided tour in Stratford.

An interesting aspect concerning all the earliest recorded visits to the town is the exclusive concentration on the church, an emphasis which extends well into the eighteenth century. William Hall, for example, arrived one evening in 1694, stayed overnight and 'ye next day went to visit ye ashes of the Great Shakespear which lye interr'd in that Church'.[8] There is no reference to the Birthplace in the handful of seventeenth-century accounts of visits to Stratford; nor for that matter is there any mention of Anne Hathaway's cottage, the grammar school, New Place (Shakespeare's retirement home which was still standing in its unaltered state until the beginning of the eighteenth century), nor of any other buildings with Shakespearian connections, apart from the church. There are several explanations for this apparent oddity.

As indicated, no biographical information of any consequence about Shakespeare had appeared in the seventeenth century, and although oral traditions existed about his Stratford background they had not yet found their way into print. Then, the fact that the church was a public place, unlike the other buildings in the town with Shakespeare connections, helped to make it the focal point of interest in the first phase of Stratford's growth as a literary shrine. Further, it would appear that until well into the eighteenth century the relatively small number of those who went in search of places associated with the famous were often more attracted to where they had been buried than where they were born. Early travellers were drawn to tombs and monuments rather than to houses that might be linked to the illustrious dead, not only because the former were often easier to identify and visit. Burial places have a special appeal simply on account of holding the mortal remains, and may offer an onlooker a degree of affinity with the deceased that is not gained elsewhere, especially if, as in Shakespeare's case, an epitaph and a portrait bust with inscriptions are present. It was at gravesides, not scenes of nativity, that the tourists of early modern England were likely to contemplate the fleeting nature of life and take some consolation in the triumph of art over death, sentiments expressed on Shakespeare's own monument. The tendency to regard Holy Trinity Church as Stratford's principal Shakespearian sight persisted even after the Birthplace in Henley Street had become a considerable attraction. The Honourable John Byng, visiting the town in 1785, checked in at the White Lion, close to the Birthplace, and after dinner, as his diary records, 'went forth to pay my obeisance at the shrine of our immortal bard: but first the house of his birth'.[9]

It is possible, of course, that some travellers did go to see the Birthplace in the seventeenth century but have left no record of their visit. If so they would have found John Shakespeare's original three-bay house turned into a sizeable inn, the Maidenhead, with William's sister, Joan Hart, living in a small adjoining part of the property until her death in 1646. Vistors could have joined the locals for a cup of sack in the inn and quizzed them about Shakespeare but it would have never entered the thinking of the landlords in the pre-Civil War era, who were members of the Hiccox family, or the owner, Shakespeare's daughter, Susanna Hall, to memorialize the house as the birthplace of the dramatist. In fact, it seems unlikely that any precedent had been set anywhere in the country at this period for turning the birthplace of a writer into a place of pilgrimage. The impulse to do so belongs to the mental world of the eighteenth century.

The Maidenhead Inn was used early in the Civil War for recruiting and billeting Parliamentary troops: a 1642 document details the expenditure incurred by the landlord for this purpose and a record relating to the following year lists items of value which had been sequestered or stolen from the inn by soldiers.[10] Bardolph and his companions would have felt at home in the Master's birthplace at this time, but few people, if any, went there because of its connections with the creator of these reprobates. However, at

1746. AS the generous proposals of the Proprietors of the two greatest Play-Houses in this Kingdom, were kindly accepted and encourag'd, in relation to each of them Acting a PLAY, for the Sole purpose of erecting a New Monument to the Memory of SHAKESPEARE, in *Westminster-Abbey*; And as the Curious Original Monument and Bust of that incomparable Poet, erected above the Tomb that enshrines his Dust, in the Church of *Stratford upon Avon Warwickshire*, Is through length of Years and other accidents become much impair'd and decay'd; An offer has been kindly made by the Judicious and much Esteem'd Mr. JOHN WARD, and his Company, To Act one of SHAKESPEARE'S PLAYS, *Viz.*

Othello, or the Moor of Venice.

At *Stratford*, on *Tuesday* the *Ninth* of this instant *September*: The Receipts arising from which Representation are to be Solely Appropriated to the Repairing the Original Monument aforesaid.

The part of Othello, to be perform'd by Mr WARD,

Jago, Cassio, Brabantio, Montano, Rodergio, Gratiano, by Mr. *Elrington*, Mr. *Redman*, Mr. *Woodward*, Mr. *Butler*, Mr. *Butcher*, Mr. *Bourne*,

Desdemona, Emilia, by Mrs. *Elrington*, Mrs. *Ward*,

With several Entertainments of SINGING, between the ACTS, by Mrs. Elrington. and Mrs. Willson.

To begin punctually at 6 o'Clock. Pit, 2 s. 6 d. Gallery, 1 s.

It is therefore humbly wish'd, that such Persons as have a taste for the Inimitable Thoughts, the Sublime Expressions, the Natural and lively Descriptions and Characters of that Great Genius, and Consequently a Value for his Memory, will Encourage the propos'd method of perpetuating it, by attending the PLAY, at that juncture, for the laudable purpose of re-beautifying his Venerable Monument and Effigies.

N. B. The Money receiv'd on this Occasion, is to be Deposited in the Hands of the Church-Wardens.

Plate 35. Playbill for the first-known staging of a Shakespeare play in Stratford, a production of *Othello* (1746) to raise money for the restoration of Shakespeare's bust in Holy Trinity Church. (Folger Shakespeare Library T.b.11)

the beginning of the eighteenth century the portion of the Birthplace used as an inn was reduced by about a third when the new inheritor of the property, Shakespeare Hart, moved into its western bay, and it was during the next fifty years that the significance of the house began to be formally recognized, with particular attention being paid by visitors to its western section, in which, it was claimed, lay the actual room in which Shakespeare had been born.

It is sometimes said that Shakespeare's Birthplace did not begin to be appreciated as such and to become a visitor attraction until David Garrick held his Shakespeare Jubilee in the town in 1769, but there was a developing interest before this event. The Birthplace features by name on the earliest street plan of Stratford, drawn by Samuel Winter and published in 1759 (Plate 27), and in 1762 a 'Letter from the Place of Shakespeare's Nativity', appearing in the *British Magazine*, recounts a stay in Stratford which included being taken by the landlord of the White Lion to see the Birthplace.[11] The landlord in question, John Payton, it would appear, was used by this time to escorting guests to view Shakespearian sights both in and around Stratford.

There are other signs, too, to show that before the Garrick Jubilee not only was the Birthplace achieving formal recognition but the town generally was wakening to the realization that it had produced a remarkable son, the protection and honouring of whose memory was a matter of civic pride, and even cash. The first recorded performance of a Shakespeare play in Stratford took place in the Town Hall, in 1746, when a company of players led by John Ward put on *Othello*, with the proceeds of the show being given to restoring the monument of Shakespeare in the church. Ten years later much ill-feeling among Stratford townspeople was aroused against the owner of New Place, the spacious house in Chapel Street bought by Shakespeare in the middle of his London career and where he later retired and died. By the mid-eighteenth century New Place was attracting, like the Birthplace, an increasing number of visitors. A particular feature of interest was an old mulberry tree in the garden, said to have been planted by the dramatist himself. The owner of New Place, a clergyman from Lichfield, the Reverend Francis Gastrell, whose threshold of patience and charity was not high, felt harassed by the mulberry tree seekers, and decided to rid himself of the nuisance by arranging, in 1756, for the tree to be felled. The axeing caused considerable anger in the community, although not everyone disapproved; the Reverend's irreverential act precipitated Stratford's first souvenir industry, thanks mainly to the initiative of one Thomas Sharp who bought the wood from the fallen tree and proceeded to carve and sell goblets, boxes, tobacco-stoppers and other items for years to come. Three years later Gastrell prompted another furore, the nature of which further reflected the growing awareness of Shakespeare's place and value in Stratford and, indeed, signalled an emerging conservation consciousness.

The chopping down of the mulberry did not stop sightseers going to look at New Place and its garden, despite the fact that the house had been substantially or entirely rebuilt since Shakespeare resided there. Pestered by visitors, and involved in a running dispute with the town authorities over the payment of poor rate contributions, Gastrell gave directions for New Place itself to be demolished and he cleared out of town 'amidst the rage and curses of its inhabitants'.[12] The bizarre events surrounding Gastrell are a clear indication that the Shakespearian heritage of Stratford was becoming significant for both locals and visitors.

Plate 36. New Place, Shakespeare's home, as remodelled by Sir John Clopton, *c.* 1700, and demolished by the Reverend Francis Gastrell in the late 1750s. There are no contemporary views: the above is the young R.B. Wheler's reconstruction, published in 1806, presumably drawing on local memory.

What lay behind this very different climate of opinion compared with seventeenth-century attitudes? Why was tourism beginning to take root at this juncture? It has much to do with increasing national interest in Shakespeare's life and works during the first half of the eighteenth century. A spate of editions of the plays, beginning with Nicholas Rowe's in 1709, made Shakespeare a widely read author for the first time and helped to establish him indisputably as a classic.[13] Importantly, Rowe added to his edition a short life of the dramatist, the first attempt at a biography, which prompted further enquiry about Shakespeare's background and career, culminating later in the century with the work of the scholar and editor, Edmond Malone, who was the first person to draw extensively on the Stratford archives. As the level of curiosity and knowledge rose concerning the circumstances of Shakespeare's life, so awareness grew of his Stratford environment and of the surviving buildings and features associated with him.

The proliferation of Shakespeare's works in the first half of the eighteenth century was both cause and effect of the dramatist's rising status, and reflects a growing demand for cheap editions of the classics, especially from middle-class readers. Their needs were also met by the publication of periodicals, usually monthly magazines, which carried news, comment and articles on a wide variety of subjects. The most successful was the *Gentleman's Magazine*, founded in 1731, which was soon printing 15,000 copies a month.[14] It was in a 1769 issue that there appeared the first printed illustration of Shakespeare's Birthplace, in conjunction with an article on the house. Information about Stratford's Shakespearian heritage was gradually being disseminated.

As the eighteenth century progressed, a growing interest in the country's past was reflected in a vogue for historical literature and the rise of antiquarian studies. Following Marlborough's victorious campaigns a spirit of chauvinism was in the air, caught in patriotic songs such as 'Rule Britannia', and cultural as well as historical figures from the past were being sought to validate the sense of national supremacy. Shakespeare, as it were, was waiting in the wings for this moment and now stepped forward onto the national stage as a representative of all that was glorious about the world of English letters. It was at this time, 1741 to be precise, that Shakespeare literally took his place in the pantheon of British worthies when his statue, commissioned from the sculptor Peter Scheemakers, was erected in Westminster Abbey.[15] Stratford's son was truly coming into his own.

In the same year that the Shakespeare statue was unveiled to public acclaim in the Abbey, David Garrick burst upon the London theatre scene, his first major role being Richard III. For the next thirty years he was to dominate the English stage, mainly through performances of Shakespearian parts, and on his death he was buried appropriately close by the Abbey's Shakespeare statue. Garrick was not only responsible in his own right, as actor, theatre manager, writer and collector, for popularizing Shakespeare and helping to make him a cult figure; he was also instrumental in uniting the build-up of interest in Shakespeare, which had been gathering pace over several decades both on the national front and at local level, by staging in Stratford his famous Shakespeare Jubilee. This one event did much to promote Stratford's rise to fame as Shakespeare's town.[16]

Arising out of a request made to him to present a statue of Shakespeare to Stratford's new Town Hall, Garrick conceived the idea of holding a festival in honour of the dramatist (and, his meaner critics said, himself). Costume-makers, carpenters and scenic staff from his Drury Lane theatre were despatched to Stratford, along with a fireworks specialist and a battery of cannons. Composers were commissioned to produce music and songs for the

Plate 37. The pavilion erected on the Bancroft for the 1769 Jubilee, as drawn by Samuel Ireland from contemporary engravings, and published in 1795 in his *Picturesque Views . . . of the Avon*.

occasion, and Garrick himself sat down to write a long ode to Shakespeare. Shortly before the Jubilee took place over three days in September 1769, an impressive wooden amphitheatre had been completed on the banks of the Avon. The programme comprised a colourful range of events intended, some more obviously than others, to do honour to Shakespeare, including public breakfasts at the Town Hall, costumed processions through the streets, an oratorio in the church, a masquerade ball in the amphitheatre, and a horse race on Shottery meadow. One missing ingredient, ironically, was any performance of Shakespeare, but those taking part had the satisfaction of seeing Garrick, aided by the Drury Lane orchestra, score a personal triumph with his rendition of his Shakespearian ode.

Heavy rain on two of the days marred the proceedings and caused some participants to regret they had ever journeyed to Stratford. Others complained at being overcharged for accommodation: the Jubilee can be said to have started, on any scale, Stratford's hotel trade. Nevertheless, despite the problems, the Jubilee was a remarkable happening and a considerable public relations success for both Garrick and Stratford. It generated much press interest, with newspapers and magazines giving coverage to both the planning and implementation of the festival, and its repercussions were widely felt. In itself the Jubilee gave further impetus to the elevation of Shakespeare as the national bard, but in some ways the greatest beneficiary was the town itself. The media attention accorded to Garrick's three-day celebration helped to fix in the public mind Shakespeare's close ties with Stratford and drew attention to the buildings associated with him other than the church, including the Birthplace itself, to which Garrick led a procession, and Anne Hathaway's Cottage, which his brother, George, visited, doubtless with other Jubilites. The local town community was never quite the same after it had experienced the Jubilee, and, though the occasion had caused some adverse comments, Garrick's ground-breaking commemoration put Stratford firmly on the cultural map and in some respects marked the beginnings of the tourist industry proper.

The success of the Jubilee did not depend solely on the fame of Shakespeare and the reputation and abilities of Garrick. The ambitious programme was planned on the assumption that many of those attending would travel to Stratford from outside the locality, and indeed many visitors were attracted from afar, including a fair sprinkling of fashionable London society. They travelled, of course, by coach. That this could happen with relative ease was due to a fairly recent communications revolution which was to have a considerable impact on the rise of Stratford as Shakespeare's town, namely the turnpiking of the major roads which went hand in hand with improvements in the quality and reliability of the coaches which used them. By 1750 the trunk roads connecting London to most major cities, including Birmingham, had been completed, and nearly all the main routes out of Stratford were turnpiked – to Birmingham, Banbury, Long Compton, Alcester and Warwick. In fact, the incentive for improving local road conditions had little to do with encouraging visitors but rather was intended to boost Stratford's role as a regional market centre.[17] Nevertheless an infrastructure was soon in place which, coinciding with Shakespeare's rise to cultural supremacy, provided the basis for an incipient tourism business to become established and for Garrick to consider holding an event such as the Jubilee. The town's strategic position in the centre of England, allied to the new communications network, turned it by the early eighteenth century into a thriving coaching centre. Coaches from London were routed through Stratford to Birmingham, Shrewsbury and Holyhead, and by 1817 at least twenty-four coaches a day were passing through Stratford to and from these destinations.[18]

An increasing number of passengers in coaches reaching Stratford were visitors intent on seeing Shakespeare's town, and inns and hotels were established to meet their needs. As early as the 1750s John Payton had created at the White Lion, situated close to the Birthplace in Henley Street, one of the most famous hostelries in the Midlands. Garrick stayed there during his 1769 Jubilee and later patrons included the Prince Regent when he visited the town in 1806. A sign from the inn dating perhaps to the eighteenth century, which still survives as a museum item, announced 'Saddle Horses with a Guide to be lett to any part of Great Britain'. Another coaching inn to achieve fame was the Red Horse in Bridge Street. Its renown was largely due to its association with Washington Irving, the American author, who first stayed there in 1815 and referred to it in his *Sketch Book*, consisting mainly of an account of his travels in England, which first appeared in parts, on both sides of the Atlantic, in 1819–20. The *Sketch Book* was reprinted many times during the nineteenth century and became one of the most popular publications of its kind. The chapter on Stratford was one of the longest and its delightful descriptions of some of the Shakespearian sights did much to ensure a steadily increasing patronage of the town by visitors from both the old world and the new.[19]

The coaching age, made possible by the 'Georgian motorways', gave people greater access to new leisure pursuits and encouraged a fashion for taking tours to view the country's landscapes and historic sites.[20] There was a particular interest in monuments, ruins and places associated with famous figures from the past, and a literature grew up in

Plate 38. The White Lion Inn in Henley Street, Stratford's leading coaching establishment, from a drawing by Captain James Saunders, *c.* 1825. (SBTRO, ER 1/82, fol. 7)

response to these interests. A publication reflecting the taste for antiquities was *The Beauties of England and Wales* (1801–1816) which included, in 1814, a long survey of Stratford's history, made mainly with reference to its Shakespearian heritage, and drawing substantially on the first history of the town, by R.B. Wheler, published a few years earlier. The direct link between the increasing awareness of Shakespeare's works during the previous hundred years and 'the public inclination to visit this favoured neighbourhood' was acknowledged.

> Until the early part of the eighteenth century polite literature was confined to so few, that the national love of Shakespeare (whose birth was so momentous an era in the fortunes of the town) was not sufficiently ardent to lead numerous pilgrims to Stratford, for the purpose of poetical devotion. But with the spread of letters inevitably kept pace the progress of Shakespeare's fame. His readers must needs become innoxious idolists; and, for very many years, Stratford has witnessed throngs of visitors, anxious to tread the ground which Shakespeare's feet had pressed in boyhood; and to express, by mournful contemplation over the spot hallowed by his ashes, their gratitude for the banquet of intellectual joys afforded by his all but superhuman talents.[21]

Notwithstanding this testimony, at the time Stratford was still a long way from being a centre of tourism on a scale which contributed significantly to its prosperity. The town in fact was suffering from economic depression in the late eighteenth and early nineteenth centuries. Although Shakespeare-inspired visitors were on the increase, boosting the hotel trade and the souvenir industry, the 'throngs of visitors' mentioned in *The Beauties* represented many hundreds rather than many thousands, and were largely confined to an affluent and leisured élite, since travel and sightseeing were beyond the earning power of the majority of the population.[22] A fairly accurate indication of the numbers coming to view the Birthplace can be gleaned from the first visitors' book which begins in 1812 and records in 1813 and 1814 close on 700 people each year who signed the album.[23] The emergence of Stratford as a major visitor attraction was a slow process, extending throughout the nineteenth century: in the early 1850s, those visiting Shakespeare's Birthplace numbered around 2,500; it was not until the turn of the century that admissions exceeded 30,000. Nevertheless, the rise of Stratford as Shakespeare's town continued unabated in Regency and Victorian times, and was linked to the benefits, social and material, brought by the Industrial Revolution, and to Shakespeare's greater cultural pre-eminence, reflected in his expanding reading and theatre-going public, both in his own country and abroad.[24] On the local front it was another key advance in communications which brought many more people to the town – the coming of the railways.

The turnpikes had furthered the commercialization of tourism but the transformation brought about by the application of the steam engine to public transport affected a much higher number of people. Between the mid-1830s and the early 1850s the main intercity railway lines of Britain were almost all completed, followed by the construction of many feeder and branch lines.[25] Stratford benefited much from accessibility by train. Osborne's *London and Birmingham Railway Guide*, published in 1840, proudly reminded its readers that: 'Many who, but a few years since, scarcely penetrated beyond the county in which they happened to have been born, are now induced to visit places far more remote, from the facility and comfort afforded them by railway transit.' The *Guide*'s concern, the London to Birmingham line, had recently been completed, in 1838, twenty years before Stratford was linked to the national network; but in addition to giving information about the places on the itinerary from Euston, travellers could read descriptions of towns off the route which could be reached by changing to a coach, including Stratford-upon-Avon.[26]

By 1860 Stratford was connected to the main system, both by a branch from Hatton Junction on the London to Birmingham line and also by a track from Honeybourne on the Oxford, Worcester and Wolverhampton railway. The railway arrived in time to boost attendance at the celebrations in the town to mark the tercentenary of Shakespeare's birth, held over a two-week period in April/May 1864. Some months before the festival the mayor, Edward Flower, had written to *The Times* announcing Stratford's claim 'in these railway times' to be the focus for national celebrations rather than London.[27]

Visitors to the celebrations were fewer than hoped for, the secretary of the organizing committee attributing this to inadequate publicity, including the rather small posters placed in railway stations. Nevertheless it was reckoned that over 100,000 people were drawn to Stratford over the fortnight period. Some of those arriving by the new steam train were pulled by an engine called 'Will Shakespeare'.[28] At the end of several festival events, including performances of *Othello, Much Ado About Nothing* and *The Merchant of Venice*, trains were waiting to take audiences home to Birmingham, Wolverhampton and Worcester. For the biggest popular entertainment, a street pageant held on two days and featuring, among other things, a procession of Shakespearian characters and some equestrian circus performers, crowds of about 30,000 thronged the town, some of whom came on cheap trains from destinations such as Gloucester, Bristol, Worcester and Birmingham.[29]

At the beginning of the steam age the Duke of Wellington had deplored the growth of railways on the grounds that they would encourage the lower classes to move about. An 1844 Act of Parliament subsequently confirmed the Duke's fears by requiring every railway company to run regular trains at fares not exceeding one penny a mile. Such opportunities for 'third-class' travel, together with the popularity of excursion trains, opened up the new transport system to most working-class people.[30] In Stratford's case, the railways did much to enlarge its role as a major visitor attraction and increase the income which it derived from tourism. From the 1860s onwards, for the rest of the century and beyond, the increasing numbers who journeyed by train represented a wide social diversity, encompassing affluent Americans, middle-class visitors staying in guest houses or small hotels, and day-trippers from the conurbations of Birmingham and Coventry. The town's railway connections improved further in the 1870s and 1880s with an east-west line linking a London route near Towcester to the Evesham and Redditch railway. Operated in due course by the Stratford and Midland Junction railway, with its own station near Old Town, the company exploited Stratford's Shakespearian appeal so as to induce sightseers to use the facility, although the carrying of goods traffic was its main purpose. The line was marketed as 'The Shakespeare Route', with the title appearing on publicity material and luggage labels, and one of the company's promotion plans aimed to attract 'Americans and Continental visitors'.[31]

Not everyone was satisfied with the rail services to Stratford. One complainant writing to the *Stratford Herald*, under the name of 'Veni, Vidi', said, 'There should be a handy convalescent home for Stratford trains as well, because many of the vehicles must be very tired, judging by the long rest they require at every station and the hours of enforced leisure at each junction'.[32] Nevertheless, whatever their shortcomings, the trains to Stratford brought countless visitors and well before the beginning of the twentieth century their services and timetables had become a feature on publicity aimed at tourists. For example, from the early years of the new Memorial Theatre, completed in 1879, publicity leaflets carried details of the special trains being run in connection with performance times.

The rise of towns and large-scale industry in the nineteenth century, transforming old communities and encroaching on the countryside, led to a growing movement to safeguard historic buildings and notable landscapes. Increasing sensitivity to preserving the past, at a time of rapid change, is reflected on the national scene by developments in the final decades of the century such as the passing of the Ancient Monuments Act in 1882, the work of the Commons Preservation Society, and the founding of the National Trust in 1896. In Stratford the second half of the century witnessed a concerted effort to protect the town's Shakespearian heritage. Whatever financial benefits might flow from such action, the impulse to conserve was a moral one, largely inspired by the view that Shakespeare – the man, the works and his environment – was a national treasure who commanded the attention of the civilized world. Shakespeare's age, too, was one with which the Victorians readily and nostalgically identified, recognizing parallels between their time and his, such as the presence of a long-lived female monarch on the throne, the imperial ambitions of colonialists, naval supremacy, an enterprise culture of merchants and businessmen, and the prevalence of a strong sense of patriotism.

Hence it was that the purchase of Shakespeare's Birthplace as a national memorial, in 1847, aroused media and other interest across the country. The sale of the house, following the death of its last private occupier Mrs Court, was conducted in London by Mr George Robins, whose poster announcing the event was not over modest in its claims: 'The truly heart-stirring relic of a most glorious period, and of England's immortal bard . . . the most honoured monument of the greatest genius that ever lived.' Despite its somewhat decrepit appearance, the Birthplace carried much symbolic value at a time when British imperial ambitions were in the ascendancy. Prior to the sale, newspapers campaigned vigorously in favour of saving the house, especially when the news broke that P.T. Barnum, the American circus owner, was interested in acquiring the building and shipping it off to New York. *The Times* thundered that the country's pride was at stake. 'We doubt whether there is in the whole kingdom an edifice of which the nation has greater reason to be proud . . . it must be rescued at all events from the desecrating grasp of those speculators.'[33] Rescued it was, by the joint effort of two committees, one in Stratford and the other in London, which raised funds by a public appeal and successfully bid £3,000 at the auction. On the next day the *Evening Sun* congratulated the committees on an achievement which constituted: 'A brilliant token of the advancement of civilization in these realms and . . . a lesson calculated to inspire the uneducated mechanic with aspirations beyond those which have, in bye-gone centuries, been prevalent throughout the humble classes of society.' The purchase of the Birthplace had 'conferred upon the Empire a boon which has been preserved by three thousand pounds, but which could not be created by the riches of the earth'.[34] Such was the popular perception of Shakespeare. He had now become an embodiment of British pride and a unique cultural asset exportable to other lands; he was part of the mental world of every educated Englishman, and with the growth of literacy and widespread educational opportunity, there were many homes up and down the land which boasted a copy of Shakespeare's works alongside the Bible.

The purchase of the Birthplace, generating as it did innumerable news items, articles and pictures, was wonderful advertising for Stratford, and constituted another milestone in its rise as Shakespeare's town. After its restoration in the 1850s, responsibility for the house, which now incorporated a museum, passed to the Shakespeare Birthplace Trust. Further moves followed to give permanent protection to other Shakespearian sites in Stratford. In 1861, following the launching of a public appeal by the Shakespeare scholar J.O. Halliwell, the site in Chapel Street, where New Place, the dramatist's family home, had stood, was bought, together with the adjoining garden area which had once formed part of the property. Some relatively recent buildings had already encroached on the garden, and Halliwell undertook his initiative to prevent the rest of the site falling into the hands of 'speculators'.[35] After the estate had been safeguarded, the offending buildings were demolished and it was given in due course to the Shakespeare Birthplace Trust. Halliwell proposed too the raising of funds for the purchase of Anne Hathaway's Cottage, which had also been threatened by new development. It was not, however, until 1892 that the Shakespeare Birthplace Trust, now operating under an Act of Parliament, acquired the Hathaway farmhouse for preservation in perpetuity.

Thus by the end of the century key sites in Stratford connected with Shakespeare had been secured. Along with the school buildings, Holy Trinity Church, Clopton Bridge and the new Memorial Theatre, they formed the principal features in a rich historical and architectural townscape which was promoted in a multitude of guides, travel books, editions of Shakespeare, and illustrative matter, and which was made physically and financially accessible to a large proportion of the population, as well as overseas visitors,

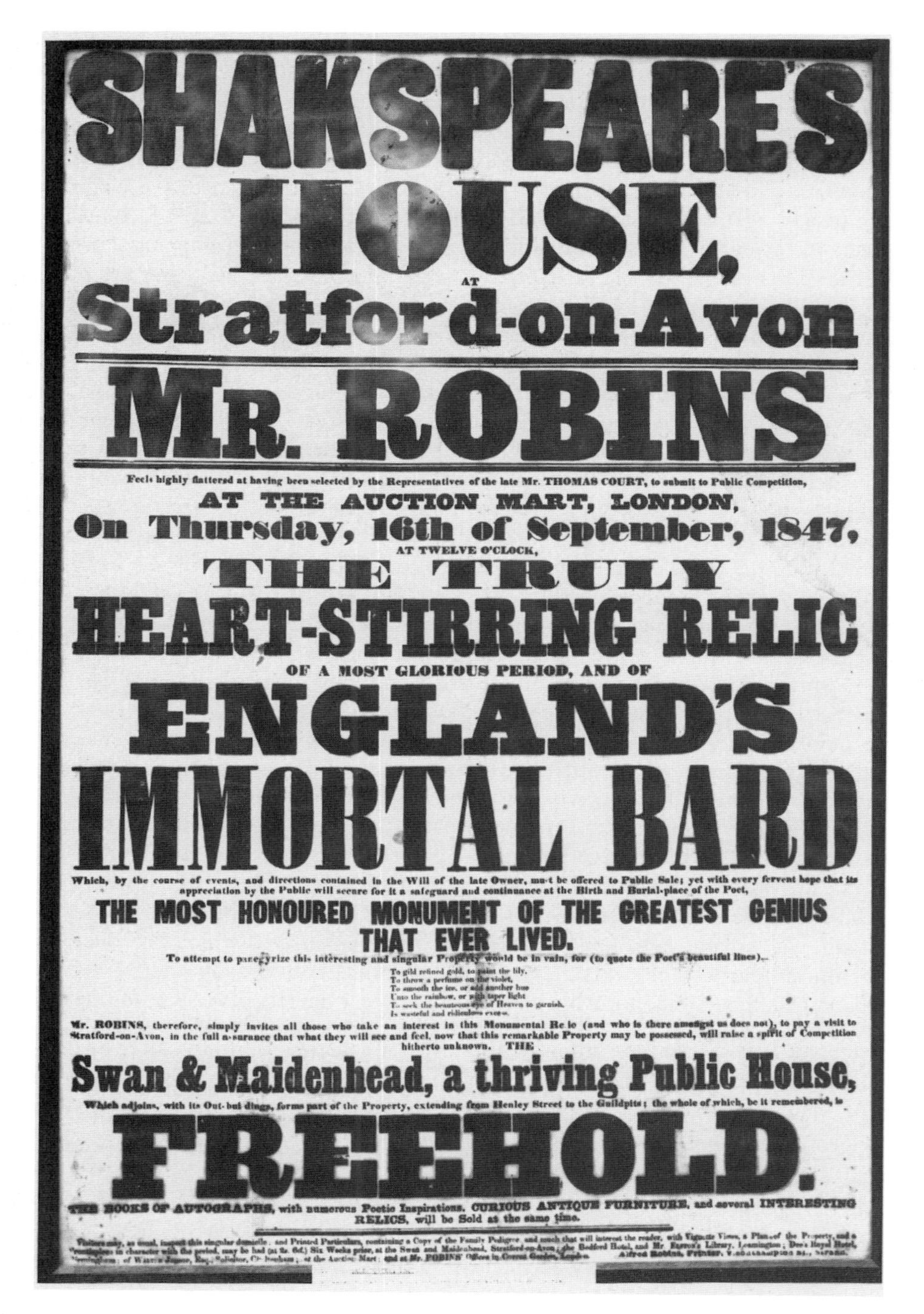

Plate 39. George Robins's sale poster for the auction of Shakespeare's Birthplace on 16 September 1847. (SBTRO, ER 1/129, fol. 11)

Plate 40. Shakespeare's Birthplace, during restoration, 1858. (Photo: Shakespeare Birthplace Trust)

thanks to easy transport, especially the railways. The era of the excursion and the conducted tour truly arrived to take advantage of the propitious circumstances. In the latter part of the century horse-drawn buses or carriages waited outside the station to take newly arrived passengers to see the sights. By about 1910 Messrs Bollands' motor car was ready to take visitors on a tour.[36] In 1911 the Great Central Railway, operating out of Marylebone, was offering an ordinary 'day trip' (its phrase) to Stratford for 6*s* 6*d*, or 12*s* 6*d* including lunch and afternoon tea, or 4*s* for a half-day trip. It was also possible on four days a week in the summer months to take 'an attractive day tour through Shakespeare Country from London (Marylebone) by train and motor car'. This involved departing from London at 10.00 a.m., arriving at Stratford at 12.20 p.m., picking up 'a private automobile' for a drive to Anne Hathaway's Cottage, arriving there at 12.35 p.m. and departing at 12.45 p.m. The brochure was honest enough to state: 'The view of the cottage from the road amply recompenses one for the journey. Time will not permit us to linger.' After a half-hour lunch in Stratford, the day tourists were whisked off to see Warwick Castle, Guy's Cliffe, Kenilworth Castle and Leamington Spa. They returned to Stratford in time for a visit to Shakespeare's Birthplace, before departing on the 4.35 p.m. train back to

London.[37] The development of facilities for Stratford-bound visitors had clearly reached dizzy new heights in the years just before the First World War. Yet further revolutions in the way people might travel paved the way for a still greater expansion of Stratford as a cultural and tourist 'mecca' (the word was increasingly used in this context from the mid-nineteenth century). The growth of motoring in the 1920s and the advent of the motor bus provided new incentives for travel and sightseeing to all except the most disadvantaged; shipping experienced a profound change as the age of sail gave way to steam-powered vessels, and, notably, it was the transatlantic passenger boats and luxury liners which first took advantage of the new technology.[38] Later, after the Second World War, the aeroplane became a major form of travel.

Improvements in transport have always been a key factor in Stratford's growing fame as Shakespeare's town. But without the enduring appeal of Shakespeare's poems and plays the story would have been very different. The seemingly inexhaustible capacity of his writings to give, in all historical periods, delight, consolation and insight into so many human dealings, has ensured the name of Stratford is synonymous with Shakespeare. The first recorded bonding of their names was in fact as early as 1630, unless one counts Leonard Digges's reference, in his poem composed for the First Folio, to 'thy Stratford monument'. Fourteen years after the dramatist's death an anonymous traveller, breaking his journey in Stratford, described it as 'a Towne most remarkeable for the birth of famous William Shakespeare'.[39]

Nor would the story have been the same had not, through accident as well as design, so much of the tangible environment associated with the birth town of this extraordinary, now world-famous, man been preserved. What good fortune to have the house of the glove-maker and mayor under whose roof the sixteenth-century writer grew up; to have, close to certainty, the classroom he sat in, the chapel in which he said prayers with his schoolmates, and the hall where his interest in drama was first whetted; to have the farmhouse where his future wife spent the first third of her life; to have the impressive medieval church where he and his children were baptized, whose services he attended, and where he was buried; to have the garden site acquired when he was thirty-three and which he enjoyed perhaps as a welcome retreat from the pressures of the London life that provided the cash for its purchase; to have the bridge he crossed over on his journeys to and from the capital. And, in addition, to have that later legacy, now stretching back well over a century, for the performance and study of his plays. At the heart of Stratford's successful rise as Shakespeare's town has been the interest and appeal wielded by the survival of this surprisingly varied and extensive heritage which links directly with his world, and to some extent the world of his plays. It is a heritage which, through sheer familiarity, is easily taken for granted.

ABBREVIATIONS

BL	British Library
DNB	*Dictionary of National Biography*
HWCRO	Hereford and Worcester County Record Office
PRO	Public Record Office
SBTRO	Shakespeare Birthplace Trust Record Office
VCH Warws	*Victoria History of the County of Warwick*, 8 vols, London 1904–69
VCH Worcs	*Victoria History of the County of Worcester*, 4 vols, London 1901–26
WCRO	Warwickshire County Record Office

INTRODUCTION

1. On this see Levi Fox, 'Shakespeare's Birthplace Library, Stratford-upon-Avon', *Archives* v 1961, 90–9.
2. Robert Bearman, *Shakespeare in the Stratford Records*, Stroud 1994, 22–31, 49–59.
3. For details see Philip Tennant, *The Civil War in Stratford-upon-Avon: Conflict and Community in South Warwickshire, 1642–1646*, Stroud 1996, 72–4.
4. *VCH Warws,* iii, 236.
5. The scheme, complete with drawings, is explained in Andrew Yarranton, *England's Improvement by Land and Sea*, London 1677, 117–37.
6. Robert Bearman, *Stratford-upon-Avon: A History of its Streets and Buildings*, Nelson 1988, 24–7, 43–6.
7. R.B. Wheler, *The History and Antiquities of Stratford-upon-Avon*, Stratford-upon-Avon 1806, 24.
8. *VCH Warws*, iii, 242, 255–7.
9. Charles Hadfield and John Norris, *Waterways to Stratford*, Newton Abbot 1968; John Norris, *The Stratford and Moreton Tramway*, Guildford 1987.
10. SBTRO, ER 1/107/71; Robert Bearman, *Education in Nineteenth-Century Stratford-upon-Avon*, Stratford-upon-Avon 1974.
11. R.I. Penny, 'The Board of Health in Stratford-upon-Avon: aspects of environmental control', *Warwickshire History* i, no. 6, Autumn 1971, 2–19.
12. For the most recent assessment of the economic impact of tourism on the town, see Stratford-upon-Avon Visitor Management Action Programme, *Stratford-upon-Avon Town Centre Visitor Survey, 1992–1993*, Stratford-upon-Avon 1994.

CHAPTER ONE

1. *Domesday Book, Warwickshire*, ed. John Morris, Chichester 1976, Ch. 3.2.
2. *The Red Book of Worcester*, ed. Marjory Hollings, Worcestershire Historical Society 1934–50, 259–62 where it is dated 1182. For a correction to this, see Mary G. Cheney, *Roger, Bishop of Worcester, 1164–1179*, Oxford 1980, 108–9. Precise counting is difficult due to the listing of identical names twice which may or may not refer to the same person.

3. *Red Book*, 471–97, from a scarce printed version, published by Sir Thomas Phillips, *c*. 1845. The medieval copy from which Phillips worked has since re-surfaced (above, p. 43), requiring some slight modifications to the figures given in E.M. Carus-Wilson, 'The First Half-century of the Borough of Stratford-upon-Avon', *Economic History Review* 2nd series xviii, 1965, 46–63, reprinted in *The Medieval Town*, ed. Richard Holt and Gervase Rosser, London 1990, 49–70 (subsequent references are to the reprinted version).
4. Chapter 3.
5. HWCRO, BA 2636/9 iv ref. 009:1, fol. 93.
6. His confirmation follows John's charter in the cartulary. Mauger was consecrated bishop in June 1200 and his confirmation is witnessed by Archdeacon William de Verdun, who died in 1210 (John Le Neve, *Fasti Ecclesiae Anglicanae, 1066–1300. II: Monastic Cathedrals*, London 1971, 108).
7. William Dugdale, *The Antiquities of Warwickshire*, London 1656, 514.
8. E.g., Carus-Wilson, 'First Half-century', 54.
9. 'Sir Simon Archer: "a lover of antiquity and of the lovers thereof" ' in Philip Styles, *Studies in Seventeenth Century West Midlands History*, Kineton 1978, 1–41. But see also, Robert Bearman, *Captain James Saunders of Stratford-upon-Avon: A Local Antiquary*, Dugdale Society Occasional Paper xxxiii, 1990, 22–5.
10. SBTRO, ER 1/101, fol. 17v: a copy, *c*. 1815, by James Saunders of one of a batch of letters since lost. For copies of the same batch by R.B. Wheler, see BL Add. ms 28564, 220–9, 231. Habington's inspection had been completed by October of the following year (SBTRO, ER 1/101, fols 18–19).
11. SBTRO, ER 1/101, fols 24–24v. See also fols 21–21v.
12. Society of Antiquaries, Habington ms 144, fol. 106.
13. This volume was a victim of the disastrous fire at Birmingham Reference Library in 1879 but had luckily been copied out, at least in part, by several early nineteenth-century antiquaries: see Bearman, *Captain James Saunders*, 22–3. The Stratford entry, as copied by R.B. Wheler, was on page 305 (SBTRO, ER 1/8, 355).
14. Folger Shakespeare Library V.b.66, fol. 2 (microfilm at WCRO, Mi 287/10).
15. SBTRO, ER 1/75, fols 54–54v.
16. They formed part of the Archer family muniments lodged with a Stratford solicitor, Thomas Hunt, when the estates were being partitioned between heiresses: Bearman, *Captain James Saunders*, 21–5.
17. The discovery was made by T.H. Lloyd: see R.H. Hilton, *The English Peasantry in the Later Middle Ages*, Oxford 1975, 83n.
18. William Thomas, *A Survey of the Cathedral-Church of Worcester*, London 1737, Appendix 18–19, from the bishop's 'White Book', HWCRO 821 BA 3814 ref. 821, fol. 42v. Dugdale has caused much confusion by misdating this charter to 25 January (*Antiquities*, 514).
19. He was consecrated on 20 October 1196 (*Radulfi de Diceto Decani Lundoniensis Opera Historica*, ed. William Stubbs, 2 vols, London 1876, ii, 146). For his election earlier in the year, see below, note 27.
20. The Bishop of Worcester from December 1193 to October 1195 was Henry de Soilli, earlier Prior of Bermondsey (1186–9) and Abbot of Glastonbury (1189–93).
21. *Annales Monastici*, ed. H.R. Luard, 5 vols, London 1864–9, ii, 64.
22. His career is neatly summarized in *DNB*, xii, 351–4.
23. For this and what follows, see F.M. Powicke, *The Loss of Normandy, 1189–1204*, 2nd edn., Manchester 1961, 112–17; L. Landon, *The Itinerary of Richard I*, Pipe Roll Society ns xiii, 1935, 106–14; F.M. Powicke, 'King Philip Augustus and the Archbishop of Rouen', *English Historical Review* xxvii, 1912, 106–16.
24. *Radulfi de Diceto*, ii, 145.

25. Le Neve, *Fasti, 1066–1300. III: Lincoln*, 1977, 36.
26. *Chancellor's Roll, 8 Richard I*, Pipe Roll Society ns vii, 1930, 207.
27. *Radulfi de Diceto*, ii, 139. The letter is undated but was placed by Diceto between documents which belong to January and April.
28. The Latin text will be published in the forthcoming *English Episcopal Acta* volume for the diocese of Worcester, edited by Mary Cheney. I am grateful to Mrs Cheney for her comments on a draft of this chapter.
29. Thomas, *Cathedral-Church of Worcester*, Appendix 18–19.
30. For this and what follows, see R.H. Britnell, 'English Markets and Royal Administration before 1200', *Economic History Review* 2nd series xxxi, 1978, 183–96; R.H. Britnell, 'The Proliferation of Markets in England, 1200–1349', *Econ. Hist. Rev.* 2nd series xxxiv, 1981, 209–21.
31. *Domesday Book, Warwickshire*, Chs 3; 16.60; 22.21–2; 36.2; *VCH Warws*, iii, 261, 263–4; v, 198.
32. Christopher Dyer, *Lords and Peasants in a Changing Society, The Estates of the Bishopric of Worcester 680–1540*, Cambridge 1980, 11.
33. *Rotuli Hundredorum*, 2 vols, Record Commission 1812–18, ii, 226; *Placita de Quo Warranto*, Record Commission 1818, 783; *Red Book*, 259.
34. On these 'casual' markets, see Britnell, 'The proliferation of markets', 211–12.
35. Chapter 3.
36. Mary Bateson, 'The Laws of Breteuil', *English Historical Review* xv, 1900, 73–8, 302–18, 496–523, 754–7; xvi, 1901, 92–110, 332–45 (especially xv, 513).
37. Bateson, 'Laws of Breteiul', xv, 302–6.
38. Dyer, *Lords and Peasants*, 64.
39. Maurice Beresford, *New Towns of the Middle Ages, Town Plantation in England, Wales and Gascony*, London 1967, 60–97, 330.
40. Dyer, *Lords and Peasants*, 60–1.
41. For this, see the seminal study, Carus-Wilson, 'The First Half-century', especially 58–63. Her figures, however, have been adjusted slightly to take account of Christopher Dyer's comment that three of the places she regarded as unidentified are probably Talton, Larkstoke and Preston-on-Stour, and that Hatton in Hampton Lucy (one of the bishop's manors) is a more likely identification than Hatton near Warwick.
42. Above, pp. 34–5.
43. The discussion is summarized in Edward Miller and John Hatcher, *Medieval England: Towns, Commerce and Crafts, 1086–1348*, London 1995, 393–4.
44. *Rotuli Chartarum in Turri Londinensi Asservati*, Record Commission 1837, 202.

CHAPTER TWO

1. Shakespeare Birthplace Trust Coin Collection Series B (Wheler) and C (Cove Jones).
2. N. Palmer, *Roman Stratford, Excavations at Tiddington 1980–81*, Warwickshire Archaeology no. 2, Warwick 1982, 5–6.
3. W.J. Fieldhouse, T. May and F.C. Wellstood, *A Romano-British Industrial Settlement at Tiddington near Stratford-upon-Avon*, Birmingham 1931.
4. G. Webster, 'The West Midlands in the Roman Period', *Transactions of the Birmingham and Warwickshire Archaeological Society*, lxxxvi, 1974, 53.
5. F.C. Wellstood, *Report of the Proceedings at the Annual Meeting of the Trustees and Guardians of Shakespeare's Birthplace*, 1935.
6. Palmer, *Roman Stratford*, 5–6.
7. W.J. Ford, 'Stratford-upon-Avon', *West Midlands Archaeological News Sheet* xii, 1969, 33.
8. W.J. Ford, 'Alveston Manor Hotel, Stratford-upon-Avon', *WMANS* xiii, 1970, 41; 'Alveston,

Stratford-upon-Avon', *WMANS* xiv, 1971, 21; 'Alveston Manor Hotel', typescript report in Sites and Monuments Record WA 1065.

9. T. Slater and C. Wilson, *Archaeology and Development in Stratford on Avon*, Birmingham 1977.
10. Palmer, *Roman Stratford*; N. Palmer, 'Tiddington Roman Settlement – an Interim Report on Excavations 1980–1', *West Midlands Archaeology* xxiv, 1981, 16–24; N. Palmer, 'Tiddington Roman Settlement, Second Interim Report', *WMA* xxvi, 1983, 36–46.
11. Palmer, 'Second Interim', 41; N. Palmer and S. Palmer, 'Stratford-upon-Avon, Tiddington Roman Settlement', *WMA* xxxi, 1988, 34.
12. D. Hooke, *Anglo-Saxon Landscapes of the West Midlands: The Charter Evidence*, British Archaeological Reports 95, Oxford 1981, 90–1, 108, 327–8; D. Hooke, *The Anglo-Saxon Landscape: The Kingdom of the Hwicce*, Manchester 1985, 202–8.
13. Palmer, *Roman Stratford*, 9; Palmer, 'Interim Report', 19.
14. A. Baker, 'Aerial Reconnaissance', *WMANS* xiii, 1970, 12.
15. Slater and Wilson, 29, n. 10.
16. Palmer, 'Second Interim', 39, 41; Palmer, *Roman Stratford*, 12; Palmer, 'Interim Report', 21.
17. Palmer, *Roman Stratford*, 12, Fig. 13; Palmer 'Interim Report', 21.
18. Palmer, *Roman Stratford*, 16, 18; Palmer, 'Interim Report', 22; Palmer, 'Second Interim', 44.
19. Warwickshire Museum, *Archaeological Evaluation at 80 Tiddington Road, Stratford-upon-Avon, Warwickshire*, Warwick 1996.
20. Confirmed by trial trenching in 1993: R. King, *Proposed Extension to Rayford Caravan Park, Tiddington Warwickshire, Archaeological Evaluation*, Cotswold Archaeological Trust 1993.
21. Palmer, 'Second Interim', 39.
22. Palmer, *Roman Stratford*, 12–15.
23. Palmer, *Roman Stratford*, 14–16; Palmer, 'Interim Report', 21–2.
24. Fieldhouse, May and Wellstood, 32–3, No. 48, Pl. IX, XII–XIII.
25. L.C. Moffett, 'Crops and Crop Processing', in N. Palmer, *Tiddington Roman Settlement*, forthcoming.
26. J. Hamilton, 'Animal Bone' in N. Palmer, *Tiddington Roman Settlement*, forthcoming.
27. Palmer, 'Second Interim', Fig. 5.
28. M. Green, 'A Miniature Bronze Axe from Tiddington, Warwickshire', *Britannia* xvi, 1985, 238–41.
29. P.M. Booth, 'Iron Age, Roman and Anglo-Saxon Pottery' in N. Palmer, *Tiddington Roman Settlement*, forthcoming.
30. N. Palmer and S. Palmer, *WMA* xxxi, 1988, 34. The interim makes no mention of the Anglo-Saxon phase as the Anglo-Saxon pottery was not recognized in a predominantly Roman assemblage until detailed analysis took place.
31. W.J. Ford, 'Alveston Manor Hotel', typescript report in SMR WA 1065.
32. A Hawkes Type Ib: S.C. Hawkes, 'Soldiers and Settlers in Britain, Fourth to Fifth Century', *Medieval Archaeology* v, 1981, 26, 49, Fig. 16.
33. Slater and Wilson, 29–30.
34. Slater and Wilson, 22, 29; A. Meany, *Gazetteer of Early Anglo-Saxon Burial Sites*, London 1964, 257, quoting Warwick Museum Records.
35. Hawkes, 'Soldiers and Settlers', 26.
36. A single skeleton was found at Bradley Lodge in 1936 but there is no mention of grave goods in the contemporary newspaper account (*Stratford-upon-Avon Herald*, 31 January 1936) and it is likely to have been another Romano-British burial. This skeleton survives in the SBT collection, but without any grave goods. Confusion may have arisen with the then recently excavated Alveston Manor material. The only finds in the article cited by Slater and Wilson, 29, n. 12, are definitely from Alveston Manor Grave 70.

37. Warwickshire Museum, *6 & 7 Tiddington Road, Stratford-upon-Avon, Warwickshire, Archaeological Evaluation*, Warwick 1992.
38. Warwickshire Museum, *Archaeological Evaluation at Woodpecker Cottage, Loxley Road, Stratford-upon-Avon*, Warwick 1996.
39. Warwickshire Museum, *Archaeological Observation at Banbury Road, Stratford-upon-Avon*, Warwick 1996.
40. It is noticeable that all the finds made so far lie in the later Alveston parish.
41. D. Hooke, *The Anglo-Saxon Landscape: The Kingdom of the Hwicce*, 204–6; information from Della Hooke; *VCH Warws*, iii, 221.
42. J.M. Kemble, *Codex Diplomaticus Aevi Saxonici*, 6 vols, London 1839–48, iii, No. 651.
43. *Domesday Book, Warwickshire*, ed. John Morris, Chichester 1976, Ch. 3.2; SMR WA 1010.
44. SMR WA 1020; R. Bearman, *Stratford-upon-Avon: A History of its Streets and Buildings*, Hendon 1988, 46.
45. Slater and Wilson, 10, Fig. 2.
46. Warwickshire Museum, *New Street, Stratford-upon-Avon, Archaeological Evaluation*, Warwick 1992; SMR WA 7215.
47. W.J. Ford, 'Stratford-upon-Avon', *WMANS* xii, 1969, 33.
48. S. Ratkai, 'Pottery from the New Vicarage Site, Stratford-upon-Avon, 1969', unpublished report in SMR WA 1031, 1994.
49. Slater and Wilson, 24; Warwickshire Museum, *Archaeological Recording in Avoncroft Gardens, Stratford-upon-Avon*, Warwick 1997.
50. *Domesday Book*, Ch. 3.
51. Slater and Wilson, 30.
52. Warwickshire Museum, *Archaeological Evaluation of Cox's Timber Yard, Bridge Foot, Stratford-upon-Avon*, Warwick 1996.
53. Slater and Wilson, 9.
54. SBT Coin Collection Series B, No. 20.
55. SMR WA 5911.

The drawings for this section were prepared by Andrew Isham.

CHAPTER THREE

1. M.R.G. Conzen, *Alnwick, Northumberland: A Study in Town-Plan Analysis* [Publications of the Institute of British Geographers, No. 27] London 1960.
2. Della Hooke, *The Anglo-Saxon Landscape: The Kingdom of the Hwicce*, Manchester 1985, 207.
3. Hooke, 204.
4. T.R. Slater and C. Wilson, *Archaeology and Development in Stratford-upon-Avon*, Birmingham 1977, 25.
5. T.R. Slater, 'The Origins of Warwick', *Midland History* viii, 1983, 1–13.
6. Slater and Wilson, 23.
7. G. Webster and B. Hobley, 'Aerial Reconnaissance over the Warwickshire Avon', *Archaeological Journal* cxxi, 1971, 1–19.
8. Christopher Dyer, *Lords and Peasants in a Changing Society: The Estates of the Bishopric of Worcester 680–1540*, Cambridge 1980, 19–20.
9. P. Rahtz, 'A Possible Saxon Palace near Stratford-upon-Avon', *Antiquity* xliv, 1970, 137–40.
10. M.E. Tomlinson, 'River Terraces of the Lower Valley of the Warwickshire Avon', *Quarterly Journal of the Geological Society* lxxxi, 1925, 137–69.
11. John Blair, 'Minster Churches in the Landscape', in Della Hooke (ed.), *Anglo-Saxon Settlements*, Oxford 1988, 35–58.

12. Hooke, 202–8.
13. *Domesday Book, Warwickshire*, ed. John Morris, Chichester 1976, Chs 18.7; 22.21–2.
14. *Domesday Book*, Ch. 3.1–2.
15. *Domesday Book*, Ch. 3.2.
16. C.C. Taylor, 'The Origins of Lichfield', *Transactions of the South Staffordshire Archaeological and Historical Society* xxii, 1969, 43–52; T.R. Slater, 'The Topography and Planning of Medieval Lichfield', *Transactions of the South Staffordshire Archaeological and Historical Society* xxvi, 1986, 11–35.
17. M.W. Beresford, *New Towns of the Middle Ages: Town Plantation in England, Wales and Gascony*, London 1967, 499.
18. T.R. Slater, 'Urban Genesis and Medieval Town Plans in Warwickshire and Worcestershire', in T.R. Slater and P.J. Jarvis (eds), *Field and Forest: An Historical Geography of Warwickshire and Worcestershire,* Norwich 1982, 173–202.
19. E.M. Carus-Wilson, 'The First Half Century of the Borough of Stratford-upon-Avon', *Economic History Review* 2nd series xviii, 1965, 46–63.
20. T.R. Slater, 'Benedictine Town Planning in Medieval England: The Evidence from St Albans', in T.R. Slater and G. Rosser (eds), *The Church in the Medieval Town*, Aldershot 1997 (forthcoming).
21. Beresford, 14–51.
22. David Friedman, *Florentine New Towns: Urban Design in the Late Middle Ages*, Cambridge, Mass., 1988, 149–66.
23. T.R. Slater, 'Ideal and Reality in English Episcopal Medieval Town Planning', *Transactions of the Institute of British Geographers* New Series xxii, 1987, 191–203.
24. Tomlinson, 'River Terraces'.
25. Slater, 'Ideal and Reality', 193.
26. Robert Bearman, *Stratford-upon-Avon: A History of its Streets and Buildings*, Nelson 1988, 2.
27. Slater, 'Ideal and Reality', 195.
28. Hooke, 206–7.
29. Beresford; Slater, 'Ideal and Reality'.
30. C.J. Bond, 'Central Place and Medieval New Town: The Origins of Thame, Oxfordshire', in T.R. Slater (ed.), *The Built Form of Western Cities: Essays for M.R.G. Conzen on the Occasion of his Eightieth Birthday*, Leicester 1990, 83–108.
31. T.R. Slater, 'The Analysis of Burgage Patterns in Medieval Towns', *Area* xiii, 1981, 211–16.
32. M.R.G. Conzen, 'The Use of Town Plans in the Study of Urban History', in H.J. Dyos (ed.), *The Study of Urban History*, London 1968, 113–30; T.R. Slater, 'English Medieval Town Planning', in D. Denecke and G. Shaw (eds), *Urban Historical Geography: Recent Progress in Britain and Germany*, Cambridge 1988, 93–108; T.R. Slater, 'English Medieval New Towns with Composite Plans: Evidence from the Midlands', in T.R. Slater (ed.), *Built Form*, 60–82.
33. Slater, 'Analysis of Burgages'.
34. Slater, 'Ideal and Reality'.
35. Beresford, 500–1.
36. *The Red Book of Worcester*, ed. Marjory Hollings, Worcester Historical Society, 1934–50, 471–97.
37. M. Biddle (ed.), *Winchester in the Early Middle Ages*, Oxford 1976, 370–4.
38. William Cooper, *Henley-in-Arden, an Ancient Market Town,* Birmingham 1946, 7.
39. Slater, 'Ideal and Reality', 195–6.
40. G. Milne (ed.), 'Timber Building Techniques in London, A.D. 900–1400', *London and Middlesex Archaeological Society Special Paper No. 15*, London 1992.
41. Bearman, 20, 36, 47.

42. *Archaeological Excavations in 1970*, HMSO, London 1971.
43. *Minutes and Accounts of Stratford-upon-Avon Corporation III*, Dugdale Society v, 1929, 105–9.
44. Bearman, 20.

CHAPTER FOUR

1. This is based on research for the forthcoming *Cambridge Urban History of Britain*.
2. Philip Styles, 'Borough of Stratford-upon-Avon', in *VCH Warws*, iii, 221–82; Levi Fox, *The Borough Town of Stratford-upon-Avon*, Stratford-upon-Avon 1953; Eleanora Carus-Wilson, 'The First Half-Century of the Borough of Stratford-upon-Avon', *Economic History Review* 2nd series xviii, 1965, 46–63, reprinted in *The Medieval Town*, ed. Richard Holt and Gervase Rosser, London 1990, 49–70 (subsequent references will be to the reprinted version); Terence Lloyd, *Some Aspects of the Building Industry in Medieval Stratford-upon-Avon*, Dugdale Society Occasional Paper xiv, 1961; Rodney Hilton, *The English Peasantry in the Later Middle Ages*, Oxford 1975, 83–4, 93–4.
3. The figure for the number of small towns comes from the forthcoming *Cambridge Urban History of Britain*. On small towns in general see Rodney Hilton, 'Small Town Society in England before the Black Death', in *The Medieval Town*, ed. Holt and Rosser, 71–96; Rodney Hilton, 'Medieval Market Towns and Simple Commodity Production', *Past and Present* 109, 1985, 3–23; David Postles, 'An English Small Town in the Later Middle Ages: Loughborough', *Urban History* xx, 1993, 7–29; Mark Bailey, 'A Tale of Two Towns: Buntingford and Standon in the Later Middle Ages', *Journal of Medieval History* xix, 1993, 351–71; Peter Clark, 'Introduction', in *Small Towns in Early Modern Europe*, ed. Peter Clark, Cambridge 1995, 1–21.
4. Carus-Wilson, 'First Half-Century'.
5. Printed in *The Red Book of Worcester*, ed. Marjory Hollings, Worcestershire Historical Society 1934–50, 471–97.
6. Winchester Cathedral Library, W40/28. I am very grateful to Dr Nicholas Vincent for alerting me to the existence of this document, and to Mr Hardacre of the Cathedral Library who allowed me to read it.
7. *Curia Regis Rolls* xiii, 246–7; *Rolls of the Justices in Eyre for Gloucestershire, Warwickshire and Shropshire, 1221, 1222*, ed. Doris Stenton, Selden Society lix, 1940, 301–2.
8. Mark Ormrod, 'The Crown and the English Economy, 1290–1348', in *Before the Black Death*, ed. Bruce Campbell, Manchester 1991, 156.
9. Christopher Dyer, 'Taxation and Communities in Late Medieval England', in *Progress and Problems in Medieval England*, ed. Richard Britnell and John Hatcher, Cambridge 1996, 175–7.
10. *Register of Simon de Montacute, Bishop of Worcester, 1334–1337*, ed. Roy Haines, Worcestershire Historical Society new series xv, 1996, 171. Wilmcote was not a rectory, so the title may be a clerical error.
11. For a similar argument about the credibility of such figures, see Richard Britnell, 'The Black Death in English Towns', *Urban History* xxi, 1994, 198–9, 204–5.
12. The estimate of the rural population is based on *Red Book*, ed. Hollings, 243–57; *The Lay Subsidy Roll for Warwickshire of 6 Edward III*, ed. W.F. Carter, Dugdale Society vi, 1926, 84–6; W.F. Carter, ed., 'Lay Subsidy Roll, Warwickshire, 1327', *Transactions of the Midland Record Society* vi, 1902, 34–5.
13. Shipston-on-Stour's population was 300–400: Christopher Dyer, 'Small-Town Conflict in the Later Middle Ages: Events at Shipston-on-Stour', *Urban History* xix, 1992, 193; see pp. 89–90 for early modern population figures.
14. Carus-Wilson, 'First Half-Century', 58–9. Her identifications need some correction – 'de

Hatton' is most likely to refer to Hatton-on-Avon in Hampton Lucy, not Hatton near Warwick, and she did not notice Talton and Barcheston, the latter because it was mis-transcribed.

15. *Records of the Borough of Leicester*, ed. Mary Bateson, i, Cambridge 1889, 233.
16. Carter, 'Lay Subsidy'; *Lay Subsidy Roll for the County of Worcester I Edward I[II]*, ed. F.J. Eld, Worcestershire Historical Society 1895; *The Taxpayers of Medieval Gloucestershire*, ed. Peter Franklin, Stroud 1993.
17. *Red Book*, ed. Hollings, 259; SBTRO, BRT 1/2/59 (deed of *c.* 1296); *Justices in Eyre*, ed. Stenton, 281.
18. *Red Book*, ed. Hollings, 259, 464.
19. *The Register of the Gild of the Holy Cross, the Blessed Mary and St John the Baptist of Stratford-upon-Avon*, ed. J. Harvey Bloom, London 1907, v–vi; the date of Giffard's document is usually given as 1269, but see Roy Haines, *Archbishop John Stratford*, Toronto 1986, 1–2; SBTRO, BRT 1/3/202; 1/2/60; 1/2/2 (deeds of the early thirteenth century and 1296); Levi Fox, *The Early History of King Edward VI School Stratford-upon-Avon*, Dugdale Society Occasional Paper xxix, 1984, 3; *Lay Subsidy Roll*, ed. Carter, 90–6; *Calendar of Patent Rolls, 1330–1334*, 210, 219, 521; Rodney Hilton, *A Medieval Society. The West Midlands at the End of the Thirteenth Century*, reprint, Cambridge 1983, 206.
20. Haines, *Archbishop*, 367–81
21. *Justices in Eyre*, ed. Stenton, 177, 301–2, 350.
22. SBTRO, BRT 1/2/34; 1/2/37; 1/2/77 (deeds of 1306, 1318 and 1327).
23. SBTRO, BRT 1/2/260; 1/2/187 (deeds of 1346 and 1341); 1/2/79 (deed of *c.* 1294).
24. *Registrum sive Liber Irrotularius et Consuetudinarius Beatae Mariae Wigorniensis*, ed. William Hale, Camden Society xci, 1865, 83a (seven cottars are listed *juxta pontem*).
25. The evidence all comes from later documents, but these must have been long standing features of the town: SBTRO, BRT 1/2/356; 1/2/430 (gardens in deeds of 1404 and 1424); 1/3/57; 1/3/134; 1/3/143 (elms in account of 1450–1, rentals of 1475 and 1485); 1/3/51 (hedges in account of 1441–2); 1/3/214 (pigs in *interlocutio* notes of 1387). On similar features in Coventry, see Hilton, *Medieval Society*, 185.
26. Again the evidence is late, but still relevant to the earlier period: SBTRO, BRT 1/2/527 (deed of 1497 mentions coal being burnt in the hearths of the almshouses); *Stratford-on-Avon Corporation Records, the Guild Accounts*, ed. [W.J. Hardy], Stratford-upon-Avon n.d., 32 (fire in Rother Street mentioned in account of 1452–3); BRT 2/1, fol. 1 (dunghills in rental of bridge-wardens).
27. *Justices in Eyre*, ed. Stenton, 348–9 (a Welshman was killed, and his brothers accused nineteen named townspeople).
28. Carus-Wilson, 'First Half-Century', 62–3; 'staff' could refer by association to his right hand.
29. SBTRO, BRT 1/2/76 (deed of *c.* 1285) and numerous others; Haines, *Archbishop*, 3–5; *Red Book*, ed. Hollings, 265–7, 276 (surveys of Hatton in 1299 and *c.* 1166).
30. Haines, *Archbishop*, 101–23.
31. The controversy is summed up in Alan Dyer, *Decline and Growth in English Towns, 1400–1640*, 2nd edition, Cambridge 1996.
32. John Sheail, 'The Regional Distribution of Wealth in England as indicated by the Lay Subsidy Returns of 1524/5' (University of London Ph.D. thesis, 1968), appendix; Richard Holt, *The Early History of the Town of Birmingham 1166–1600*, Dugdale Society Occasional Paper xxx, 1985, 15–16; *English Gilds*, ed. Toulmin Smith, Early English Text Society, Original Series xl, 1870, 222. The calculation of the town's population in 1546 is based on the assumption that 1,500 communicants represents some 1,900 people in the parish, and that the rural population would have been about 400 (as well as the general population decline since 1300, four of the villages had been deserted). I am grateful to Alan Dyer for his advice on these documents.
33. HWCRO, ref. 009:1 BA2636/176 92498; /177 92503; /40 43814; ref. 899:49 BA 8789 (accounts of Stratford borough, 1496–1525). From 1433 the receivers' accounts give totals of

cash paid by Stratford officials to the central administration of the estate. These documents are listed in Christopher Dyer, *Lords and Peasants in a Changing Society: The Estates of the Bishopric of Worcester, 680–1540*, Cambridge 1980, 391–2.

34. SBTRO, tenement histories compiled by adult education classes.
35. SBTRO, BRT 1/2/372; 1/2/380; 1/2/392; 1/2/426; 1/2/463; 1/2/484; 1/2/406; 1/2/414; 1/2/520.
36. Terence Lloyd, 'The Mediaeval Gilds of Stratford-on-Avon and the Timber-Framed Building Industry' (University of Birmingham MA thesis, 1961), 77–8; HWCRO, ref. 009:1 BA2636/37(iii) 43806, fols 207–9 (lease of 1537).
37. E.g. SBTRO, BRT 1/3/216 (memorandum of an arbitration in 1429); *Corporation Records*, ed. Hardy, 39 (account with costs of settling discord in 1464–5); Dyer, *Lords and Peasants*, 280; *Select Cases before the King's Council in the Star Chamber*, ed. I.S. Leadam, Selden Society xvi, 1902, 230–4.
38. SBTRO, BRT 1/3/114, 111; *Register of the Gild*, ed. Bloom, 6–7, 188–96; *Corporation Records*, ed. Hardy, 56.
39. Maurice Beresford and John Hurst, *Deserted Medieval Villages*, London 1971, 204–6. The problems of finding tenants and collecting rents in the manor of Old Stratford are vividly displayed in the manorial account of 1464–5; Berkeley Castle muniment room, select roll no. 63.
40. HWCRO, ref. 009:1 BA 2636/40 43814; Dyer, *Lords and Peasants*, 280.
41. For the later mill rents, the manuscripts cited in notes 36 and 39 above; for the 1290s, *Red Book*, ed. Hollings, 244, 258.
42. Lloyd, 'Mediaeval Gilds', 94–6; SBTRO, tenement histories.
43. SBTRO, BRT 1/2/447, 1/2/518; 1/3/32.
44. *VCH Warws*, iii, 223, 227–9; Robert Bearman, 'A History of Stratford's Finest Mediaeval House', *Warwickshire History* i, no. 2, 1969, 25–36; Stephen Cracknell, '"Bard's Walk", Wood Street, Stratford-upon-Avon. Medieval Structures Excavated in 1989', *Transactions of the Birmingham and Warwickshire Archaeological Society* xcvii, 1991–2, 57–75.
45. Levi Fox, 'Some New Sidelights on Stratford-upon-Avon's Medieval Guild Buildings', *Transactions of the Birmingham Archaeological Society* lxx, 1952, 48–59; SBTRO, BRT 1/3/42 (account of 1431–2); *VCH Warws,* iii, 269–78.
46. College revenues: *Valor Ecclesiasticus*, Record Commission 1817, iii, 94; SBTRO, BRT 1/3/72 (rental of 1455–6).
47. Lloyd, 'Mediaeval Gilds', 33–4; SBTRO, BRT 1/3/5 (account 1390–1); 1/2/339 (deed, 1396); Carus-Wilson believed that a surname in 1251/2 indicated oil processing at that date, but the name seems to derive from the Christian name Ilger. For plaster pits: HWCRO, ref. 009:1 BA 2636/175 92480 (receiver's account); for plastermonger, *Register of the Gild*, ed. Bloom, 101.
48. PRO, E101/258/1. I am grateful to Drs Jim Galloway and Margaret Murphy for this reference.
49. Rodney Hilton, 'The Small Town and Urbanisation – Evesham in the Middle Ages', in Rodney Hilton, *Class Conflict and the Crisis of Feudalism*, London 1985, 190.
50. Lloyd, *Building Industry*, 12–16.
51. SBTRO, BRT 1/3/40. A quarter of expenditure went on bread, while ale and fish accounted for two-thirds.
52. Charles Phythian-Adams, 'Urban Decay in Late Medieval England', in *Towns in Societies*, ed. Philip Abrams and E.A. Wrigley, Cambridge 1978, 166–7; Martha Carlin, *Medieval Southwark*, London 1996, 53.
53. Alan Everitt, 'The Primary Towns of England', in Alan Everitt, *Landscape and Community in England*, London 1985, 93–107.
54. *Calendar of Ancient Deeds*, iii, 91.
55. Della Hooke, 'Village Development in the West Midlands', in *Medieval Villages*, ed. Della Hooke, Oxford 1985, 127–49.

56. Worcestershire had four towns by 1086, and others were probably growing in the twelfth century. South of Warwick only Alcester may have existed before 1196.
57. *VCH Warws*, iii, 237.
58. Dyer, 'Small-Town Conflict'.
59. Hilton, *English Peasantry*, 93–4; *VCH Warws*, iii, 247.
60. *Register of Simon Montacute*, ed. Haines, 172–81; HWCRO, ref. 009:1 BA 2636/175 92483 (receiver's account with donation to church fabric, 1460–1); /177 92503 (bailiff's account of borough, 1517–18); SBTRO, BRT 1/3/38; 1/3/119 (accounts with expenses of bishops' visits, 1427–8, 1436–7); BRT 2/1 fol. 5 (gift to bridge, 1527); Maidstone, Centre for Kentish Studies, Sackville of Knole U269 M73 (Stratford borough court rolls).
61. SBTRO, DR 75/4, 7, 8; Christopher Dyer, 'Market Towns and the Countryside in Late Medieval England', *Canadian Journal of History* xxxi, 1996, 17–35.
62. *Corporation Records*, ed. Hardy, 55; *Register of the Gild*, ed. Bloom, 117; Sackville of Knole, U269 M73.
63. Rodney Hilton, 'Winchcombe Abbey and the Manor of Sherborne', in Hilton, *Class Conflict*, 20.
64. PRO, SC6/ 1038/4, 5; 1042/7; 947/2, 3, 5 (accounts of Bidford, Radbourne, Catesby); JUST 1/977 (assize roll). I owe the Catesby references to Dr Jane Laughton.
65. Dyer, *Lords and Peasants*, 212; Christopher Dyer, 'Were there any Capitalists in Fifteenth-Century England?', in Christopher Dyer, *Everyday Life in Medieval England*, London 1994, 318.
66. BL ms Add. 34739; SBTRO, BRT 1/2/525.
67. Magdalen College, Oxford, 35/9; David Farmer, 'Marketing the Produce of the Countryside, 1200–1500', in *Agrarian History of England and Wales*, iii, 1348–1500, ed. Edward Miller, Cambridge 1991, 413; PRO, SC6/ 947/ 1, 3.
68. For purchases of iron and leather goods recorded in manorial accounts, Magdalen College, Oxford, 35/9; PRO, SC6/1038/5; for Shelfeld, 'Extracts from the . . . De Banco Rolls and Coram Rege Rolls of Richard II and Henry IV', ed. G. Wrottesley, *Collections for a History of Staffordshire* xvi, 1895, 60. Grain was being traded from Stratford to Birmingham, Coleshill, Dudley and Walsall in 1401: *Calendar of Patent Rolls 1399–1401*, 552–3; for the pottery, Cracknell, '"Bard's Walk"', 62–73 (specialist report by Stephanie Ratkai).
69. PRO, SC6/ 1042/ 3; *Household Accounts from Medieval England*, ed. Christopher Woolgar, part 2, British Academy Records of Social and Economic History xviii, Oxford 1993, 448.
70. *Corporation Records*, ed. Hardy, 16, 20, 26, 42, 43.
71. Christopher Dyer, *Warwickshire Farming. Preparations for Agricultural Revolution*, Dugdale Society Occasional Paper xxvii, 1981, 9–12.
72. Hilton, *Medieval Society*, 172–3. For Wootton, *West Midlands Archaeology* xxxi, 1988, 40–1.
73. Wendy Barker, 'Warwickshire Markets', *Warwickshire History* vi, no. 5, 1986, 161–75; Hilton, *Medieval Society*, 192–3.
74. WCRO, CR 1886/143 (Alcester borough court roll); Worcester Cathedral Library, C788 (Shipston rental).
75. e.g. PRO, KB27/576 m.cccxvii (King's Bench plea roll, 1405); CP 40 / 332 m. ccxvi (Common Pleas plea roll, 1342); *Register of the Guild of the Holy Trinity, John the Baptist and St Katherine of Coventry*, ed. Mary Dormer Harris, Dugdale Society xiii, 1935, 41.
76. *Register of the Gild*, ed. Bloom, 117; SBTRO, BRT 1/2/408 (deed of 1474).
77. SBTRO, DR 98/ 90, 92, 93, 96; 'Some Ancient Indictments in the King's Bench Referring to Kent, 1450–1452', ed. Roger Virgoe, in *Kent Records. Documents Illustrative of Medieval Kentish Society*, ed. F.R.H. Du Boulay, Kent Archaeological Society Records Publication Committee xviii, 1964, 218–19, 258–60.
78. PRO, PROB 11/6 9 Wattys; *Register of the Gild*, ed. Bloom, 77.
79. *Register of the Gild*, ed. Bloom, 88–156; *Corporation Records*, ed. Hardy, 27; *Exchequer, Augmentation Office, Calendar of Ancient Deeds*, List and Index Society xcv, 1970, B4806.

80. See above, p. 57; SBTRO, BRT 1/3/76 (account of 1464–5); Sackville of Knole, U269 M73.
81. SBTRO, BRT 1/3/61 (account of 1453–4); PRO, PROB 11/6 9 Wattys; *Warwickshire Feet of Fines*, III, 1345–1509, ed. L. Drucker, Dugdale Society xviii, 1947, 179; HWCRO, ref. 009:1 BA 2636/176 92493; /191 92625 9/12.
82. PRO, PROB 11/13 32 Blamyr.
83. Hilton, *English Peasantry*, 94.
84. Gervase Rosser, 'Going to the Fraternity Feast: Commensality and Social Relations in Late Medieval England', *Journal of British Studies* xxxiii, 1994, 430–46.
85. *Leland's Itinerary in England and Wales*, ed. Lucy Toulmin Smith, 5 Vols reprint, London 1964, ii, 48–50, shows the strong impression the buildings made on one visitor. For the clocks SBTRO, BRT 1/2/406 (deed of 1473); 1/3/68; 1/3/90 (accounts of 1460–1, 1478–9); *Corporation Records*, 44, 53.
86. *Register of the Gild*, ed. Bloom.
87. SBTRO, BRT 1/3/22, 23, 25, 27, 28, 30.
88. *Register of the Gild*, ed. Bloom, viii–ix; SBTRO, BRT 1/3/72 (rental of College 1455–6); 2/1 fol. 38.
89. Thomas Fisher, *A Series of Antient Allegorical, Historical and Legendary Paintings . . .*, London 1836; Wilfred Puddephat, 'The Mural Painting of the Dance of Death in the Guild Chapel of Stratford-upon-Avon', *Transactions of the Birmingham Archaeological Society* lxxvi, 1958, 29–35. See also Clifford Davidson, *The Guild Chapel Wall Paintings at Stratford-upon-Avon*, New York 1988.
90. SBTRO, BRU 15/3/10.
91. Giving medieval prices modern values is always dangerous, but as 6*d*, the fee for the feast, represented 1.5 days work by a skilled worker, this would be £60 in the money of 1997.

I wish to thank Terence Lloyd and John Sheail for permission to use information from their theses. Helpful information was provided by Alan Dyer, Jim Galloway, Jane Laughton, Margaret Murphy, Stephanie Ratkai and Nicholas Vincent. Robert Bearman has helped and encouraged this work at every stage. Andrew Isham and Cathleen Millwood prepared illustrations.

CHAPTER FIVE

1. The books are A. Brown, *Popular Piety in Late Medieval England: the Diocese of Salisbury 1250–1550*, Oxford 1995; V. Bainbridge, *Gilds in the Medieval Countryside: Social and Religious Change in Cambridgeshire* c. *1350–1550*, Woodbridge, forthcoming; B. Kümin, *The Shaping of a Community: the Rise and Reformation of the English Parish* c. *1400–1560*, St Andrews Studies in Reformation History, Aldershot 1996. The main reading on religious guilds is otherwise W.R. Jones, 'English Religious Brotherhoods and Medieval Lay Piety', *The Historian* xxxvi, 1974, 646–59; C.M. Barron, 'The Parish Fraternities of Medieval London', *The Church in Pre-Reformation Society*, ed. Barron and C. Harper-Bill, Woodbridge 1985, 13–37; C. Burgess, '"By Quick and by Dead": wills and pious provision in late medieval Bristol', *English Historical Review* cii, 1987, 837–58; G. Rosser, 'Communities of Parish and Guild in the Late Middle Ages', in *Parish, Church and People: Local Studies in Lay Religion 1350–1750*, ed. S. Wright, London 1988, 29–55; M. Rubin, *Corpus Christi: the Eucharist in Late Medieval Culture*, Cambridge 1991; B. Hanawalt and B. McRee, 'The Gilds of *Homo Prudens* in Late Medieval England', *Continuity and Change* vii, 1992, 163–79; B. McRee, 'Charity and Gild Solidarity in Late Medieval England', *Journal of British Studies* xxxii, 1993, 195–225; G. Rosser, 'Going to the Fraternal Feast: commensality and social relations in late medieval England', *Journal of British Studies* xxxiii, 1994, 430–46. I must thank Professor Christopher Dyer for commenting on this paper and saving me in particular from the errors of a non-native of Warwickshire.

2. C. Phythian-Adams, 'Ceremony and the Citizen: the communal year at Coventry 1450–1550', in *Crisis and Order in English Towns 1500–1700*, ed. P. Clark and P. Slack, London 1972, 57–85; M. James, 'Ritual, Drama and Social Body in the Late Medieval English Town', *Past and Present* xcviii, 1983, 3–29; B. McRee, 'Religious Gilds and Civic Order: the case of Norwich in the later Middle Ages', *Speculum* lxvii, 1992, 69–97; B. McRee, 'Peacemaking and its Limits in Later Medieval Norwich', *English Historical Review* cix, 1994, 831–66. H. Swanson, 'The Illusion of Economic Structure: craft guilds in the late medieval urban economy,' *Past and Present* cxxi, 1988, 29–48, and H. Swanson, *Medieval Artisans: an Urban Class in Late Medieval England*, Oxford 1989 are purely economic studies of urban guilds.
3. E. Duffy, *The Stripping of the Altars: Traditional Religion in England 1400–1580*, Yale 1992. This and R. Swanson, *Church and Society in Late Medieval England*, 2nd edn, Oxford 1993, sum up and refer to all but the most recent work in this field (for which see n. 1). An earlier contribution, which has a lot to say about the Stratford Guild, is J.J. Scarisbrick, *The Reformation and the English People*, Oxford 1984.
4. This message is especially important in the work of Scarisbrick, Duffy, Rosser and Kümin.
5. New work of this kind can be pursued through the synthesis of one of its most distinguished contributors in R. Britnell, *The Commercialisation of English Society 1000–1500*, Cambridge 1993. An important urban study of this sort published since then is M. Kowaleski, *Local Markets and Regional Trade in Medieval Exeter*, Cambridge 1995. See also the remarks, pertinent to the subject of this paper, in M. Rubin, 'Religious Culture in Town and Country: reflections on a great divide', in *Church and City 1000–1500: Essays in Honour of Christopher Brooke*, ed. D. Abulafia, M. Franklin and Rubin, Cambridge 1992, 3–22. A notable recent West Midlands contribution is C. Dyer, 'Small-town Conflict in the Later Middle Ages: events at Shipston-on-Stour', *Urban History* xix, 1992, 183–210.
6. R.H. Hilton, *The English Peasantry in the Late Middle Ages*, Oxford 1975, 93–4.
7. But they do get some discussion in G. Rosser, 'The Town and Guild of Lichfield in the Late Middle Ages', *Transactions of the South Staffordshire. Archaeological and Historical Society* xxvii, 1985–6, 39–47 and Rosser, 'Going to the Fraternity Feast', 440–2. However, Rosser's promise to deal with guilds in 'the sphere of local politics' ('Communities of Parish and Guild', 55 n. 101) has yet to be redeemed.
8. R. Horrox, 'Urban Patronage and Patrons in the Fifteenth Century', in *Patronage, the Crown and the Provinces in Later Medieval England*, ed. R. Griffiths, Gloucester 1981, 145–66; R. Horrox, 'The Urban Gentry', in *Towns and Townspeople in the Fifteenth Century*, ed. J.A.F. Thomson, Gloucester 1988, 22–44.
9. McRee, 'Religious Gilds and Civic Order'; *The Register of the Guild of the Holy Trinity, St Mary, St John the Baptist and St Katherine of Coventry*, ed. M.D. Harris, Dugdale Society xiii, 1935; Rosser, 'Town and Guild of Lichfield'; Horrox, 'Urban Patronage', 156; Scarisbrick, 22; *The Register of the Gild of the Holy Cross, the Blessed Mary and St John the Baptist of Stratford-upon-Avon*, ed. J.H. Bloom, London 1907.
10. McRee, 'Religious Gilds and Civic Order', 95; Rosser, 'Communities of Parish and Guild', 33–4; Rosser, 'Going to the Fraternity Feast', 431–3, 438–9; *Stratford Register*, 5; *English Gilds*, ed. Toulmin Smith, Early English Text Society 1870, 217.
11. See the works in n. 2 and also Rosser, 'Going to the Fraternity Feast', 430–3 and Rubin, 257–71 (the quotation is from Rubin, 259).
12. McRee, 'Religious Gilds and Civic Order', 79. For landowners' social attitudes, see pp. 74–5..
13. On noble and gentry participation in feasts, see Rosser, 'Going to the Fraternity Feast', 440, 442, which comes to a similar conclusion; also Horrox, 'Urban Patronage', 156. See C. Phythian-Adams, *Desolation of a City: Coventry and the Urban Crisis of the Late Middle Ages*, Cambridge 1979, 140 on attendance at meetings.

14. But see above, p. 71. For references to these various guild functions, see the literature cited in n. 1.
15. Phythian-Adams, *Coventry*, 140.
16. G. Rosser, 'Parochial Conformity and Popular Religion in Late Medieval England', *Transactions of the Royal Historical Society* 6th series i, 1991, 173–89.
17. See especially Horrox, 'Urban Gentry'.
18. For more on this, see above, p. 75.
19. C. Carpenter, *Locality and Polity: a Study of Warwickshire Landed Society, 1401–1499*, Cambridge 1992, 223.
20. Carpenter, *Locality and Polity*, 347–8; J. Watts, *Henry VI and the Politics of Kingship*, Cambridge 1996, 64–5, 70.
21. For the structures of power in late-medieval England, see Carpenter, *Locality and Polity*, Part II, esp. Chap. 9(i) and 10(i); C. Carpenter, 'Gentry and Community in Medieval England', *Journal of British Studies* xxxiii, 1994, 344–53; Watts, Chaps 2 and 3.
22. Toulmin Smith, 453–4; McRee, 'Religious Gilds and Civic Order', 79 and 'Peacemaking', 849–66; Watts, Chaps 5 and 6.
23. Rosser, 'Gild of Lichfield', 41–2, 46; Carpenter, *Locality and Polity*, Chap. 15.
24. References for printed Guild material are *Stratford Register* and *Stratford-on-Avon Records: the Guild Accounts*, ed. W.J. Hardy, Stratford 1886. F.C. Wellstood, 'A Calendar of the Medieval Records Belonging to the Mayor and Corporation of Stratford-upon-Avon' (1941) is in typescript and held at SBTRO. General statements about the Guild made below, unless accompanied by particular references, are substantiated from the works listed here. Since this is a foray into a largely untouched field and my research into the Stratford Guild records has been relatively limited, my answers are on the whole speculative and provisional. I have gone through the sources above but I have by no means read all the originals. While I have looked with some care at Bloom's printed edition of the register, I am aware that it is suspect, not just in its accuracy but in the possible omission of entries. There may thus be noble or gentry members missed by Bloom, whom I would not have picked up unless they feature in the Guild accounts.
25. There is some uncertainty about the date of the Guild's feast. Given the name of the Guild, it should have occurred on one of the festivals of the Holy Cross but this appears not to have been the case. According to the returns of 1389, the feast occurred 'in Easter week' (Toulmin Smith, 217) but, according to Bloom, 'The common feast was originally held on the Sunday after the Feast of the Ascension' and was moved in 1526 (*Stratford Register*, xi: this statement is unreferenced). Dr Eamon Duffy has advised me that, if the feast was moved out of Easter week because of overcrowding of liturgical events, the Sunday after Ascension, as the first free Sunday after Easter, would be the logical place to put it. A reference to entertainment offered on Monday 'the morrow of the feast of the gild' (*Guild Accounts*, no. 42) substantiates the existence of a Sunday feast. That there was more than one feast in the year is shown by *Guild Accounts*, no. 39, and Bloom maintains that there were four (*Stratford Register*, ix). It is possible that when the Guild was refounded in 1403 the feast was moved to the later date and that the other, presumably lesser, feasts were for patronal days of the guilds incorporated into the Holy Cross Guild which appear in its full name (*VCH Warws.*, iii, 247; *Stratford Register*, viii).
26. I am most grateful to Dr Miri Rubin for explaining the purposes of the hoods to me and discussing how they could bear on gentry activities in guilds. Rosser, 'Going to the Fraternity Feast', 439; the Guild accounts cited by Rosser give numbers but not personnel.
27. *Guild Accounts*, no. 39.
28. *Guild Accounts*, no. 42.
29. *Stratford Register*, 3.
30. *Stratford Register*, 84.
31. *Stratford Register, passim.*

32. For the Cloptons, see William Dugdale, *The Antiquities of Warwickshire*, 2 vols, London 1730, ii, 698 and for Hugh, *VCH Warws*, iii, 224, 262, 275; Dugdale, 696, 699; *Stratford Register*, 144, 175, 176, 189.
33. *Stratford Register*, 78, 80. For the Harewells, see *The History of Parliament: the House of Commons 1386–1421*, ed. J.S. Roskell, L. Clark and C. Rawcliffe, 4 vols, Stroud 1992, iii, 290–3, and Carpenter, *Locality and Polity*, 656, 686 and *passim*.
34. C. Dyer, *Lords and Peasants in a Changing Society: the Estates of the Bishopric of Worcester 680–1540*, Cambridge 1980, 11.
35. For power and politics in Warwickshire in the fifteenth century, see Carpenter, *Locality and Polity, passim*. For the distribution of the lands of the earldom see map on 449 and for Warwick dominance over this part of the county and the neighbouring parts of Warwickshire and Gloucestershire, see especially 31, 313, 360–1. For the Berkeley and Despenser acquisitions, see also *The Complete Peerage*, ed. V. Gibbs, H.A. Doubleday etc., 13 vols, London 1910–40, xii II, 381–2; the former were by no means acquired in their entirety (see A. Sinclair, 'The Great Berkeley Law-Suit Revisited 1417–39', *Southern History* ix, 1987, 34–50). For affinities, see K.B. McFarlane, *England in the Fifteenth Century: Collected Essays*, London 1981, especially introduction by G.L. Harriss; Carpenter, *Locality and Polity*, Part II and Carpenter, 'Gentry and Community', 356–65, all of which include references to the large literature on this theme.
36. After a rather cursory look at the Guild in the course of doing a much larger study of landed society in Warwickshire in the fifteenth century, I originally placed too much emphasis on the role of the Warwick affinity in the Guild. Now, after a less impressionistic examination, I think the gentry members of the Guild look rather less like the Beauchamp affinity at prayer – or perhaps at dinner – than I originally thought. Carpenter, *Locality and Polity*, 339.
37. Dugdale, ii, 856.
38. For Burdet, Neville and Bishopestone and the Guild, see above, p. 71. For incomes in 1436, see H.L. Gray, 'Incomes from Land in England in 1436', *English Historical Review* xlix, 1934, 607–39 and the full return for Warwickshire, PRO E179 (Exchequer KR, Subsidy Rolls etc.) /192/59, supplemented with other returns for that year: E179/200/68, 238/90, 240/266; E163/7/31 Part I. See also further discussion of the tax and Warwickshire gentry incomes in Carpenter, *Locality and Polity*, 52–3, 56–79.
39. See maps in Carpenter, *Locality and Polity*, 54, 519.
40. *The Register of the Guild of Knowle*, ed. W.B. Bickley, Walsall 1894. The entries start at 1451 only, but the catchment area, as far as lesser figures are concerned, is very clear and therefore unlikely to have been different before. However, see below, n. 54 for the apparently peculiar role of Knowle in relation to some of its greater members.
41. *Register of the Trinity Gild, passim*; Phythian-Adams, *Coventry*, Chap. 8.
42. For Bishopstone and the Guild, see above, p. 71.
43. *Stratford Register*, 78, 93, 147; J.T. Driver, 'A Fifteenth-Century Leicestershire Lawyer and Parliamentary Knight of the Shire: Thomas Palmer of Holt (*c.* 1400–1475)', *Transactions of the Leicestershire Archaeological and Historical Society* lxix, 1995, 43, 57; Carpenter, *Locality and Polity*, esp. 117–18, 191–3 and Part II, *passim; Register of the Trinity Guild, passim* and 94 (with an incorrect date for his death in the accompanying note). Catesby's local guild in the part of west Warwickshire where he did have lands (see Carpenter, *Locality and Polity*, 117–18, 191–3) was Knowle, of which he was a member (*Knowle Register*, 48).
44. *Stratford Register*, 147; Hilton, 93.
45. *Stratford Register*, 124; *Guild Accounts*, no. 60. His second wife was Joan Barre, a widow of Herefordshire (J.S. Roskell, 'William Catesby' in J.S. Roskell, *Parliament and Politics in Medieval England*, ii, London 1981, 313). The wording of the accounts entry could suggest that Catesby was married in Stratford but this seems improbable and it is more likely that the Guild gave him a celebratory drink when he was passing through the town at some later date.

46. *Stratford Register*, 144, 169; *Guild Accounts*, no. 39. As Professor Dyer pointed out to me, all three houses held land in the vicinity of Stratford, which could well be sufficient reason for the affiliation (*VCH Warws*, iii, 43–4, 53, v, 4; *VCH Worcs.*, ii, 128–9).
47. *Guild Accounts*, no. 74; Dyer, *Lords and Peasants*, 154.
48. *Stratford Register*, 59, 143, 159; *Guild Accounts*, no. 39. For their episcopal offices, see Dyer, *Lords and Peasants*, 11, 380.
49. *VCH Warws*, viii, 479; H.A. Cronne, *The Borough of Warwick in the Middle Ages*, Dugdale Society Occasional Paper x, 1951.
50. For all these, see Carpenter, *Locality and Polity*, Appendix 3, which is the source for all further reference to membership of Warwickshire affinities.
51. SBTRO, BRT 1/3/70: undated but the dating can be established from the names of the Guild proctors on the account, William Beoley and John Weoley (see *Stratford Register*, 54); above, pp. 73–4.
52. *Guild Accounts*, no. 20; *History of Parliament*, iv, 814. The others were Thomas Burdet, Ailred Trussell, his son William, Thomas Lucy, John and Thomas Harewell and Burdet's son, presumably Nicholas.
53. *Stratford Register*, 59, 60, 62. For Wollashull and the earl, see *History of Parliament*, iv, 889–90; for Curson, see e.g. Longleat, ms of the Marquess of Bath 6414, Misc. IX; BL, Add. Charter 11678; WCRO, Warwick Castle ms 373; Warwick Corporation Records W19/5. For Warwick's power in Warwickshire at this time and for his relations with Mountford, see Carpenter, *Locality and Polity*, Chaps 9 and 10; for Mountford's standing in the county, see *Locality and Polity*, 61, 65, 101. See also *History of Parliament*, iii, 797–800.
54. However, he may have been a member of the Guild at Knowle, for which there are no records of members before 1451. This was in the parish of Hampton-in-Arden, the centre of the Peche estate that William acquired by marriage to the heiress (Dugdale, i, 55). It was certainly the guild joined by almost all the members of the Mountford family from 1461 and the surprisingly high rank and wide geographical distribution of its members in the later fifteenth century may well reflect the widening influence of the Mountfords – first in central and western Warwickshire and ultimately over most of the county – that is one of the most significant developments in Warwickshire politics in the fifteenth century: certainly, many of the names coincide with contacts that the Mountfords were making in these decades (see *Knowle Register, passim* and esp. 41, 46, 62, 64 and Carpenter, *Locality and Polity*, Chaps 12–15, although the author did not realize the significance of the Knowle membership at the time). The Mountfords failed to found their projected chantry at Coleshill and the Knowle Guild, to which a college of twelve priests was added in 1417–18, may ultimately have been considered an adequate substitute (Carpenter, *Locality and Polity*, 228; *Knowle Register*, x–xi).
55. *Stratford Register*, 62. He is likely to be William's uncle, who must be the cleric referred to in William's settlement of his property of 1417 (Birmingham Reference Library, Wingfield Digby ms A473), as his younger son William, named in the same document, would then have been too young to be a cleric and the next known Mountford rector of Ilmington, who *was* probably William's son, was called Richard (*Warwickshire Feet of Fines*, ed. L. Drucker, iii, Dugdale Society xviii, 1943, no. 2648). For Mountford ownership of the benefice, see Dugdale, i, 629–30.
56. SBTRO, DR 37 (Archer Collection) Box 73 (Mountford account) for evidence that the family was spending part of the year at Ilmington in 1432–3: this is now printed in *Household Accounts from Medieval England*, ed. C.M. Woolgar, British Academy Records of Social and Economic History new series xvii, xviii, 1992–3, ii, 433–51; see also Carpenter, *Locality and Polity*, 158, 177.
57. *Stratford Register*, 159, 163. For the political background, see Carpenter, *Locality and Polity*, 516–22 and Carpenter, 'The Duke of Clarence and the Midlands: a study in the interplay of

local and national politics', *Midland History* xi, 1986, 23–48. As these accounts make clear, Stafford was a follower of somewhat dubious value. For the participation of the Stratford area in the death of Ankarette, see *Calendar of Patent Rolls 1476–85*, 72–3.

58. For reference, see immediately above, n. 57.
59. *Guild Accounts*, no. 90; Carpenter, *Locality and Polity*, Chap. 14; Dyer, *Lords and Peasants*, 154; M.A. Hicks, 'The Changing Role of the Wydevilles in Yorkist Politics to 1483', in *Patronage, Pedigree and Power*, ed. C. Ross, Gloucester 1979, 75–9; D.E. Lowe, 'Patronage and Politics: Edward IV, the Wydevills, and the council of the Prince of Wales', *Bulletin of the Board of Celtic Studies* xxix, 1980–2, 545–73.
60. *Stratford Register*, 26.
61. Carpenter, *Locality and Polity*, 439; *Stratford Register*, 14, 65. Her husband had entertained some notables himself in 1437–8 (*Guild Accounts*, no. 46).
62. *Guild Accounts*, no. 60; Carpenter, *Locality and Polity*, 446, 466.
63. *Guild Accounts*, no. 62.
64. Dugdale, ii, 685; *Complete Peerage*, xii II, 383–4.
65. Dyer, *Lords and Peasants*, 115–16, 153–4, 156–7, 211, 373; R.B. Dobson, *Durham Priory 1400–1450*, Cambridge 1973, 183–202; PRO, SC6 (Special Collections: Ministers' Accounts) /1039/18; E. Miller and J. Hatcher, *Medieval England: Rural Society and Economic Change 1086–1348*, London 1978, 172–3, 191–2. For a summary of the development of gentry control of local government, see A.L. Brown, *The Governance of Late Medieval England 1272–1461*, London 1989, Chap. 7.
66. Above, nn. 48 and 53; Dyer, *Lords and Peasants*, 50; *History of Parliament*, iv, 606, 892–3.
67. William Dugdale, *The Baronage of England*, 2 vols, London 1675–6, i, 247; Dyer, *Lords and Peasants*, 154; *Cal. Pat. Rolls 1416–22*, 305–6; *Cal. Pat. Rolls 1441–6*, 241; *Calendar of Close Rolls 1419–22*, 156.
68. *Stratford Register*, 83; *Guild Accounts*, no. 50; *Complete Peerage*, xii I, 420; Carpenter, *Locality and Polity*, Chap. 11. Note that Boteller joined the Stratford Guild despite the fact that there was a guild at Henley which he himself refounded (W. Cooper, *The Records of Beaudesert, Henley-in-Arden, co. Warwick*, Leeds 1931, lviii–ix).
69. *Stratford Register*, 33, 35; Carpenter, *Locality and Polity*, 373–91.
70. McRee, 'Religious Gilds and Civic Order', 95; Hilton, 83–4, 93–4; Dyer, *Lords and Peasants*, 280; see Wellstood, 'Calendar of Medieval Records of Stratford-upon-Avon' for some evidence of gentry land ownership and land transactions in Stratford; *Guild Accounts*, nos 66, 89; also, above, pp. 66–7.
71. See *Guild Accounts* and Wellstood, 'Calendar of Stratford Records', *passim*. In discussing the relations of these people with the Guild, only particular instances cited in the text will be separately referenced in the notes.
72. On purgatory, see C. Burgess, '"A Fond Thing Vainly Invented": an essay in Purgatory and pious motive in later medieval England', in *Parish, Church and People*, ed. Wright, 56–84, and Duffy, *Stripping of the Altars*, Chap. 10. From a number of works examining the gentry and the parish church, see M. Vale, *Piety, Charity and Literacy among the Yorkshire Gentry, 1370–1480*, Borthwick Papers 1, 1976; P. Fleming, 'Charity, Faith and the Gentry of Kent 1422–1529', in *Property and Politics*, ed. A.J. Pollard, Gloucester 1984, 36–58; Carpenter, 'The Religion of the Gentry of Fifteenth-Century England', in *England in the Fifteenth Century*, ed. D. Williams, 53–74; Carpenter, *Locality and Polity*, 222–43.
73. A point made in D.M. Palliser, 'Introduction: the parish in perspective', in *Parish, Church and People*, ed. Wright, 10–11, and by the respondents to Henry VIII's commission of enquiry (Toulmin Smith, *English Gilds*, 221–2).
74. *VCH Warws*, iii, 260.
75. Scarisbrick, 20.

76. *Guild Accounts*, no. 50 and e.g. no. 74; on *obits*, see Brown, *Popular Piety*, 101–2.
77. Dugdale, *Warwickshire*, ii, 701.
78. Dugdale, *Warwickshire*, ii, 856.
79. *Stratford Register*, 74 (although, in the accounts, he and his wife are listed as joining in 1431–2: *Guild Accounts*, no. 42); e.g. *Guild Accounts*, nos 52, 53, 56, 58.
80. *Guild Accounts*, no. 58.
81. Dugdale, *Warwickshire*, ii, 772–3; *VCH Warws*, ii, 60; iii, 19; Carpenter, *Locality and Polity*, 229–40, 255.
82. *Cal. Pat. Rolls 1441–6*, 422, 480; *Cal. Pat. Rolls 1446–52*, 270.
83. See references in n. 79.
84. Carpenter, *Locality and Polity*, 309.
85. *VCH Warws*, iii, 19.
86. Both Neville and Beauchamp are known to have had dealings with the abbey, which highlights further their apparent neglect of it (WCRO, Warwick Castle ms 114, 117A, B).
87. Dugdale, *Warwickshire*, ii, 739; e.g. *Guild Accounts*, nos 56, 57; *Complete Peerage*, ii, 47; Watts, Chap. 5; Carpenter, *Locality and Polity*, 309–10, 331–2, 412 and Chap. 11, *passim*; *Calendar of Fine Rolls 1445–52*, 10.
88. *VCH Warws*, iii, 260; PRO, C139 (Chancery, Inquisitions *Post Mortem*) /115/27, /145/9; Dugdale, *Warwickshire*, ii, 809; Carpenter, *Locality and Polity*, 656.
89. PRO, C139/145/9; *Stratford Register*, 71; Dugdale, *Warwickshire*, ii, 810. It should also be noted that William Harewell leased the bishopric's Stratford demesne between 1464 and 1500 (Dyer, *Lords and Peasants*, 215).
90. Above, p. 65; Carpenter, *Locality and Polity*, Chaps. 10–12, Appendix 3. The Guild of Knowle may have absorbed more of the family's energies later on, as they were almost equidistant from Knowle and Stratford and several members of the family, including William, joined (see *Knowle Register* for 1468, 1480, 1486).
91. *Guild Accounts*, no. 60.
92. William's will, ordaining his place of burial, is printed in Dugdale, *Warwickshire*, i, 505, where reference is also made to the place of his wife's burial. For his wife's will, see PRO, PROB 11 (Prerogative Court of Canterbury Wills) /10, fol. 167.
93. Dugdale, *Warwickshire*, i, 498–504, 505; PRO, PROB 11/11, fol. 177v.; Carpenter, *Locality and Polity*, 228–9.
94. See above, n. 48.
95. For the family history of the Burdets, see Dugdale, *Warwickshire*, ii, 846–9.
96. Carpenter, *Locality and Polity*, 535–8; *Stratford Register*, 166.
97. Carpenter, *Locality and Polity*, 521, 535–6; Carpenter, 'Duke of Clarence', 38–9 (further references will be found to both these remarkable events in these works). The dating of the annulment is problematical: in 1456 Burdet obtained a royal licence to marry the woman who became his second wife, but it seems from Dugdale that the annulment was in fact obtained between 1464 and 1466, while the fact that the children of the second marriage were not of age at Burdet's death in 1477 would support the later date (*Cal. Pat. Rolls 1452–61*, 427; Dugdale, *Warwickshire*, ii, 849; Carpenter, *Locality and Polity*, 536 and n. 46).
98. *Guild Accounts*, no. 74.
99. Dugdale, *Warwickshire*, ii, 851.
100. Carpenter, *Locality and Polity*, 535–6.
101. *Guild Accounts*, no. 50. The entry does not make clear whether the *obit* was in the abbey or parish church. If the abbey, it was almost at rock-bottom at this point (Dugdale, *Warwickshire*, ii, 773).
102. Wellstood, 'Calendar', I/427. This is on the assumption that the deed is not part of some complex transaction in which Burdet was merely an intermediary.

103. See works in n. 72, above.
104. Brown, *Popular Piety*, 110.
105. For lordship, gentility and the gulf between those who had lordship and those who did not, see Carpenter, *Locality and Polity*, Chap. 3 and 'The Stonor Circle in the Fifteenth Century' in *Rulers and Ruled in Late Medieval England: Essays Presented to Gerald Harriss*, ed. R. Archer and S. Walker, London 1995, 198–9.
106. *Guild Accounts*, nos 33, 42.
107. SBTRO, BRT 1/3/26. See Rosser, 'Going to the Fraternity Feast', 442, where the harpist is said to be supplied for the Guild feast, but there is no indication in the record that this was for this occasion; nor is there any suggestion in the record that the hoods were distributed 'on this occasion' (n. 49). In fact, as this account covers six years, it is not possible to tell when any particular item of expenditure was made unless a specific date is given.
108. *Guild Accounts*, no. 50.
109. *Stratford Register*, 81. It must be Middleton's stepson, Thomas Straunge, as he married a daughter of Wode; the register entry, referring to Middleton as 'Lord of Walton' and his wife as Elizabeth, combined with the will of Thomas Straunge senior, dating to 1436, and showing that his wife's name was Elizabeth, are the main pieces of evidence establishing that Middleton married the Straunge widow (*History of Parliament*, iv, 893; WCRO, CR133 (Mordaunt of Walton Collection) /15).
110. SBTRO, BRT 1/3/54.
111. *Guild Accounts*, no. 86; *Stratford Register*, 92; Dugdale, *Warwickshire*, ii, 707; Carpenter, *Locality and Polity*, 110–11, 113n. 65, 492, 517, 531–2. The marriage, to the Cokesey heiress (John's mother in fact), had been made long before but it was only in 1445 that the death of her brother without heirs made her the heiress.
112. See, by way of introduction, Carpenter, *Locality and Polity*, Chap. 9; Carpenter, 'Stonor Circle'; Carpenter, 'Gentry and Community', 340–80. Extensive reference to further reading, both historical and anthropological, will be found in these works.
113. See the general references in n. 24 above and, more specifically, from Wellstood, 'Calendar', I/427, 473, 501, 502, 503; II/83 and cf. Carpenter, *Locality and Polity*, 303–4, 309–10, 331–2 and Chaps. 13–16.
114. S. Reynolds, *An Introduction to the History of English Medieval Towns*, Oxford 1977, 154–5; Cronne, *Borough of Warwick*, 18–19.
115. See for example the itinerations of the Countess of Warwick in the earl's absence in France in 1420–1 in Longleat ms Misc. IX, discussed in C. Ross, 'The Household Accounts of Elizabeth Berkeley, Countess of Warwick', *Transactions of the Bristol and Gloucestershire Archaeological Society* lxx, 1951, 81–105.
116. See Carpenter, *Locality and Polity*, Chaps. 13–15.
117. For a discussion of possible meeting points in Warwickshire, including the town of Warwick, see Carpenter, *Locality and Polity*, 336–44.
118. For further discussion of this point, see Carpenter, *Locality and Polity*, 312–21; Carpenter, 'Gentry and Community', 356–65.
119. See p. 76.
120. Wellstood, 'Calendar', I/442.
121. This was Thomas Straunge (see above, n. 109).
122. Thomas Middleton.
123. This is very much the theme of Carpenter, *Locality and Polity*; see especially Chap. 2.
124. But see the comments on Knowle's peculiarities, above, n. 54.
125. *VCH Warws*, iii, 42; Dugdale, *Warwickshire*, ii, 695, 838, 936–7, 938; PRO, PROB 11/14, fol. 147v. The Guild's own record of the transaction suggests that this may have been a sale, even if perhaps a preferential one (*Guild Accounts*, no. 93).

126. Horrox, 'Urban Patronage'; see particularly her perceptive remarks on the expenditure on wine etc. which has featured largely in this paper (152–3).
127. *Stratford Register*, 40; Carpenter, *Locality and Polity*, 302–3.
128. *Guild Accounts*, no. 28.
129. *Guild Accounts*, no. 60.
130. *Guild Accounts*, no. 56.
131. *Guild Accounts*, no. 52. Mountford was twice commissioned in 1445–6 as a tax assessor, by virtue of having been MP in the parliament of 1445–6 (*Cal. Fine Rolls 1437–45*, 324; *Cal. Fine Rolls 1445–52*, 31). He was also a JP throughout this period but the justices did not usually sit at Coventry and would not usually be referred to as anything other than justices (*Cal. Pat. Rolls 1441–46*, 480; *Cal. Pat. Rolls 1446–52*, 596). For Mountford as local officer, see *History of Parliament*, iii, 797.
132. *Guild Accounts,* no. 52; *Cal. Fine Rolls 1445–52*, 10.
133. *Guild Accounts*, no. 54; *Cal. Pat. Rolls 1441–6*, 480; *Cal. Pat. Rolls 1446–52*, 596; *Cal. Fine Rolls 1445–52*, 103. These confirm that Bate held these offices at this time. Bermingham's commission is on *Cal. Pat. Rolls 1446–52*, 299.
134. There is no single reference to the local importance of both these men (but see *History of Parliament*, ii, 236–7 for Bermingham's father) but both receive a number of mentions in Carpenter, *Locality and Polity, passim*. Bermingham's father had been associated with Richard Beauchamp's affinity and Bate had joined the Duke of Buckingham's following which was inheriting much of Beauchamp's power in north Warwickshire and hence some of his north Warwickshire followers: these included Thomas Mollesley, who had participated in one of the Guild's transactions (Wellstood, 'Calendar', I/442). Both were before long to be linked in local politics with Mountford (Carpenter, *Locality and Polity*, 405, 453).
135. Horrox, 'Urban Patronage', 158–60.
136. Carpenter, *Locality and Polity*, 315–21, 368–93; *History of Parliament*, i, 665.
137. For listing of these officers, see *List of Sheriffs for England and Wales*, ed. A. Hughes, PRO Lists and Indexes, Main series ix, London, HMSO, rpt N. York 1963, 145–6; the appendices to the *Calendars of Patent Rolls* (for JPs); *Return: Members of Parliament*, 2 vols., London, House of Commons 1878; J.C. Wedgwood, *History of Parliament: Register . . . of the Members of both Houses 1439–1509*, London 1938, 699–700; A.C. Wood, *Typescript List of Escheators for England and Wales*, List and Index Society lxxii, rpt N. York 1971, 169–71.
138. See Carpenter, *Locality and Polity*, Chap. 9 (i) and 10 (i).
139. See the remarks above, p. 68.
140. *Guild Accounts*, no. 60. Warwick was also in a more powerful position in the country from late 1453 because of the rise to power at the centre of his ally, the Duke of York, largely as a result of the king's illness (see Carpenter, *Locality and Polity*, 448–75 and Watts, 301–15).
141. Carpenter, 'Duke of Clarence', 39; above, p. 69. Thomas Burdet's treason, a rather murky contributory factor in Clarence's fall, would also have been an embarrassment to the Guild, even if it seems that Burdet himself was not entirely *grata* with the Guild at the time (Carpenter, 'Duke of Clarence', 38–9; above, pp. 73–4).
142. For the events and their context and Warwickshire's particular role, see Watts, 350–62 and Carpenter, *Locality and Polity*, 475–86.
143. *Guild Accounts*, no. 69; Carpenter, *Locality and Polity*, 478–83, 484 and n. 159, 486n. 162 (John Hugford's appearance for Edward IV at the battle of Towton: things might have been different for John had Edward lost), 496. *Locality and Polity* has extensive further discussion of Verney's and Hugford's activities in Warwickshire.
144. Horrox, 'Urban Patronage', 156.
145. See a similar suggestion, but in relation to guilds alone, not to their external membership, in G. Rosser, 'The Essence of Medieval Urban Communities: the vill of Westminster 1200–1540', in *The Medieval Town 1200–1540*, ed. R. Holt and G. Rosser, London 1990, 232.

146. McRee, 'Religious Gilds and Civic Order', 92–5; McRee and Hanawalt, 'Guilds of *Homo Prudens*', 74–5; *VCH Warws*, viii, 258–64 (showing that, despite the existence of corporate institutions since the mid-fourteenth century, the 'Prior's half' remained administratively separate and independent; but see also Phythian-Adams, *Coventry*, 118 n. 1 for discussion of this vexed question).
147. Rosser, 'Town and Guild of Lichfield', 44–5; Horrox, 'Urban Patronage', 143, 156; Bainbridge, *Gilds in the Medieval Countryside*. Hence perhaps some of the hostility to Guilds which produced Richard II's enquiries of 1388–9 (Hanawalt and McRee, 'Guilds of *Homo Prudens*', 172).
148. McRee, 'Religious Gilds and Civic Order'; McRee, 'Peacemaking and its Limits'; Hanawalt and McRee, 'Guilds of *Homo Prudens*'. The troubles in Norwich are also discussed in P. Maddern, *Violence and Social Order: East Anglia 1422–1442*, Oxford 1992, 175–225 and R.L. Storey, *The End of the House of Lancaster*, London 1966, 217–25. Both these accounts emphasize the importance of conflict between town and priory in these affairs (see especially Maddern, 201–3 for the symbolic role of guild processions in this), something which would add force to the interpretation offered here. However, McRee, the most recent and most thorough historian of the internal politics of the town, downplays the prior's role.
149. Most recently and notably Kümin, in *Shaping of a Community*. See also Bainbridge, *Gilds in the Medieval Countryside*.

CHAPTER SIX

1. *Selected Cases before the King's Council in Star Chamber (1477–1544)*, ed. I.S. Leadam, Selden Society xvi, 1903, 230–3.
2. *Valor Ecclesiasticus* iii, 219.
3. *Calendar of Patent Rolls, Edward VI, 1548–1549*, 255.
4. *Calendar of State Papers Domestic, Edward VI, 1547–1553*, revised edn, 1992, 87.
5. *The House of Commons 1509–1558*, ed. S.T. Bindoff, London 1982, i, 116, 187, 189.
6. *Acts of the Privy Council, 1552–4*, 226; *Cal. of Pat. Rolls, Edward VI, 1553*, 279.
7. There is little sign in Edward's reign that the politicians saw the granting of town charters as a means of creating political allies in the country, despite the shock of widespread revolt in 1549; the much larger number of Mary's charters do seem to have been regarded as a means to increase political support for the regime.
8. The quatercentenary was celebrated with style in 1953.
9. *Evesham Borough Records of the Seventeenth Century, 1605–1687*, ed. S.K. Roberts, Worcestershire Historical Society new series xiv, xii–xiv.
10. E.A. Wrigley and R.S. Schofield, *The Population History of England 1541–1871*, Cambridge 1989, 52.
11. J. Jones, *Family Life in Shakespeare's England: Stratford-upon-Avon 1570–1630*, Stroud 1996, 22–3.
12. *VCH Warws*, iii, 241.
13. *Letters and Papers Henry VIII*, 12, ii, 909; see above p. 82.
14. Jones, *Family Life*, 22–3.
15. J.O. Halliwell, *A Descriptive Calendar of the Ancient Manuscripts . . . of the Corporation of Stratford-on-Avon*, London 1863, 88.
16. Much the same thing was true of Warwick, where plotting the origins of debtors recorded in the probate inventories of shopkeepers reveals a similar extension over the territories of Southam and Kineton: A. Dyer, 'Warwickshire Towns under the Tudors and Stuarts', *Warwickshire History* iii, no. 4, 1977, 126.
17. *Minutes and Accounts of the Corporation of Stratford-upon-Avon, V*, ed. Levi Fox, Dugdale Society xxxv, 1990, 133.
18. *VCH Warws*, iii, 236.

19. A 1607 law case over a consignment of 186 cheeses must reflect this under-recorded trade: Halliwell, 210.
20. Map based on the Bishop's Census of 1563, BL ms Harleian 595, fols 212–212v.
21. Dyer, 124–5, 134.
22. *Minutes and Accounts*, V, 133.
23. C. Hadfield and J. Norris, *Waterways to Stratford*, Newton Abbot 1968. For more on the regional road network at this time see Robert Bearman, *Shakespeare in the Stratford Records*, Stroud 1994, 44–8.
24. *VCH Warws*, iii, 238.
25. 1546 estimate based on chantry certificate claim of 1,500 communicants for the whole parish (clearly rounded), assuming that the town had about 80–5 per cent of the parish's population and that the missing young were 25 per cent of the total population (J.E. Jones, 'A community study of sixteenth-century Stratford-upon-Avon', University of Birmingham M.Phil. thesis, 1991, 12–26; Wrigley and Schofield, 565–6). 1563: 320 families excluding Luddington, assuming 5.0 per family and removing 150 to allow for the rest of the rural area outside the town (BL ms Harl 595 fol. 212). Average baptisms from Table 1, assuming a birth rate of *c.* 33 per thousand (Wrigley and Schofield, 531) and allowing for the non-urban element in the parish. 1591: a claim of 3,000 inhabitants in the parish, reduced for the rural element; 1598: an allegation of almost 2,000 communicants; assuming this means 1,950, 35 per cent were too young to communicate (Wrigley and Schofield, 569) and the usual allowance for the rural element. Both the estimates for the 1590s are based on claims in petitions with a vested interest in exaggeration and very rounded figures, and so could be too high (*Minutes and Accounts, IV*, Dugdale Society x, 1929, 127; Jones, thesis, 17).
26. Judging by the way in which baptismal figures hold up until 1640 (Table 1), the reduction came after that date; see below.
27. *VCH Warws,* iii, 222, assuming about 4.2 people per house.
28. R.B. Wheler, *History and Antiquities of Stratford-upon-Avon*, Stratford 1806, 16–17.
29. J.M. Martin, 'A Warwickshire Market Town in Adversity', *Midland History* vii, 1982.
30. *The Registers of Stratford-on-Avon*, ed. R. Savage, Parish Register Society vi, xvi, lv, 1897, 1898, 1905.
31. Estimates have been made for the years where entries are deficient, principally 1558–60, 1570–2, 1581 and 1591.
32. Children are indicated by the use of the word 'infant', or the expression 'son of . . . ' or 'daughter of . . . ' in the register; these latter terms can be used right up to the child's marriage, and so must include some young adults, but the distortion here will be minimal, especially as the clerk may sometimes have forgotten to use them, thus distorting the figures in the other direction.
33. R.M. Smith, 'Population and its Geography in England 1500–1730', in *An Historical Geography of England and Wales*, ed. R.A. Dodgson and R.A. Butlin, London 1978, 210–11.
34. 'Hic incepit pestis', *Registers of Stratford, Burials*, 9.
35. *Minutes and Accounts V*, xxii. For a more detailed account of these events, and Shakespeare's possible involvement, see Bearman, *Shakespeare in the Stratford Records*, 23–31.
36. Wrigley and Schofield, 670–2.
37. *Minutes and Accounts V*, xix–xx.

CHAPTER SEVEN

1. *Minutes and Accounts of the Corporation of Stratford-upon-Avon and Other Records 1553–1566*, Dugdale Society i, 1921, 128.
2. R.B. Wheler, *History and Antiquities of Stratford–upon-Avon*, Stratford 1806, 98–105. The

pictures were rediscovered during repairs to the Chapel in 1804.

3. Patrick Collinson, 'William Shakespeare's Religious Inheritance and Environment', in Collinson, *Elizabethan Essays*, London 1994, 219–52 (especially 246).
4. *Minutes and Accounts . . . 1553–1566*, xiv–xxvii; P. Styles, *The Borough of Stratford-upon-Avon and the Parish of Alveston* (reprinted from the *VCH Warws*, iii).
5. For general accounts of religious change see, Collinson, 'William Shakespeare's Religious Inheritance'; Collinson, *The Birthpangs of Protestant England: Religious and Cultural Change in the Sixteenth and Seventeenth Centuries*, London 1988; Diarmaid MacCulloch, *The Later Reformation in England, 1547–1603*, London 1990; and for the unpopularity of many of the changes, Eamon Duffy, *The Stripping of the Altars: Traditional Religion in England 1400–1580*, New Haven and London 1992.
6. For Puritanism see, among a vast and controversial literature, Patrick Collinson, *The Elizabethan Puritan Movement*, London 1967; Peter Lake, 'Calvinism and the English Church, 1570–1635', *Past and Present*, 114, 1987, 32–76; P. Lake, 'Defining Puritanism – again?' in *Puritanism: Transatlantic Perspectives on a Seventeenth-Century Anglo-American Faith*, ed. F.J. Bremer, Boston, Mass, 1993, 3–29; and Nicholas Tyacke, *The Fortunes of English Puritanism, 1603–1640*, Friends of Dr Williams Library, 44th Lecture, London 1990.
7. *Minutes and Accounts . . . 1553–1566*, xix–xx.
8. Collinson, 'William Shakespeare's Religious Inheritance', 247; E.R.C. Brinkworth, *Shakespeare and the Bawdy Court of Stratford*, Chichester 1972, 21; *Minutes and Accounts of the Corporation of Stratford upon Avon 1593–1598*, Dugdale Society xxxv, 1990, xix. Bayly was vicar of nearby Shipston-on-Stour in the 1590s and at Evesham from 1600.
9. For important discussions about religion, literacy and oral communication see, for example, Paul Seaver, *Wallington's World: A Puritan Artisan in Seventeenth Century London*, London 1985, 74, where Wallington's mother provides an example; Margaret Spufford, *Small Books and Pleasant Histories: Popular Fiction and its Readership in Seventeenth Century England*, Athens, Georgia, 1981; Adam Fox, 'Ballads, Libels and Popular Ridicule in Jacobean England', *Past and Present* 145, 1994, 47–83; Tessa Watt, *Cheap Print and Popular Piety, 1550–1640,* Cambridge 1991.
10. Jeanne Jones, *Family Life in Shakespeare's England: Stratford-upon-Avon 1570–1630*, Stroud 1996, 65.
11. *Minutes and Accounts . . . 1566–1577*, Dugdale Society iii, 1924, 46–8; Collinson, 'William Shakespeare's Religious Inheritance', 246–7.
12. Edgar Fripp, *Shakespeare. Man and Artist*, 2 vols, Oxford 1938, 194–5; Collinson, 'William Shakespeare's Religious Inheritance', 248–51. Collinson's account of John Shakespeare has been preferred to that given by Fripp in *Minutes and Accounts 1566–1577*, 76–7, or in *Shakespeare Man and Artist*, 306, where John's presentment for not coming to church, said to be 'for fear of process', is interpreted as 'obstinate' Puritanism.
13. *Minutes and Accounts of the Corporation of Stratford upon Avon 1586–1592*, Dugdale Society x, 1929, 148–9, 159–61.
14. For Badger's recusancy see, for example, Fripp, *Shakespeare Man and Artist*, 795–6; Brinkworth, *Shakespeare and the Bawdy Court,* 50, 148. For the problems in the Corporation, *Minutes and Accounts 1593–1598*, 86, 105–10, 115.
15. Fripp, *Shakespeare Man and Artist*, 638–42.
16. *Minutes and Accounts 1566–1577*, 47, 54; *Minutes and Accounts 1586–1592*, 32. For later improvements to the Guild Chapel see SBTRO, BRU2/2 (Council Minute Book), 123, August 1605, when the windows were (again) glazed and a pigcote near the chapel walls demolished.
17. *Minutes and Accounts 1586–1592*, xv, xxvii, 17, 31 for payments of the chamberlains to Cartwright including 3*s* for wine for him and Throckmorton in 1586. Patrick Collinson, *The Elizabeth Puritan Movement* is the classic account of developments in these years.
18. Extracts from the survey are printed in *Minutes and Accounts . . . 1586–1592*, 2–8.
19. Bramhall was succeeded by Richard Byfield, a member of an eminent Puritan family. The

seventeenth-century ministers, John Rogers (1605–19) and Thomas Wilson (1619–38), both had various difficulties with the town authorities, as discussed below, but there is no reason to doubt their zealous Protestantism: cf. Ann Hughes, 'Religion and Society in Stratford upon Avon, 1619–1638', *Midland History* xix, 1994, 58–84.

20. *Minutes and Accounts . . . 1586–1592*, 127.
21. *Minutes and Accounts . . . 1577–1586*, Dugdale Society v, 1926, 98, 119, 136–7, 149; *Minutes and Accounts . . . 1586–1592*, 16–17, 31–2, for payments by the chamberlains.
22. SBTRO, BRU2/2, 95, 17 December 1602. For Baker see below, and for evidence of his conscientious approach to local government a memorandum book kept while Bailiff, November 1602 – September 1603: SBTRO, ER2/25.
23. SBTRO, BRU2/2, 220.
24. SBTRO, BRU4/1 (Chamberlains' accounts), Richard Hathaway.
25. *Minutes and Accounts . . . 1577–1586*, 152 and n.
26. Brinkworth, *Shakespeare and the Bawdy Court*, 120–1.
27. Brinkworth, *Shakespeare and the Bawdy Court*, 123–6. I have excluded routine licensing and presentments of churchwardens for neglect from this analysis.
28. Brinkworth, *Shakespeare and the Bawdy Court*, 122–3. These cases are from 1590.
29. Alan Dyer's essay covers these issues fully. For measures taken by the Corporation on alehouses, inmates and companies, see *Minutes and Accounts 1593–98*, 101, 103, 148, April 1597–September 1598; SBTRO, BRU2/2, 99–100, for restrictions on trade and apprenticeship in 1603.
30. *Minutes and Accounts 1593–98*, 59–69; Robert Bearman, *Shakespeare in the Stratford Records*, Stroud 1994, 27–31.
31. SBTRO, BRU2/2, 108.
32. Hughes, 'Religion and Society', 60–1.
33. Hughes, 'Religion and Society', 76–7 for the relationship with the lord of the manor. For troubles with Greville: *Minutes and Accounts 1593–98*, 13; SBTRO BRU2/2, 70, 74–5, 83, 89. Richard Quyney, of course, whose election as bailiff was opposed by Greville, died of injuries suffered in a brawl with the lord's servants in 1602: Fripp, *Shakespeare Man and Artist*, 577–8. For Cranfield's involvement with the Wilson disputes: SBTRO, ER1/1/88; Maidstone, Centre for Kentish Studies, U269/Warwickshire Estate Correspondence, Miscellaneous Box, Stratford folder. The originals of the ecclesiastical court act books, calendared by Brinkworth, are among the Cranfield family papers, part of the Sackville manuscripts at the Centre for Kentish Studies.
34. Brinkworth, *Shakespeare and the Bawdy Court*, 124, 127, 136, 145.
35. *Minutes and Accounts 1593–98*, 113–14; SBTRO, BRU2/2, 71–2, 104–5. From the 1590s to the early seventeenth century there were several examples of reluctance to take office: even the conscientious Daniel Baker had to be threatened with a fine before he would become an alderman in 1598: *Minutes and Accounts 1593–98*, 141–5.
36. Brinkworth, *Shakespeare and the Bawdy Court*, 128.
37. Jones, *Family Life in Shakespeare's England*, 65–6, 109–10.
38. Patrick Collinson, 'Ecclesiastical Vitriol: Religious Satire in the 1590s and the Invention of Puritanism', in *The Reign of Elizabeth I: Court and Culture in the Last Decade*, ed. J.A. Guy, Cambridge 1995, 150–70, is a stimulating discussion of the general phenomenon.
39. Brinkworth, *Shakespeare and the Bawdy Court*, 48.
40. Brinkworth, *Shakespeare and the Bawdy Court*, 135–7.
41. A full account of the disputes over Wilson is offered in Hughes, 'Religion and Society'.
42. PRO, STAC8/26/10, for the events of 1619.
43. SBTRO, ER1/115/13, 14, 15 for presentments by churchwardens June–October 1619; STAC 8/26/10 for the libels. For similar incidents in Nottingham and Dorchester, see C.J. Sisson, *Lost Plays of Shakespeare's Age*, Cambridge 1936, 201–3; David Underdown, *Fire from Heaven:*

Life in an English Town in the Seventeenth Century, London 1992, 27–8.

44. SBTRO, BRU2/2, 430, 509; BRU15/13/81 for Wilson's stipend and the lecture; BRU2/2, 467, 493 for the chapel; *The Vestry Minute Book of the Parish of Stratford-on-Avon from 1617 to 1699 AD*, ed. G. Arbuthnot, London 1899, for the repairs of the church.
45. There are two Act Books for Wilson's incumbency. One, covering 1622 and 1624, is calendared in Brinkworth, *Shakespeare and the Bawdy Court*; the original is in Centre for Kentish Studies, U269/Q24. The second, for 1633–4, is SBTRO, BRU15/13/103. There are extensive churchwardens' presentments in SBTRO, ER1/115; BRU15/7/78; BRU15/13/97; BRU15/17/26; ER1/1/95; BRU15/11/4. The May 1622 session is in Brinkworth, 148–52; the associated presentments are ER1/115/31, 33, 35.
46. For examples see SBTRO, ER1/115/35, 40, 47, all cases of premarital pregnancy.
47. Centre for Kentish Studies, U269/Q27/2, 3 for the Corporation's views on the court as expressed in petitions to Lord Brooke. SBTRO, BRU2/2, 378, 386, 467–8, 472; BRU4/1, accounts of Chamberlain William Smith, 1619–20, and BRU4/2, accounts of Chamberlain William Shaw, 1625–6, for defence of Wilson at Worcester.
48. SBTRO, BRU2/2, 475 for the expulsion; ER1/115/48, 50, 51, for the presentments.
49. SBTRO, BRU2/3, 14, 34; BRU4/2, chamberlains' account of Nathaniel Duppa (1630–1), Richard Tyler (1631–2) for Wilson and Harris in 1629–31. For attempts to obtain Harris as Wilson's successor see BRU2/3, 166; Centre for Kentish Studies, U269/Warwickshire Estate Correspondence, Miscellaneous Box, Stratford Folder, Corporation to Cranfield, 6 December 1638.
50. SBTRO, BRU15/5/153.
51. The main sources for the Chancery suit, besides the Corporation minute book SBTRO, BRU2/3, are: BRU15/8/303, the bill of Hall and Wilson; BRU14/1 a volume containing the Corporation's answer, the plaintiffs' replication and many depositions; BRU15/8/1, further depositions. For a fuller account see Hughes, 'Religion and Society', 68–75.
52. SBTRO, BRU15/8/303; cf BRU15/11/30, an additional memorandum by Wilson and Hall; Centre for Kentish Studies, U269/Q28/1, 'Mr Wilson's argument'.
53. This is based on the Corporation minute books and Chamberlain's accounts, SBTRO, BRU2 and BRU4, *passim*.
54. PRO, SP16/320/59.
55. PRO, SP16/293/128; SBTRO, BRU14/1, fol. 210r.
56. PRO, SP16/320/59; SBTRO, ER1/1/97.
57. SBTRO, ER1/1/95, BRU15/13/97 for presentments in 1628 and 1633; BRU15/13/103 for an Act Book from 1633.
58. SBTRO, BRU2/3, 52, 62–5, 72, 84; BRU15/13/103, fos 8v–9r.
59. SBTRO, BRU2/3, 100, 127, 134.
60. See for example, W. Hunt, *The Puritan Moment: The Coming of Revolution in an English County*, Cambridge, Mass. 1983; K. Wrightson, *English Society 1580–1680*, London 1982, especially Chapter 7.
61. Brinkworth, *Shakespeare and the Bawdy Court*, 150, 152, 163; SBTRO, ER/1/115/44. The morris dancers presented in May 1622 confessed in July they had 'committed the lyke offence againe'.
62. A.G. Matthews, *Walker Revised*, Oxford 1948, 366.
63. SBTRO, BRU15/7/78; ER1/1/95.
64. Arbuthnot, *Vestry Minutes*, 35–6.

CHAPTER EIGHT

1. The evidence is widely scattered: in private and estate correspondence, reports of various committees and councils of war, like the King's (BL ms Harl. 6802, 6804, 6851–2), military correspondence (e.g. Prince Rupert's, Sir Samuel Luke's, BL mss Add. 18980–2, Stowe 190;

Egerton 785–7), but especially in the weekly newsletters and pamphlets forming the Thomason collection (BL, E references) and the list of Stratford's war compensation claims submitted in 1646 to the Parliamentary authority at Coventry (BL mss Add 28565; PRO, SP 28/136/50–1; copies at SBTRO). For further discussion of these sources and their reliability, see Philip Tennant, *The Civil War in Stratford-upon-Avon*, Stroud, 1996, xii–xvi, 176, n. 5, 6.

2. Details of these events are given in Philip Tennant, *Edgehill and Beyond: The People's War in the South Midlands 1642–1645*, Stroud 1992.
3. For a different view, see Ann Hughes, *Politics, Society and Civil War in Warwickshire 1620–1660*, Cambridge 1987, 151: 'Stratford seems to have been royalist in sympathy, if anything . . . ' The eternal issue must always be to decide how representative is the evidence from isolated cases, and Philip Styles's wry comment is pertinent: 'It cannot be said that the townsmen as a whole showed much enthusiasm for either side during the struggle . . . and the many changes down to 1660 seem to have been accepted with equal readiness' (*VCH Warws*, iii, 236). For one interesting discussion of the problems in trying to establish urban allegiance, see Roger Howell, 'Neutralism, Conservatism and Political Alignment in the English Revolution: the Case of the Towns, 1642–9', in *Reactions to the English Civil War, 1642–1649*, ed. John Morrill, London 1982.
4. BL, E.109(3), 'Some Speciall Passages from Warwickshire', 4 August 1642; SBTRO, BRU 2/3, fol. 209; BRU 4/2, fol. 175.
5. SBTRO, BRU 2/3, fos 205, 261, 265, 279, 283; BRU 4/2, fol. 195.
6. Nash records accommodating (not necessarily all at once) Lord Brooke, Cols John and Nathaniel Fiennes, Capt. James Sheffield, Capt. John Hampden, Col. John Hutchinson, Sir Philip Stapleton, Sir William Balfour, Sir James Ramsey, Lord Willoughby of Parham and other lesser commanders at the time of Edgehill, and others during the course of the war: PRO, SP 28/136/51, fos 330–1.
7. Tennant, *Stratford*, 50–60.
8. BL, E.85(9).
9. The Civil War is largely ignored in the Warwickshire volumes of the *VCH*, one notable exception being the useful (if selective) summary of Stratford's experience by the late Philip Styles. Modern histories of Stratford give very few details. Ann Hughes, *Politics*, contains much incidental information on Stratford while analysing local politics in detail.
10. Tennant, *Edgehill* and *Stratford*.
11. *Minutes and Accounts of the Corporation of Stratford-upon-Avon, IV,* Dugdale Society Publications x 1929, 115; *Minutes and Accounts, V*, Dugdale Society Publications xxxv, 1990, 3; SBTRO, BRU 15/5/157; BRU 15/7/114, 116; *Quarter Sessions Order Book, Michaelmas 1637 to Epiphany 1650* ed. S.C. Ratcliff and H.C. Johnson (Warwick County Records ii, 1936), 205, 223, 226–7. Wills: Jeanne Jones, *Family Life in Shakespeare's England: Stratford–upon-Avon 1570–1630*, Stroud 1996, xviii–xix, 121. Fires: summary in *VCH Warws*, iii, 223; *Minutes and Accounts, V*, xix–xx; Stephen Porter, 'Fires in Stratford-upon-Avon in the 16th and 17th Centuries', *Warwickshire History*, iii, no. 3, 1976. George Willis: *The Wyllys Papers*, Connecticut Historical Society, xxi, Hartford, Connecticut, 1924, 9.
12. *Calendar of State Papers, Domestic (CSPD), 1640*, 327 (the Lunsford riots of 22 June 1640; original at PRO, SP 16/457 fol. 91); cf. J.F. Larkin, ed., *Stuart Royal Proclamations*, 2 vols, Oxford 1983, ii, 716–8. Popish Plot: W.H. Coates, ed., *The Journal of Sir Simonds d'Ewes*, Yale 1942, 144, 146, 172; *Journals of the House of Lords*, iv, 439–41, 449, 455; Hughes, *Politics*, 135. Watch: *CSPD 1641–3*, 166; *Quarter Sessions Order Book*, 116; SBTRO, BRU 2/3, fos 203, 209; BRU 4/2, fos 164–5.
13. Riots: *Historical Manuscripts Commission, Fifth Report*, 1876, Appendix 43, and *House of Lords Journals*, v, 298, 17 August. Stratford musters: BL, E.109(3), 669 f.6(50), and PRO, SP 23/170/153 (Kittermaster case); Tennant, *Edgehill*, 19–24.
14. Centre for Kentish Studies, Maidstone, U269/1 (Sackville mss, Cranfield Papers), E126, 23

July and 23 September 1642, Robert Fawdon to the Earl of Middlesex; BL, E.108(6), E.109(3).

15. Sackville ms U269/1, E126, 16 September 1642. Combe: PRO, SP 28/247, fol. 485; Combe was later accused of 'disaffection' by a mischief-maker for having warned against fortifying Warwick and criticized Lord Brooke for 'raising the Militia' and ignoring instructions to surrender the county magazine to the King's representative, the Earl of Northampton, at Banbury early in August 1642.
16. G.M. Trevelyan, *History of England*, London 1952, 407: 'In the end the King lost the war for lack of money'; D.H. Pennington. 'The Accounts of the Kingdom 1642–1649', in *Essays in the Economic and Social History of Tudor and Stuart England*, ed. F.J. Fisher, Cambridge 1961, 182: 'The war was won by [finance] committees'.
17. Warwickshire's official assessment (including Coventry) was exactly £600 per week (BL, E.90(26)), though actually much more, nearer £1,000, compared to its pre-war Ship Money figure of £4,000 per annum. The county Parliamentary committee itself protested to Westminster at unfair treatment relative to adjacent counties: 'it hath bene much impoverished . . . and is not able to beare above £500 a weeke' (BL ms Harl. 158, fol. 277; compare Leicestershire's £187 10*s*, Staffordshire's £212 10*s*, Northamptonshire's £425: *Acts and Ordinances of the Interregnum 1642–1660*, ed. C.H. Firth and R.S. Rait, 3 vols, 1911, i, 85–8). For general discussion of Warwickshire's tax burden, see Ann Hughes, 'Parliamentary Tyranny? Indemnity Proceedings and the Impact of the Civil War. A Case Study from Warwickshire', *Midland History* xi, 1986, 49–52; and for other comment, G.E. Aylmer, *Rebellion or Revolution? England 1640–1660*, Oxford 1986, 71.
18. Ship Money: SBTRO, BRU 2/3, fols 140, 145, 153–4, 167, 169, 183; cf. Hughes, *Politics*, 115–16. Coat and Conduct: PRO, SP 16/456/12 (the constables of several parishes including Stratford and Old Stratford refused to submit complete returns).
19. Tennant, *Stratford*, 9–10. Poll Tax: PRO, SP 28/248; of the £55, Thomas Nash paid a lion's share of £10 0*s* 6*d*.
20. SBTRO, BRU 2/3, fol. 209, 3 June 1642. The episode remains obscure, but the charges were denied and not pursued; there is no clear suggestion that 'royalist' soldiers were involved.
21. Loans: Tennant, *Stratford*, 22–5. Woolmer: Sackville ms U269/1, E126, Robert Fawdon to Earl of Middlesex, 1 August 1642. Brooke: SBTRO, BRU 2/3, fol. 209a; BRU 4/2, fol. 165, and Tennant, *Stratford*, 13–14. Ronald Hutton, *The Royalist War Effort 1642–1646*, London 1982, 4.
22. Stratford's tax assessment is precisely itemized at PRO, SP 28/136/51, fols 334–5. The initial £20, beginning 23 July 1643, was reduced by degrees, to £14 after only three months, then to £12 after another four months and £10 after another four, and finally to £8 lasting until 30 January 1646. This reflects common practice: Shottery and Old Stratford's sum was similarly reduced from an initial £12 to £9 10*s* and below, Great Alne's from £5 15*s* eventually to £3, Luddington's from £6 to £4. These 'abatements' were often won by the villagers through petitioning the Coventry authorities; cf. Kineton: 'Upon petition to the Committee wee had an abatement of xxs. a weeke' (PRO, SP 28/182). It is unclear to what extent the initial over-assessment was deliberate policy, but the universal and drastic reductions suggest Coventry's recognition of the justice of the local community's case.
23. Corporation rents: *VCH Warws*, iii, 236. Poor: A.L. Beier, 'Poor Relief in Warwickshire, 1630–1660', *Past and Present* 35, 1966, 78, 85, 87, 89–90, 92–4.
24. The Earl of Middlesex's estate revenues were reduced by more than one-half of their pre-war value by 1644: M. Prestwich, *Cranfield: Politics and Profits under the Early Stuarts*, Oxford 1966, 568–70. For the total destruction of Milcote house, see Tennant, *Stratford*, 107, 111, 116–17. Doubling of Milcote rents: ' . . . and now the burthen is growen intollerable, for they have dubled the monthlie payments . . . ': Sackville ms U 269/1, E.126, 20 April 1643.
25. Sackville ms U269/1, E.126, 10 February 1645.
26. Tyler: SBTRO, BRU 2/3, fol. 276. Combe: *Wyllys*, 122. For general discussion of the impact on

estates, see Christopher Clay, 'Landlords and Estate Management in England: The Civil War and Interregnum', in *The Agricultural History of England and Wales V*, ed. Joan Thirsk, Cambridge 1985; for the Cotswolds, Ian Roy, 'England turned Germany? The Aftermath of the Civil War in its European Context', in *Trans. Royal Hist. Soc.*, 5th series, xxviii, 1978; and for Warwickshire, Hughes, *Politics*, 255–71 and Tennant, *Edgehill*, 135–40.

27. Earl of Northampton: PRO, SP 28/184 (Packwood); SP 28/182 (Tachbrook); BL, E.85(9). SBTRO, BRU 2/3, fos 280, 315, 323, 385, 389, and for comment, Tennant, *Stratford*, 145–6.
28. To these figures could be added other similar sums, like the excise of meat which affected several residents. The excise caused riots in Worcester in 1647: BL, E.425(19). All sums and the following illustrations are taken from the Stratford compensation claims (see note 1).
29. Thomas Nash was easily the wealthiest citizen, but his claims are incomplete and list no taxes paid to Warwick; and his colleague William Combe submitted no claim at all. The highest tax figure extant is the £33 of William Lindon, the lowest hovering around £1 for some dozen residents. A rough calculation using these and poll tax figures suggests that Nash was about thirty times wealthier than Lindon, and Lindon thirty times those assessed at £1. For comment on relative incomes of the previous generation, see Jones, *Family Life*, Chapter 2.
30. Apart from the Quarter Sessions cases the very poor, of course, are virtually absent from the records altogether. Tithes: submission of the town's 'Chamber', PRO, SP 28/136/51, fol. 321 and BL, ms Add. 28565 fol. 23 ('Paid to Warr Garrison out of the tythes wch was given to pious uses'). Poor: *Quarter Sessions Order Book*, 140, 182, 205, 223, 226–7 and many other cases.
31. Robert Ashton, 'From Cavalier to Roundhead Tyranny: 1642–9', in *Reactions to the English Civil War*, ed. John Morrill; also cf. G.E. Aylmer, *Rebellion or Revolution? England 1640–1660*, Oxford 1986, 71.
32. For details of the manoeuvrings before the battle, see Tennant, *Edgehill*, Chapter 4; and for the battle itself, Peter Young, *Edgehill 1642*, Kineton 1967. Stragglers: Sackville ms U 269/1, E.110.
33. Sir Edward Nicholas to Prince Rupert, 11 July 1645: BL ms Add. 18982 fos 68–9.
34. Nehemiah Wharton, a subaltern in Essex's army, letter of 30 August 1642, Coventry: *The Edgehill Campaign and the Letters of Nehemiah Wharton*, ed. S. Peachey, Leigh-on-Sea 1989. Rupert: BL, E.96(2). Wasperton and Warwick: PRO, SP 28/184; BL ms Harl. 6804, fol. 55.
35. Wounded: Tennant, *Edgehill*, 66–8; shrouds: SBTRO, BRU 4/2, fol. 175. There are no Stratford burials recorded between 23 March 1642 and 29 April 1645.
36. Sackville ms U 269/1, E.126 (23 September 1642, 7 August 1643, 13 July 1645); *CSPD 1644*, 64, Sir Edward Nicholas to Earl of Forth, 21 March 1644; BL, E.260(12).
37. PRO, SP 28/186 (Binton).
38. PRO, SP 28/183 (Charlecote).
39. *CSPD 1644*, 97, 6 April 1644.
40. Tyler PRO, SP 28/136/50 (Shottery); Nash SP 28/136/51, fol. 331; Sheldon SP 28/184 (Temple Grafton); Peers SP 28/183 (Alveston).
41. BL, E.301(2). Sackville ms U269/1, E.126, 31 September, Fawdon to Middlesex.
42. The Stratford figure of £3,000+ is roughly comparable to those for, say, the smaller communities of Kineton, Brailes and the Tysoes. Kineton (half Stratford's size, with 100 houses to Stratford's 210) paid £1,200 plus an approximate further £500 to support the garrison at Compton Wynyates at £5 per week for 2 years, i.e. a total of £1,700. Brailes and Tysoe, with about 70 houses each, paid £1,660 and £1,590 respectively. Losses attributed to free quarter and theft commonly equalled or, in many cases, far exceeded, totals for formal taxation, twice as much in Cheshire and three times as much in Buckinghamshire (John Morrill, *Cheshire 1630–1660*, Oxford 1974, 97–111; David Underdown, *Revel, Riot and Rebellion: Popular Politics and Culture in England 1630–1660*, Oxford 1985, 150). For

South Warwickshire the disparity is usually less dramatic:

Brailes	tax	£851	other	£809
Packwood	tax	270	other	279
Exhall, Alcester	tax	122	other	192
Southam	tax	815	other	800
Wolfhampcote	tax	759	other	730

(PRO, SP 28/182–4, 201, 247; the last two examples from Ann Hughes. 'Parliamentary Tyranny?', 49–50). It must be stressed again that such figures represent losses inflicted by one side only, the Parliamentarian.

43. BL, E.411(11).
44. Space excludes consideration of these. Some (like the street mugging of a former Parliamentary soldier and others, including the charges against the vicar and other Royalist 'delinquents') are described in Tennant, *Stratford*, 15–16, 146–52, others in Hughes, *Politics*, 207–8, 278, 303.
45. *Wyllys*, 89, 97, 122; see Tennant, *Stratford*, 189 note 20.
46. Stratford Jury Presentment, January 1647: SBTRO, BRT 4/1/1/36; Sackville ms U 269/1, E.120, E.127.

CHAPTER NINE

1. Warwickshire County Record Office, QS 11.
2. William Dugdale, *The Antiquities of Warwickshire*, 2 vols, London 1730, ii, 697.
3. *Correspondence of the Reverend Joseph Greene*, ed. Levi Fox, Dugdale Society Publications xxiii, 1965, 157; using a multiplier of five per household.
4. *VCH Warws*, ii, 185; SBTRO, BRT 8/203.
5. SBTRO, ER1/8, 507–25.
6. *VCH*, iii, 255.
7. *VCH*, iii, 281.
8. *Universal British Directory of Trade, Commerce, and Manufacture*, 1793–8, iv (1), 537–9; iv (2), 694–7; v, 169.
9. WCRO, QS 39/10.
10. *Medical Registers*, ed. Sanuel Foart Simmons, London 1779 and 1783.
11. SBTRO, BRT 8/203. This is particularly disappointing, since eighteenth-century overseers' accounts have survived for 115 of Warwickshire's historic 215 parishes, while a further thirteen have accounts for the seventeenth century.
12. SBTRO, BRT 8/203; SBTRO, DR 243/1.
13. Greene, *Correspondence*, 38.
14. Greene, *Correspondence*, 116.
15. Greene, *Correspondence*, 133.
16. Greene, *Correspondence*, 80.
17. Charles Shuckburgh, *A Treatise upon the Inoculation of the Smallpox*, n.d.
18. WCRO, DR 446.
19. WCRO, N4.
20. R.B. Wheler, *History and Antiquities of Stratford-upon-Avon*, Stratford-upon-Avon 1806, 50.
21. J.M. Martin, *The Rise in Population in Eighteenth-century Warwickshire*, Dugdale Society Occasional Paper xxiii, 1976, 29, 36.
22. WCRO, DR 325/Box 5.
23. Gloucestershire Record Office, P 353 OV2/2.
24. WCRO, DR432/30.

25. WCRO, DR166/20.
26. WCRO, DR325/Box 5.
27. SBTRO, BRT 8/203.
28. P.J. and R.V. Wallis, *Eighteenth-Century Medics*, Newcastle-upon-Tyne 1988, 66.
29. WCRO, DR468/34 and DR 325/Box 5.
30. WCRO, DR468/34 and DR432/29.
31. Wallis, *Eighteenth-Century Medics*, 402.
32. Greene, *Correspondence*, 109.
33. SBTRO, PR 117.
34. Wallis, *Eighteenth-Century Medics*, 479.
35. Greene, *Correspondence*, 149.
36. SBTRO, ER5/435.
37. Wallis, *Eighteenth-Century Medics*, 66.
38. *Medical Register*, 1783, 114–5.
39. *Medical Register*, 1783, 117–8.
40. SBTRO, ER1/8, 415–26. This is a rate assessment, annotated with biographical memoranda by R.B. Wheler.
41. Greene, *Correspondence*, 3.

CHAPTER TEN

1. Nicholas Fogg, *Stratford-upon-Avon: Portrait of a Town*, Chichester 1986, 101–2.
2. Fogg, *Stratford-upon-Avon*, 125.
3. Fogg, *Stratford-upon-Avon*, 126.
4. Owen Chadwick, *The Victorian Church, Part One*, 70.
5. *Warwick Advertiser*, 9 May 1835.
6. *Warwick Advertiser*, 25 June 1836.
7. *Warwick Advertiser*, 8 September 1836.
8. *Warwick Advertiser*, 18 September 1836.
9. *Warwick Advertiser*, 19 November 1836 for this and what follows.
10. *Warwick Advertiser*, 4 November 1837.
11. Anthony Trollope, *Barchester Towers*, London 1857.
12. Benjamin Disraeli, *Lothair*, London 1870.
13. *Stratford-upon-Avon Herald*, 16 August 1899.
14. *Warwick Advertiser*, 4 November 1848, and 1 and 10 November 1849.
15. *Stratford-upon-Avon Herald*, 17 May 1868.
16. Chadwick, *Victorian Church*, 150.
17. *Warwick Advertiser*, 15 July 1837.
18. *Warwick Advertiser*, 1 March 1849, 25 July 1850.
19. *Warwick Advertiser*, 14 April 1855.
20. *Warwick Advertiser*, 1838.
21. F.S. Attenborough, *Life of Joseph Arch*, Leamington 1872.
22. Joseph Arch, *The Story of His Life, Told by Himself*, London 1896.
23. Reg Groves, *Sharpen the Sickle*, 1949.
24. Arch, *Story of His Life*.
25. *Stratford Herald*, 27 June 1873.
26. *Stratford Herald*, 19 August 1872.
27. Fogg, *Stratford-upon-Avon*, 186.
28. Flora Thompson, *Lark Rise to Candleford*, 1945, 54–5.
29. *Stratford Herald*, 11 April 1890.

30. Fogg, *Stratford-upon-Avon*, 201.
31. *Warwick Advertiser*, 21 May 1831.
32. *Warwick Advertiser*, 23 February 1833.
33. *Stratford Herald*, 21 July 1865.
34. *Stratford Herald*, 12 May 1865.
35. *Stratford Herald*, 27 November 1868.
36. Robert Bearman, *Education in Stratford-upon-Avon*, Stratford-upon-Avon 1976.
37. *Stratford Herald*, 3 March 1884.
38. *Stratford Herald*, 21 March, 1884.
39. *Stratford Herald*, 14 November 1884, 4 March 1898, 30 August 1899.
40. *Stratford Herald*, 20 November 1896.
41. *Stratford Herald*, 10 March 1899.
42. *Stratford Herald*, 7 March 1899.
43. *Stratford Herald*, 24 March 1899.
44. Fogg, *Stratford-upon-Avon*, 204–8.
45. For this and what follows, see *Stratford Herald*, 9, 16, 23, 30 March 1899.
46. Angela Hewins, ed., *The Dillen*, London 1981, 69.
47. For this and what follows, see especially, *Stratford Herald*, 28 June 1901, and J.D. Browne, '"A Seat Lost to the Government is a Seat Gained by the Boers": an account of the Stratford-upon-Avon by-election of 1901', *Warwickshire History* v, no. 1, Summer 1981, 15–29; J.D. Browne, 'The Stratford By-election of 1901: a further note', *Warwickshire History*, v, no. 5, Summer 1983, 157–63.
48. *Stratford Herald*, 14 August 1908.
49. Fogg, *Stratford-upon-Avon*, 222.
50. *Stratford Herald*, 13 November 1897.

CHAPTER ELEVEN

1. For an account of Shakespeare's reputation in the seventeenth century, see Irvin Leigh Matus, *Shakespeare, IN FACT*, New York 1994, 167–89.
2. Gary Taylor, *Reinventing Shakespeare*, London 1991, 32.
3. Quoted by E.K. Chambers, *William Shakespeare: A Study of Facts and Problems*, 2 vols, Oxford 1930, ii, 235.
4. Chambers, ii, 243.
5. *The Life, Diary, and Correspondence of Sir William Dugdale*, ed. William Hamper, London 1827, 99.
6. Chambers, ii, 249–50.
7. Chambers, ii, 259.
8. Chambers, ii, 260.
9. *The Torrington Diaries*, ed. C. Bruyn Andrews, London 1934, 244.
10. Philip Tennant, *The Civil War in Stratford-upon-Avon*, Stroud 1996, 14, 60.
11. Chambers, ii, 286.
12. R.B. Wheler, *History and Antiquities of Stratford-upon-Avon*, Stratford-upon-Avon 1806, 136–38.
13. For an account of Shakespeare's reputation in the eighteenth century, see Michael Dobson, *The Making of the National Poet*, Oxford 1992.
14. Paul Langford, *A Polite and Commercial People: England 1727–1783*, Oxford 1989, 91.
15. Dobson, 139.
16. A detailed account of the Jubilee is given in Christian Deelman, *The Great Shakespeare Jubilee*, London 1964; see also Martha W. England, *Garrick's Jubilee*, Ohio 1964, and Johanne

M. Stocholm, *Garrick's Folly*, London 1964.

17. *VCH Warws*, iii, 242–3.
18. *VCH Warws*, iii, 243.
19. *Stratford-upon-Avon from 'The Sketch Book' of Washington Irving*, ed. Richard Savage and W.S. Brassington, Stratford-upon-Avon 1900. This edition includes extensive notes on Irving's text.
20. The phrase 'Georgian motorways' is Roy Porter's. See his *English Society in the Eighteenth Century*, London 1990, 191.
21. *The Beauties of England and Wales: Warwickshire*, ed. John Britton and others, London 1814, 226.
22. Travel via the turnpikes was not cheap: coaches charged 2*d* or 3*d* a mile. See Porter, 192.
23. SBTRO, DR185/1.
24. For an account of Shakespeare's reputation in the nineteenth century, see Gary Taylor, Chapter 4.
25. John Walton, *Late Georgian and Victorian Britain*, London 1989, 148.
26. *Osborne's London & Birmingham Railway Guide*, Birmingham [1840], 192–3.
27. Robert E. Hunter, *Shakespeare and Stratford-upon-Avon . . . the Tercentenary Celebration*, London 1864, 114.
28. Hunter, 59.
29. Richard Foulkes, *The Shakespeare Tercentenary of 1864*, London 1984, 36.
30. For a succinct summary of the social impact of the railways, see Asa Briggs, *A Social History of England*, London 1983, 208–16.
31. Arthur Jordan, *The Stratford-upon-Avon and Midland Junction Railway*, Oxford 1982, 7–14.
32. *Stratford-upon-Avon Herald*, 2 September 1910.
33. *The Times*, 21 July 1847.
34. *Evening Sun*, 17 September 1847.
35. SBTRO, ER 1/47, fols 101, 119.
36. Jordan, 51.
37. Jordan, 83.
38. Steam-powered transatlantic crossings began as early as the 1830s. See Briggs, 222.
39. *The Shakspere Allusion-Book*, ed. John Munro, 2 vols, London 1932, i, 347, quoting from *A Banquet of Jeasts or Change of Cheare*, 1630.

Further Reading

Much has been written on the history of Stratford and in no sense is the list which follows intended to be a bibliography. It does not, for instance, include early works or editions of original source material. The emphasis, instead, is on more modern books and articles which explore in more detail many of the issues raised in this current volume.

Bearman, Robert. *Shakespeare in the Stratford Records*, Stroud 1994.

— *Stratford-upon-Avon: a History of its Streets and Buildings*, Nelson 1988.

Brinkworth, E.R.C. *Shakespeare and the 'Bawdy Court' of Stratford*, Chichester 1972.

Carus-Wilson, E.M. 'The First Half-century of the Borough of Stratford-upon-Avon', *Economic History Review* 2nd series xviii, 1965, 46–63 (reprinted in *The Medieval Town*, ed. Richard Holt and Gervase Rosser, London 1990, 49–70).

Davies, Jamie. *Shakespeare's Avon: the History of a Navigation*, Headington 1996.

Deelman, Christian. *The Great Shakespeare Jubilee*, London 1964.

Dyer, Alan. 'Warwickshire Towns under the Tudors and Stuarts', *Warwickshire History* iii, no. 4, Winter 1976/77.

Dyer, Christopher. *Lords and Peasants in a Changing Society: the Estates of the Bishopric of Worcester, 680–1540*, Cambridge 1980.

Fogg, Nicholas. *Stratford-upon-Avon: Portrait of a Town*, Chichester 1986.

Foulkes, Richard. *The Shakespeare Tercentenary of 1864*, London 1984.

Fox, Levi. *The Borough Town of Stratford-upon-Avon*, Stratford-upon-Avon 1953.

— *The Early History of King Edward VI School, Stratford-upon-Avon*, Dugdale Society Occasional Paper xxix, 1984.

Hadfield, Charles & John Norris. *Waterways to Stratford*, Newton Abbot 1968.

Hughes, Ann. 'Religion and Society in Stratford upon Avon, 1619–1638', *Midland History* xix, 1994, 58–84.

Jones, Jeanne. *Family Life in Shakespeare's England: Stratford-upon-Avon 1570–1630*, Stroud 1996.

Lane, Joan. *John Hall and his Patients: the Medical Practice of Shakespeare's Son-in-Law*, Stroud 1996.

Lloyd, Terence H. *Some Aspects of the Building Industry in Medieval Stratford-upon-Avon*, Dugdale Society Occasional Paper xiv, 1961.

Macdonald, Mairi. *The Town Hall, Stratford-upon-Avon*, Stratford-upon-Avon 1986.

McFarland, Patricia. *A Dynasty of Town Clerks: the Hunt Family of Stratford-upon-Avon*, Dugdale Society Occasional Paper xxxvii, 1996.

Martin, J.M. 'A Warwickshire Market Town in Adversity: Stratford-upon-Avon in the Sixteenth and Seventeenth Centuries', *Midland History* vii, 1982.

Morriss, Richard K. & Hoverd, Ken, *The Buildings of Stratford-upon-Avon*, Stroud 1994.

Norris, John. *The Stratford and Moreton Tramway*, Guildford 1987.

Penny, R.I. 'The Board of Health in Victorian Stratford-upon-Avon', *Warwickshire History*, i, no. 6, Autumn 1971.

Porter, Stephen. 'Fires in Stratford-upon-Avon in the 16th and 17th centuries', *Warwickshire History* iii, no. 3, Summer 1976.

Pringle, Marian. *The Theatres of Stratford-upon-Avon, 1875–1992*, Stratford-upon-Avon 1994.

Styles, Philip. *The Borough of Stratford-upon-Avon and the Parish of Alveston*, London 1946 (reprinted from *VCH Warws* iii, 1945).

Tennant, Philip. *The Civil War in Stratford-upon-Avon: Conflict and Community in South Warwickshire 1642–1646*, Stroud 1996.

Index

Numbers in italics refer to illustrations.
Places are in Warwickshire unless otherwise specified.
Streets are in Stratford-upon-Avon.